Paleobotany, Paleoecology, and Evolution

PALEOBOTANY, PALEOECOLOGY, AND EVOLUTION

VOLUME 1

edited by

Karl J. Niklas

PRAEGER

PRAEGER SPECIAL STUDIES • PRAEGER SCIENTIFIC

Library of Congress Cataloging in Publication Data
Main entry under title:

Paleobotany, paleoecology, and evolution.

Includes bibliographical references and index.
1. Paleobotany.   2. Paleoecology.   3. Evolution.
I. Niklas, Karl J.
QE905.P29   560'.45   81-1838
ISBN 0-03-059136-8 (v. 1)   AACR2
ISBN 0-03-056656-8 (v. 2)
ISBN 0-03-060038-3 (set)

Published in 1981 by Praeger Publishers
CBS Educational and Professional Publishing
A Division of CBS, Inc.
521 Fifth Avenue, New York, New York 10175 U.S.A.

© 1981 by Praeger Publishers

123456789   145   987654321

Printed in the United States of America

LIST OF CONTRIBUTORS

Elso S. Barghoorn, Harvard University, Cambridge, Massachusetts.

Charles B. Beck, Museum of Paleontology and Division of Biological Sciences, University of Michigan, Ann Arbor, Michigan.

Gillian Cooper-Driver, Biological Science Center, Boston University, Boston, Massachusetts.

William A. DiMichele, Department of Botany, University of Washington, Seattle, Washington.

Andrew H. Knoll, Department of Geology, Oberlin College, Oberlin, Ohio.

Tom L. Phillips, Botany Department, University of Illinois, Urbana, Illinois.

Greg Retallack, Department of Biology, Indiana University, Bloomington, Indiana.

Thomas J. M. Schopf, Department of the Geophysical Sciences, and Committee on Evolutionary Biology, University of Chicago, Chicago, Illinois.

Tony Swain, Biological Science Center, Boston University, Boston, Massachusetts.

Harlan P. Banks

AN APPRECIATION—HARLAN P. BANKS

It is indeed appropriate that this volume consisting of such a broad range of scientific papers should be published in honor and recognition of the continuing contributions of Harlan P. Banks to paleobotany. For if there can be one hallmark that characterizes the broad spectrum of his scientific career, it is the amazing productivity and the wide-ranging ramifications of his energies and interests, which are so well mirrored by the present volume.

Harlan Banks is prolific, not only in the papers he produces, the seminars and lectures he gives, the botanists and paleobotanists he has launched, but also in the large numbers of young minds he has filled with the love of botany. These are only some of the many facets of his impressive career, but they are the activities for which we feel he will be long remembered with respect, admiration, and affection.

Harlan P. Banks is a major worker and synthesizer in the area of earliest vascular plants and their significance to land plant evolution. He early advocated a high standard of rigorous and exhaustive study of plant fossil materials, to wrest the maximum information from recalcitrant materials. Such studies applied by various workers to early vascular plant fossils led in 1968 to what has become a classic paper in paleobotany. In this paper, Dr. Banks reorganized the old Order Psilophytales, which had become a taxonomic repository for many early land plants of diverse characteristics. He excluded a number of taxa that were clearly not referable to the group, and separated the remainder into three categories: the rhyniophytes, the zosterophyllophytes, and the trimerophytes. He established definitive criteria for each category, and for the major subdivisions within these categories. He resolved what was then a bewildering and diverse array of early plants into clearly related groups based on their morphological, anatomical, and reproductive features; and equally clearly, he revealed those areas that were in need of further work and new insights. In 1975 he modified the classification and discussed many of the new studies and contributions that the earlier paper had engendered. Although future studies may bring modifications, these two papers and the concepts they embody are landmarks in Paleozoic paleobotany. Dr. Banks alone, and in collaboration with his colleagues and students, has produced numerous papers that represent many of the major thrusts and significant achievements in the area of early vascular plants. A selected list of such papers is appended.

Harlan Banks has had a strong influence on the field of paleobotany, which extends beyond the papers he has authored or coauthored. He early grasped the importance of stratigraphic control to paleobotanical studies that provide immediate benefits to paleobotanists, paleontologists, and stratigraphers alike, and that eventually accrue to evolutionists, paleoclimatologists, and paleogeographers, as is witnessed by several papers in this symposium. He foresaw the potential that the fledgling field of palynology could provide to independent temporal control of the megafossil record.

Harlan Banks is a plantsman, and, perhaps because of this and his New England background, an inveterate peddler of the love of botany and paleobotany. His Yankee conscience and drive is reflected in the service he has given botany at many levels. He has served the Botanical Society of America in numerous capacities on committees, as Secretary-Treasurer, Vice-President, and President.

Harlan Banks strongly believes in the international cooperation of paleobotanists and, to that end, has promoted cooperation, exchanges, and visits at the international level. His efforts have been recognized by various fellowships abroad such as Fulbright Research Scholar, Liège, Belgium; Corresponding Member, Geological Society of Belgium; Guggenheim Fellow at University of Liège and Cambridge University; and Fellow of Clare Hall, Cambridge University, England. He has served as Vice-President and President of the International Organization of Paleobotany and is a member of various editorial boards.

Besides his direct contributions to the broad range of international paleobotany, Harlan Banks has played a major role in enlisting and training graduate students in both botany and paleobotany. He transmits his own enthusiasm and excitement, and, in an era of sputnik and molecular biology, he has conveyed to students that rigor, accomplishments and intellectual satisfaction in science need not belong only to the current fashion to be significant. He has always encouraged young paleobotanists, while at the same time he exhorts them to excel, to develop their evidences, and to suspend judgement until their evidence is in. His own horizons are not confined and he opens vistas to others. Thirty some prospective students received twenty-one doctorates and thirteen masters degrees under his able guidance. The subjects of these degrees were as wide-ranging as his interests and reflect a broad perspective of botanical approaches encompassing the technical, floristic, taxonomic, and anatomic-morphologic disciplines of living and extinct botany. Many of these thirty students, now active colleagues of Dr. Banks, convey his message and enthusiasm for botany in over twenty different schools or research institutions, and continue active research in paleobotany.

Probably the most intangible legacy accorded the botanical community is the influence Harlan Banks has had, not only on his own graduate students, but on the thousands of undergraduate students who were first introduced to the world of plants in his excellent general botany course. In this course the students were exposed to an extraordinary teacher who could take any topic and make it spring to life, become interesting, exciting, and truly relevant. Many of these young lives were changed and/or redirected because of Harlan Banks's talent as a teacher and storyteller. In some ways this is his most important contribution—one that has touched all of us who are priviliged to know him. For Harlan Banks is a TEACHER in the finest and best sense of the word.

In all aspects of his career, in research, writing papers, and student interactions, Harlan Banks is teaching. He has the talent to hold an audience in the palm of his hand from the moment he begins, whether it is directed to a group of distinguished scholars or to a general botany class. No matter his message—"The Rhyniophytina, Zosterophyllophytina, and Trimerophyllophytina," "The worldwide distribution in the Devonian of toothy cuticles," or "Plants are fun"—he weaves a spell and transmits knowledge, enthusiasm, and motivation. We wish him many more years of continued opportunity to weave such superb spells.

Patricia M. Bonamo

James D. Grierson

SELECTED BIBLIOGRAPHY

Banks, Harlan P. 1944. A new Devonian lycopod genus from southeastern New York. *Amer. J. Bot.* 31:649–659.

Zimmerly, Bessie C. and Harlan P. Banks. 1950. On gametophytes of *Psilotum. J. Bot.* 37(8):668. (abstr.)

Fry, Wayne L. and Harlan P. Banks. 1955. Three new genera of algae from the Upper Devonian of New York. *J. Paleont.* 29:37–44.

Banks, Harlan P. 1959. The stratigraphic occurrence of Devonian plants with applications to phylogeny. *Proc. IX Int. Bot. Congress* II:17–18.

Banks, Harlan P. 1960. Notes on Devonian lycopods. *Senckenbergiana lethaea* 41(1–6):59–88.

Banks, Harlan P. 1961. The stratigraphic occurrence of Devonian plants with applications to phylogeny. In *Recent Advances in Botany.* Univ. Toronto Press, pp. 963–968.

Leclercq, Suzanne and Harlan P. Banks. 1962. *Pseudosporochnus nodosus* sp. nov., a Middle Devonian plant with cladoxylalean affinities. *Palaeontographica B* 110:1–34.

Banks, Harlan P. 1962. *The Invasion of the Land.* Film 7 of Part VII. A.I.B.S. Secondary School Biological Film Series. New York: McGraw-Hill.

Grierson, J. D. and Harlan P. Banks. 1963. Lycopods of the Devonian of New York. *Palaeontographica Americana* 4(31):219–295.

Banks, Harlan P. 1964. Putative Devonian Ferns. *Mem. Torrey Bot. Club* 21(5):10–25.

Banks, Harlan P. 1964. Upper Devonian plants with gymnospermous anatomy and pteridophytic foliage. Invitation paper. *X Internat. Botanical Congress.* Abstracts, p. 32.

Banks, Harlan P. 1965. Some recent additions to the knowledge of the early land flora. *Phytomorphology* 15(3):235–245.

Banks, Harlan P. 1966. Devonian flora of New York State. *Empire State Geogram* 4(3):10–24.

Banks, Harlan P. 1966. Early land plants and some of their relatives. *Bio Sci* 16(6):432–433.

Carluccio, Leeds M., F. M. Hueber, and Harlan P. Banks. 1966. *Archaeopteris macilenta*, anatomy and morphology of its frond. *Amer. J. Bot.* 53(7):719–730.

Bonamo, P. M. and Harlan P. Banks. 1966. *Calamophyton* in the Middle Devonian of New York State. *Amer. J. Bot.* 53(8):778–791.

Matten, Lawrence C. and Harlan P. Banks. 1966. *Triloboxylon ashlandicum* gen. et sp. nov. from the Upper Devonian of New York. *Amer. J. Bot.* 53:1020–1028.

Hueber, F. M. and Harlan P. Banks. 1967. *Psilophyton princeps:* the search for organic connection. *Taxon* 16:81–85.

Banks, Harlan P. 1967. Plant fossils in central New York. *The Cornell Plantations* 22:55–63.

Matten, Lawrence C. and Harlan P. Banks. 1967. Relationship between the Devonian progymnosperm genera *Sphenoxylon* and *Tetraxylopteris*. *Bull. Torrey Bot. Club* 94:321–333.

Bonamo, P. M. and Harlan P. Banks. 1967. *Tetraxylopteris schmidtii:* Its fertile parts and its relationships within the Aneurophytales. *Amer. J. Bot.* 54:755–768.

Banks et al. 1967. In Chap. 1, Thallophyta, Part 1; Chap. 4, Pteridophyta, Part 1; Chap. 5, Pteridophyta, Part 2. In *The Fossil Record*. W. B. Harland, et al. (eds.). London: Geological Society, pp. 163–180, 219–231, 233–245.

Banks, Harlan P. 1968. The stratigraphic occurrence of early land plants and its bearing on their origin. In *Internat. Symposium on the Devonian System*. D. H. Oswald (ed.) (1967) Vol. 2. Calgary, Canada: Alberta Soc. Petroleum Geologists, pp. 721–730.

Banks, Harlan P. 1968. The early history of land plants. In *Evolution and Environment*. Ellen T. Drake (ed.). New Haven and London: Yale University Press, pp. 73–107.

Banks, Harlan P. and J. D. Grierson. 1968. *Drepanophycus spinaeformis* Goppert in the early Upper Devonian of New York State. *Palaeontographica B.* 123:113–120.

Banks, Harlan P. 1968. Anatomy and affinities of a Devonian *Hostinella*. *Phytomorphology* 17:321–330.

Banks, Harlan P. 1968. Devonian Plants, pp. 1355–1356. In *Developments, trends and outlooks in paleontology*. R. C. Moore (ed.). *J. Paleontol.* 42:1327–1377.

Banks, Harlan P. 1969. Richard Krausel (1890–1966). *Phytomorphology* 18:178–179.

Banks, Harlan P. and M. R. Davis. 1969. *Crenaticaulis*, a new genus of Devonian plants allied to *Zosterophyllum*, and its bearing on the classification of early land plants. *Amer. J. Bot.* 56:436-449.

Matten, Lawrence C. and Harlan P. Banks. 1969. *Stenokoleos bifidus* sp. n. in the Upper Devonian of New York State. *Amer. J. Bot.* 56:880-891.

Banks, Harlan P. 1969. Early Land Plants: Time of Origin and Rate of Change. *J. Paleont.* 43:880. Abstr. No. Amer. Paleont. Conf. Chicago. Sept. 1969.

Banks, Harlan P. Organizer and Chairman. 1970. Symposium on Major Evolutionary Events and the Geological Record of Plants, for XI International Botanical Congress 1969. *Biological Reviews* 45(3):317-454. (Specific authorship: Introduction pp. 317-318; Summary pp. 451-454.)

Banks, Harlan P. 1970. *Evolution and Plants of the Past.* Belmont, California: Wadsworth Pub. Co., Inc. 170 pp.

Banks, Harlan P. 1970. Loren Clifford Petry (1887-1970). *Plant Sci. Bull.* 16(3):10-11.

Banks, Harlan P. 1970. Chipping away at early land plants: of people, places and perturbations. *Plant Sci. Bull.* 16(4):1-6.

Scheckler, S. E. and Harlan P. Banks. 1971. Anatomy and relationships of some Devonian progymnosperms from New York. *Amer. J. Bot.* 58:737-751.

Scheckler, S. E. and Harlan P. Banks. 1971. *Proteokalon* a new genus of progymnosperms from the Devonian of New York State and its bearing on phylogenetic trends in the group. *Amer. J. Bot.* 58:874-884.

Banks, H. P. 1972. The stratigraphic occurrence of early land plants. Palaeontology 15(2):365-377.

Banks, H. P. 1972. The scientific works of Suzanne Leclercq. *Rev. of Palaeobotany & Palynology.* 14:1-5.

Banks, H. P., P. M. Bonamo and J. D. Grierson. 1972. *Leclercqia complexa* gen. et sp. nov., a new lycopod from the Late Middle Devonian of eastern New York. *Rev. of Paleobotany & Palynology* 14:19-40.

Banks, H. P. 1972. Silurian-Devonian Boundaries and early land plants. Twenty-fourth Int. Geol. Congress, Montreal. Abstracts, p. 214.

Skog, J. E. and H. P. Banks. 1973. *Ibyka amphikoma*, gen. et sp. n., a new protoarticulate precursor from the late Middle Devonian of New York State. *Amer. J. Bot.* 60:366-380.

Banks, H. P. 1973. Occurrence of *Cooksonia*, the oldest vascular land plant macrofossil, in the upper Silurian of New York State. *J. Indian Bot. Soc. Golden Jubilee Volume* 50A:227-235.

Scheckler, S. E. and H. P. Banks. 1974. Periderm in some Devonian plants. In *Advances in Plant Morphology. Prof. V. Puri Commem. Vol.* Y. S. Murty, B. M. Johri, H. Y. Mohan Ram, and T. M. Varghese (eds.). Meerut City, U.P. India: Prabhat Press, pp. 58-64.

Banks, H. P., Suzanne Leclercq and F. M. Hueber. 1975. Anatomy and Morphology of *Psilophyton dawsonii* sp. nov. from the Late Lower Devonian of Quebec (Gaspe), and Ontario, Canada. *Palaeontographica Americana* VIII(48):73-127.

Banks, H. P. 1975. The oldest vascular land plants: a note of caution. *Rev. Palaeobot. Palynol.*, 20:13-25.

Banks, H. P. 1975. Palaeogeographic implications of some Silurian-Early Devonian floras. In *Gondwana Geology.* K. S. W. Campbell (ed.). Canberra: Australian

National University Press, pp. 75–97.

Banks, H. P. 1975. Reclassification of Psilophyta. *Taxon* 24:401–413.

Banks, H. P. 1975. Early vascular land plants: Proof and Conjecture. *Bio. Sci.* 25:730–737.

Banks, H. P. 1977. Plant Macrofossils. pp. 298–300. In *The Silurian Devonian Boundary.* A. Martinsson (ed.). I U G S Series A. No. 5. Stuttgart.

Banks, H. P. 1977. Stratigraphic occurrences of Silurian-Devonian megafossils. *J. Paleont.* 51(2 supp.):2.

Stubblefield, Sara and H. P. Banks. 1978. The cuticle of *Drepanophycus spinaeformis* a long-ranging Devonian lycopod from New York and eastern Canada. *Amer. J. Bot.* 65:110–118.

Fairon-Demaret, Murial and H. P. Banks. 1978. Leaves of *Archaeosigillaria vanuxemii.* a Devonian lycopod from New York. *Amer. J. Bot.* 65:246–249.

Serlin, Bruce S. and Harlan P. Banks. 1978. Morphology and anatomy of *Aneurophyton* a progymnosperm from the Late Devonian of New York. *Palaeontographica Americana* 8(51):343–359.

Banks, H. P. 1979. Plant evolution: Study of macrofossil floras. In 1979 Yearbook of Science and Technology. D. N. Lapedes (ed.). New York: McGraw-Hill, pp. 296–298.

Hueber, F. M. and H. P. Banks. 1979. *Serrulacaulis furcatus* gen. et sp. nov., a new zosterophyll from the lower Upper Devonian of New York State. *Rev. Palaeobot. Palynol.* 28:169–189.

Banks, H. P. 1979. Pteridophyta. In *The Encyclopedia of Paleontology.* R. W. Fairbridge and D. Jablonski (eds.). Stroudsburg, Pa: Dowden, Hutchinson and Ross, (886 pp.), pp. 665–669.

Banks, H. P. 1980. The role of *Psilophyton* in the evolution of vascular plants. *Rev. Palaeobot. Palynol.* 29:165–176.

Hartman, Christine M. and Harlan P. Banks. 1980. Pitting in *Psilophyton dawsonii,* and Early Devonian trimerophyte. *Amer. J. Bot.* 67:400–412.

Banks, H. P. (In press). Time of appearance of some plant biocharacters during Siluro-Devonian time. *Bull. Canadian Botanical Association* (supp.).

Banks, H. P. (In press). Floral assemblages in the Siluro-Devonian. In *Biostratigraphy of Fossil Plants: Successional and Palaeoecological Analyses.* D. Dilcher and T. N. Taylor (eds.). Stroudsburg, Pa: Dowden, Hutchinson and Ross.

Banks, H. P. (In press). Peridermal activity (wound repair) in an Early Devonian (Emsian) trimerophyte from the Gaspe Peninsula, Canada. *The Paleobotanist.*

PREFACE

Although it is a truism that the search for the generalized aspects of evolution necessarily involves the perspective gained from diverse areas of specialization and varying levels of abstraction, it is a curiosity that very few paleobiological studies are multidisciplinary. In light of this, a symposium was organized and held at Cornell University on November 16 and 17, 1979. This volume, and its companion, represent 13 of the 14 papers presented and reflect an effort to focus on the nature, direction, and rate of change in evolution.

For various reasons, the symposium emphasized aspects of plant evolution. Perhaps the foremost reason was the initial impetus for its organization—to honor a great paleobotanist, Dr. Harlan P. Banks. In a career spanning five decades, Dr. Banks has contributed much to our understanding of early vascular plant evolution, not merely by his persistent attention to detail, but also because of his innovative approach. A less altruistic but nevertheless equally strong motive for organizing the symposium was the conviction that studies falling under the rubric of paleobotany are undergoing a renaissance and are expanding to include topics in chemistry, genetics, ecology, climatology, and the rigorous quantification of evolutionary theory. This symposium draws attention to an innovation in approach currently seen in fossil plant studies, which, it is hoped, carries on the tradition exemplified by Dr. Banks. The papers collected here demonstrate that the understanding of evolution is a paleo*biological* concern.

The papers are presented in two volumes and are organized in a chronological sequence from the Precambrian to the Tertiary. Volume 1 contains papers dealing with the "formative years" in plant evolution. In addition to contributions relative to specific time periods or relatively circumscribed sets of organisms, some chapters deal with more abstract or theoretical topics. Thus in Volume 1, two chapters on early and late Precambrian biota are followed by discussions on the genesis of fossil soils, biochemical scenarios in early land plant evolution, and the implications of genetic theory on the appearance and longevity of species. With these chapters the stage is set for the diversification of plant life in terrestrial environments, as well as for an appreciation of how many potential species of fossil organisms were never represented in the fossil record. Volume 1 concludes with a treatment of the phyletic implications of *Archaeopteris* and a paleoecologic reconstruction of a Pennsylvanian coal ball swamp. Volume 2 deals predominantly with such megatopics in Mesozoic and Cenozoic plant evolution as the pollination biology of some early seed plants and angiosperms, patterns of land plant diversity, continental drift, and paleoclimatology.

A synthesis of the various chapter topics would be both presumptuous and illogical since their collective scope is evolution. Yet even upon a casual glance, certain leitmotives become evident in the approach taken by the authors. Perhaps the most conspicuous approach is the implicit desire to view fossil organisms as dynamic entities, both in their own life space (in terms of growth, development, and reproduction) and within the context of evolutionary time. A second common approach is the desire to view fossils within their ecosystems—thus, both biotic and abiotic factors are explored in their relationship to functional morphology and evolution. Third, considerable effort is made wherever possible to quantify the data, whether they be morphologic, ecologic, or phyletic. While none of these leitmotives are unique to the literature, they can be placed in apposition to a larger body of earlier studies best described as purely descriptive and lacking in a perspective of temporal change.

The paleobiologist's perception of evolution is most often constrained by the extent to which the morphology of a fossil organism is preserved. There are at least three potentially useful levels of abstraction whereby morphology may be understood. These are the organism's physical properties, its ecologic relationships to other contemporary taxa, and its genotypic and phenotypic potential, which may best be described as "phyletic legacy." Each is reflected in some or all of the papers published here. Various theoretical and applied fields of study bridge the three approaches to understanding a fossil. Developmental patterns, both onto- and epigenetic, link phyletic legacy to the environment and hence to the organisms's ecological role. Functional morphology relates the ecology of a plant or animal to its architecture, while molecular and genetic theory place the biosynthetic capacity of an organism within the context of its evolutionary history and capacity to change. These "bridge concepts" and their respective scientific disciplines require a multidisciplinary approach to evolutionary phenomena and justify the "truism" set forth in the preamble to this introduction.

Like all cooperative efforts, *Paleobotany, Paleoecology, and Evolution* is the product of many people and their hard work. The patience, stamina, and intense motivation of the contributors are the principle reasons for any success that these volumes may enjoy. The College of Agriculture and Life Sciences and the Section of Botany, Genetics and Development of Cornell University are gratefully acknowledged for their financial support, as is The Boyce Thompson Institute for Plant Studies for providing its spacious lecture hall for the formal presentations. We are grateful to President Frank Rhodes, who took time from a busy schedule to welcome all the participants. Mss. Barbara Bernstein, Brenda Colthart, Lois Geesey, Sandra Kisner, Joan Miller, Esther Spielman, and Joan Wilen are to be congratulated and thanked for their assistance and support during and after the symposium. I also wish to thank Dominick Paolillo, Jr., the symposium co-organizer. And, finally, we all wish to thank Dr. Harlan P. Banks, for without the deep love and respect that he engendered during his career such a symposium would not have been possible.

Karl J. Niklas

CONTENTS

PALEOBOTANY, PALEOECOLOGY, AND EVOLUTION

ASPECTS OF PRECAMBRIAN PALEOBIOLOGY: THE EARLY PRECAMBRIAN

Elso S. Barghoorn

INTRODUCTION

The earliest record which allows even conjecture as to the existence of life on earth occurs in the oldest dated rocks now known, the Isua supracrustal metamorphic belt, a small arcuate belt at the edge of the inland ice cap in Greenland (3.7–3.8×10^9 yrs) (Moorbath, O'Nions, and Pankhurst 1975). The evidence is purely geochemical and inferential. In virtually unmetamorphosed units in parts of the Swaziland Supergroup complex of South Africa, however, organic structures occur which can reasonably be interpreted as fossils despite their great antiquity (about 3.4–3.5×10^9 yrs) and have been reported by a number of investigators (e.g., Jahn and Shih 1974). Although there is no consensus that these discrete entities and associated organic lamellae are truly fossil evidence of life, no coherent hypothesis of their origin by abiological mechanisms has been proposed. Organic structures of comparable age have been reported recently from Western Australia. In sediments of younger Precambrian sequences many of these Archean "fossils" would be readily accepted as bona fide fossils, based on morphological criteria, sedimentary context, and the geochemistry of stable carbon and sulfur isotopes. The existence of stromatolitic structures of algal origin has recently been determined in sediments more than 3×10^9 years in carbon-rich cherts of the Pilbara Block of Western Australia. The evidence for the existence of an early Archean biosphere is discussed in this chapter, especially with reference to the Swaziland Supergroup of South Africa.

I approach this subject with some trepidation rendered no less by my increasing realization of how little we can infer or deduce concerning a science of Precambrian biology, much less the paleoecology of the primitive earth. It is encouraging, however, that the subject can now at least be addressed, a situation scarcely possible a few decades ago.

To contain this discussion within reasonable limits and coherence, I shall forego the temptation to indulge in speculation on such intriguing intellectual problems as chemical evolution in the origin of life, and on the possible physical parameters of the prebiotic earth. This limits us to the interval in earth history between the earliest occurrences of putatively biogenic carbonaceous sediments to the time of appearance of relatively diverse true fossils in the Proterozoic. The totality of time involved approaches 2 billion (2×10^9) years, an appreciable portion of the history of the planet earth. It is in this interval of time, however, that primitive life originated, evolved through a sequence of nonrandom processes—natural selection—and attained ultimately a distinctly diversified level of morphological, as well as physiological complexity, especially the remarkable capacity of photolysis of H_2O and release of (O_2 and the autotrophic reduction of CO_2 through photosynthesis. I would like to present in perspective some documentation of Precambrian life in the order of its decreasing age, and increasing complexity of biological organization.

THE ARCHEAN EARTH AND ITS EVIDENCE OF LIFE

In an intriguing account of the narrative of early life on the primitive earth, M. G. Rutten (1971) distinguished three main stages in the history and evolution of life: (1) pre-life; (2) early life in an anoxic world, and; (3) later life in an oxygenic world. This subdivision neatly encapsulates three basic and sequential concepts in the evolution of the earth and its biosphere. To paraphrase Rutten, we must recognize the fact that every scheme or mode of natural processes entails some falsification, or at least arbitary delimitation, either in time or degree of precision. For example, the transition from pre-life, the realm of chemical evolution, must have overlapped living systems, with their insatiable appetite for high energy C-H bonded compounds, presumably available in the ancient ambient environment. Whether or not the earliest, self-replicating systems arose in the overwhelming stress of incipient starvation in the dilute broth of a "primordial soup" or in a benevolent enclave of concentrated organics in protected basins, is a question we shall probably never be able to answer. The fact, however, that life is never in equilibrium with its physical environment seems persuasive evidence that it arose in a geological setting of benign environmental parameters, perhaps under physical conditions that we may call geobioge-netic for lack of a better term.

The vision or specter of an earth devoid of life is difficult to conceive unless the earth were either molten or frozen, two conditions which are inimical to the transition from pre-life to life. To a biologist the view of the contemporary earth is one of an almost infinite number of ecological systems, econiches, and adaptive biological mechanisms for overcoming the vicissitudes of the environment—in essence, a network of nonequilibrium counterbalances triggered and favored by natural selection. When and where the ultimate and irreversible transition from the abiological to the biological world transpired remains obscure, but it is not beyond the scope of scientific inquiry. The problem has certainly been elevated from the realm of pure speculation in which it was so long embedded. Perhaps I should leave this area of conjecture with the thought that the history of carbon and the history of life on earth are so intertwined that we may regard the origin and early development of life as an aspect of carbon chemistry in its association with liquid water and the lighter elements that feature all living systems.

As stated previously, the earth's oldest now known sedimentary rocks are exposed in the Isua supracrustal complex in Greenland, 3.7–3.8×10^9 years (Moorbath, O'Nions, and Pankhurst 1975). (For further discussion of the geology, isotopic dating, and structural relations of the Isua complex see Bridgwater, Collerson, and Myers [1978].) Although moderately to highly metamorphosed, the Isua complex contains a quite varied suite of sedi-ments, certainly indicative of deposition under conditions of flowing water which is germane to the question of the possible existence of life at the time of deposition. Among the lithologies are graphitic metasediments (originally shales?) and iron formation, possibly indicative of photosynthetically in-duced oxidation. Despite its tenuous nature, the most suggestive evidence for a possibly biologically induced carbon cycle in Isua time lies in a significant degree of fractionation of the two stable isotopes of carbon, ^{13}C and ^{12}C, ($\delta^{13}C$ in the reduced (graphitic) carbon and the carbonate carbon, respectively. In a well-reasoned discussion of the stable carbon isotope geochemistry of 124 samples of carbonates and 13 samples of reduced carbon-bearing sediments from the Isua supracrustal rocks Schidlowski et al. (1979) have concluded that "The terrestrial carbon cycle was virtually stabilized" at the time of Isua sedimentation and that "this would imply an extremely early origin on earth of both life itself and photosynthetic activity." It should be noted in this connection that photosynthetic activity in the microbial world may be either oxygenic or nonoxygenic, though in both modes of CO_2 reduction C isotope fractionation is involved, namely, varying amounts of depletion of the heavy isotope ^{13}C along the biochemi-cal pathways of photosynthetic metabolism.

Although these arguments are contestable and may be challenged on various grounds of metamorphic geochemical processes, the very fact that there is considerable depletion of ^{13}C in the reduced carbon as opposed to the carbonate carbon in the Isua metasediments is difficult to explain except as the result of biological processes involving CO_2 reduction by photosynthesis. The existence of relatively massive amounts of banded iron formation is temptingly suggestive of localized production of oxygen in basinal environments. As in the case of other later Archean banded iron formation the presence of these oxidized primary chemical precipitates can scarcely be explained as evidence of a worldwide oxygenic atmosphere and hydrosphere. Indeed, there is abundant evidence as discussed later, that the earth's atmosphere remained highly reducing for more than 1.5 billion years after Isua time. Both the isotopically fractionated reduced carbon and the oxidized ferruginous sediments in the Isua sequence, hence, remain geochemical enigmas of the earliest Archean rocks of the earth. In the absence of fossils, the Isua complex impinges only peripherally on our consideration of Precambrian paleobiology. The importance lies in the possibility that it may represent a stage in the earth's biological history between pre-life and early life. If we accept the graphite of these ancient rocks as truly biological in origin, it focuses attention on the somewhat startling conclusion that within only a few hundred million years after the differentiation of the earth as a planet, following the major meteoritic bombardment (? 4 billion years ago), life had originated.

Unfortunately, the question of a truly biological record possibly represented by geochemical indicators in the Isua metasediments has recently been confused by the publication of alleged microfossils found in quartzitic units of these rocks (Pflug 1978; Pflug and Jaeschke-Boyer 1979). Examination, in thin section, of these same metaquartzites collected independently in the field in 1979 by Clifford Walters and Cyril Ponnamperuma of the University of Maryland, from immediately adjacent and abutting rock samples, shows conclusively that the structures described as microfossils and designated by the taxon *Isuasphaera*, are in fact fluid inclusions within as well as between quartz crystals. As such, the structures are quite evidently of metamorphic origin and irrelevant to any paleontological interpretation.

The earliest geological and geochemical evidence of a widespread and biologically productive early Precambrian ecosystem now known is contained in the column of diverse carbonaceous sediments, volcanics, and conglomerates comprising the Swaziland Supergroup of the eastern Transvaal of South Africa and adjacent Swaziland. The basal volcanics of the Swaziland Supergroup have been dated at about 3.4 to 3.5×10^9 years (Jahn and Shih 1974). A comprehensive review of the geochronology of the Swaziland Sequence is presented by Anhaeusser (1978). Certain sedimentary facies, in particular the black cherts, contain carbonaceous structures reasonably interpretable as three-dimensionally preserved remains of microorganisms and the organic mats in which they are preserved (Schopf and Barghoorn 1967). Indeed, structures that are highly suggestive of cells in varying stages of binary division have been observed and which, for a variety of reasons, provide cognitive evidence of morphologically preserved populations of microorganisms (Knoll and Barghoorn 1977). The geochemistry of the stable carbon and sulfur isotopes in these same carbonaceous sediments also provides further presumptive evidence of biological activity as inferred from fractionation and depletion of the heavier stable isotopes of these two elements. This is consistent with the postulated existence of biochemical pathways in the microbial populations from which were derived the carbon of the black shales and cherts (Eichmann and Schidlowski 1975). Whether these microorganisms were oxygenic or nonoxygenic in metabolism, or both, is not possible to determine. The presence in the Swaziland Sequence of locally abundant banded iron formation (BIF) attests to, though does not prove, the existence of populations of photosynthetic organisms producing free oxygen in localized environments of shallow water basins.

The Swaziland Supergroup is an isolated block of supracrustal rocks consisting of interbedded sediments, volcanics, and locally metamorphosed rocks in which are intercalated virtually unmetamorphosed units of organic rich cherts, graywackes, and shales indicative of shallow water subsiding basinal deposition. The entire Supergroup was successively injected and uplifted by several granitic bodies that are dated at about 3×10^9 years (Anhaeusser 1978). Fortuitiously, the tectonic processes attending uplift resulted in minimal thermal alteration (275°C) and structural deformation so that many of the sedimentary units were preserved with remarkably little or no metamorphic change for rocks of such great age. In a sense the entire System is a complex of superposed rock units, volcanics, and sediments, floated on a sea of granite with much of its lithological integrity preserved and decipherable, though much altered where in contact with subsequent igneous intrusives.

Stratigraphically, the Swaziland Sequence is a Supergroup divisible into three groups of formations: (1) the lowermost Onverwacht Group (15,230 m in thickness), (2) the middle Fig Tree Group (2,150 m), and (3) the uppermost Moodies Group (3,150 m). It is possible that the entire Supergroup, both sedimentary and volcanoclastic facies, was formed within a time span of only 200 to 300 million years, although more precise limits are not possible to define with present radiogenic dates. Ages for the lower Onverwacht Group (Komati Formation) have been determined as 3,500 ± 220 million years (m.y.) (Jahn and Shih 1974). The upper age limit of the Moodies Group is not well established, but is clearly older than the aforementioned intrusive granites.

The most convincing evidence of microorganisms comprising two distinct size classes of fairly well-defined modal distribution occurs in cherts of the "Swartkoppie Zone" transitional between the uppermost Onverwacht and the basal Fig Tree Sheba Formation (Knoll 1977; Knoll and Barghoorn 1977). During the past decade and from various laboratories more than a dozen reports have been published describing microfossils from chert units of both the Onverwacht and the Fig Tree cherts (Reimer 1975; Muir 1978). Divergent views as to the true biogenicity of these microstructures have been expressed by Schopf (1977) and more recently by Cloud (1979), for a variety of reasons, but primarily statistical, with respect to the size of the Swaziland microstructures, which are considered anomalously large for prokaryotic organisms of such antiquity. This criticism may be taken seriously with respect to the relatively large isolated organic microstructures, described as *Archaeosphaeroides barbertonensis* (Schopf and Barghoorn 1967), whose size range between 15 μm and 23 μm shows a pronounced peak at 18 μm. These structures must be evaluated, however, also in terms of their sedimentary context which is that of highly carbonaceous black cherts, featured by parallel bedded organic layers and also other amorphous dispersed organic matter. It should be noted in this connection that the much smaller, abundant microstructures from the Swartkoppie, interpreted as showing stages of cell division (Knoll and Barghoorn 1977), are not subject to question as true fossils on the basis of anomalously large size. These instead conform closely to many taxa of small extant cyanophytes (Desikachary 1959) and meet other criteria for biogenicity as well, namely: (1) comparable general morphology to that of geologically younger microorganisms, (2) size frequency distribution comparable to that of both fossil and extant microbial populations, (3) occurrence in a sedimentary context similar to that in which Proterozoic fossils now well recognized and accepted as bona fide have been found, and (4) the microstructures have been preserved in the configuration of binary division. These lines of evidence collectively constitute cogent evidence for a biological population rather than a random accumulation of carbon from nonbiological sources.

As previously noted (Knoll and Barghoorn 1977), the only structures that closely resemble the Swartkoppie spheroids are indeed microfossils; it is also true that the simple morphology of these ancient microstructures makes their 100 percent unequivocal determination as biological entities virtually impossible. However, the distribution of reduced carbon in Archean sediments (Dimroth and Kimberley 1976) and the stable carbon isotope ratios of these Archean carbon fractionations (Eichmann and Schidlowski 1975) are virtually identical to the patterns observed in younger rocks in which their origin is clearly biologically controlled. It seems consistently logical to conclude that in the Swaziland basins, just as in Proterozoic and Phanerozoic basins, photosynthetic organisms, whether oxygenic or nonoxygenic, thrived, and under favorable conditions of silica deposition (chemically precipitated chert) could have been preserved as discrete microbial populations.

It has long seemed of great importance to me that the sheer volume of reduced carbon in Archean rocks in conjunction with other geochemical and sedimentological parameters provides presumptive evidence of a synchronously ancient productive biosphere. To quantitate and evaluate this problem in a well-delineated Archean basin had not been possible, however, until comprehensive data became available from the intensive study of a single depositional sequence. Fortunately, such data are now available from the Swaziland Supergroup, namely, in the Sheba Formation of the Fig Tree Group (Reimer 1975). Analysis of the relevant information with respect to carbon in the Sheba Formation, its amount, dispersed continuity, and sedimentological relations has been made recently (Reimer, Barghoorn, and Margulis 1979). From sedimentological considerations the extent of the original Sheba sediments may be inferred to have been about 4,000 km^2, with an average thickness of 700 m. Measurements of the reduced carbon in the sediments, primarily graywackes and shales, with minor chert units, calculate to 0.42 percent of the rock column. This value when extrapolated to the inferred cubic volume of total Sheba Formation sediments calculates to 52×10^9 metric tons of reduced carbon.

Although these data are no more than a best fit to available chemical analyses of 19 samples from the Sheba Formation they are highly significant in the context of the general problem of how to explain the amount of reduced carbon in Archean rocks, not only the Swaziland Supergroup, but elsewhere. If we eliminate allochthonous sources of graphitic carbon from weathering of igneous rocks (for which there is little or no petrographical evidence in the cherts or graywackes of the Sheba rocks) we have three possible sources: (1) extraterrestrial origin, such as from carbonaceous chondrites, (2) abiological carbon produced or fixed by electric discharge and other atmospheric processes induced by radiation, or (3) biologically fixed carbon produced by photosynthetic (oxygenic or nonoxygenic) or chemoautotrophic microbial processes. As stated previously (Reimer, Barghoorn, and Margulis 1979), I would like to reemphasize that I cannot entertain seriously the first two alternatives, that is, the reduced carbon in the Sheba Formation or in the other rocks of the Swaziland System is abiological in origin. Its degree of sedimentological dispersion and occurrence in shale and chert units, as well as graywackes, seem clearly to indicate a biogenic and microbial origin. This conclusion is also consistent with the isotopic fractionation of $^{13}C/^{12}C$. The $\delta^{13}C$ values of various reduced carbon samples from the Swaziland Supergroup range from approximately -25 to -30 (Eichmann and Schidlowski 1975), consistent with biogenic origin. When viewed in this larger context of organic geochemistry, the problem of interpreting putative organic structures as true microfossils, or as "dubio-fossils" is placed in a different perspective, favoring a paleontological interpretation.

In connection with the interpretation of Archean life and paleobiology in the Barberton Mountainland, recent discoveries in the early Archean of Western Australia of what appears to be evidence of a microbiota, in rocks of comparable age, should be considered (Dunlop et al. 1978). Although these microstructures are surely carbonaceous, they are less well preserved than those of the Swaziland Sequence, and accordingly, less convincingly microbial. They occur, however, in a geological context that is consistent with a biological origin, namely, organic-rich black bedded cherts which, significantly, also show evidence of possible stromatolitic structure (Walter 1978).

Until further evidence is forthcoming concerning the possible stromatolitic nature of the Pilbara cherts of Western Australia, the most convincing evidence of early Archean stromatolites is found in sediments of the Pongola Supergroup of South Africa (Mason and Von Brunn 1977). These structures occur in carbonate units (dolmitic) of a thick (2,500 m) sequence of volcanic-sedimentary rocks exposed in the eastern Transvaal and northern Natal states of South Africa and in Swaziland. The structures are domal and undulatory, of low relief and small size (1–4 cm), and show fine laminations reminiscent of extant algal mat stromatolitic structure, although it cannot be proven that they are of cyanophycean origin, and hence, presumably photosynthetic. The presence in the upper units of the Pongola rocks of thin banded iron formation is again presumptive, though not conclusive evidence of an oxygenic microbiota. Whatever their microbial composition, the significance of the Pongola stromatolites lies in the clear evidence that mat building, and hence, colonial autotrophic life, had clearly evolved well back in Archean time. A succinct and provocative statement concerning the possible limits of early Archean autotrophic life has been published by Knoll (1979), and a general review of the problem will not be restated here.

The existence of relatively large amounts of carbonaceous matter in the Witwatersrand Supergroup, associated with gold-bearing sands and conglomerates, has been known for many years (Garnier 1896; Young 1909). It has been consistently shown that the organic matter is of biogenic origin (Snyman 1965; Prashnowsky and Schidlowski 1967; Hoefs and Schidlowski 1967; Pretorius 1974) and as such gives strong evidence that a flourishing biota existed in the shallow water and alluvial fans, at least on this part of the earth's surface about 2,600 m.y. ago. According to the models proposed by Pretorius (1974), the detrital gold settled in the mid-fan facies of the erosional debris entrapped in part by microbial (algal?) subaqueous growths, and that colloidal gold, or gold from solution was precipitated along the margins and base of the fan. If this model is even approximately correct, it would account for the frequent intimate association of the kerogen-like carbonaceous units and the gold associated with them, as well as the detrital gold in the auriferous sandy units (now quartzites) devoid of carbonaceous matter. In a series of studies on the nature of the organic matter in the gold-bearing unit of the Witwatersrand sediments (the carbon leader), Hallbauer (1973, 1975) (Hallbauer and van Warmelo 1974) postulated the presence of fossil organisms that are present in both the carbonaceous sheets and fibers, as well as in the surface of the base of the alluvial fan deposits. Using a variety of techniques, including x-ray photography of rock slabs, microincineration of the carbonaceous lenses (which range in thickness from <1 mm to several centimeters), and other chemical maceration procedures, Hallbauer has demonstrated what appear to be biological structures. The structures in the ash are preserved as gold encrustations on single fibers or aggregates of fibers, thin encrustations of uranium dioxide (UO_2) on fibers, and silicified filamentous aggregates. Whether one can regard these remains, certain of which conform closely in size and organization to filamentous blue-green algae or filamentous bacteria, as fossils, is open to question. If mineralization by silica occurred rapidly, as is certainly the case in many modern sedimentary environments (Leo and Barghoorn 1976), it is conceivable that the mineralized remnants of the organisms that produced the biogenic carbon of the "carbon leader" are truly fossil. Unfortunately, the assignment of certain of the larger columnar structures to supposed lichen-like affinity has cast doubt on the biogenicity of *all* the alleged "fossils" in the Witwatersrand sediments. We are on the horns of a dilemma in rejecting the morphological evidence of the filamentous "fossils," which occur in a context which we can well accept as biogenic on geochemical and sedimentological grounds. This situation plagues the interpretation of all Archean and many early Proterozoic putative fossils (Cloud 1976, 1979). Probably the most convincing evidence of the true biogenicity of certain of the structures figured by Hallbauer (1974, 1975) is of those which consist of hollow filaments possessing silica walls and those fiber-like gold filaments revealed by stereo x-ray photography of whole rock samples. "The structure of the fibrous gold within the columnar carbonaceous material is totally different from gold particles found in the footwall contact or in typical sedimentary reef deposits. . . ." (Hallbauer and van Warmelo 1974). In view of this, it seems reasonable to regard the fibrous structures as true fossils of filamentous bacteria, flexibacteria, or protocyanophycean algae, in which the cell walls have been emplaced with gold precipitation from true solution or colloidal solution. Such a process has been observed experimentally in fungi in which the cell walls of both living and dead colonies were permineralized by gold (Williams 1918). Whatever the final verdict on the controversial "fossils" of the Witwatersrand "carbon leader," it seems to me it would scarcely be scientific to dismiss them out of hand as having nothing to do with the remains of former organisms.

Of approximately the same age as the Witwatersrand System sediments (2,500–2,600 m.y.), stromatolitic structures widely accepted as biogenic are known from the Bulawayan Group in southern Rhodesia. The Bulawayan structures were first noted by Macgregor in the 1930s and described by him subsequently in a brief but highly significant account (Macgregor 1940). This work received little serious attention from geologists and paleontologists, as was the case with much of the early work on Precambrian algal fossils in the first half of this century. In retrospect, it seems probable that Precambrian paleontology was not ready for serious attention until the development of a reasonable framework of geochronometric control, and the demonstration of morphologically acceptable true fossils. These two circumstances did not come about until the early 1950s with the discovery of the Gunflint microbiota, to be considered later in this chapter.

Although none of the now known half dozen or more late Archean and Proterozoic stromatolite occurrences (preceding the Transvaal Group ca. 2,200 m.y.) have yielded morphologically preserved microfossils, geochemical evidence from stable carbon isotope ratios and greater knowledge of stromatolite sedimentology and morphology has rendered acceptable the biogenicity of these early cryptalgal structures (Schopf et al. 1971; Schindewolf 1956).

The existence of extensive black shales in many Proterozoic sequences of the Lake Superior district has long been known (Van Hise, Bayley, and Smyth 1897), but their significance as indirect paleontological evidence of early life was not appreciated. A rejuvenation of interest in presumptive evidence of life in the form of coaly carbonaceous residues in Precambrian sediments was stimulated by Rankama (1948) in a reexamination of carbonaceous blebs in finely laminated sediment from Finland. It was concluded by him, on the basis of stable carbon isotope ratios as well as what little could be surmised from morphology, that *Corycium enigmaticum* Sederholm was indeed a fossil. An interesting historical review of this important turn of events in Precambrian paleontology is presented by Rankama (1954). Following the discovery by Stanley A. Tyler, in 1952, of a coaly sediment interbedded in the black shales of the Michigamme Formation of northern Michigan, a full-scale effort was made to investigate the geology, geochemistry, and sedimentology of this unexpected occurrence (Tyler, Barghoorn, and Barrett 1957). This study provided ample evidence for the biogenicity of the Michigamme coal, and some evidence of its algal origin. It also provided stimulus for intensive study of the chronologically, nearly contemporaneous, Gunflint Formation algal cherts, containing a profusion of preserved microorganisms (Tyler and Barghoorn 1954; Barghoorn and Tyler 1965).

It is with a brief discussion of the Gunflint chert that I wish to end this narrative of selected aspects of Precambrian paleobiology. The existence of fossil microorganisms in sedimentary rocks of the western Lake Superior region were made known by Cayeux (1911) and also by Gruner (1922), but attracted little notice probably in good part because both the stratigraphy and geochronology of the complex Huronian (Animikiean) System were so poorly known at the time. Probably, also, the general prejudice and scepticism about Precambrian fossils among paleontologists and biologists played an important role. The widespread occurrence of gross algal stromatolitic and cryptalgal structures likewise attracted little attention among paleontologists and biologists. The discovery by S. A. Tyler, in the summer of 1953, of a virtually unmetamorphosed outlier of the Gunflint Formation near its easternmost outcrop provided the key to understanding the nature of the stromatolitic cherts. This discovery made shortly after completion of the field work on the Michigamme coal described previously, started a long series of collaborative field and laboratory studies, which I carried out with Tyler until the time of his death in 1963. The cherts from the easternmost exposures of the Gunflint Formation, although very limited in occurrence, are remarkable for the quality of preservation of the contained delicate microbial structures. An element of scepticism as to the authenticity of the Gunflint microfossils (i.e., as to whether they were truly indigenous to the dense black cherts, or postdepositional contaminants) prevailed for some time after their discovery. Continued study of the cherts, and the wealth and diversity of its microbiota, however, resulted in the general acceptance of the Gunflint assemblage as a genuine index of the level of evolution and diversity of life about 2,000 m.y. ago. Corroboratory evidence from geochemistry, sedimentology, and stable carbon isotope studies give the Gunflint biota some status as a "bench mark" of Precambrian life in the early Proterozoic. In a tabulation of the Gunflint biota (Awramik and Barghoorn 1977), a total of 28 taxa proposed by various authors are reviewed. Certain of these are of dubious authenticity as fossils, a number are poorly preserved and should not have been assigned taxonomical status, but there remain 16 morphological entities that seem unambiguously valid taxonomically. An additional two taxa were subsequently added (Knoll, Barghoorn, and Awramik 1978), yielding an impressive assemblage of microorganisms in toto.

Attempts to assign affinity of these fossils to extant groups, of course, involves subjective judgment based purely on morphology. We suggest that three major categories are present: eight species of cyanophytes, four species of budding bacteria, and six species of uncertain, or unassignable, affinity. Whatever future additions may be made to the Gunflint microbiota, it is apparent from what we now know that it represents a morphologically quite diverse population; and, if the taxonomical assignments are correct, this would translate into a presumed physiological diversity as well. Thus, it may be assumed that a complex biocoenose existed in Gunflint time, featured by oxygenic cyanophytes functioning as energy accumulators and scavenging, or heterotrophic microorganisms, functioning as agents of degradation. The well-developed stromatolites of the Gunflint contain primarily associations of cyanophycean-like microfossils of benthonic habit and probably shallow water. There were, however, subordinate numbers of other microfossils in the total assemblage, of which some were probably planktonic and, hence, allochthonous in their contribution to the well-developed stromatolitic columns. In the upper part of the Gunflint sedimentary sequence nonstromatolitic cherts, containing taxonomically depauparate but locally rich populations of a few other microorganisms occur. These comprise a biota distinct from the algal cherts that probably existed in an environment of deeper, quieter water, of hypersaline chemistry, favoring formation of evaporites (Knoll, Barghoorn, and Awramik 1978). It is this facies of the Gunflint chert which contains locally profuse populations of the organism *Eoastrion* Barghoorn. *Eoastrion* is a trichospheric colonial organism morphologically virtually identical to the extant budding bacterium *Metallogenium personatum* Perfil'ev. It occurs in the completely nonclastic cherts in elongate zones of concentration in which the colonies have been measured in concentrations averaging 7,500 per mm^3 in the exceptionally transparent hyaline chert (Barghoorn 1977). From the gross structure and lithology of the chert it is apparent that the dense parallel zones of *Metallogenium*-like colonies (*Eoastrion*) were concentrated in the aqueous phase horizontal to the water surface before precipitation of the silica from solution. There is no evidence of a solid clastic substratum, with respect to the colonial aggregates, and it is possible that the "suspension" of these laterally elongated masses of the organisms were the result of concentration on a chemocline, as has been shown for modern *Metallogenium* in lakes (Klaveness 1977). There is no evidence that the metallic encrustations on the Gunflint chert *Eoastrion* colonies is manganese rather than iron, a question now being investigated.

This discussion of the *Eoastrion-Metallogenium* analogy and possibly actual phylogenetic homology is brought in here to exemplify and accentuate the fact that by Gunflint time a series of morphological and possibly physiological analogs to extant microbial systems had already evolved.

On the basis of morphology alone, the bulk of the Gunflint taxa can be assigned to extant existing groups of microorganisms. Of those which are not assignable certain are poorly preserved, or represent degradational stages of other taxa. Only one entity, *Eosphaera tyleri*, of very distinct morphology appears to be wholly unrelated to any living organism. It is not common in the assemblage, but is conspicuous because it is of relatively large size (28 to 40 μm). *Eosphaera* was probably planktonic in habit, hence allochthonous to the algal stromatolites. There is no evidence whatsoever that *Eosphaera*, or any of the associated microorganisms in the Gunflint assemblage, was eucaryotic in organization.

RESUMÉ

By way of a résumé, the following generalizations are suggested:

1. The isolated spheroidal carbonaceous structures described from several formations of the Swaziland Supergroup are fossils and indicative of the existence of an active CO_2 assimilative biosphere in the early Archean. By the same token, the bulk of the detrital organic matter in these sediments is interpreted to be of biogenic origin. Sedimentological and geochemical evidence (Stable C and S isotope fractionation), as well as the occurrence of appreciable amounts of banded iron formation and jasper-rich cherts, tend to support this conclusion. No one of these criteria in itself may seem conclusive, but collectively they appear to be compelling evidence of biological activity.

2. Less controversial evidence of widespread late Archean, and very early Proterozoic biological activity derives from the occurrence of carbonate stromatolites from various parts of the world. There is a consensus that these structures are Precambrian analogs of later, if not of modern day, carbonate mats and stromatolites. Unfortunately, the organisms responsible for their formation are not cellularly preserved.

3. Certain of these structures preserved in sediments of the Witwatersrand System are here regarded as bona fide fossils. They require judicious interpretation since some of these alleged "fossils" are certainly nonbiological. If we accept the most convincingly biological structures as fossils, it follows that the filamentous habit of growth had evolved by the late Archean, a level of specialization that is suggested, but not provable, in the coeval stromatolites referred to previously in item 2.

4. The widespread and persistent occurrence and relative abundance of reduced carbon in Archean and Proterozoic sediments—shales, graywackes, and cherts—is interpreted as evidence of a vigorous autotrophic microbial biota existing on earth since the early Archean (3.4 billion years [b.y.] ago).

5. The varied assemblage of microorganisms comprising the Gunflint microbiota provides an index of the level of evolution of life on the primitive earth about 2 billion years ago and demonstrates the complexity of the ecosystems which had evolved by that time in the early history of life on the earth.

REFERENCES

Anhaeusser, C. R. 1978. The geological evidence of the primitive earth—evidence from the Barberton Mountain Land. In *Evolution of the Earth's Crust* (D. H. Tarling, ed.). New York: Academic Press, pp. 71–106.

Awramik, S. M., and E. S. Barghoorn. 1977. The Gunflint microbiota. *Precambrian Res.* 5:121–42.

Barghoorn, E. S. 1977. Eoastrion and the *Metallogenium* problem. In *Chemical Evolution of the Early Precambrian* (C. Ponnamperuma, ed.). New York: Academic Press, pp. 185–86.

Barghoorn, E. S., and S. A. Tyler. 1965. Microorganisms from the Gunflint chert. *Science* 147:563–77.

Bridgwater, D., K. D. Collerson, and J. S. Myers. 1978. The development of the Archaean Gneiss Complex of the North Atlantic Region. In *Evolution of the Earth's Crust*. (D. H. Tarling, ed.). New York: Academic Press, p. 19.

Bridgwater, D., J. H. Allaart, J. W. Schopf et al. 1981. Microfossil-like objects from the Archaean of Greenland: A cautionary note. *Nature* 289:51–53.

Cayeux, L. 1911. Existence des restes organiques dans les roches ferrugineuses associées aux minerais de fer huroniens des Etats-Unis. *C. R. Acad. Sci.* (Paris) 153:910–12.

Cloud, P. 1976. Beginnings of biospheric evolution and their biogeochemical consequences. *Paleobiology* 2:351–87.

———. 1979. On microbial contaminants, micropseudofossils, and the oldest records of life. *Precamb. Res.* 9:81–91.

Desikachary, T. V. 1959. Cyanophyta. *Ind. Counc. Agricult. Res.* (New Delhi), pp. 1–686.

Dimroth, E., and M. M. Kimberley. 1976. Precambrian atmospheric oxygen: evidence in the sedimentary distribution of carbon, sulfur, uranium and iron. *Can. J. Earth Scis.* 13:1161–85.

Dunlop, J. S. R., M. D. Muir, V. A. Milne, and D. I. Groves. 1978. A new microfossil assemblage from the Archean of Western Australia. *Nature* 274:674:676–78.

Eichmann, R., and M. Schidlowski. 1975. Isotopic fractionation between coexisting organic carbon-carbonate pairs in Precambrian sediments. *Geochim. Cosmochim. Acta* 39:585–95.

Engel, A. E. J. 1970. The Barberton Mountain Land: Clues to the differentiation of the earth. In *Adventures in Earth History* (P. Cloud, ed.). San Francisco: W. H. Freeman, pp. 431–45.

Garnier, J. 1897. Gold and diamonds in the Transvaal and the Cape. *Trans. Geol. Soc. S. Africa.* 2:91–120.

Gruner, J. W. 1922. The origin of sedimentary iron formations: The Biwabik Formation of the Mesabi range. *Econ. Geol.* 64:407–60.

Hallbauer, D. K. 1973. In Research Review, Chamber of Mines of S. Africa PRO Series No. 175:27–34.

———. 1975. The plant origin of the Witwatersrand 'carbon.' *Min., Sci. and Eng.* (S. Africa) 7:111–31.

Hallbauer, D. K., and K. T. van Warmelo. 1974. Fossilized plants in thucolite from the Precambrian rocks of the Witwatersrand, South Africa. *Precamb. Res.* 1:199–212.

Hoefs, J., and M. Schidlowski. 1967. Carbon isotope composition of carbonaceous matter from the Precambrian of the Witwatersrand System. *Science* 155:1096–97.

Jahn, B., and C. Y. Shih. 1974. On the age of the Onverwacht Group, Swaziland Sequence, South Africa. *Geochim. Cosmochim. Acta* 38:873–85.

John, B. M., and C. Y. Shih. 1974. On the age of the Onverwacht Group, Swaziland Sequence, South Africa. *Geochim. Cosmochim. Acta* 38:873–85.

Klaveness, D. 1977. Morphology, distribution and significance of the manganese-accumulating microorganism *Metallogenium* in lakes. *Hydrobiologia* 56:25–33.

Knoll, A. H. 1977. Studies in Archean and early Proterozoic paleontology. Ph.D. dissertation, Harvard University.

———. 1979. Archean photoautrophy: some alternatives and limits. *Origins of Life* 9:313–27.

Knoll, A. H., and E. S. Barghoorn. 1977. Archean microfossils showing cell division from the Swaziland System of South Africa. *Science* 198:396–98.

Knoll, A. H., E. S. Barghoorn, and S. M. Awramik. 1978. New microorganisms from the Aphebian Gunflint iron formation, Ontario. *Paleontology* 52(5):976–92.

Leo, R. F., and E. S. Barghoorn. 1976. Silicification of wood. *Bot. Museum Leaflets* (Harvard University) 25:1–47.

Macgregor, A. M. 1940. A Precambrian algal limestone in Southern Rhodesia. *Trans. Geol. Soc. S. Africa* 43:9–15.

Mason, T. R., and V. Von Brunn. 1977. 3-Gyr-old stromatolites from South Africa. *Nature* 266:47–49.

Moorbath, S., R. K. O'Nions, and R. J. Pankhurst. 1975. The evolution of Early Precambrian crustal rocks at Isua, West Greenland—geochemical and isotopic evidence." *Earth Plan. Sci. Lett.* 27:229–39.

Muir, M. D. 1978. Occurrence and potential uses of Archean microfossils and organic matter. In *Archean Cherty Metasediments: Their Sedimentology, Micropaleontolgy, Biogeochemistry and Significance to Mineralization*. Geology Dept. and Extension Services. University of Western Australia.

Pflug, H. D. 1978. Yeast-like microfossils detected in oldest sediments of the earth." *Naturwissenschaften* 65:611–15.

Pflug, H. D., and H. Jaeschke-Boyer. 1979. Combined structural and chemical analysis of 3,800-Myr-old microfossils." *Nature* 280:483–86.

Prashnowsky, A. A., and M. Schidlowski. 1967. Investigation of Precambrian thucolite." *Nature* 216:560–63.

Pretorius, D. 1974. Gold in the Proterozoic sediments of South Africa: Systems, paradigms and models. *Univer. Witwatersrand Econ. Geol. Res. Unit Inf.* (circular) 87:1–22.

Rankama, K. 1948. New evidence of the origin of Pre-Cambrian carbon. *Geol. Soc. Am. Bull.* 59:389–416.

———. 1954. *Isotope Geology*. London: Pergamon Press, pp. 199–206.

Reimer, T. O. 1975. Untersuchungen über Abtragung, Sedimentation und Diagenese in frühen Praecambrium am Beispiel der Sheba Formation (Südafrika). *Geolog. Jhb.* Reihe, B 17:3–108.

Reimer, T. O., E. S. Barghoorn, and L. Margulis. 1979. Primary productivity in an early Archean microbial ecosystem. *Precamb. Res.* 9:93–104.

Rutten, M. G. 1971. *The Origin of Life by Natural Causes*. Amsterdam: Elsevier.

Schidlowski, M., W. U. Appel, R. Eichmann, and C. E. Junge. 1979. Carbon isotope geochemistry of the 3.7×10^9-yr-old Isua sediments, West Greenland: Implications for the Archaean carbon and oxygen cycles. *Geochim. Cosmochim. Acta* 43:189–99.

Schindewolf, O. H. 1956. Über Präkambrische Fossilien. Geotektonisches Symposium zu Ehren von Hans Stille (Fr. Lotze, ed.). Munster: *Deutsche Geologischen Gesellschaft, der Geologisches Verinigung und der Paleontologischen Gesellschaft*, pp. 455–80.

Schopf, J. W. 1977. Are the oldest "fossils" fossils? *Origins of Life* 7:19–36.

Schopf, J. W., and E. S. Barghoorn. 1967. Alga-like fossils from the Precambrian of South Africa. *Science* 156:508–12.

Schopf, J. W., D. Z. Oehler, R. J. Horodyskiand, K. A. Kvenvolden. 1971. Biogenicity and significance of the oldest known stromatolites. *J. Paleont.* 45:477–85.

Snyman, C. P. 1965. Possible biogenetic structures in Witwatersrand thucolite. *Trans. Geol. Soc. S. Africa* 68:225–35.

Tarling, M. R. 1978. *Evolution of the Earth's Crust*. New York: Academic Press, pp. 1–17.

Tyler, S. A., and E. S. Barghoorn. 1954. Occurrence of structurally preserved plants in Pre-cambrian rocks of the Canadian Shield. *Science* 119:606–8.

Tyler, S. A., E. S. Barghoorn, and L. P. Barrett. 1957. Anthracitic coal from Precambrian Upper Huronian black shale of the Iron River district, northern Michigan. *Geol. Soc. Am. Bull.* 68:1293–1304.

Van Hise, C. R., W. S. Bayley, and H. L. Smyth. 1897. The Marquette iron-bearing district of Michigan. *U.S. Geol. Survey Mon.* 28:1–580.

Walter, M. R. 1978. Recognition and significance of Archean stromatolites. In *Archean Cherty Metasediments: Their Sedimentology, Micropaleontology, Biochemistry and Significance to Mineralization*. Geology Dept. and Extension Services, University of Western Australia 2:1–10.

Williams, M. 1918. Absorption of gold from colloidal solutions by fungi. *Ann. Bot.* 32:531–34.

Young, P. B. 1909. Further notes on the auriferous conglomerates of the Witwatersrand with a discussion of the origin of the gold. *Trans. Geol. Soc. S. Africa* 12:82–101.

PALEOECOLOGY OF LATE PRECAMBRIAN MICROBIAL ASSEMBLAGES

Andrew H. Knoll

By censusing the microfossils preserved in individual lamellae of flat, laminated stromatolites from the late Precambrian (740–950 m.y. [million years]) Bitter Springs Formation, Australia, one can establish that certain microbial taxa characteristically occur together, forming recurrent associations. This information, when coupled with observations on the spatial relationships of individuals within populations and taphonomic considerations, allows the subdivision of the Bitter Springs biota into at least five distinct paleocommunities: a microbial mat association dominated by the filamentous cyanobacterium *Eomycetopsis*; a second mat association having as its principal builder the thin filamentous blue-green *Tenuofilum*; an *Eoentophysalis* dominated mat association; an association composed of several sheathless oscillatorian cyanobacteria which on rare occasions covered mat surfaces in the Bitter Springs basin; and a low diversity planktonic assemblage. Similar associations occur in cherts of the approximately coeval Draken Conglomerate, Svalbard; however, the planktonic component of the Svalbard biota is significantly more diverse than its Australian counterpart. Associations of taxa in the late Precambrian Narssârssuk Formation, Greenland, are quite different from those of the other two formations. All benthos examined are prokaryotic, while the plankton includes both cyanobacteria and probable eukaryotes. Heterotrophic protists are present in the late Precambrian of Svalbard. Collectively, these several communities and biotas reflect a measure of the biological heterogeneity of late Precambrian environments. Paleoecology provides a means of refining our ideas of Precambrian biological diversity and the factors that influenced microbial distribution on the early earth.

INTRODUCTION

Students of Precambrian paleontology have, in general, stressed the "verticality" of the early fossil record. Major research emphasis has been placed on the comparison of microbiotas of differing ages in an effort to establish the chronology of early evolution. In its emphasis on microbial variation within a single time plane, paleoecology provides a different, and complementary, approach to the record. This "horizontal" perspective is valuable for several reasons:

1. The existing Precambrian microfossil record reflects systematic environmental biases of preservation. Postmortem cellular degradation is more likely to be arrested at an early stage in some habitats, for example hypersaline tidal flats, than it is in others, including well-oxygenated shelf bottoms (Knoll and Golubic 1979). An understanding of the true nature and extent of this environmental bias is fundamental to the interpretation of the preserved record.

2. Within the limits imposed by item 1, the lateral approach to Precambrian paleontology allows one to recognize patterns of microbial diversity and distribution, thus providing an improved sense of ancient biological associations and the ecological factors that influenced their organization.

3. Recognition of the ecological relationships of early organisms can significantly improve the resolution of vertical analyses of Precambrian fossils. That is, by filtering out the environmental components of variation among microfossil assemblages, paleoecology can help to determine the role of evolution in shaping the early fossil record. Needless to say, the horizontal perspective is also essential in Precambrian biostratigraphy.

A variety of approaches to Precambrian paleoecology are possible. The specific question to be addressed in this chapter is, Can internal patterns of species distributions be recognized *within* individual microbiotas? That is, can one define recurrent associations of taxa in Precambrian sedimentary rocks? The principal focus of this study is the well-known biota of the late Precambrian Bitter Springs Formation, Australia (Schopf 1968; Schopf and Blacic 1971). Conclusions drawn on the basis of Bitter Springs fossils will then be critically augmented from observations on two additional late Precambrian microfossil assemblages,[1] the Draken Conglomerate of Svalbard (Knoll 1979) and the Narssârssuk Formation, Greenland (Strother and Knoll 1979). All samples came from coastal carbonate sequences, although details of environmental setting vary from one formation to the next, a fact of major importance in the interpretation of the microbiotas. Prokaryotes (cyanobacteria) dominate the benthic microbial mat communities of each assemblage, while cooccurring planktonic microfossils include probable prokaryotes, eukaryotes, and a variety of spheroidal taxa whose affinities remain unclear.

MATERIALS AND METHODS

Silicified, flat laminated, microbial stromatolites from the Ross River locality of the late Precambrian (approximately 740–950 m.y.) Bitter Springs Formation were chosen for this investigation because their microfossils are unusually well preserved and they have been extensively studied (Barghoorn and Schopf 1965; Schopf 1968). In addition, the Bitter Springs microbiota is an appropriate assemblage for this initial analysis because of its central role in the historical development of our ideas about Precambrian paleobiology. Thin sections analyzed include all type sections of Ross River material, as well as preparations made from other samples collected by E. S. Barghoorn in 1965 and J. W. Schopf in 1968. All materials are housed in the Paleobotanical Collections of Harvard University. The general geological setting of the Bitter Springs Formation has been described by Wells et al. (1970), Schopf (1968), Walter (1972), and Stewart (1979), and need not be reiterated here. Suffice it to say that the Bitter Springs shales and carbonates accumulated on a marine platform beneath a warm, shallow sea. Early stage barred basin conditions gave way to less restricted marine environments in later Bitter Springs time. It is in these younger deposits that the Ross River fossils are found.

The microbiotas chosen for comparison to the Bitter Springs assemblage are currently being studied in detail. The Draken Conglomerate samples were collected by Colin Wilson under the auspices of the 1953 Cambridge Spitsbergen Expedition, W. B. Harland, director, and were made available through the courtesy of Mr. Harland. P. K. Strother and I collected the Narssârssuk materials in the summer of 1978. Because the geological settings of these formations are germane to the consideration of their microbial remains, discussion of sedimentary environments is presented in a later section of this chapter.

The procedure used to gather data is simple. In the silicified stromatolites whose contained microfossils constitute a major element of the Precambrian fossil record, each lamination represents a single time interval. Thus, by censusing the preserved assemblages found along individual laminae, it is possible to test for the occurrence of distinct microbial associations. In the Bitter Springs analysis, I have employed the systematic classification of Schopf (1968), with several exceptions. Following the emendation of Knoll and Golubic (1979), I have recognized only a single species of *Eomycetopsis*, not two. Spheroidal unicells 7 to 15 μm in diameter assigned by Schopf to the three species *Glenobotrydion aenigmatis*, *Myxococcoides minor*, and *Caryosphaeroides pristina* were, for reasons to be discussed later, grouped together as "spheroidal unicells." No attempt was made to distinguish among the three described species of *Biocatenoides*. Finally, the coccoidal cyanobacterial species *Eosynechococcus amadeus*, recently described by

Knoll and Golubic (1979) from the Ellery Creek locality of the Bitter Springs Formation, was recognized in the Ross River material and, thus, added to Schopf's (1968) species list. The data matrix in Table 2.1 gives census data for 3-cm lengths of 54 laminae from 21 thin sections; hundreds of additional laminae from dozens more thin sections were examined, but these merely confirm the trends evident in the table. Thus, the data displayed in the matrix are considered to be representative of the locality as a whole. Absolute values are probably not very significant; it is the relative abundances of species within laminae that are important.

MICROFOSSIL ASSOCIATIONS IN THE BITTER SPRINGS FORMATION

Perusal of Table 2.1 reveals that certain taxa are consistently associated in Bitter Springs laminae. For example, *Eomycetopsis robusta* Schopf, a 2 to 5 μm in diameter, nonseptate tube that represents the hydrated polysaccharide external sheath of a *Lyngbya* or *Phormidium* type of filamentous cyanobacterium, consistently occurs with the spheroidal unicells. *Tenuofilum septatum* Schopf, despite its name another tubular sheath, but only about 1 μm in cross-sectional diameter, is also commonly associated with these unicellular microfossils; however, in most cases, where *Tenuofilum* is abundant, *Eomycetopsis* is rare or absent and vice versa. A distinctly different association of taxa includes the species *Palaeolyngbya barghoorniana* Schopf, *Oscillatoriopsis obtusa* Schopf, *Calypotothrix annulata* Schopf, *Cephalophytarion grande* Schopf and *C. minutum* Schopf, and *Caudiculophycus rivularioides* Schopf. All of these fossils are sheathless trichomes of oscillatorian cyanobacteria.

A cooccurrence matrix can be constructed from the data in Table 2.1, and a distilled version of this matrix is presented in Table 2.2. Displayed in this form, the data confirm the inference drawn from Table 2.1 that the Ross River cherts contain three distinct taxonomic associations (Table 2.3). Under the microscope, the spatial distinctness of the three associations is clear.

Having determined that recurrent associations exist, one must ask *why* certain species consistently occur together. Three explanations are possible: (1) the species lived together in a microbial community association; (2) the species occur together because of transportation to a common site of burial; (3) the species are synonymous, representing different morphological or degradational variants of a single biological entity. All three factors are applicable in the explanation of the Bitter Springs distributions.

The *Eomycetopsis* Association

Eomycetopsis robusta specimens commonly occur as scattered, short lengths of tubular sheaths; however, in well-preserved pockets within the

TABLE 2.1: **Occurrence of Microfossil Taxa in Laminae of Silicified, Flat Laminated Stromatolites from the Ross River Locality, Bitter Springs Formation**

	BS 7-1 L-1	BS 7-1 L-2	BS 7-1 L-3	BS 7-1 L-4	BS 7-1 L-5	BS 6-6 L-1	BS 6-6 L-2	BS 6-6 L-3	BS 6-6 L-4	BS 6-6 L-5	BS 6-6 L-6
Eomycetopsis robusta	17	6	18	30	8	17	6	1	1	32	
"Spheroidal unicells"	7	46	64	6	61	19	125	75	104	9	17
Myxococcoides inornata			7		20	8				1	
Tenuofilum septatum						6	5	45			
Siphonophycus kestron						5	10	4	1	3	
Palaeolyngbya barghoorniana											7
Oscillatoriopsis obtusa											1
Calyptothrix annulata											1
Cephalophytarion grande											29
C. minutum											21
Cyanonema attenuatum											
Contortothrix vermiformis[a]											1
Halythrix nodosa											
Caudiculophycus rivularioides											
Anabaenidium johnsonii											
Heliconema australiense											
Archaeonema longicellulare											
Biocatenoides sp.										50	13
Archaeotrichion contortum					2		3				
Globophycus rugosum											
Gloeodiniopsis lamellosa											
Zosterosphaera tripunctata											
Sphaerophycus parvum											
Eosynechococcus amadeus											
Unidentified coccoids											

(continued)

21

Table 2.1 (continued)

	BS 6-6 L-7	BS 6-1 L-1	BS 11-1 L-1	BS 11-1 L-2	BS 11-1 L-3	BS 6-5 L-1	BS 6-5 L-2	BS 6-5 L-3	BS 6-5 L-4	BS 6-5 L-5	BS 6-5 L-6
Eomycetopsis robusta	150		19	4	5		2	35	9	2	2
"Spheroidal unicells"			79	51	196	200	330	480	93	44	19
Myxococcoides inornata				4				4			
Tenuofilum septatum			12[a]	6	21		16		1	41	
Siphonophycus kestron											
Palaeolyngbya barghoorniana		4									2
Oscillatoriopsis obtusa		3									19
Calyptothrix annulata											
Cephalophytarion grande		17									22
C. minutum		12									19
Cyanonema attenuatum		2									10
Contortothrix vermiformis[b]											
Halythrix nodosa											2
Caudiculophycus rivularioides											1
Anabaenidium johnsonii											
Heliconema australiense											4
Archaeonema longicellulare											1
Biocatenoides sp.	12	5							6		4
Archaeotrichion contortum		2							2	3	
Globophycus rugosum											
Gloeodiniopsis lamellosa											
Zosterosphaera tripunctata											
Sphaerophycus parvum											
Eosynechococcus amadeus											
Unidentified coccoids											

(continued)

Table 2.1 (continued)

	BS 6-7 L-1	BS 6-7 L-2	BS 6-7 L-3	BS 6-4 L-1	BS 6-4 L-2	BS 6-3 L-1	JS 68-1 L-1	JS 68-2 L-1	JS 68-3 L-1	JS 68-4 L-1	JS 68-5 L-1
Eomycetopsis robusta	50		2				256	21	23	52	100
"Spheroidal unicells"	22	3	22				2	59	8	95	
Myxococcoides inornata											
Tenuofilum septatum			19	20				2	1		
Siphonophycus kestron								1	1		
Palaeolyngbya barghoorniana		8				8					
Oscillatoriopsis obtusa		16			24	22					
Calyptothrix annulata		10			3						
Cephalophytarion grande		75			37	72					
C. minutum		86			17	28					
Cyanonema attenuatum		2				2					
Contortothrix vermiformis[b]		4									
Halythrix nodosa		13									
Caudiculophycus rivularioides											
Anabaenidium johnsonii						7					
Heliconema australiense						3					
Archaeonema longicellulare											
Biocatenoides sp.		31			4	17			5		
Archaeotrichion contortum					1		1				
Globophycus rugosum											
Gloeodiniopsis lamellosa							4				
Zosterosphaera tripunctata											
Sphaerophycus parvum				40			10				
Eosynechococcus amadeus							3				
Unidentified coccoids							15				

(continued)

23

Table 2.1 (continued)

	BS 12-5 L-1	BS 12-5 L-2	JS 68-6 L-1	JS 68-6 L-2	BS 1 L-1	BS 1 L-2	BS 1 L-3	BS 10-1 L-1	BS 11-3 L-1	BS 11-3 L-2	BS 11-3 L-3
Eomycetopsis robusta	2	9	84	31				6	30		30
"Spheroidal unicells"	75	10		2	46	107	58	51	49		113
Myxococcoides inornata	1										
Tenuofilum septatum						7	7	25	2	24	
Siphonophycus kestron											
Palaeolyngbya barghoorniana											
Oscillatoriopsis obtusa											
Calyptothrix annulata											
Cephalophytarion grande											
C. minutum											
Cyanonema attenuatum											
Contortothrix vermiformis [b]											
Halythrix nodosa											
Caudiculophycus rivularioides											
Anabaenidium johnsonii											
Heliconema australiense											
Archaeonema longicellulare											
Biocatenoides sp.		2									
Archaeotrichion contortum		1	5				8	3			
Globophycus rugosum											
Gloeodiniopsis lamellosa											
Zosterosphaera tripunctata											
Sphaerophycus parvum											
Eosynechococcus amadeus											
Unidentified coccoids											

(continued)

24

Table 2.1 (continued)

25

	BS 11-3 L-4	BS 12-1 L-1	BS 6-2 L-1	BS 6-2 L-2	BS 6-2 L-3	BS 6-2 L-4	BS 6-2 L-5	BS 11-2 L-1	BS 11-2 L-2	BS 11-2 L-3
Eomycetopsis robusta	2	1			50	1		5	17	40
"Spheroidal unicells"	30	42	15	11	200	99	1	35	82	42
Myxococcoides inornata										
Tenuofilum septatum	37	270	300	75				175	37	10
Siphonophycus kestron									3	
Palaeolyngbya barghoorniana							2			
Oscillatoriopsis obtusa							11			
Calyptothrix annulata							3			
Cephalophytarion grande							20			
C. minutum							36			
Cyanonema attenuatum							1			
Contortiothrix vermiformis [b]										
Halythrix nodosa							1			
Caudiculophycus rivularioides							1			
Anabaenidium johnsonii										

(continued)

Table 2.1 (continued)

	BS 11-3 L-4	BS 12-1 L-1	BS 6-2 L-1	BS 6-2 L-2	BS 6-2 L-3	BS 6-2 L-4	BS 6-2 L-5	BS 11-2 L-1	BS 11-2 L-2	BS 11-2 L-3
Heliconema australiense										
Archaeonema longicellulare										
Biocatenoides sp.							1			
Archaeotrichion contortum										
Globophycus rugosum								1		
Gloeodiniopsis lamellosa										
Zosterosphaera tripunctata										
Sphaerophycus parvum		35						200		
Eosynechococcus amadeus	1									
Unidentified coccoids										

[a]Listed as *Contortonema vermiformae* in Schopf and Blacic (1971).
[b]Segregated in a distinct cluster within the lamina.

TABLE 2.2: Partial Cooccurrence Matrix for Major Taxa of Ross River Locality

	Eo	Te	SU	SO
Eomycetopsis robusta	39	20(8)	37(25)	0
Tenuofilum septatum		25	23(19)	0
"Spheroidal unicells"			46	3(1)
Sheathless oscillatorians*				7

Note: Diagonal indicates number of occurrences of each taxon or group. Other numbers indicate total cooccurrences (the number in parenthesis indicates numbers of cooccurrences in which the less abundant taxon is represented by at least four individuals).

**Cephalophytarion grande*, *C. minutum*, *Oscillatoriopsis obtusa*, *Palaeolyngbya barghoorniana*, and associated taxa.

silicified mats, large populations of loosely interwoven individuals can be observed (Figs. 2.4, 2.5, 2.8). Schopf (1968, p. 685) noted that *Eomycetopsis* filaments were "commonly gregarious, sinuously interlaced in a loosely woven prosenchyma-like mass." The choice of adjectives here reflects the original interpretation of *Eomycetopsis* as possible fungal hyphae, a view that has been abandoned with the discovery of partially degraded oscillatorian cellular trichomes inside *E. robusta* sheaths (Hofmann 1976; Knoll and Golubic 1979). Occasionally, these filamentous arrays are laterally persistent and display a distinctive microfabric in which members of the population are oriented parallel to the bedding plane in one lamina, turn upward to a vertical position (perpendicular to bedding) in the overlying band, and then

TABLE 2.3: Recurrent Associations

1. *Eomycetopsis robusta*
   "spheroidal unicells"
      Tenuofilum septatum
      Siphonophycus kestron

2. *Tenuofilum septatum*
   "spheroidal unicells"
      Siphonophycus kestron
      Eomycetopsis robusta
      Sphaerophycus parvum
      Eosynechococcus amadeus

3. *Cephalophytarion grande*
   Cephalophytarion minutum
   Oscillatoriopsis obtusa
   Calyptothrix annulata
   Palaeolyngbya barghoorniana
   Cyanonema attenuatum
   Contortothrix vermiformis
   Anabaenidium johnsonii
   Caudiculophycus rivularioides
   Halythrix nodosa
   Heliconema australiense
   Archaeonema longicellulare
   Biocatenoides sp.

Note: Minor members of the associations—those species that are found in less than half of the association occurrences, but which do generally occur in the same laminae as major taxa in the association—are indented.

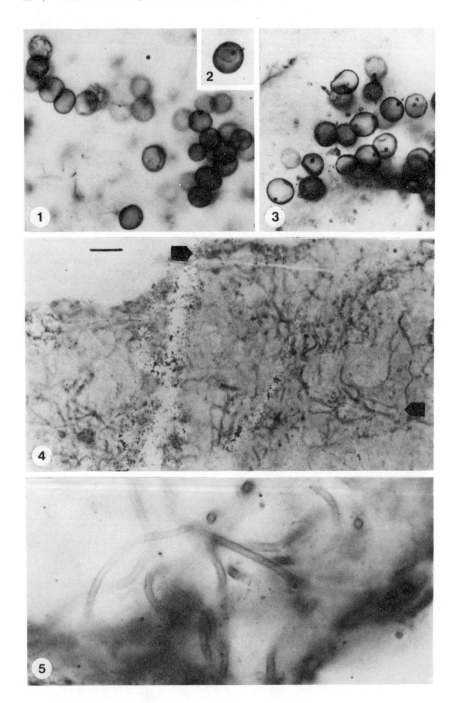

return to a bedding-parallel orientation (Figs. 2.4, 2.8). This microfabric is quite similar to the noctidiurnal growth patterns of *Phormidium hendersonii* Howe in modern stromatolites from Andros Island, Bahamas (Monty 1965, 1976); Bermuda (Golubic and Focke 1978); Bonaire; Florida (Golubic and Focke 1978); and the Great Barrier Reef of Australia (Monty 1978). In *P. hendersonii* mats, vertical sheaths record phototactic daytime growth, while the alternating horizontal individuals reflect noctural layering (Monty 1976; Golubic and Focke 1978).

The distinctive orientation of *Eomycetopsis* sheaths in the Bitter Springs Formation demonstrates that in some areas of the late Precambrian Bitter Springs sea, *E. robusta* was a primary mat builder. The preservation of this fabric further suggests that in this specific zone, the filaments were supported by a sediment matrix during early stages of diagenesis. In the absence of mineral support, compaction would have altered the vertical orientation pattern, (Horodyski, Bloeser, and Vander Haar 1977), as it evidently has in other *Eomycetopsis*-dominated portions of the Bitter Springs cherts.

The organisms most frequently found in association with *Eomycetopsis* are spheroidal unicells originally assigned to the species *Myxococcoides minor*, *Caryosphaeroides pristina*, and *Glenobotrydion aenigmatis* (Schopf 1968). These remains occur as isolated individuals and colonies of a few to several hundred cells scattered more or less randomly throughout the silicified stromatolites. On the basis of this distribution, Schopf (1972) suggested that these common Bitter Springs microfossils are the remains of *planktonic* algae that lived in the water column above the accreting mats, occasionally spreading across a mat surface, an interpretation with which I concur. The *Eomycetopsis* association therefore represents not a single community, but two ecologically distinct groups. This, in turn, prompts further observations.

Preserved mat-dwelling microbes or subordinate mat builders are rare in this association, although occasional, apparently in situ sheaths of *Tenuofilum septatum* or *Siphonophycus kestron* Schopf occur. This does not necessarily mean that no other microorganisms lived in the *Eomycetopsis* mats. Indeed, in modern stromatolitic communities, a wide range of bacteria thrive (e.g., Krumbein et al. 1979). Preservation is selective, however, and most mat-dwelling bacteria do not become incorporated into the fossil record. Further, as Horodyski, Bloeser, and Vander Haar (1977)

FIGURES 2.1–2.5 **2.1–2.3.** Planktonic unicells from the Ross River locality of Bitter Springs Formation, Australia: **2.1.** *Myxococcoides minor* Schopf or *Glenobotrydion aenigmatis* Schopf; **2.2.** *Caryosphaeroides pristina* Schopf; and **2.3**, *G. aenigmatis* Schopf. **2.4.** Low magnification view of *Eomycetopsis robusta* population showing horizontal (arrows) and vertical orientation of sheaths. **2.5.** Higher magnification view of *E. robusta* showing intricate interweaving of individuals. Bar in 2.4 = 50 μm for 2.4, and 15 μm for 2.1–2.3, and 2.5.

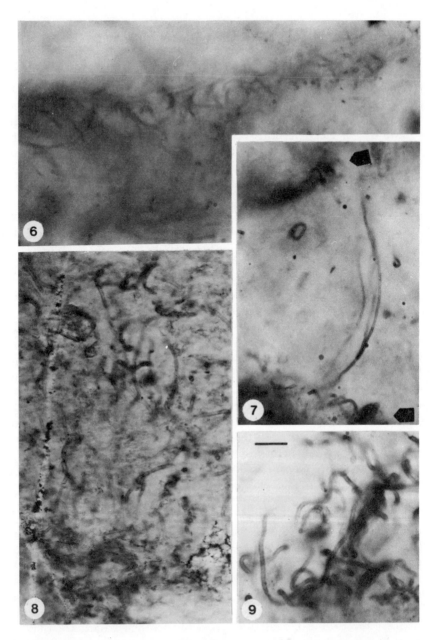

FIGURES 2.6–2.9 **2.6** Population of *Tenuofilum septatum* showing densely woven mat fabric which is clearly visible even though overall preservation of the population is ghost-like. **2.7.** *T. septatum*, showing portions of two densely woven horizontal mat laminae (arrows) with vertical sheaths in between. **2.8.** *Eomyceptopsis robusta*, enlarged view of a portion of Figure 2.4. **2.9.** *T. septatum*, a dense cluster of sheaths. Bar in 2.9 = 15 µm for 2.6. and 2.7, 30 µm for 2.8, and 10 µm for 2.9.

have demonstrated, selective preservation can also shift the apparent abundance ratios of mat-building cyanobacterial filaments. In certain recent stromatolites from Baja California, *Microcoleus chthonoplastes* Thuret is the major mat builder; but because this taxon suffers rapid postmortem degradation, the less abundant (but better preserved) associated cyanobacterium *Lyngbya aestuarii* Liebm. is predominant in buried horizons. One cannot rule out the possibility that other microbes were important contributors to the accretion of these Bitter Springs stromatolites; however, the density and orientation of *Eomycetopsis* in well-preserved sections does indicate that this taxon was a dominant organism in mat formation. The vertical differentiation of taxa along light and oxygen gradients characteristic of modern mat communities (Golubic 1976; Krumbein, Cohen, and Shilo 1977; Krumbein et al., 1979) has not been recognized in the fossil record (Awramik, Gebelein, and Cloud 1978).

A second consideration involves the apparently planktonic spheroidal unicells. These fossils are among the most abundant elements of the Ross River microbiota, and it is of interest to inquire into their taxonomic diversity. Schopf (1968) recognized three major species (*Myxococcoides minor*, *Glenobotrydion aenigmatis*, and *Caryosphaeroides pristina*), as well as several additional rare taxa. Because the three major taxa are similar in many respects, Hofmann (1976) raised the question of whether or not they constitute distinct biological entities.

The species cannot be distinguished unequivocally by the spatial patterns of cell populations. In all three cases, cells can occur as solitary individuals or in a variety of distinctive or irregular packing arrangements (Schopf 1968). The most consistent differences among these forms relate to their internal structures. In *Caryosphaeroides*, a consistently small internal spot of dense organic matter is surrounded by an irregular organic sac (Fig. 2.2). *Glenobotrydion* differs in the absence of the sac (Fig. 2.3), and in *Myxococcoides* neither spot nor sac are present (Fig. 2.1). Unfortunately, the criterion of internal morphology cannot be rigidly applied to fossil populations. Implicit in Schopf's (1968, p. 681) diagnosis of the genus *Glenobotrydion* as "cells, spherical, spheroidal, or ellipsoidal, *commonly* with prominent, circular, small organic structure on inner surface of cell wall" (italics mine) is the recognition that in the Ross River cherts there exist cells that in size, shape, divisional patterns, and clustering patterns are identical to the type population of *G. aenigmatis*, but which have *no* internal bodies. Indeed, Hofmann (1976) has noted that *G. aenigmatis*, *M. minor* and *C. pristina* have nearly identical distributions in Bitter Springs rocks and that more than one internal structural type can be present in a single cluster of cells. Hoffmann's suggestion is that variations in internal morphology are products of postmortem degradation (see also Awramik, Golubic, and Barghoorn 1972).

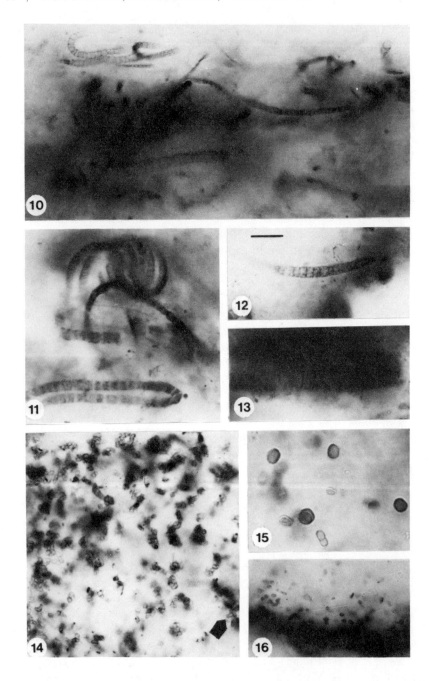

Cells within a single cluster are usually consistent in the presence or absence of an internal spot (Oehler 1977), although as mentioned previously, it is common to observe two clusters that are identical *except* for the single character of an internal bleb (cf. Figs. 2.1 and 2.3). If one accepts Schopf's (1968) interpretation that these are the fossils of green algae, then one can further hypothesize that the internal blebs may be partially degraded starch granules that in life were positioned about the pyrenoid. (This is not the same as equating the blebs to the pyrenoid itself.) Morphologically distinctive starch bodies have been identified in permineralized Pennsylvanian seeds (Baxter 1964), and recent experiments on the postmortem degradation of green algae suggest that starch grains are much more likely to be preserved than organelles (Francis et al. 1978). This hypothesis readily explains the consistent size, position, and number of spots in an individual, as well as the significant presence-absence phenomenon in otherwise identical clusters of cells. Under the terms of this argument, the presence or absence of an internal bleb is considered to be a function of biology (starch storage) as much as of degradation, but the internal structure is not useful in species identification. (Two notes of caution. Although this idea is appealing in its consistent explanation of the observed facts, I cannot prove that the internal bodies are anything more than coalesced cytoplasm. Further, the arguments obtain *only* for the Bitter Springs populations herein considered and cannot be extrapolated to a general explanation of organic bodies in fossil microorganisms. Indeed, *most* such bodies are probably shrunken cell contents.)

Size frequency distributions for the three taxa as distinguished by internal contents also support a hypothesis of biological identity. Measurements of a sample population of 422 individuals from a single thin section yield the following data: *M. minor*: n = 255, mean diameter = 10.0 μm, standard deviation = 2.4 μm; *G. aenigmatis*: n = 150, $\overline{X}$ = 9.5 μm, s = 2.0 μm; *C. pristina*: n = 17, $\overline{X}$ = 9.8 μm, s = 3.6 μm. Three Student's *t*-tests can be performed to compare means, and of these only the *G. aenigmatis–M. minor* comparison fails at the 5 percent level. Failure occurs because the *Myxococcoides* size frequency distribution is bimodal, containing a secondary peak at about 13 μm, in addition to the major mode at 9 to 10 μm. This indicates that the *Myxococcoides* population is heterogeneous, a fact recognized by

FIGURES 2.10–2.16   2.10, 2.11. Views of *Cephalophytarion* association. 2.12. *C. grande* Schopf. 2.13. *Palaeolyngbya barghoorniana* Schopf. 2.14. Portion of a thin lamina dominated by *Eosynechococcus amadeus* Knoll and Golubic. Arrows denote cylindrical or rod shape of cells. Distinct clustering arrangements reflect both division patterns and the confining effects of extracellular mucilage. 2.15. *Sphaerophycus parvum* Schopf. 2.16. Same, showing distribution of *S. parvum* population along a bedding plane. Bar in 2.12 = 11 μm for 2.10 and 2.11; 8 μm for 2.12, 2.13, and 2.15; 15 μm for 2.14; and 25 μm for 2.16.

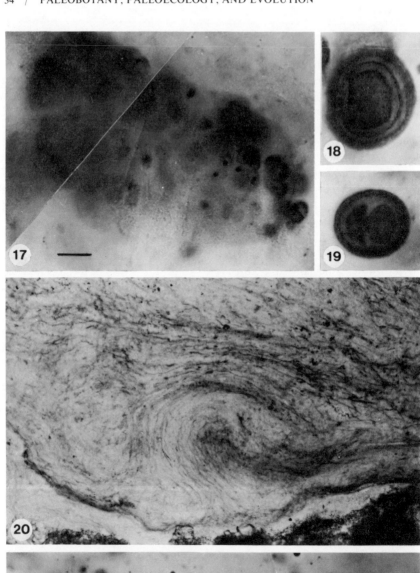

Schopf in the diagnosis of the species *M. reticulata* for *Myxococcoides* specimens in the size range of 12 to 15 μm. When the secondary peak is removed, Student's *t*-test is easily passed at the 5 percent level.

Although they do not correspond closely to the distributions of internal cell structures, distinctive size classes and division and clustering patterns do exist in the Ross River assemblage. In an attempt to gauge the diversity of the Bitter Springs plankton assemblage, several populations of presumably planktonic cells, including *all* apparently planktonic individuals and not only those in the 7- to 15-μm range, were censused. Using size frequency distributions and packing arrangements as taxonomic criteria, I estimated the number of species present and counted the number of specimens in each taxonomic entity. Because many uncertainties exist in this procedure, Table 2.4 displays three separate distributions for each sample: a "minimum" count that is taxonomically conservative, that is, all morphological classes that could possibly be grouped together were "lumped"; a "maximum" count in which "splitting" was favored; and an "estimated" column that gives a best estimate of true distribution. For each tabulation, values for species richness and dominance were calculated, as was the Shannon-Wiener index, an equitability function that serves as a general index of diversity (Whittaker 1975). Samples BS 6-7, BS 6-6, and BS 11 (Table 2.4) are from the Ross River locality of the Bitter Springs Formation, and all three present a similar picture of plankton diversity. If the "minimum" estimate is correct, the plankton assemblage, insofar as can be detected from fossils, is almost completely dominated by a single taxon. Even in the "maximum" and "estimated" cases, few species are present (S = 4–7) and one or two species are strongly dominant (C = 0.4–0.7, where 1.0 indicates a monospecific assemblage). A fourth sample from the Ellery Creek locality of the same formation (Schopf and Blacic 1971) similarly shows an assemblage of low species richness with dominance concentrated in the same taxa that are so abundant in the Ross River samples.

In part, this low diversity may stem from preservational convergence of originally distinguishable microbial taxa through loss of differentiating characters during fossilization. Additionally, differential degradation may have removed certain species altogether, thereby augmenting the apparent importance of those that were preserved. Still, the diversity of this system is

FIGURES 2.17–2.21 **2.17.** Broadly hemispherical cluster of *Eoentophysalis cumulus* Knoll and Golubic from the Ellery Creek locality of the Bitter Springs Formation. **2.18, 2.19.** Specimens of *Gloeodiniopsis lamellosa* Schopf em. Knoll and Golubic found in association with *E. cumulus* mats. **2.20.** Densely woven mats built by an as yet unnamed *Lyngbya* or *Phormidium*-like sheathed cyanobacterium from the Draken Conglomerate, Svalbard. **2.21.** Higher magnification view of an individual belonging to the population illustrated in 2.20. Note degradation of sheath at right. Bar in 2.17 = 7 μm for 2.17–2.19, 10 μm for 2.20, and 14 μm for 2.21.

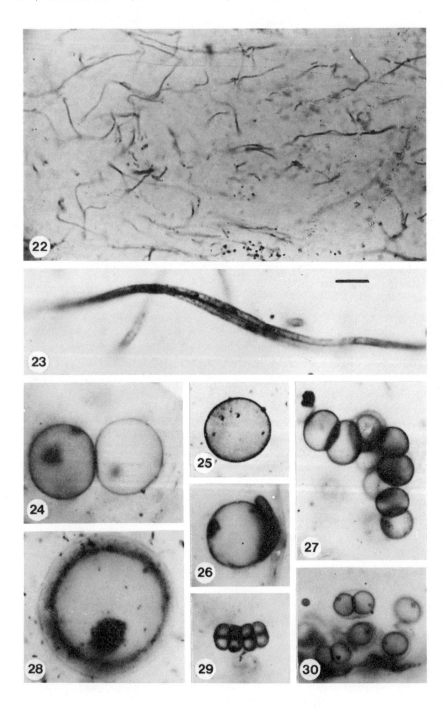

notably low relative to those of some other late Precambrian plankton assemblages (Table 2.7), and this may indicate partial restriction of water circulation between the Bitter Springs environment and the open ocean. In modern coastal environments, low plankton diversity can be related to elevated salinity, eutrophication, and/or the inhibition of potential algal competitor by the production of allelochemics (Whittaker and Feeny 1971). Salinity may have been important in restricting the number of taxa present in the Bitter Springs water column.

The *Tenuofilum* Association

In the Ross River stromatolites, *Tenuofilum* sheaths are common, and large populations are found "entangled in sub-parallel oriented groups" (Schopf 1968, p. 679). The dense interweaving of filaments (Figs. 2.6, 2.7, 2.9) leaves no doubt that *T. septatum*, like *E. robusta*, was a mat-building organism. *Eomycetopsis* individuals are sometimes found in the same laminae as *Tenuofilum* populations (and vice versa), but when present they tend to occur as short, broken lengths of (transported?) sheaths. That is to say, the *Eomycetopsis* and *Tenuofilum* mats are distinct. Nonetheless, the two associations appear to be related environmentally. Several lines of evidence support this observation: (1) there is significant overlap (Table 2.2) in the lamellar distribution of the two taxa (the cooccurrence helps establish that *Tenuofilum* is not merely a shrunken *Eomycetopsis*; (2) abundant planktonic unicells are found in both associations; and (3) in some Ross River cherts, the two associations occur in alternate laminations within a single hand specimen. Application of Walther's law on a very small scale suggests that the two associations are related along an environmental gradient. Alternation of mat builders can occur as pools or channels shift laterally through time (Golubic, personal communication), and transgression or regression will also result in the superimposing of one community on the remains of another.

In modern microbial mats, "mat dwelling" or "guest" species (Golubic 1976) occasionally proliferate locally in response to favorable microenvironmental conditions, covering a small patch of mat surface for a short period of time. These proliferation "events" can sometimes be recognized in permineralized stromatolites as thin lenses, on the order of 10^1 μm thick and

FIGURES 2.22–2.30 2.22. Loosely interwoven sheaths of *E. robusta* from the Draken Conglomerate, Svalbard. **2.23.** Higher magnification view of individuals from the population illustrated in **2.22. 2.24–2.28, 2.30.** Apparently planktonic microbes from the Draken Conglomerate illustrating a small measure of the morphological diversity exhibited by this assemblage. **2.29.** As yet unnamed mat-dwelling cyanobacteria, found locally along bedding laminae in Draken mat shards. Bar in 2.23 = 15 μm for 2.23, 60 μm for 2.22, and 10 μm for 2.24–2.30.

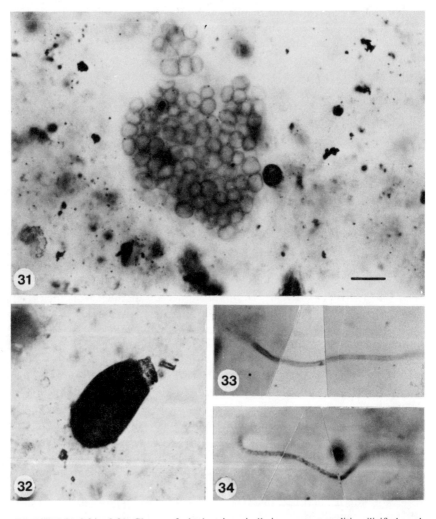

FIGURES 2.31–2.34 **2.31.** Cluster of planktonic unicells in nonstromatolitic, silicified mud clasts from the Draken Conglomerate. Note the differences in matrix texture between this figure and 2.20 or 2.22. **2.32.** Vase-shaped heterotrophic protist from Backlundtoppen Formation, Svalbard. **2.33, 2.34.** Poorly preserved individuals from *Tenuofilum septatum* population in the Draken Conglomerate. Bar in 2.31 = 30 μm for 2.31, 20 μm for 2.32, and 10 μm for 2.33, 2.34.

10^2 and 10^3 μm wide, of distinctive microorganisms. In *Tenuofilum*-dominated sections of the Ross River stromatolites, populations of the coccoidal cyanobacteria *Sphaerophycus parvum* Schopf (Figs. 2.15, 21.6) and *Eosynechococcus amadeus* Knoll and Golubic (Fig. 2.14) conform to this spatial distribution. Other mat dwellers are rare.

TABLE 2.4: Planktonic Diversity in Bitter Springs Cherts

BS 6-7 (N = 1100)

Min	Max	Est
1065	792	792
33	273	273
1	30	33
1	3	1
	1	1
	1	

S = 3.64 S = 5.45 S = 4.55
C = 0.94 C = 0.59 C = 0.59
H' = 0.15 H' = 0.70 H' = 0.70

JWS 68-22 (N = 954)

Min	Max	Est
913	579	679
40	209	209
1	70	45
	45	20
	30	1
	20	
	1	

S = 3.14 S = 7.34 S = 5.24
C = 0.93 C = 0.43 C = 0.56
H' = 0.18 H' = 1.17 H' = 0.81

BS 6-6 (N = 1309)

Min	Max	Est
1270	693	693
39	537	537
	40	40
	33	33
	6	6

S = 1.53 S = 3.82 S = 3.82
C = 0.94 C = 0.45 C = 0.45
H' = 0.13 H' = 0.92 H' = 0.92

BS 11 (11-1 + 11-2) (N = 1016)

Min	Max	Est
907	585	860
95	185	95
8	99	35
2	95	20
1	20	8
	20	3
	3	1
	3	
	3	
	2	
	1	

S = 4.92 S = 10.83 S = 6.89
C = 0.81 C = 0.38 C = 0.73
H' = 0.38 H' = 1.30 H' = 0.62

Note: For each sample, the number of individuals belonging to each species is tabulated. (For explanation of minimum, maximum, and estimated distributions, see text.) S = number of species/1000 individuals; C = Simpson's Index of Dominance Concentration =

$$\sum_{i=1}^{s} \left[\frac{n_i}{N}\right]^2 ,$$

where n_i = number of specimens of species i, and N = number of specimens in the total sample population; H' = Shannon-Wiener Index =

$$- \sum_{i=1}^{s} \frac{n_i}{N} \ln \left[\frac{n_i}{N}\right] .$$

The Cephalophytarion Association

Of the 24 taxa listed in Table 2.1, 13 occur exclusively (with the rare exception of scattered trichome fragments) in the association of sheathless oscillatorian cyanobacteria here designated by the name of the dominant genus (Figs. 2.10, 2.11). This association is notable not only for its high apparent diversity relative to other Bitter Springs groupings, but also because it is encountered so infrequently. In an aggregate thickness of approximately 1 m of Ross River cherts examined, no more than 1 mm contains this assemblage. All type specimens come from closely spaced intervals of a single lamina or, locally, pair of laminae.

The criteria used to differentiate species in this assemblage include cell size and shape, apical tapering, terminal cell shape, and presence or absence of coiling—all morphological attributes employed in the determination of modern cyanobacterial taxa (Schopf 1968). In the 1960s, the common assumption was that many of the permineralized microbes in Precambrian cherts had been preserved in more or less pristine condition; thus, it made sense to consider the various morphological features of microfossils as primary biological structures. Recognition of the pervasiveness of postmortem degradation and the significant ways in which it can alter microbial morphologies (Awramik, Golubic, and Barghoorn 1972; Golubic and Barghoorn 1977; and many other specific reports) now suggests that some of the morphological features used in the differentiation of taxa in this association may be of diagenetic origin. For example, Awramik, Golubic, and Barghoorn (1972) have demonstrated that a common postmortem change in specimens of modern *Oscillatoria* is the progressive shrinkage of cells near the ends of trichomes, producing tapering morphologies similar to some Bitter Springs microfossils assigned to the Rivulariaceae.

Within local populations of fossil cyanobacteria, the degree to which postmortem degradation has progressed can vary markedly from individual to individual (Hofmann 1976; Golubic and Hofmann 1976; Knoll and Golubic 1979). This variation can be used to infer both patterns of cellular decomposition and, by mentally "running the machine in reverse," the nature of the original microbial population. A degradational continuum is clearly evident in the constituent remains of the Ross River *Cephalophytarion* assemblage. Specimens assigned to *Cephalophytarion grande* Schopf are almost fully turgid, while trichomes of *Biocatenoides* sp. consist of chains of tiny (<1 μm), shrunken organic blebs.[2] Individuals showing various intermediate degrees of postmortem shrinkage can be found throughout the *Cephalophytarion*-dominated laminae.

No formal synonymy is attempted here; however, it seems probable that as many as six of the taxa listed in the *Cephalophytarion* association belong to a single biological population. It is also apparent that other morphologies found in the association cannot be fitted into this population. *Palaeolyngbya barghoorniana* Schopf (Fig. 2.13), for example, is a distinct entity. Cell size and shape also seem to distinguish *Oscillatoriopsis obtusa* Schopf, *Cyanonema attenuatum* Schopf, and *Archaeonema longicellulare* Schopf from the *Cephalophytarion* population.

Taxonomically, then, it appears that the *Cephalophytarion* association contains two abundant taxa and four, or perhaps five, rarer elements. Ecologically, this thin zone clearly records a short-lived environmental shift. Although sheathless oscillatorians are known to participate with other cyanobacteria in the formation of modern stromatolites (Gebelein 1969), they rarely weave coherent mats on their own (Golubic 1976). In Solar Lake, Sinai, the metabolically versatile *Oscillatoria limnetica*[3] forms a flocculose carpet during seasonal periods of anoxic bottom conditions (Krumbein, Cohen, and Shilo 1977). By analogy, it could be hypothesized that the Bitter Springs *Cephalophytarion* association reflects temporary basin stagnation. Alternately, the abundant amorphous organic matter associated with this paleocommunity may be degraded mucilage from diffluent sheaths of what were, in fact, mat-building cyanobacteria. In either case, an environmental perturbation of some type is apparent.

The Eoentophysalis Association

A second fossiliferous locality of the Bitter Springs Formation was described from Ellery Gorge by Schopf and Blacic in 1971. Although much of the "Ellery Creek" material that I have been able to examine contains microbial associations similar to those of the Ross River biota, it is evident from the work of Schopf and Blacic (1971), as well as from the discussion of Schopf (1972), that certain elements of the Bitter Springs microflora are not present in both localities. Principal among these is an assemblage characterized by mat-building entophysalidacean cyanobacteria found in Ellery Creek cherts (Knoll and Golubic 1979).

Entophysalis, a colonial, gel-producing, coccoid blue-green, is known to form mammillate microbial mats in the Persian Gulf (Golubic 1973); Shark Bay, Australia (Golubic 1976); Baja California (Horodyski and Vander Haar 1975); and, to a lesser extent, on intertidal algal flats of Andros Island, Bahamas (Golubic and Awramik 1974). The fossil genus *Eoentophysalis* is morphologically indistinguishable from the modern taxon and, like living *Entophysalis*, it built essentially monospecific (in terms of mat-building cyanobacteria) stromatolites having a distinctive billowy microstructure. By analogy to the modern examples, *Eoentophysalis cumulus* Knoll and Golubic is interpreted as having grown in the lower intertidal zone bordering the Bitter Springs sea, a conclusion supported by the absence of "spheroidal unicell" plankton in this association. Microorganisms that are associated with *Eoentophysalis* include rare populations of the coccoid mat dweller *Eosynechococcus amadeus*, as well as abundant and well-preserved specimens of chrococcacean cyanobacteria assigned to the genus *Gloeodiniopsis* Schopf. The *Gloeodiniopsis* populations are found not within the entophysalid billows, but in thin bands and lenses just above mat-builder concentrations. According to the interpretation of Knoll and Golubic (1979), these cells lived or were trapped in evanescent tidal pools dammed by the relief of the accreting entophysalidacean stromatolites.

Some linkage to the previously discussed associations may be provided by two thin (100 μm) horizons within the *Eoentophysalis* stromatolites in which densely woven sheaths of *Eomycetopsis* predominate. As in the case of the Ross River *Cephalophytarion* laminae, these thin zones record transitory environmental shifts.

Community Diversity in the Bitter Springs Environment

Interpretations of the recurrent associations of taxa found in silicified stromatolites from the Bitter Springs Formation are summarized in Table 2.5. Five communities (Table 2.6) can be distinguished. Three were responsible for the accretion of mats in different subtidal and intertidal areas of the Ross River and Ellery Creek environments; one covered subtidal mat surfaces during rare, brief periods of environmental perturbation; and one inhabited the shallow water column above the benthic associations. While the Bitter Springs biota can be viewed in the aggregate as a relatively diverse assemblage of microfossils, it can also be understood as a collection of taxonomically and environmentally distinct microbial communities, each represented by relatively few preserved species. It should be borne in mind that the true microbial diversity of the benthic communities was probably significantly higher than the fossil record indicates. Modern microbial mat ecosystems contain a host of metabolically diverse bacteria. Fossilization permits us to observe elements of the mat-building cyanobacteria that lived at or near the upper surface of the active mat, as well as a few mat dwellers,

TABLE 2.5: Interpreted Associations

1. *Eomycetopsis* built mats
   closely related to

2. *Tenuofilum* built mats

3. Sheathless oscillatorian surfaces — five or six species, dominated by two

4. Low-diversity plankton assemblage dominated by
   Myxococcoides-Glenobotrydion algae

5. *Eoentophysalis* built mats

TABLE 2.6: Cooccurrence Matrix for Major Bitter Springs Taxa, Including *Eoentophysalis*

	Em	*T*	*C*	*Ee*	*P*
Eomycetopsis	31	8	0	0	25
Tenuofilum		21	0	0	19
Cephalophytarion			7	0	1
Eoentophysalis				5	0
Plankton					42

Note: In this table, only occurrences in which at least four specimens are present were tallied. Occurrence counts include data for one thin section of Ellery Creek *Eoentophysalis*-bearing chert.

but the photosynthetic and heterotrophic bacteria that almost assuredly thrived in below the cyanobacterial horizon have not been preserved. Detailed sedimentological data on the carbonate units from which these samples were collected will improve our understanding of the factors responsible for the ecological partitioning of the Bitter Springs sea floor.

These communities do not exhaust the ecological diversity of the Bitter Springs biota; additional Ellery Creek taxa described by Schopf and Blacic (1971), but not discussed here, probably represent further communities. In a recent publication, Oehler, Oehler, and Steward (1979) have also described an assemblage of microfossils from an evaporitic facies in the lower part of the formation, adding significantly to the range of associations and environments for which information is available.

ASSOCIATIONS IN THE DRAKEN CONGLOMERATE

Having established the existence of certain distinctive microbial associations in the Bitter Springs Formation, it is important to ask whether or not these patterns have any application outside the Amadeus Basin. Microfossils in silicified microbial mats from the late Precambrian Draken Conglomerate, Svalbard (Knoll 1979, 1981) suggest that they do. The Draken Conglomerate is exposed in nunataks in the glaciated interior of Ny Friesland, northern Spitsbergen, where it forms part of the well-known Hecla Hoek sedimentary sequence (Harland and Wilson 1956). On the basis of palynological, stromatolitic, and oncolitic biostratigraphical evidence (Krassil'shchikov 1970, 1973; Raaben and Zabrodin 1969; Knoll unpublished data), the age of deposition is considered to be uppermost Riphean—that is, 700 to perhaps 800 m.y. Thus, the Draken Conglomerate is approximately correlative with the Bitter Springs Formation.

According to Wilson (1961), the formation consists predominantly of dolomite, often stromatolitic; intraformational conglomerates are common. The fossiliferous strata under discussion in this chapter consist of an unusual lithology termed a "flake conglomerate" by Wilson. Thin (<1 cm) shards of black chert are set in a matrix of coarse sand- to grit-sized, rounded clasts of carbonate mud, some of which have also been silicified. Microscopical examination shows the shards to be silicified fragments of microbial mats. One can infer that the mat-building communities became established in a shallow, subtidal marine environment of limited water movement, perhaps a lagoon separated from open shelf waters by some type of barrier. Periodic storms breached this barrier, ripping up the mats and redepositing them with the carbonate clasts.

In thin section, the Draken mat shards reveal a familiar picture. Filamentous sheaths assignable to *Eomycetopsis robusta* (Figs. 2.22, 2.23) form loosely woven mats in some fragments, although the vertical-horizontal pattern noted in the Bitter Springs chert is not in evidence here. Compaction may have altered the original orientation, or vertical alignment of filaments may not have been established in the Draken mats. The presence of *E. robusta* in both Australian and Svalbard cherts does not necessarily mean that a single biological species, or, perhaps more appropriately, clone (Gould and Eldredge 1977) is represented. *Eomycetopsis* is a form genus of sorts, and a variety of extant cyanobacterial taxa secrete sheaths of the same approximate size and shape. Rare cellular trichomes preserved within sheaths from both locations demonstrate that the constituent cells of these populations were indeed similar, but partial degradation makes detailed comparisons impossible.

On the other hand, many modern cyanobacterial taxa have cosmopolitan distributions; *Phormidium hendersonii*, for example, builds mats in the Persian Gulf, Australia, and Bermuda. Support for a hypothesis of biological similarity comes from other Draken mat shards in which thin sheaths referable to *Tenuofilum septatum* (Figs. 2.33, 2.34) are displayed in interwoven arrays. It is interesting to note that sheaths of the comparatively large (10–12 μm cross-sectional diameter) *Lyngbya*-like cyanobacterium *Siphonophycus kestron* Schopf (1968) occur sporadically in these *T. septatum* mats, much as they do in the Bitter Springs Formation. The mat shards in the "flake conglomerate" are all locally derived, thus, it is apparent that in the Draken Conglomerate, as in its Australian counterpart, two communities containing *Lyngbya-Phormidium* type cyanobacteria, *E. robusta* and *T. septatum*, occupied distinct, but environmentally closely related portions of the shallow sea floor. While the question of genetic correspondence must remain open, one can say that among late Precambrian mat-building microbes of widely differing geographical position, similar environmental problems begat similar morphological solutions.

A third mat builder, not yet recognized from the Bitter Springs

Formation, characterizes several Draken mat shards. The fossils, once again, are oscillatorian sheaths, but of a distinct size class (4–8 m cross-sectional diameter, Fig. 2.21). The thick, tightly woven fabric of this association (Fig. 2.20) demonstrates the nature of this additional component of ecological complexity in the Draken lagoon. Mat dwellers of various types are present among the Draken mat taxa and, interestingly enough, they differ from their ecological counterparts in the Bitter Springs stromatolites. In modern microbial mat communities, mat dwellers may be similarly variable.

Draken Plankton

While differences in mat-dwelling microbes stand in contrast to the basic similarities of the Draken and Bitter Springs mat-building associations, it is in the plankton that the strongest differences between the two microbiotas are seen. Species richness in the Draken plankton is two to three times that of the Bitter Springs (Table 2.7); dominance concentration is much lower; and so, correspondingly, the Shannon-Wiener index of overall diversity is significantly higher for the Draken assemblage. The greater planktonic diversity evident in the Svalbard biota may be related to the storms that periodically affected the Draken lagoon. The same waves that ripped up the mat clasts also brought in plankton from the open shelf and mixed the restricted lagoonal waters with sea water of normal salinity. There is little evidence for this type of activity in the fossiliferous Bitter Springs cherts.

In the Bitter Springs Formation, a planktonic mode of life was inferred from the spatial distribution of spheroidal unicells within stromatolitic cherts. The silicified carbonate mud clasts found in the Draken "flake conglomerate" provide independent support for this hypothesis. Silicified muds do not contain the woven fabric characteristic of the mat fragments; instead, more or less featureless organic debris is distributed evenly throughout the clasts (Fig. 2.31). No lamination is apparent. Whilte the filaments comprising the mat-building communities are absent, the spheroidal cells, inferred from their scattered distribution in mats to be planktonic, are relatively abundant, a demonstration of the relative facies independence characteristic of organisms living in the water column.

Discussion

The "flake conglomerate" of the Draken Conglomerate corroborates and extends the paleoecological distribution interpreted for the Bitter Springs Formation. Through a fortunate circumstance of sedimentation, different rock clasts containing distinct microbial mat associations and/or a

TABLE 2.7: Planktonic Diversity in Draken Cherts

Draken W839-B
(N = 850)

Min	Max	Est
485	303	409
189	125	125
90	90	90
80	64	64
40	47	47
3	45	40
2	40	40
1	40	20
	25	9
	21	3
	20	2
	10	1
	6	
	5	
	3	
	3	
	2	
	1	

S = 9.41	S = 21.17	S = 14.12
C = 0.40	C = 0.17	C = 0.27
H′ = 1.30	H′ = 2.11	H′ = 1.65

Note: See Table 2.4 for explanation.

planktonic assemblage are preserved together, providing a strong spatial confirmation of the statistically derived taxonomic associations of the Bitter Springs biota. Preliminary studies of a large volume of Svalbard Precambrian rock collected by the author in 1979 from the Murchison Bay area of Nordaustlandet indicate further that the communities found in the Draken Conglomerate constitute but a small subset of the preserved late Precambrian Svalbard biota. Different bottom habitats supported other benthic communities, and the plankton of the open shelf sea differed significantly from that of the Draken lagoon.

All the fossils with which I have dealt in this chapter are algal in the broad sense of the term; that is, they are oxygenic photoautotrophs. There must also have been heterotrophic protists in late Precambrian marine environments, and evidence for this can be found in carbonates of the

Backlundtoppen Formation which conformably overlies the Draken Conglomerate in Svalbard. Here large (60–150 μm long) vase-shaped organic walled microfossils occur in abundance (Fig. 2.32). Distinct collar regions, variously circular or polygonal in cross-section, characterize the open apical end of these remains, although the collar is not always preserved. Among the extant microbiota certain ciliate protists, including the Tintinnida, form loricas of similar shape. A few testate amebae also secrete coverings of similar shape and size, although in some of the most vase-like taxa, for example, *Euglypha*, the test is composed of imbricate siliceous scales (Sleigh 1973, pp. 166–72). Most of these testate amebae live in fresh water or damp soil environments, but a few marine Foraminifera form single-chambered, bottle-shaped, organic tests. The extinct Chitinozoa also bear comparison with the Svalbard fossils (Bloeser et al. 1977). Whatever the true taxonomic affinities of these remains, it is clear that they add a significant paleoecological dimension to the Svalbard Precambrian biota.

It should be mentioned here that early protists similar in morphology to the above-mentioned fossils have been found in other rocks of comparable age. They were first described from the late Precambrian Galeros Formation of the Grand Canyon, U.S.A. (Bloeser et al. 1977) and have subsequently been reported from Brazil (Fairchild, Barbour, and Haralyi 1978), East Greenland (Vidal 1979), Saudi Arabia (Binda and Bokhari 1980), and Sweden (Knoll and Vidal 1980), suggesting that heterotrophic protists were geographically widespread in the late Precambrian.

MICROBIAL DISTRIBUTION
IN THE NARSSÂRSSUK FORMATION

The similarities between the Bitter Springs and Draken microbiotas are striking, but lest one be tempted to generalize from these two series of communities, it is useful to look briefly at the microorganisms preserved in the late Precambrian Narssârssuk Formation of the Thule region, northwestern Greenland (Strother and Knoll 1979, and in press 1981). The Narssârssuk sedimentary sequence consists of cyclic carbonates, sandstones, and nonmarine red siltstones recording the repeated progradation of a sabkha-like plain over a shallow lagoonal area. The western coast of the Persian Gulf provides a reasonable modern environmental analog. On the basis of acritarch biostratigraphy, Vidal and Dawes (1980) suggest a Vendian (570–650 m.y.) age of deposition for the sequence.

Following Walther's law, one can interpret the vertical series of lithologies comprising each Narssârssuk cycle as representative of a lateral environmental gradient. The stratigraphically upward progression from limestone through dolomite and gypsiferous dolomite to redbeds documents coastal environments ranging from shallow subtidal to supratidal and terrestrial. The presence of such sedimentary indicators of water movement as ripple marks, channel-fill structures, and cross beds in the upper member of the sequence and their total absence in lower Narssârssuk cycles allow one to superimpose a second environmental variable, water movement, onto the onshore-offshore variation.

Eleven distinct stromatolite morphologies have been observed in Narssârssuk carbonates, and the environmental position of each can be fixed with respect to current activity and position relative to tidal range. The recurring lithological sequence of the lower cycles is matched by the repetition of a characteristic stromatolite sequence. The same is true of the upper portion of the formation, but because of the aforementioned differences in current activity, the microbial structures in the two parts of the formation are entirely different.

Each stromatolite macrostructure in the Narssârssuk Formation has its own characteristic microstructure. Because microstructure is determined by the constituent mat-building community (Gebelein 1974; Monty 1976; Bertrand-Sarfati 1976), each stromatolite can be considered as indicative of a discrete microbial association. This can be confirmed, in part, by the examination of fossil microorganisms preserved in silicified patches of some of these structures. Five benthic microbial communities are represented in Narssârssuk cherts. None of these fossil associations—in fact, none of the fossil taxa in these associations—is found in the Draken Conglomerate. The only similarity between the Bitter Springs microbiota and that of the Narssârssuk is the presence of some type of entophysalidacean mat-building community; however, the entophysalid species present in the two formations are quite different, as are accessory taxa occurring with them.

A full account of the Narssârssuk microbiota will appear elsewhere, but in this brief overview, there are three points worth underscoring. The sedimentary environmental matrix (derived independently of any paleontological data) provides a proper context for the analysis of microbial community distribution within a formation. Although a practice of long standing in invertebrate paleontology (e.g., Walker and Laporte 1970), the marriage of detailed sedimentological information and fossil distributional data has not been a primary focus of Precambrian paleobiological research. Hofmann (1976) and Oehler, Oehler, and Stewart (1979) have successfully employed sedimentary data in their discussions of benthic microbial paleoecology, and Knoll, Blick, and Awramik (1981) have done the same for certain late Precambrian plankton assemblages.

Although stromatolite macrostructure can be influenced significantly by environmental factors (Horodyski 1976a, 1976b, 1977), microstructure appears to be controlled by the mat-building community (Gebelein 1974). Thus, the distribution of stromatolite microstructural types within an environmental matrix provides important information on the distribution of ancient microbial associations. In the Narssârssuk Formation, community distribution is controlled primarily by water movement and frequency and duration of subaerial exposure, the major factor of consequence in the supratidal-subtidal gradient. Park (1977) has presented a good discussion of wetting frequency as a primary determinant of intertidal mat distribution in the present-day Persian Gulf.

Organically preserved microfossils in several of the Narssârssuk stromatolites corroborate this interpretation of microbial community distribution along an environmental gradient and enlarge the total picture of the late Precambrian microbial distribution by providing a set of environments and microorganisms different from those characteristic of the other formations discussed in this chapter. Microfossils from subtidal columnar stromatolites (e.g., Schopf and Sovietov 1976) and other open-shelf associations, including plankton (Vidal 1976), further demonstrate the complexity of microbial distribution patterns in the late Precambrian.

SUMMARY

Three sources of data are available for the paleoecological investigation of Precambrian microbes: (1) the spatial distribution and orientation of organisms in the rock (as seen in thin section); (2) the grouping of taxa in recurrent associations interpretable in terms of community patterns, transportation and mixing, and postmortem degradation patterns; and (3) the relationship of these associations to the sedimentary environment.

The application of these approaches casts discussions of Precambrian microbial diversity in a new light as it becomes possible to look at taxonomic diversity within a community, community distribution within an environment, and environmental heterogeneity on the ancient earth.

It is evident the microbiotas available for any single time plane will represent a variety of environmental settings, although the selective effects of postmortem degradation will insure that this is only a subset of true habitat diversity. (Common sense, as well as a large body of ecological and invertebrate paleontological literature, tells us this must be true; the problem is one of recognition.) In comparing the fossil records of different times periods, then, rates of evolution can be discerned only by comparing microbiotas from similar environments.

The close correspondence in morphology between Bitter Springs and modern stromatolitic microbes was noted by Schopf (1968) more than a decade ago. The paleoecological considerations briefly set forth in this study extend this observation by demonstrating that late Precambrian cyanobacteria of benthic coastal environments had diversity levels and distributional patterns similar to those of their extant counterparts. Physiologically, this means that ancient cyanobacteria, like living blue-greens, had varying tolerances for such environmental variables as water depth (wetting frequency), current strength, pO_2, and rate of detrital influx. Because the dispersal abilities of modern cyanobacteria are quite considerable, it can be inferred that competition among organisms of different physiological capabilities determined microbial distributions in late Precambrian habitats. Certainly, evolution has affected cyanobacteria during the past 700 m.y., and it is unlikely that any living blue-green is genetically identical to its remote ancestors. Nevertheless, it does appear that the organisms constituting late Precambrian microbial mat communities can, in general, be understood in terms of the ecology and physiology, as well as morphology, of modern stromatolitic microbes.

NOTES

1. Following Kauffman (1974), I reserve the term "assemblage" for accumulations of organisms representing several communities. "Association" as used here denotes groups of taxa that occur together throughout the censused laminae. "Communities" are considered to be microbial populations that actually lived together in the same habitat.

2. I do not mean to imply that no occurrences of *Biocatenoides*-like morphologies should be interpreted as filamentous bacteria, but the localization of many Ross River *Biocatenoides* specimens in the *Cephalophytarion* association, coupled with the presence of a degradational continuum within that association, strongly suggests that the individuals found in this lamina are indeed highly degraded cyanobacteria.

3. Golubic (1978) has found evidence for sheath formation in populations of *Oscillatoria limnetica* grown under conditions of reduced salinity, suggesting that the filaments should properly be assigned to the genus *Phormidium*. Under the conditions of high salinity and anoxic water characteristic of Solar Lake, no sheaths are formed.

ACKNOWLEDGMENTS

I thank E. S. Barghoorn of Harvard University for making available the Bitter Springs material used in this study. I am also grateful to W. B. Harland of Cambridge University for providing samples of the Draken "flake conglomerate." E. S. Barghoorn, S. Golubic, and T. Phillips provided helpful criticisms of an early draft of this manuscript.

Field work in Greenland and Svalbard was supported by NSF Grant DPP77-06993. Additionally, Svalbard field work was greatly facilitated by the generous support of the Cambridge Spitsbergen Expedition.

REFERENCES

Awramik, S. M., S. Golubic, and E. S. Barghoorn. 1972. Blue-green algal cell degradation and its implication for the fossil record. *Geol. Soc. Am., Abst. with Prog.* 4(7):438.

Awramik, S. M., C. D. Gebelein, and P. Cloud. 1978. Biogeologic relationships of ancient stromatolites and their modern analogs. In *Environmental Geochemistry and Geomicrobiology* (W. Krumbein, ed.). Ann Arbor: Ann Arbor Science. Vol. 1, pp. 165–78.

Barghoorn, E. S., and J. W. Schopf. 1965. Microorganisms from the late Precambrian of central Australia. *Science* 150:337–39.

Baxter, R. W. 1964. Paleozoic starch in fossil seeds from Kansas coal balls. *Kansas Acad. Sci. Trans.* 67:418–22.

Bertrand-Sarfati, J. 1976. An attempt to classify late Precambrian stromatolite microstructures. In *Stromatolites* (M. R. Walter, ed.). Amsterdam: Elsevier, pp. 251–59.

Binda, P., and M. M. Bokhari. 1980. Chitinozoan-like microfossils in a late Precambrian dolostone from Saudi Arabia. *Geology* 8:70–71.

Bloeser, B., J. W. Schopf, R. J. Horodyski, and W. J. Breed. 1977. Chitinozoans from the late Precambrian Chuar Group of the Grand Canyon, Arizona. *Science* 195:676–79.

Fairchild, T. R., A. P. Barbour, and N. L. E. Haralyi. 1978. Microfossils in the "Eopaleozoic" Jacadigo Group at Urucum, Mato Grosso, southwest Brazil. *Boletino IG. Instituto Geosciencias, Universidado de São Paulo* 9:74–79.

Francis, S., L. Margulis, and E. S. Barghoorn. 1978. On the experimental silicification of microorganisms. II. On the time of appearance of eukaryotic organisms in the fossil record. *Precambrian Res.* 6:65–100.

Gebelein, C. D. 1969. Distribution, morphology, and accretion rate of recent subtidal algal stromatolites, Bermuda. *J. Sediment. Petrol.* 39:49–69.

———. 1974. Biologic control of stromatolite microstructure: implications for Precambrian time stratigraphy. *Am. J. Sci.* 274:575–98.

Golubic, S. 1973. The relationship between blue-green algae and carbonate deposits. In *The Biology of the Blue-Green Algae* (N. S. Carr and B. A. Whitton, eds.). Oxford: Blackwell Scientific, pp. 434–72.

———. 1976. Organisms that build stromatolites. In *Stromatolites* (M. R. Walter, ed.). Amsterdam: Elsevier, pp. 113–26.

———. 1978. The adaptational value of microbial halotolerance vs. halophily. *Abstracts of the 4th College Park Colloquium on Chemical Evolution*, p. 22.

Golubic, S., and S. M. Awramik. 1974. Microbial comparison of stromatolitic environments: Shark Bay, Persian Gulf and the Bahamas. *Geol. Soc. Am., Abst. with Prog.* 6(7):759–60.

Golubic, S., and E. S. Barghoorn. 1977. Interpretation of microbial fossils with special reference to the Precambrian. In *Fossil Algae* (E. Flügel, ed.). New York: Springer, pp. 1–14.

Golubic, S., and J. W. Focke. 1978. *Phormidium hendersonii* Howe: Identity and significance of a modern stromatolite building microorganism. *J. Sediment. Petrol.* 48:751–64.

Golubic, S., and H. J. Hofmann. 1976. Comparison of Holocene and mid-Precambrian Entophysidaceae (Cyanophyta) in stromatolitic algal mats: cell division and degradation. *J. Paleont.* 50:1074-82.

Gould, S. J., and N. Eldredge. 1977. Punctuated equilibria: the tempo and mode of evolution reconsidered. *Paleobiology* 3:115-51.

Harland, W. B., and C. B. Wilson. 1956. The Hecla Hoek succession in Ny Friesland, Spitsbergen. *Geol. Mag.* 93:265-86.

Hofmann, H. J. 1976. Precambrian microflora, Belcher Islands, Canada: Significance and systematics. *J. Paleont.* 50:1040-73.

Horodyski, R. 1976a. Stromatolites of the upper Siyeh Limestone (Middle Proterozoic), Belt Supergroup, Glacier National Park, Montana. *Precambrian Res.* 3:517-36.

———. 1976b. Stromatolites from the Middle Proterozoic Altyn Limestone, Belt Supergroup, Glacier National Park, Montana. In *Stromatolites* (M. R. Walter, ed.). Amsterdam: Elsevier, pp. 587-97.

———. 1977. Environmental influences on columnar stromatolite branching patterns: examples from the Middle Proterozoic Belt Supergroup, Glacial National Park, Montana. *J. Paleont.* 51:661-71.

Horodyski, R., and S. P. Vander Haar. 1975. Recent calcareous stromatolites from Laguna Mormona (Baja California) Mexico. *J. Sediment. Petrol.* 45:894-906.

Horodyski, R., B. Bloeser, and S. Vander Haar. 1977. Laminated algal mats from a coastal lagoon, Laguna Mormona, Baja California, Mexico. *J. Sediment. Petrol.* 47:680-96.

Kauffman, E. G. 1974. Cretaceous assemblages, communities, and associations: western interior United States and Caribbean Islands. In *Principles of Benthic Community Analysis* (A. M. Ziegler et al., eds.). University of Miami: Miami, Florida, p. 122.

Knoll, A. H. 1979. Silicified microorganisms from the late Precambrian Draken Conglomerate, Svalbard. *Geol. Soc. Am., Abst. with Prog.* 11(7):459.

———. 1981. Microbiota of the late Precambrian Draken Conglomerate, Svalbard. *J. Paleont.* (in press).

Knoll, A. H., N. Blick, and S. M. Awramik. 1981. Stratigraphic and ecologic implications of late Precambrian microfossils from Utah. *Am. J. Sci.* 281:247-63.

Knoll, A. H., and S. Golubic. 1979. Anatomy and taphonomy of a Precambrian algal stromatolite. *Precambrian Res.* 10:115-51.

Knoll, A. H., and G. Vidal. 1980. Protistan microfossils in phosphate nodules from the late Precambrian Visingsö Beds of central Sweden. *Geol. Fören. Stockholm Förh.* 102:207-11.

Krassil'shchikov, A. A. 1970. Scheme for the Precambrian and Lower Paleozoic Stratigraphy of the Spitsbergen archipelago. *Doklady, Acad. Sci.* (USSR) *Earth Sci. Sec.* 194:97-100.

———. 1973. Stratigraphy and paleotectonics of the Precambrian and early Paleozoic of Spitsbergen. *Trans., Sci. Res. Inst. Arctic Geol.* 172 (in Russian).

Krumbein, W. E., P. Cohen, and M. Shilo, 1977. Solar Lake (Sinai). 4 Stromatolitic cyanobacterial mats. *Limnol. Oceanog.* 22:635-56.

Krumbein, W. E., H. Buchholz, P. Franke, D. Giani, C. Giele, and K. Wonneberger, 1979. O₂ and H₂S coexistence in stromatolites. *Naturwissenschaften* 66:381–89.
Monty, C. L. V. 1965. Recent algal stromatolites in the Windward lagoon, Andros Island, Bahamas. *Ann. Soc. Géol. Belg.* 88:269–76.
———. 1976. The origin and development of cryptalgal fabrics. In *Stromatolites* (M. R. Walter, ed.). Amsterdam: Elsevier, pp. 193–249.
———. 1978. Scientific reports of the Belgian expedition on the Australian Great Barrier Reefs, 1967. Sedimentology: 2 Monospecific stromatolites from the Great Barrier Reef tract and their paleontological significance. *Ann. Soc. Géol. Belg.* 101:163–71.
Oehler, D. Z. 1977. Pyrenoid-like structures in late Precambrian algae from the Bitter Springs Formation of Australia. *J. Paleont.* 51:885–901.
———. 1978. Microflora of the middle Proterozoic Balbirini Dolomite (McArthur Group) of Australia. *Alcheringa* 2:269–309.
Oehler, D. Z., J. H. Oehler, and A. J. Stewart. 1979. Algal fossils from a late Precambrian, hypersaline lagoon. *Science* 205:388–90.
Park, R. K. 1977. The presentation potential of some recent stromatolites. *Sedimentology* 24:485–506.
Raaben, M. Ye., and V. Ye. Zabrodin. 1969. Biostratigraphic characteristics of the upper Riphean in the Arctic. *Doklady, Acad. Sci.* (USSR) 184:676–79.
Schopf, J. W. 1968. Microflora of the Bitter Springs Formation, late Precambrian, central Australia. *J. Paleont.* 42:651–88.
———. 1972. Evolutionary significance of the Bitter Springs (late Precambrian) microflora. *Proc. 24th Inter. Geol. Cong.*, (*Montreal*), Sec. 1:68–77.
Schopf, J. W., and J. M. Blacic. 1971. New microorganisms from the Bitter Springs Formation (late Precambrian) of north-central Amadeus Basin, Australia. *J. Paleont.* 45:925–60.
Schopf, J. W., and Yu. K. Sovietov. 1976. Microfossils in *Conophyton* from the Soviet Union and their bearing on Precambrian biostratigraphy. *Science* 193:143–46.
Sleigh, M. 1973. *The Biology of Protozoa.* New York: American Elsevier, pp. 166–72, 211–14, and 261–64.
Stewart, A. J. 1979. A barred-basin marine evaporite in the Upper Proterozoic of the Amadeus Basin, central Australia. *Sedimentology* 26:33–62.
Strother, P. K., and A. H. Knoll. 1979. A late Precambrian microflora from the Thule Basin, Greenland. *Bot. Soc. Am., Misc. Pub.* 157:39.
———. 1981. Microbiota of the late Precambrian Narssârssuk Formation, north-western Greenland. *Palaeontology* (in press).
Vidal, G. 1976. Late Precambrian microfossils from the Visingsö Beds in southern Sweden. *Fossils and Strata* 9.
———. 1979. Acritarchs from the Upper Proterozoic and Lower Cambrian of East Greenland. *Grönlands Geologiske Undersögelse Bull.* 134.
Vidal, G., and P. R. Dawes. 1980. Acritarchs from the Proterozoic Thule Group, North-West Greenland. Grönlands Geologiske Undersögelse Rapp. 100.
Walker, K. R., and L. F. Laporte. 1970. Congruent fossil communities from Ordovician and Devonian carbonates of New York. *J. Paleont.* 44:928–44.

Walter, M. R. 1972. Stromatolites and the biostratigraphy of the Australian Precambrian and Cambrian. *Palaeont. Ass. Lond. Spec. Pap.* 11.

Wells, A. T., D. J. Forman, L. C. Ranford, and P. J. Cook. 1970. Geology of the Amadeus Basin, central Australia. *Aust. Bur. Min. Res. Bull.* 100.

Whittaker, R. H. 1975. *Communities and Ecosystems.* New York: Macmillan, pp. 94–104.

Whittaker, R. H., and P. P. Feeny. 1971. Allelochemics: chemical interactions between species. *Science* 171:757–70.

Wilson, C. B. 1961. The upper middle Hecla Hoek rocks of Ny Friesland, Spitsbergen. *Geol. Mag.* 98:89–116.

3

FOSSIL SOILS: INDICATORS OF ANCIENT TERRESTRIAL ENVIRONMENTS

Greg Retallack

INTRODUCTION

The study of fossil soils, particularly those older than Pleistocene, is now gaining widespread recognition as an emerging area of earth science. Such studies have great potential for reconstructing ancient environments. Fossil soils can provide evidence for the size and structure of ancient vegetation and its location relative to sedimentary environments, for paleo-topography, for depth to the water table and its chemistry, for rates of relative sedimentation, subsidence and uplift, and for paleoclimate. Fossil soils are proving abundant and widespread in nonmarine rocks of all ages and are the only aspect of the geology of many areas remaining completely undescribed. Studies of fossil soils may commonly be combined with existing studies of fossil plants and vertebrates, sedimentary environments, paleocurrents, and paleoclimates to give a detailed impression of ancient environments and ecosystems.

As research on older fossil soils gains impetus, there is also the prospect of documenting the diversification of the world's soils through geological time. Studies of fossil soils may provide critical evidence for understanding the development of the modern atmosphere during the Precambrian and early Paleozoic, the origin of terrestrial organisms during the late Precambrian and early Paleozoic, the first vascular land plants and the first forests of the mid-Paleozoic, the emergence and spread of savanna and grassland during the Tertiary, and the recent impact of human beings on the land surfaces of the earth.

Compared to other branches of earth sciences so little is known of fossil soils, particularly those older than Pleistocene, that a review of them does not cover an impossibly large literature. This review is biased toward my personal conviction that interpretation of ancient environments is the most promising future direction for studies on fossil soils. Pleistocene buried soils and altered rocks at major geological unconformities are the best known fossil soils, but they are discussed here in less detail than well-preserved fossil soils within thick sedimentary sequences that also preserve other kinds of fossils. Because of difficulties peculiar to Pleistocene fossil soils and geological unconformities, the study of older fossil soils has often been approached timidly or avoided in the past. Caution is certainly needed, especially in unraveling the complex effects of sedimentation, volcanism, diagenesis, and metamorphism from ancient soil-forming processes. However, more and more studies of older fossil soils are overcoming these obstacles. It is now apparent that careful studies of fossil soils can provide evidence for many features of ancient environments that were previously indeterminable and can also support and integrate conclusions from a number of other earth sciences into surprisingly detailed reconstructions of the past. It is also becoming apparent that fossil soils are much more abundant in nonmarine rocks than generally realized. Many enigmatic kinds of rocks, masquerading under a variety of uninformative names are now turning out to be (at least partly) fossil soils. Among these are redbeds, variegated beds, badlands, cornstone, ganister, tonstein, underclay, and fireclay (Williamson 1967; Steel 1974; McBride 1974; Retallack 1977a, 1979).

What are fossil soils and how are they recognized? The most practical definition of a fossil soil (also called a paleosol) is a former soil buried by later deposits. The main difficulty with this definition arises, not from its fossil nature, but from the concept of modern soil, which is different for engineers, agriculturists, geologists, and soil scientists (Ruhe 1965; Hunt 1972). I prefer to broadly define soil as material on the surface of a planet altered by physical or chemical weathering, the action of organisms, or all of these. Fossil soils can be recognized by any of the features of modern soils. For older fossil soils the most diagnostic feature is the remains of fossil roots preserved in growth position. Other features include leached or reddened, massive-looking and clay-rich layers, prismatic or blocky jointed layers, and a variety of trace fossils, mottles, nodules, and concretions. The micromorphology of the fossil soil in thin section and its clay mineralogy and geochemistry are also useful in the study of older fossil soils, if interpreted with care.

THREE MAJOR KINDS OF FOSSIL SOIL

Fossil soils occur naturally in three different geological settings. Each has been studied from different perspectives, related to their particular problems and possibilities.

In Quaternary Sediments

Fossil soils of Pleistocene and Recent age have been used for stratigraphical mapping in many parts of the world (Ruhe 1965; Gibbs 1971; Paepe 1971; Jessup and Norris 1971). The "Sangamon soil" of North America has been mapped from Ohio through Illinois to Texas over a distance of more than 3,000 km. This and other fossil soils are useful correlation surfaces in complex glacial and periglacial sediments. As mapping units these have usually been labeled "soil," in accordance with the American Code of Stratigraphic Nomenclature (American Commission on Stratigraphic Nomenclature 1961). Suggested alternative names include "pedoderm" (Brewer, Crook, and Speight 1970), "geosol" (Morrison 1968), and "profile"; the latter specifically for deeply weathered rock units of uncertain relationships (Senior and Mabbutt 1979). The problems of mapping Quaternary paleosols are ably discussed by Ruhe (1965). Similar fossil soils may have formed under similar conditions and may not be the same age everywhere. Soil formation may be progressively or locally interrupted by sedimentation at different times and places. Particular care must be taken when following fossil soils along strike as they may change character where they formed in different parts of the landscape.

Quaternary paleosols have also been used to reconstruct ancient environments. Ruhe (1970) found that the evidence of fossil soils was in agreement with palynological and other evidence that much of North America now under prairie was wooded and received more rainfall during the last interglacial. Similarly, Ložek (1967) has reconstructed the changing Pleistocene climate and vegetation of Czechoslovakia, largely on the basis of fossil soils. One great advantage in interpreting younger fossil soils is that they can often be matched closely with modern soils.

The problems with interpreting ancient environments from Quaternary paleosols are due largely to their occurrence on stable cratonic areas. Such land surfaces may be so stable that the same surficial material is altered in different ways by successively changing climates and vegetation. Such soils, formed under conditions unlike those of today, are called relict soils. The different phases of weathering in them can be very difficult to disentangle. As many cratonic areas subside only slowly or may even be rising, paleosols may only be partly buried or even exhumed. Even soils that are completely buried may be covered by such a thin layer of sediment that they are subjected to additional weathering at depth. Quaternary paleosols are not easy to interpret, although they are geologically young. These various difficulties make it easy to become pessimistic about studies of older paleosols. These difficulties apply to all fossil soils, but fortunately they are not as severe in other geological settings.

At Major Unconformities

Fossil soils are also commonly recognized at major unconformities. The original geological unconformity, first recognized by Hutton in 1787, shows several features of Siluro-Devonian soil formation. The surface has topographical relief of at least 400 m and is reddened and fissured, with fissure fills of red, calcareous, sandy breccia (Friend, Harland, and Gilbert-Smith 1970). Other examples of paleosols at unconformities are the "lateritic" paleosols which have been widely recognized at the unconformable contact between Cretaceous and early Tertiary rocks in many parts of the western United States (Wanless 1923; Pettyjohn 1966; Abbott, Minch, and Peterson 1976; Thompson, Fields, and Alt 1977).

Although easy to recognize, because they indicate millions of years of erosion and nondeposition, this in itself is a problem for their interpretation. Many features of these paleosols may be relicts of soil formation under a climate and vegetation very different from those just before burial. A more serious problem with such paleosols arises from the way unconformities commonly juxtapose rocks of different porosity, mineralogy, and other characters. Unconformities are especially susceptible to later modification by hydrothermal alteration, diagenetic or metamorphic changes involving reaction between the contrasting materials, and leaching or precipitation of minerals by intrastratal solutions or groundwater. The difficulties of unequivocally distinguishing between later modification and original weathering are well illustrated by the disagreement of Lewan (1977) and Kalliokosi (1977) over the nature of altered rocks underlying the 1-billion-year-old Jacobsville Sandstone, north of Marquette, Michigan. The need for caution can also be seen from the following example. In the driftless area of southwestern Wisconsin, successive early Paleozoic sandstones may have strongly silicified and ferruginized crusts and mottled and pallid zones immediately below each capping carbonate unit. Evidence presented by Dury and Haberman (1978) indicates that these are not early Paleozoic paleosols, but were more likely produced by deep weathering during the late Cretaceous and early Tertiary.

In Thick Terrestrial Sedimentary Successions

The ideal situation for the preservation of fossil soils is in sedimentary basins subsiding at such a rate that soils are covered and sink below the water table shortly after reaching the greatest differentiation possible, given the parent material, vegetation, and climate at the time. As discussed by Allen (1974b), this may occur without episodic basin-wide subsidence and sedimentation. The covering of soils at long intervals is a natural consequence of the restricted supply routs of sediment, such as mudflows and streams, in many terrestrial environments. Streams constantly change course or meander laterally, but any given portion of their floodplains is infrequently reworked by the stream channel or covered by thick near-channel flood deposits. With slow steady subsidence large numbers of fossil soils may become superimposed. The buried Eocene forests of the northeastern part of Yellowstone National Park, Wyoming, consist of about 27 successive buried surfaces containing petrified tree trunks in about 400 m of stream gravel, mudflows, and tuffs (Fig. 3.1). Although some of the petrified trunks may have been transported (Fritz 1979), at least two of the surfaces (which I have personally examined on Specimen Ridge) have a leached horizon overlying a clay-rich horizon and large petrified tree trunks in growth position. Dorf (1964) has counted as many as 500 growth rings in some of these buried stumps, indicating at least that many years of soil formation on some of the surfaces.

Recognizing and interpreting paleosols in such sedimentary settings is not without problems. Some features of a fossil soil may be relicts from the formation of another fossil soil (or pedorelicts in the terminology of Brewer 1964). For example, nodules or clods of an older soil may have been eroded and incorporated in the parent material of a younger soil. If the sediment overlying a buried soil was only thin, the upper portion of the buried soil may also have been altered by soil formation at the higher land surface. This may result in a B horizon of one soil containing structures of the relict A horizon of an older buried soil, as documented in the type Long Reef clay paleosol in the Triassic rocks near Sydney, Australia by Retallack (1977b). In immature paleosols many sedimentary features of the parent material may not have been obliterated. These sedimentary relicts (as they are termed by Brewer 1964) are most commonly bedding and ripple-drift cross-lamination. The upper layers of fossil soils may also have been removed by erosion. This soil material may have been transported and deposited to form a pedolith (in the sense of Gerasimov 1971), a rock unit with sedimentary organization but soil mineralogy and clast microstructure. In some sedimentary successions pedoliths are difficult to distinguish from ordinary sediments, in others they are distinct. Fortunately, subsidence rates in many sedimentary basins are such that these various problems are not insuperable. In such basins, not only fossil soils, but also fossil plants and animals may be well preserved. These can then be integrated into surprisingly detailed reconstructions of past environments (Fig. 3.2). Fossil soils in thick sedimentary successions have been the least studied in the past, but show most promise for the future.

Roeschmann (1971) has indicated that later alteration by diagenesis, metamorphism, or intrastratal solution can also be an obstacle to the interpretation of older paleosols in sedimentary sequences. Each feature of the fossil soil must be assessed separately to determine whether it is due to original soil formation or later alteration. Physical field relations and petrographical textures are usually more convincing evidence in such deliberations than mineralogy or geochemistry. For example, in the Avalon

	alluvium		tuff		petrified trees
	basalt		breccia & conglomerate		basement rocks

FIGURE 3.1. The Eocene buried forests of Yellowstone National Park, Wyoming. About 27 horizons bearing petrified stumps occur in 400 m of fossiliferous rock. (Modified from Dorf. E. April 1964. The petrified forests of Yellowstone Park. *Scientific American* 210. Copyright © 1964 by Scientific American, Inc. All rights reserved.)

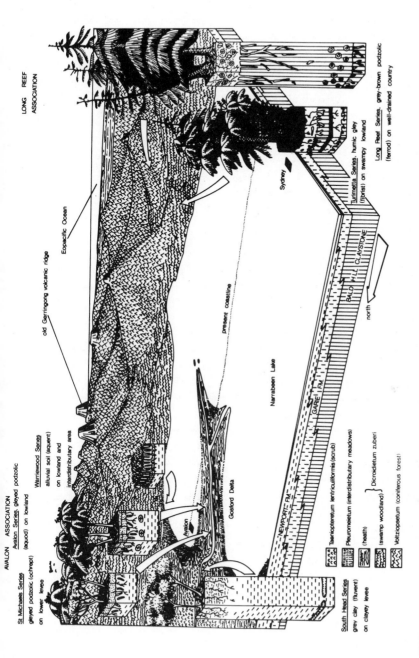

FIGURE 3.2. A reconstruction of the landscape, soils, and vegetation of the Sydney area, Australia during the later Early to earlier Middle Triassic. Lithological symbols as for Figure 3.11. (Redrawn from Retallack [1977b] with permission from the *Journal of the Geological Society of Australia*.)

61

Series paleosols of the Triassic near Sydney, Australia, the best evidence that siderite nodules were formed in place during soil formation was the rare occurrence of sand-filled insect burrows approaching the nodules from above, but sidling right around them, rather than passing through them (McDonnell 1974; Retallack 1977a). After detailed consideration of all their features, these Triassic paleosols proved impressively well preserved for their age and the few diagenetic alterations found were not critical to interpretation of the paleosols.

METHODS OF STUDY

Although theoretically recognized by all the features of modern soils, different methods of study are needed for older fossil soils than for Quaternary and modern soils. As a general rule, mineralogy and geochemistry, although necessary to consider, are the features of paleosols most susceptible to later alteration and should play a subordinate role to detailed field observations, the nature of horizons and soil peds, micromorphology, and associated fossil plants and animals in the study of older fossil soils.

Fieldwork

There is no substitute for detailed fieldwork in the study of fossil soils. The most striking feature of fossil soils from a distance is often their color, especially bright red and brown horizons. The most diagnostic feature is evidence of fossil roots in place. Other features include clayey, leached, massive prismatic, blocky-jointed or slickensided layers, and a variety of trace fossils, mottles, nodules, and concretions. Some concepts of paleosol horizons' parent material, and of special features, such as later fills of surficial holes left by felled trees (Fig. 3.3), need to be assessed in the field, before they can be confirmed by laboratory studies. Color should also be taken in the field, using a Munsell or other soil color chart, rather than any of the existing rock color charts.

For interpretative, as opposed to stratigraphical, studies of fossil soils, I have found that the soil mapping units of the United States Department of Agriculture (Soil Survey Staff 1951, 1962) are best for several reasons. The names do not imply anything of the nature or origin of the fossil soil and are not dependent on modern soil classification, whose criteria cannot always be applied to paleosols or unequivocally distinguished from diagenetic modifications. A separate name can be given to each particular paleosol. Part of the name relates it to other paleosols of a similar kind in the same area. The paleosols can be interpreted at several conceptual levels within a hierarchy of classification. There is no confusion between paleosols from different areas

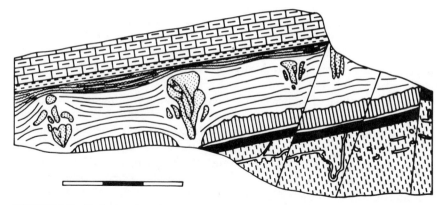

FIGURE 3.3. Scale drawing of a well-differentiated Early Permian paleosol at the contact between the Minnekahta Limestone (brick pattern) and the underlying Opeche Formation, near Boulder Park, Black Hills, South Dakota. The fossil soil is overlain by siltstone (horizontal dashes) and contains conspicuous cradle knolls (stipple). The profile includes an upper leached zone with thin ferruginized surfaces (wavy lines), yellow shale with relict bedding (long lines), red shale (vertical lines), and dark purple shale (black). Brick-red siltstone (vertical dashes) with numerous white mottles forms the parent material of the paleosol. Scale in meters, with no vertical exaggeration.

or rocks of different nature or age, as might arise if paleosols were named by letters or numbers, as is often a way of naming sedimentary facies (for example by Turner 1970; Miall 1977; Gorter 1978). Finally, the units of classification are already defined and widely accepted by soil scientists.

By this system, paleosols of a similar kind are grouped into a series named after a locality, such as the Avalon Series paleosols (of Retallack 1977b). The series is a most convenient unit for classification of paleosols in the field. Individual paleosols may be named by combining the series name with a term for the grainsize distribution in its A horizon, such as the Avalon silt loam paleosol. If individual paleosols need to be distinguished on bases other than the grainsize distribution in the A horizon, then variants and stages can be named from a variety of soil features, for example the Avalon silt loam egg-cup variant paleosol. On the other hand, series of paleosols can be grouped into associations on the basis of unifying characters, such as the Avalon Association paleosols.

Petrographical Thin Sections

Perhaps the most useful method of studying lithified older fossil soils is by petrographical thin sections. Microscopical features are often extremely helpful in deciding which features of the paleosol are original and which are due to later alteration. In addition, particular micromorphological features, such as sepic plasmic fabrics (Figs. 3.4, 3.5), may be diagnostic of soils and soil-forming processes. The terminology developed by Brewer (1964) for micromorphological features of soils has been widely accepted in studies of older fossil soils (Terrugi and Andreis 1971; Allen 1974b; Retallack 1977a; McPherson 1979).

Well-consolidated and cemented fossil soils may be difficult to disaggregate accurately for analysis of the proportions of sand, silt, and clay at different levels of the profile (Spalletti and Mazzoni 1978). Such quantitative information is of great value in assessing the nature of soil horizons and degree of illuviation, and also in naming paleosols. Grainsize distribution is best determined by counting measured grains under a microscope using a point counter. Friedman (1958, 1962) has shown that counts of the long axes of about 500 grains gives results very close to that of sieving fractions of unconsolidated sediments, and that even more accurate statistical parameters of the distribution can be obtained by converting the data with regression equations. Be aware, though, that the widely used Wentworth grainsize scale of geologists is not the same as that usually used by soil scientists. The grainsize scale and textural classes used by the United States Department of Agriculture (Soil Survey Staff 1975, p. 470) are better suited to textural studies of fossil soils.

FIGURE 3.4. Clino-trimasepic plasmic fabric from the A horizon of a well-differentiated paleosol in the latest Eocene to early Oligocene lowermost Chadron Formation (11.6 m in Figure 3.13); Pinnacles area, Badlands National Monument, South Dakota. × 50.

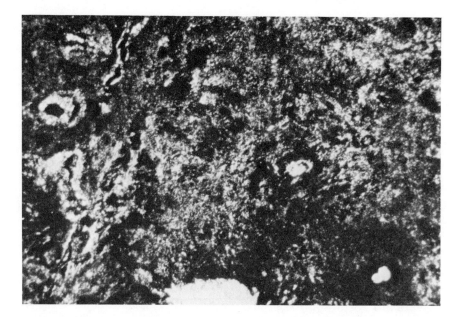

FIGURE 3.5. Omnisepic plasmic fabric with numerous channel organo-sesquans (after roots) in the B horizon of a well-differentiated paleosol in the mid-Cretaceous upper Dakota Formation, in bluffs 10 m above the river bank north of the Saline River, near U.S. highway 281, north of Russell, Kansas. × 50.

Geochemistry and Mineralogy

As with modern soils, an understanding of the mineralogy and geochemistry of fossil soils is important to their interpretation, although not always diagnostic (Power 1969). Mineralogical determinations are usually based on elemental chemical analysis and on optical properties in petrographical thin sections. The ratios of heavy minerals separated from the fossil soil and its parent material may also be useful in indicating the degree of weathering. For example, zircon and tourmaline are more rapidly weathered than amphibole and pyroxene (Ruhe 1965). X-ray diffraction analysis of clay minerals is also very useful. Clay in the upper horizons of fossil soils commonly gives broader, more diffuse peaks on an x-ray diffractometer trace than clays lower in the same profile or in adjacent sediments. This is probably due to small crystallite size, poor crystallization and mixed-layering common in the upper horizons of soils (Retallack 1977a) and can be another useful indicator of weathering. Such weathered minerals may be more difficult to identify than fresh ones. The geochemical conditions for the stability and origin of each mineral phase must be carefully cross-checked for consistency and to determine which are due to original soil formation and which due to later alteration.

Fossils

Trace fossils, bones, shells, coprolites, plant fossils, or any other vestige of former life associated with fossil soils should be collected and prepared by appropriate techniques. Fortunately, a great deal of basic paleontological work has already been done on terrestrial and near marine organisms, and this may only need to be integrated with study of the fossil soil, in order to reconstruct the soil, its setting, and the ecosystem it supported.

COMMON DIAGENETIC MODIFICATIONS

Unraveling the effects of diagenesis and original weathering can be a major stumbling block in the interpretation of older fossil soils. It is helpful to be aware of diagenetic modifications common in older paleosols. The following is my own list of troublesome diagenetic modifications. Undoubtedly others will be added as research continues.

Reddening of Ferric Oxide Minerals

The diagenetic inversion of yellow and brown ferric gel and goethite to brown or red limonite and hematite causes an appreciable reddening of fossil soils. The reason why paleosols of the last interglacial are commonly redder than those presently forming in the same areas may be partly because of higher temperature and humidity when they formed (Ruhe 1965). However, it is probably also partly due to long-term diagenetic inversion to redder ferric oxide minerals (Walker 1974). In most pre-Tertiary paleosols with horizons stained with ferric oxide, this is mostly hematite. Even the B horizons of humic gley (fibrist) paleosols from the Triassic near Sydney, Australia (Retallack 1977b), are brightly colored. These fossil soils may not have originally been as red as they appear today. Such paleosols may have originally been a variety of pale yellowish, brownish or pinkish colors, and were not necessarily oxisols or lateritic podzolic soils.

Siderite Pseudogley

Siderite nodules may form in waterlogged portions of modern soils (Kanno 1962; Degens 1965) and were evidently an original feature of the B horizons of gleyed podzolic (aquod) paleosols from the Triassic near Sydney, Australia (Retallack 1977a, 1977b). However, even previously nonwaterlogged soils become waterlogged when they subside below the water table. Such early diagenetic gleization is the best explanation for siderite nodules, spherulites, crystal tubes, and replacement of the walls of earthworm burrows in the A and organic horizons of others of the Triassic paleosols mentioned. Diagenetic gleization (or pseudogley of Roeschmann 1971) may also be responsible for the greenish and bluish hue of many older pedoliths and unoxidized soil horizons interbedded with redbeds. There is no evidence from the Triassic study cited that diagenetic gleization proceeded to the extent of reducing original ferric oxide minerals. This is in agreement with other studies indicating that ferric oxide minerals, once formed, are highly insoluble and unlikely to be reduced by the action of normal groundwater alone (Eaton 1942; Millot 1970).

Clay Diagenesis

Clay minerals are notoriously susceptible to diagenetic alterations of such a scope and complexity (Millot 1970) that it is very difficult to be certain of the original clay mineralogy of older paleosols. In Carboniferous clayey paleosols of the Ruhr district of West Germany, chlorite has been regarded as a diagenetic alteration product of montmorillonite, vermiculite and biotite, and kaolinite has been regarded as an alteration product of illite and muscovite (Roeschmann 1971).

Silicification

A variety of cherty rocks, cemented by silica, are found in or were formed by ancient soils. The silcretes of Australia, South Africa, the United States, and Europe are the most problematic of these. The cementing silica as well as the cemented orthoquartzites of silcretes may be derived from the weathering of stable land surfaces over long periods of geological time. In some cases it seems that the silica was transported great distances from where it was leached out of a variety of soils, so it is not necessarily genetically related to the material which it has transformed into a massive flinty rock. This process is probably at least partly diagenetic, although not yet completely understood. Different views on the nature and origin of silcretes have been conveniently collected in a volume edited by Langford-Smith (1978).

Ganister is a coal miner's term for indurated silicified sandstone, no thicker than 1.5 m, with over 90 percent angular grains of quartz in the grainsize range 0.5 to 0.15 mm. They commonly contain fossil roots and underlie coal seams in the Carboniferous coal measures of England (Williamson 1967). These are evidently the upper horizons of fossil soils and could not have supported the vegetation, indicated by the fossil roots, in their present indurated state. From my study of Triassic ganisters from near Sydney, Australia (Retallack 1977a), I concluded that the silica cement was derived largely from the early diagenetic mobilization and reprecipitation of opal phytoliths from plants, fecal pellets, and airborne dust in the original soil.

Similarly, the induration and complete silicification of petrified peats is probably also partly diagenetic. Kidston and Lang (1921) regarded the dead areas, wound reactions, and unequal enlargement of cells in otherwise well-preserved stems of *Rhynia major* from the early Devonian Rhynie chert of Scotland, as responses of living plants to the infiltration of silica-rich groundwaters from nearby fumaroles. Substantial influx of silica into this petrified peat was probably coincident with more aquatic conditions which destroyed the *Rhynia* marshes. The peaty substrate with well-preserved remains of these plants in growth position is overlain by layers with abundant crustaceans, algae, and the more aquatic vascular plant *Horneophyton* (emended from the original name of Kidston and Lang, by Barghoorn and Darrah [1938]). The living plants probably did not live in extremely high silica concentrations, nor in the indurated chert of today. The chert must have been silicified and indurated very early in diagenesis. This is apparent from the exceptional preservation of uncrushed herbaceous remains, and anatomical detail, in this and other petrified peats of various geological ages (Schopf 1970; Ting 1972; Basinger and Rothwell 1977; Runnegar 1977).

Sharpened Boundaries

The delineation of nodules, concretions, and horizons is often much sharper in older fossil soils than in modern soils. This may be in part a diagenetic segregation of chemically incompatible parts of the paleosol. Particularly noticeable is the often sharp delineation of gray reduced areas around fossil roots within horizons stained red with ferric oxide minerals, in older paleosols (Fig. 3.6).

The superficial appearance of sharp contacts can also be due to differential weathering of more indurated portions of a paleosol. In the Avalon and Warriewood Series paleosols of the Triassic of the Sydney Basin (Retallack 1977a), the lower boundaries of the silicified A horizons (ganisters), never prove to be as distinct in polished slabs as they appear in the field.

Physical Compaction

Depending on the depth and other conditions of burial, fossil soils may be flattened or develop jointing or other structures. According to Roeschmann (1971), the gleyed paleosols underlying Carboniferous coals of the Ruhr district of West Germany were compacted from 25 percent in sandy to 70 percent in clayey sediments. Such values need to be derived independently for each particular case, using deformation of structures and comparing the bulk density of the fossil soil with that of analogous modern soils.

Slickensides and prismatic jointing can form both at the surface in a soil, and during deep burial. The nature of the bounding surfaces (cutans) in petrographical thin sections is the best way of discriminating whether they were formed in the original soil or during later diagenesis. On this basis, the tessellated pavements and prismatic jointing in massive B horizons of the Long Reef Series paleosols from the Triassic near Sydney, Australia appear to be diagenetic in origin (Retallack 1977a).

Copper, Uranium, and Vanadium Mineralization

Certain metals are commonly mobilized and reprecipitated in fossil soils during diagenesis. Within the Long Reef Series paleosols mentioned previously, paratacamite, atacamite, and rare native copper may fill the cleat of coalified stick debris and the central portion of gray root mottles.

The uranium and vanadium ores of the Chinle and Morrison Formations of the western United States may be similar. Most of the mottled beds and redbeds of these units which I have seen are fossil soils, although not generally recognized as such. Many of the fossil logs in these formations, sometimes heavily mineralized, are scattered about on the surface of these fossil soils. Some of the impervious layers which confined ore-bearing

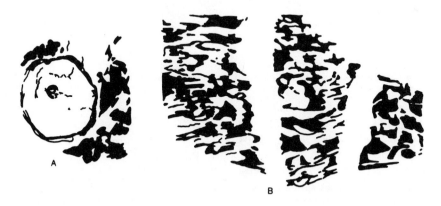

FIGURE 3.6. Ferric mottles (black) outlining gray mottles after roots, from the later Early to earlier Middle Triassic, Turimetta clay slightly eroded phase paleosol, north of Sydney, Australia: **A,** horizontal section including a root with clay-filled cortex, separating carbonaceous remnants of woody stele and periderm. **B,** vertical section. Natural size. (Redrawn from Retallack [1977a] with permission from the *Journal of the Geological Society of Australia*.)

solutions and also some of the organic layers which have been mineralized, are also probably fossil soils. The minerals are thought to have been dissolved in groundwater draining from uranium-bearing crystalline or volcanic rocks in uplands, and precipitated at a "redox front" (a transitional zone from positive to negative Eh or oxidizing to reducing conditions) in the lowlands (Stanton 1972; Granger and Warren 1978). This may have occurred during the formation of the fossil soils in these deposits, as well as during their later diagenesis. Basin-wide studies of these fossil soils, and particularly interpretations of their ancient water tables, may prove to be a powerful exploration tool. To my knowledge, this has not yet been suggested or attempted.

INTERPRETATION

Some aspects of ancient terrestrial environments can only be interpreted from the study of fossil soils. For other aspects, the study of fossil soils may be a valuable independent check on conclusions reached by other kinds of research. The study of fossil soils has lagged far behind other geological and paleontological studies, such as analysis of sedimentary basins, sedimentary petrography, heavy mineralogy, sedimentology, paleocurrents, palynology, paleobotany, paleontology, and paleoecology. In areas where these other studies have already been completed, a study of fossil soils may serve as a critical focus to integrate other information into a more detailed concept of a particular ancient terrestrial ecosystem than was hitherto possible.

Water Table

The nature and depth to the B horizon of some kinds of paleosols is a reasonable guide to the depth of the water table, or at least the zone about which it most commonly fluctuated. Frequent wet periods are indicated by siderite nodules or spherulites in the B horizon (as with all these features they must be demonstrated to be original), by asepic or undulic plasmic fabrics, by an apedal or massive structure, by shallow root systems with thicker roots spreading laterally rather than downward, and also by more humified organic matter at the surface. More frequent dry periods may be indicated by reddish mottled or nodular B horizons stained with ferric oxide minerals, by well-differentiated peds, by animal burrows, by deeper root systems, and by less humified organic matter at the surface. Even better drained and more arid conditions are indicated by soils without a clear B horizon or with other indicators, such as caliche nodules. It is also possible that this last kind of paleosol was so immature before burial that there was not enough time to form a B horizon. If this is the case, then sedimentary relicts and other indications of immaturity should also be in evidence.

Soil Chemistry

Assessing the original chemistry of a fossil soil is often a major obstacle to interpretation. Features such as base saturation, cation exchange capacity, and pH are critical to parts of classifications of modern soils. These chemical features are irreparably changed upon burial, and further changed during compaction, diagenesis, and metamorphism. For example, buried Quarternary soils in Iowa are often completely saturated with bases throughout the profile, but analogous modern soils are only 40 percent saturated in the B horizon, but completely saturated at depths of about 1.5 m in the C horizon. The pH is usually over 6.0 throughout the buried soils, but in analogous modern soils it is 5.3 in the A horison, 4.0 in the B, and 5.0 in the C horizon (Ruhe 1965).

These chemical features are better assessed from the mineralogical phases thought to have been in the original soil. The original pH or Eh can be assessed from the ranges of values in which these minerals form or are stable, as outlined by Krumbein and Garrels (1952) and Baas-Becking, Kaplan, and Moore (1960). Acidic conditions (neutral to low pH) are indicated by kaolinite, by ganister or other siliceous A horizon without carbonate, and by red ferric oxide mottles, concretions, nodules, surface crust, and diffusion ferrans. Alkaline conditions (neutral to high pH) are indicated by carbonate (including siderite nodules) and by other features indicated by Northcote and Skene (1972). Oxidizing conditions (positive Eh) are indicated by red ferric oxide mottles, concretions, nodules, surface crust, and diffusion ferrans. Reducing conditions (negative Eh) are indicated by gley colors, by pyrite framboids, and by siderite nodules, intercalary crystals, spherulites, and crystal tubes. Sodic and saline soils (with Na^+ as the dominant exchangeable cation) may be characterized by surface salt crusts or casts of such crystals in sediment, by prominent domed columnar peds in an argillic B horizon or by other features indicated by Northcote and Skene (1972). Additional investigations into these and other indicators of original soil chemistry would be of great value for identifying fossil soils.

Soil Fauna

The variety of traces of soil fauna discovered in fossil soils to date include Triassic burrows of earthworms, cicada-like insects and large vertebrates (Retallack 1977a), Eocene dung beetle boli (Andreis 1972), and Oligocene land snails and coprolites (Wanless 1923; personal observations). The spectacular vertical corkscrew-like burrows (called *Daemonelix*) often more than 10 m deep in the early Miocene Harrison Formation of north-western Nebraska (Fig. 3.7) have even been found with entombed skeletons of burrowing rodents. The *Daemonelix* burrows indicate that the water table in these soils was seldom closer than 10 m below the surface, for otherwise the rodents would have drowned. The nature and occurrence of traces of soil fauna can supply useful constraints in the interpretation of fossil soils. Further studies of these traces can be expected to reveal much about the evolution of such animals as earthworms and ground-dwelling social insects and rodents.

Vegetation

The former vegetation of some fossil soils, particularly gleyed and organic soils, may be preserved in or around their upper surface. Plant material is usually not preserved in more oxidized fossil soils. However, poorly preserved pollen in oxidized Triassic fossil soils proved sufficient to gain an idea of its vegetation (Retallack 1977b). As a general rule, fossil plants are much better preserved in flood, pond, or lake deposits than in direct association with fossil soils. More detailed understanding of fossil plants gained from such better preserved material is often useful also in interpreting fossil soils. The fossil plants may indicate whether the vegetation was a forest, savanna or grassland, and also show adaptations to conditions such as aridity, salinity, or waterlogging. This may serve as an independent check on deductions from their likely fossil soil. The study of fossil soils and plants can be combined to gain a better understanding of both.

FIGURE 3.7. *Daemonelix,* burrow system of a rodent from the early Miocene Harrison Formation of Nebraska. Reduced one-tenth natural size. (Redrawn from Barbour [1897].)

In relating occurrences of well-preserved fossil plants to fossil soils I make one basic assumption: As in the modern world, different kinds of fossil soils probably supported different communities of plants, and the same soils supported similar vegetation. Some quantitative approaches have been devised for reconstructing Carboniferous plant communities from their dispersed compression remains (Scott 1977, 1978, 1979) and from their representation in peats petrified in calcareous coal balls (Phillips et al. 1974). In my own studies of Triassic fossil soils and plants of eastern Australasia (Retallack 1977a, 1977b, 1977c, 1978), I found that interpretation of communities from named recurrent fossil associations of plants gave a more balanced appraisal of different kinds of vegetation. This largely qualitative approach was particularly effective when the named associations were based on specific collections of fossil plants which did not appear to have been transported far, and also when combined with studies of fossil soils and depositional sedimentary environments. The different kinds of fossil plant associations and fossil soils can then be matched according to their nature, or preferably by direct correlation with plant fragments associated with the fossil soil.

Type of Soil

If a fossil soil can be identified with a modern soil, then presumably it formed under similar conditions of topography, drainage, vegetation, and climate. Even if complete identification is not possible because of later alteration or lack of diagnostic features, comparison with modern soils may still provide useful information about the ancient environment. Interpretations of fossil soils based on this principle of uniformitarianism have been presented by many authors (Ložek 1967; Ruhe 1970; Allen 1974b; Retallack 1977b).

There is still some debate concerning the classification of modern soils. Some of these uncertainties should be considered when interpreting fossil soils, but ultimate identification of a fossil soil in a classification of modern soils rests on a literal interpretation of a cited authority. The classification of the United States Department of Agriculture (Soil Survey Staff 1975), the more conventional Australian classification (Stace et al. 1968), and the nongenetic classification of Northcote (1974) represent a range of viewpoints on soil classification. The so-called "ecological method" of Duchafour (1978) also shows much promise, particularly if expanded into a more comprehensive form.

Fossil soils should not be strained to fit into a classification of modern soils, as some kinds of soils once formed on the earth are now extinct. The only extinct kinds of paleosol reported to date are the Precambrian paleosols thought to have formed in an anoxic atmosphere (Roscoe 1968;

Frarey and Roscoe 1970; Rankama 1955). Other more subtle kinds of extinct paleosols may be discovered in the future.

Some kinds of fossil soil horizons such as caliche and laterite have been widely identified in the past on too little evidence, without any indication of the nature of the profiles or any attempt to demonstrate that the features observed were original rather than diagenetic. This is especially apparent from reexamination of so-called laterites of the area around Sydney, Australia by Hunt, Mitchell, and Paton (1977). Close attention to detail is necessary if studies of fossil soils are to realize their evident potential.

Basin Tectonics

The nature of fossil soils and their distribution within sedimentary sequences may give otherwise unattainable information on rates of sedimentation, subsidence, uplift, and basin topography. In my work on Triassic paleosols north of Sydney, Australia (Retallack 1977a, 1977b), the distribution of paleosols indicated all these things. The Bald Hill Claystone, 18 m thick, at the base of the succession contains about eight confusingly superimposed and well-differentiated paleosols. The area probably received little sediment for 16,000 years or more because it was very slowly subsiding, freely drained, rolling land. By contrast, the paleosols are completely separated by sediment in the overlying Garie Formation. These humic gley (fibrist) paleosols indicate increased subsidence culminating in deposition of subaqueous lagoonal shale. In the overlying Newport Formation, paleosols are also well separated by sediment, but show several indications of immaturity, such as widespread sedimentary relicts within the profiles. This would indicate a steady subsidence rate of about a meter every 2,000 years. Higher within the Newport Formation, paleosols are seldom preserved. Paleosols are very rare in the overlying braided stream deposits of the Hawkesbury sandstone. This probably is due to very low rates of subsidence, allowing extensive lateral migration of streams and almost total reworking of floodplain deposits.

Allen (1974b, 1974c) has developed several theoretical models to explain the distribution of paleosols and channel deposits expected under varying conditions of subsidence, stream behavior (laternal migration as opposed to channel avulsion), and climatic fluctuations. Slow subsidence of the order of a meter every 5,000 years and periodic channel avulsion may best explain the distribution of paleosols in the Anglo-Welsh outcrop of the Siluro-Devonian Old Red Sandstone.

Climate

Temperature and rainfall are such important factors in forming modern soils that many modern soils are restricted to particular climatic zones.

However, caution is advisable when interpreting climate from fossil soils for at least two reasons. Firstly, the climatic regime of a soil, particularly of the broader categories at the level of a suborder (of Soil Survey Staff 1975), is usually a generalization which may not apply strictly to each case. Secondly, climate is only one of a number of other factors which must be considered: time of formation, topographical position, soil fauna, vegetation, and parent material.

Caliche-bearing paleosols have been widely considered to indicate warm, semiarid conditions (Allen 1974b; Hubert 1977a, 1977b), and lateritic paleosols to indicate hot, seasonally humid conditions (Abbott, Minch, and Peterson 1976; Peterson and Abbott 1979). While broadly true, there are complications and exceptions to these generalizations which must be considered before applying them to specific paleosols (Reeves 1970; Paton and Williams 1972). As another example, the dominance of podzolic paleosols, even on a variety of parent materials, as well as evidence from associated flora and paleolatitude indicated by paleomagnetic data, indicate that the climate of the area around Sydney, Australia was moderately humid and cool temperate during the early Triassic (Retallack 1977b). Until fossil soils can be identified with greater precision, only such general impressions of paleoclimate will be gained from them.

DIVERSIFICATION OF SOILS THROUGH TIME

Much can be learned from the uniformitarian interpretation of fossil soils. Perhaps the most exciting prospect of continuing paleoenvironmental studies of fossil soils will be gaining a better understanding of the diversification of soils through geological time. As knowledge of fossil soils has lagged so far behind that of other geological and paleontological sciences, such studies can be expected to integrate evidence from a variety of sources into a better understanding of the evolution of terrestrial ecosystems. The critical events for such a scenario were probably the evolution of the atmosphere, the origin of terrestrial organisms, the emergence of rooted plants, the development of woody plants, the expansion of grasslands, and the impact of human beings on the land surfaces of the world. Broadly similar scenarios have been postulated by Yaalon (1971) and Hunt (1972). Existing studies of fossil soils pertinent to these critical events are few, but show much promise for the future.

Abiotic Soils of the Precambrian

Precambrian fossil soils are difficult to recognize with certainty, because one of the most diagnostic features of Devonian and later fossil soils, roots in growth position, are not found in them. Most Precambrian paleosols recognized to date have been below major unconformities. The many problems of this kind of geological setting have already been discussed. There is a need for more earnest theoretical modeling of the likely weathering effects of different hypothetical Precambrian atmospheres and also for more detailed micromorphological and geochemical studies of Precambrian paleosols.

Collins (1925), Roscoe (1968), and Frarey and Roscoe (1970) have described a fossil soil, about 2.45 billion years old, developed on pre-Huronian crystalline rocks underlying the various basal formations of the Elliot Lake Group in the area between Sudbury and Elliot Lake, north of Lake Huron, Canada. This is a zone, up to 16 m thick, of altered biotite granite and greenstone on the pre-Huronian surface. Above unaltered pink biotite granite, there is a thick white rock with granitic texture containing highly altered mafic minerals, plagioclase almost entirely altered to sericite, and scattered inclusions of unaltered granite. Higher in the profile granitic texture is no longer present, even microcline is partly replaced by sericite and only quartz grains persist unaltered. The highest part of the profile is a greenish rock with quartz grains and remnants of microcline floating in a structureless matrix of sericite (mica-illite). Accessory minerals persisting in the altered rock include hematite, magnetite, pyrite, rutile, zircon, monazite, thorogummite (probably thorite originally), garnet, and amphibole. Thinner (about 1 m) profiles, developed on greenstone, consist of a greenish, gray or pale yellowish rock with a high sericite content. Pyrrhotite (or sometimes other sulfide minerals) may form a thin layer, up to 3 cm thick, immediately below the unconformity on these greenstone profiles. The pre-Huronian land surface was evidently leached of most of its CaO, SrO, and MnO, much of its MgO, Na_2O, FeO, and Fe_2O_3, and perhaps a little SiO_2 and Al_2O_3. Strangely, water, Rb_2O_3, and K_2O appear to have accumulated. Other aspects of this alteration are comparable with modern weathering, apart from the general loss of iron, the greater loss of Fe_2O_3 than FeO, and the extreme loss of MnO. These differences are probably due to the absence of oxygen in the atmosphere at that time. An anoxic atmosphere is also indicated by pyritic conglomerates containing placers of detrital uranium minerals, such as uraninite and brannerite, in the overlying Elliot Lake Group. Lack of oxygen is in good accord with modern theory that the Precambrian atmosphere was largely derived from degassing of the earth's interior from volcanic vents and so consisted largely of gases such as CH_4, NH_3, CO_2, H_2, H_2O, H_2S, and N_2 (Berkner and Marshall 1965).

Another paleosol, possibly formed in an oxygen-poor atmosphere about 1.8 billion years ago, has been found in the Tampere area of Finland (Rankama 1955; Eskola 1963). This is a breccia of diorite with a gray schist matrix developed on fresh diorite and overlain unconformably by varved mica schist. Analysis of all these rocks showed a preponderance of FeO over Fe_2O_3, as in the pre-Huronian paleosols north of Lake Huron.

Although some oxygen in the primitive atmosphere may have come from the photodissociation of water by ultraviolet light, a more productive source of oxygen was probably photosynthesis by marine microorganisms (J. W. Schopf 1975, 1978). There is much that could be learned about this process from fossil soils. Was there more oxygen in and near the sea than on land? Was oxygen dispersed or limited to certain areas? With very low amounts of oxygen, were some elements and minerals of Precambrian soils affected more than others?

The atmosphere evidently contained appreciable amounts of oxygen by about 2 billion years ago, as redbeds began to appear at about that time. In the Huronian sequence north of Lake Huron the advent of a more oxygenated atmosphere is indicated by monazite-rich, hematitic conglomerates of the Lorrain Formation, about 2.1 billion years old (Roscoe 1968). Other Precambrian redbeds of about this age are mentioned by Davidson (1965). Some of these may prove to be paleosols. All deserve more critical attention. Donaldson (1969) and Fraser et al. (1970) have reported a hematitic altered zone on crystalline basement underlying the Athabasca Formation, probably 1.7 billion years old, in northwestern Saskatchewan, Canada. Hematite-stained, altered zones are also widespread just below the base of the Grand Canyon Series in the Grand Canyon, Arizona (Sharp 1940), at a surface older than 1.15 billion years and possibly as old as 1.4 billion years (Livingston and Damon 1968). Other paleosols which may provide evidence on the nature of primitive atmospheres are those mentioned by Hoffman, Fraser, and McGlynn (1970) interbedded with volcanic flows of the Seton Formation, 2.0 to 1.75 billion years old, in the Great Slave fold belt, Northwest Territory, Canada and also by Blades and Bickford (1979) from a 1.5-billion-year-old sequence of volcaniclastic sediments and rhyolitic ash-flows in Missouri, U.S.A.

By about 1 billion years ago, weathering was becoming more like it is today. Williams (1968) has described a fossil soil from the Cape Wrath district of northwest Scotland, probably about a billion years old (Anderson 1965). This was developed on an old topographical surface of Lewisian biotite gneiss, amphibolite, and microcline pegmatite with a relief of at least 600 m, and covered by Torridonian alluvial fan deposits (Fig. 3.8). In the profile developed on biotite gneiss, the upper 30 cm is usually stained very dark red and is massive. Underlying this is a bleached zone of very pale green or grayish green rock with relict gneissic foliation. The bleached zone passes gradationally into light gray, fresh gneiss. The altered zone extends 1 to 3 m below the surface, and up to 6 m locally along joints and around unaltered corestones. Quartz and microcline persist throughout the profile with some corrosion and cracking, but biotite and plagioclase of the original gneiss are extensively altered. The profile developed on greenish black amphibolite is a soft dark greenish gray rock, 1.0 to 1.3 m thick and laced with veins of white carbonate up to 5 mm wide. Quartz and microcline are also little altered in

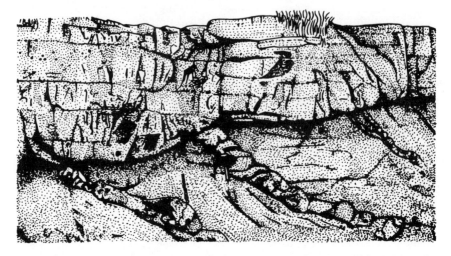

FIGURE 3.8. One-billion-year-old fossil soil on Lewisian gneiss with prominent pegmatite veins, unconformably overlain by Torridonian conglomerate and sandstone, at Sheigra, northwest Scotland. The reddish surface of the fossil soil is shown in heavier stipple. Hammer gives scale. (Redrawn from Williams [1968] with permission from the *Scottish Journal of Geology.*)

this profile, but all the original hornblende and most of the plagioclase have been altered to a pale green micaceous mass with patches of chlorite, carbonate, and iron oxide. Pegmatite veins were little altered. These and the foliation were bent at the unconformity in some outcrops, interpreted by Williams as evidence of Precambrian soil creep. Both the red and bleached portions of the profile on the biotite gneiss have lower SiO_2, FeO, CaO, and Na_2O and higher Fe_2O_3 and K_2O than fresh gneiss. In the red portion of the profile, Al_2O_3, Fe_2O_3, K_2O, TiO_2, and P_2O_5 are at maximum and SiO_2, FeO, and Na_2O at a minimum. Williams believed that the red portion of the profile was a remnant of a thicker, probably podzolic soil. There is no evidence of any different higher horizon, nor is it necessary. The accumulation of aluminium, iron and potassium and comcomitant desilication was more likely produced by lateral flow of ground and surface water, rather than by illuviation more characteristic of modern forested soils. These paleosols were probably developed on freely drained, rolling parts of valleys in a warm, moderately humid climate and oxygenated atmosphere.

Kalliokosi (1975) has described comparable paleosols of similar age from Presque Isle, north of Marquette, Michigan, developed on granodiorite, diabase, and serpentinized periodotite, where these are unconformably overlain by late Keweenawan Jacobsville Sandstone. He interpreted the dolomite-quartz layers in these fossil soils as caliche horizons, indicating semiarid climate. The exact nature of these altered rocks has been disputed

(Lewan 1977; Kalliokosi 1977). Paleosols have also been found in several parts of the Grand Canyon of Arizona at the unconformity immediately below early and middle Cambrian sandstones (Sharp 1940; McKee 1969). Patel (1977) has reported another paleosol at the unconformity covered by early Cambrian rocks in the Saint John District of New Brunswick.

Compared to earlier times, these later Precambrian and Cambrian paleosols were leached of more silica and accumulated more iron, especially Fe_2O_3. This had a considerable effect on shallow marine sedimentation. Banded iron formations became much less common. Silicified shallow marine stromatolites, often including exquisitely preserved microorganisms, became more common (Hargraves 1976; Schopf 1975). More intense terrestrial weathering is probably also a partial explanation, besides long time of formation, for the supermature quartose sandstones deposited in rivers, beaches, and shallow marine continental shelves the world over during the late Precambrian and Cambrian.

Later Precambrian Microbially Influenced Soils

It is likely that the land was partly colonized by algae, bacteria, and viruses, and perhaps even fungi, lichens or liverworts long before the first vascular plants. The green slime of shallow Precambrian seas has been studied in some detail (J. W. Schopf 1978), but did it venture out to become the "scum of the earth"? There is little firm evidence for this idea, and still a need for more perceptive and detailed speculation.

Many of the kinds of microorganisms found in cyanobacterial mats of modern desert crusts were well represented in later Precambrian marine rocks (Campbell 1979). In modern deserts these organisms are capable of withstanding high salinity and long desiccation, with instant reactivation after rain. They are also capable of traveling overland by mechanical expulsion of trichomes during rehydration and by self-propelled gliding wherever there is moisture. Many are of a size easily transported by wind. Fischer (1965) and Sagan (1965) speculated that the high ultraviolet radiation during the earlier Precambrian prevented organisms from colonizing the surface of the ocean, the intertidal zone, and land. They also postulate that radiation was only reduced to tolerable levels by the increasing amounts of oxygen in the atmosphere. Schopf (personal communication 1980) doubts the severity of this radiation on the basis of very old stromatolites and likely planktonic organisms. But even allowing such radiation, microorganisms could have still survived on land below the surface in unconsolidated diaphanous materials and also in "shade oases" of crevices and overhangs. Small outposts of life on land may have been important centers of organic evolution.

The effects of the first soil organisms on soil formation would have been enormous. Erosion resistance of cyanobacterial mats of modern deserts was demonstrated by Booth (1941), who found that runoff from them was clear, while that of adjacent areas was muddy. Today these mats may precipitate carbonate crusts in arid areas (Campbell 1979). As in modern soils (Bloomfield 1964; Zajic 1969), Precambrian microorganisms were probably capable of forming soluble metal chelates (particularly of iron) which could then be transported in solution to other parts of the profile or washed out entirely. Like modern microbes, they were probably also active in decomposing aluminosilicate minerals, releasing different elements at different rates and controlling other chemical processes by regulation of pH. Local oxygen produced by soil microorganisms may have been critical in the formation of insoluble oxides of aluminium and iron, thus fixing these elements within the soil.

Campbell (1979) has suggested that microbial influence of soils may have begun as long as 2.4 billion years ago, on the basis of 0.25 percent reduced organic matter informally reported to her by D. Grandstaff from a paleosol of that age in the Blind River Formation of Ontario, Canada. It is also possible, although presently impossible to prove, that the oxidized surface and likely caliche of younger Precambrian paleosols, and perhaps the surficial sulfides of older ones, owe their clear differentiation to the action of soil organisms. Direct evidence of Precambrian soil microbiota is inconclusive. Cherts filling cracks into basement rocks unconformably underlying the Pokegama Quartzite, a little more than 2 billion years old, contain nostocacean cyanobacteria and also possible budding bacteria (Cloud 1976). However, it is uncertain how often, or if, this material was exposed when the organisms lived. There are similar problems with the supposed terrestrial fungi described by Hallbauer and Van Warmelo (1974) from the base of the 2.3–2.7-billion-year-old Witwatersrand Group of South Africa. Although the carbon is evidently biogenic, the structures are more likely artifacts of their preparation procedures, as are several other such claims (Cloud 1976; Barghoorn, Chap. 2 [this volume]).

Future micromorphological studies of Precambrian terrestrial rocks may be more revealing, judging from discoveries of soil microorganisms in younger rocks. The symbiotic relationship between land plants and endotrophic fungi may be as old as early Devonian, as fungi of that age are preserved within vascular land plants of the Rhynie chert in Scotland (Kidston and Lang 1921; Pirozynski 1976). In the late Devonian Caballos Novaculite, near Marathon, Texas, a variety of filamentous cyanobacteria, green algae, and possible fungi were found in jasper-filled cracks of a paleosol developed on older sabkha deposits (Fairchild, Schopf, and Folk 1973), although these identifications were later doubted by Schopf (1975). *Callixylon* wood found in the Caballos Formation indicates that trees also grew in the area, but it is unclear if, or which, vascular plants grew in the jasper-bearing paleosol (McBride and Folk 1977). Finally, *Microcodium* is a widespread microfossil commonly preserved in caliche-bearing paleosols. Klappa (1978) has interpreted it as a fungus, possibly mycorrhizal, and has discussed numerous occurrences dating back to Jurassic times.

Early Paleozoic Advent of Soils of Vascular Land Plants

The study of fossil soils may make a fundamental contribution to the current debate on when the first vascular land plants appeared. Some (Gray and Boucot 1977) feel that dispersed trilete spores, tracheid-like bodies, and cuticle fragments found in rocks as old as late Ordovician are the first evidence of vascular land plants. Others (Banks 1975a, 1975b; J. M. Schopf 1978; Edwards, Basset, and Rogerson 1979) are only prepared to accept as evidence of the first vascular land plants the complete megafossils of late Silurian age. The debate has opened some very difficult, perhaps insoluble, questions. To what extent do specific structures of fossil plants necessarily indicate their affinities or paleoenvironment? Is the adaptive value of such structures in living plants the same as it was to the first land plants? Which and how many features are important indicators of terrestrial habitat? Were some of the earliest land plants adapted to partial or periodic exposure to the air? Studies of the fossil substrates supporting these early plants should give a more definitive and detailed perspective on the problem. The holdfasts, rhizoids, rhizomes, and roots of primitive plants may be well-preserved in aquatic shales and cherts. Although not preserved as well in more oxidizing environments, such structures may significantly modify soil material. They promote the obliteration of relict structures from the parent material and development of sepic plasmic fabrics, cutans, and glaebules, or leave more obvious pedotubules (this terminology is after Brewer 1964).

Early Paleozoic redbed sequences should be examined in more detail with this aim in mind. First on my list are the Ordovician and Silurian paleosols described by Boucot et al. (1974) from the Arisaig area of Antigonish County, Nova Scotia. Here paleosols cap several columnar-jointed andesite flows in the late Ordovician Dunn Point Formation. The 1.3 m thick profiles consist largely of a homogeneous aggregate of granular hematite and clay, which extends deeper into cracks within the spheroidally-weathered andesite (Fig. 3.9). The lower portion of this altered zone contains upward fining andesite corestones. This is overlain by an horizon with poorly developed spherulitic texture. The upper portion of the red material is blocky, with nodules and irregular patches of chalcedony and carbonate. Near the surface of the profile there are small white reduction spots and irregular pockets, about 1 m wide and 20 cm deep, filled with bedded, redeposited red material. Plastically deformed fragments of the red paleosols are commonly entrained in overriding andesite and ignimbrite flows. The

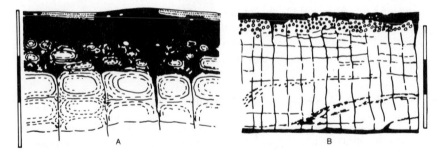

FIGURE 3.9. Late Ordovician paleosols from the Dunn Point Formation, near Arisaig, Nova Scotia; **A,** red soil material (black), with surficial hollows filled with redeposited soil material (stipple) and near surface reduction spots (white ovals), overlying spheroidally weathered andesite. **B,** red soil material swept up into overriding andesite flow. Scales in meters. (Redrawn from Boucot et al. [1974] with permission from the author and the *Geological Society of America.*)

unconsolidated red soil was also prone to slumping, as it forms thick rubbly mudflows filling in ancient channels. The original soils were evidently exposed to the surface with no overlying horizons, and were also unindurated. For these reasons, they should not have been called laterites (by Dewey, in Boucot et al. 1974), as that term is usually understood (McFarlane 1976). Without additional details these fossil soils cannot be accurately identified, but are probably better compared with some of the less differentiated oxisols (Soil Survey Staff 1975) or red earths, calcareous red earths, or krasnozems (Stace et al. 1968). It is quite possible, as suggested by Dewey, that the reduction mottles and the surficial erosion scours indicate clumps of vegetation. This also deserves further attention.

There are also fossil soils in the Red Member of the Moydart Formation of likely latest Silurian age, also in the Arisaig area (Boucot et al. 1974). These consist of about 2 m of red micaceous siltstone with numerous very light gray ellipsoidal calcareous nodules which become more numerous and even fused toward the top of the profile. This kind of fossil soil is also characteristic of Devonian rocks such as the middle Downtonian to middle Dittonian Knoydart Formation, also in the Arisaig area (Boucot et al. 1974) and in many other parts of the late Silurian and Devonian Catskill and Old Red facies of the Northern Hemisphere (Friend, Harland, and Gilbert-Smith 1970; Woodrow, Fletcher, and Ahrnsbrak 1973; Allen 1973, 1974a, 1974b; Leeder 1976). These paleosols resemble modern soils with caliche horizons, forming in warm to hot regions (mean annual temperature 16–20°C) of limited rainfall (mean annual rainfall 100–500 mm). Tepee structures in some of these paleosols indicate periodic wetting, probably during more than one season of the year (Fig. 3.10). These fossil soils also have numerous vertical and branching pedotubules and crystal tubes up to several millimeters in diameter, probably formed by both plant roots and burrowing

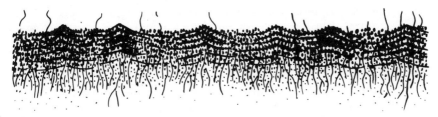

FIGURE 3.10. Schematic drawing of tepee structure in Devonian caliche-bearing paleosols of the Anglo-Welsh outcrop of the Old Red Sandstone. The carbonate nodules (black ellipses) and tubular structures (lines) are largely confined to an horizon about 2 m thick. (Redrawn from Allen [1974b].)

animals. They were evidently vegetated, at least sparsely. Much has been learned of the evolution, anatomy, and morphology of the primitive plants associated with these paleosols (Banks 1968), but it is too early yet to say what kinds of plant communities vegetated these various fossil soils.

McPherson (1979) has made a detailed study of similar fossil soils from the Late Devonian (probably Famennian) Aztec Siltstone of southern Victoria Land, Antarctica. These are riddled with small root casts and burrows, calcareous nodules, and vein networks, and also show tepee structures and color mottling. Sepic plasmic fabrics (as in Fig. 3.4) are common in these paleosols. The down profile decrease in SiO_2 and increase in Al_2O_3, K_2O, and TiO_2 indicates that there was significant illuviation of clay. Increasing total iron (Fe_2O_3 + FeO), CaO, and MnO with depth, is related to a down profile increase in hematite and carbonate. These changes indicate very rudimentary development of A and B horizons, as found, although much better differentiated, in modern forested soils. McPherson compares these Devonian paleosols with red or brown clays, red brown earths, calcareous red earths, and red earth soils of the Australian classification (Stace et al. 1968). Only a few fragmentary lycopod fossil plants have been found in Devonian rocks of Antarctica (Plumstead 1964). Judging from later representatives of this group of plants, these probably colonized wetter habitats than these fossil soils, whose vegetation is still unknown.

As discussed by Schumm (1968), the emergence of a land flora had a great effect on stabilizing stream channels, particularly in promoting meandering rather than braided stream courses. It also served to delay and lessen the devastation of flash flooding after rains in some parts of the landscape. As a result, soil formation on the interfluves was less frequently and less critically interrupted by sedimentation.

Mid-Paleozoic Appearance of Woodland Soils

The first woodlands and forests would have had a considerable impact on the world's land surfaces. In some ways their greater biomass would have accentuated soil-forming processes associated with preexisting vegetation of lesser stature. With woodlands and forests appeared the first well-differentiated soils, such as podzols (of conventional terminology) or spodosols, ultisols, and alfisols (of the U.S. Dept. of Agriculture classification, Soil Survey Staff 1975). These are soils with two clearly recognizable layers, an upper or A horizon leached of materials such as iron, aluminum, and clay, and a lower or B horizon in which these materials accumulate. Further study of such midpaleozoic paleosols may clarify how, when, and where the first woodlands and forests arose.

Theoretically this could have happened during the mid-Devonian. At this time there were many plants with limited amounts of secondary wood (Banks 1968). Large, poorly preserved stumps of *Eospermatopteris* have been found in later Middle Devonian (Givetian) rocks of New York State (Banks 1966). The more massive progymnosperm wood, *Callixylon*, may also be as old as the late Givetian (Banks 1968). During the Late Devonian this wood was widespread, and individual trees grew up to 1.6 m in diameter (Beck 1971). This is not to say that these trees necessarily formed woodland communities, although this is likely. Among outcrops of Late Devonian rocks in the area of New York and Pennsylvania described by Woodrow and Fletcher (1967), I recently discovered a number of intriguing, well-differentiated paleosols during preliminary fieldwork with J. D. Grierson. This would be a particularly suitable area for a study of fossil soils and plant paleoecology, as the fossil plants from here are exceptionally well understood (as reviewed by Banks 1966, with continuing contributions by Skog and Banks 1973; Grierson 1976; Bonamo 1977).

Paleosols with distinct leached A horizons and reddish B horizons are common and widespread in Carboniferous and younger terrestrial sedimentary rocks. As an example, the type Long Reef clay paleosol (Fig. 3.11) evidently formed under coniferous forest on volcanogenic sandstone in moderately well-drained rolling land near Sydney, Australia during the earlier Triassic (Retallack 1977a, 1977b). This has a thin brownish yellow (Munsell color 9YR6/8) surface crust (A_1), overlying 33.5 cm of very coarse subangular blocky and slickensided greenish gray (8G6/1) claystone with vomasepic porphyroskelic fabric. This passes gradationally down into 20 cm of weak red (1YR4/2) fine clayey sandstone (B_{1ir}) with isotic porphyroskelic fabric, penetrated by numerous light greenish gray (8GY7/1) vermicular mottles of sandy material around old root channels. Deeper in the B horizon there is 41 cm of apedal red material with only rare gray mottles (B_{2ir}) and below that, 67 cm of dusky red (3YR3/2) claystone (B_{3ir}). This lowest level contains relict pedotubules and undulic porphyroskelic fabric of the A horizon of an underlying paleosol, the rest of which forms a C horizon to the type Long Reef clay paleosol, more than 181.5 cm below its preserved surface. Clays of the paleosol are mainly kaolinite, probably weathered from

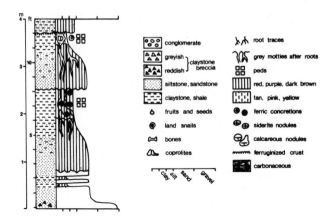

FIGURE 3.11. Later Early or earlier Middle Triassic type Long Reef clay paleosol north of Sydney, Australia. The ferruginized lower B horizon of the type profile includes pedorelicts of the A horizon of an underlying paleosol.

soft volcanic sand grains better preserved lower in the profile. The reddish material with isotic fabric in lower horizons is mainly hematite and goethite, with some siderite. Soil-forming processes have resulted in considerable accumulation of total iron (Fe_2O_3 + FeO) in the B horizon, a moderate accumulation of Al_2O_3 in the A and B horizon, and loss of CaO, MgO, Na_2O, and K_2O throughout the profile. These paleosols were identified as gray brown podzolic (of Stace et al. 1968), ferrods (of Soil Survey Staff 1975), and Uf2 (of Northcote 1974).

I have seen similar fossil soils, not yet studied in detail, in the late Mississippian or early Pennsylvanian Manning Canyon Formation, across Utah Lake, from Provo, Utah; in the early Permian uppermost Opeche Formation, near Boulder Park, in the Black Hills of South Dakota (Fig. 3.3); in the late Triassic Lockatong Formation of the Newark Basin, near Phoenixville, Pennsylvania; in the Late Triassic Chinle Formation of the Petrified Forest National Monument, Arizona; in the early Cretaceous Otway Group of southern Victoria, southeastern Australia; in the mid-Cretaceous upper Dakota Formation in Russell County, Kansas; and in the Eocene Clarno Formation, on Camp Hancock, near Clarno, Oregon. Other aspects of the geology and paleontology of these various places are discussed by Tidwell (1967), Tranter and Petter (1963), Olsen (1978), Wycoff et al. (1972), Douglas (1969), Hattin, Seimers, and Stewart (1978), Baldwin (1976), and references therein. Similar well-differentiated reddish paleosols have also been reported from the Pennsylvanian of Colorado (Hubert 1960); the Permian and Triassic of southern Germany (Ortlam 1971); the Permian and Triassic of the U.S.S.R. from the southwestern flanks of the Ural Mountains south to the Donetz Basin (Danilov 1968; Chalyshev 1969); from the early Cretaceous of England and France (Allen 1959; 1976; Batten 1973; Meyer 1976); from the late Cretaceous of Mexico (McBride 1974); and the Eocene and Miocene of South Carolina (Johnson and Heron 1965). Laterites may be formed in several ways, but are apparently initiated as an horizon of deep forested soils (McFarlane 1976). Such soils were evidently widespread during the Cretaceous and early Tertiary (Phillobos and Hassan 1975; Singer 1975; Abbott, Minch, and Peterson 1976; Thompson, Fields, and Alt 1977; Nilsen 1978; Nilsen and Kerr 1978; Blank 1978, McGowran 1979; Cox 1979). The so-called "karst bauxites" may be genetically similar to laterites and have been extensively reviewed by Nicholas and Bildgen (1979).

Organic soils (or histosols of the U.S. Dept. of Agriculture) are evidently more ancient than trees. The early Devonian Rhynie chert of Scotland is a petrified peat with remains of vascular land plants in growth position (Kidston and Lang 1921). However, the appearance of swamp forests and woodlands was probably a great stimulus to the development of thick organic horizons in wetland soils. The paleosols of the Euramerican Carboniferous coal measures have been given a number of nongenetic names, such as underclay, seat earth, fire clay, tonstein, and ganister (each explained by Williamson 1967). These fossil soils are limited in variety. Many of them were forested and most of them more or less gleyed (Huddle and Patterson 1961; Roeschmann 1971; Feofilova 1977).

Thick organic horizons and oxidized forest soils were additions to an expanding array of soils forming on the earth after the Devonian, but more ancient kinds of soils continued to form on other parts of the landscape. Caliche-bearing paleosols have been found in Permian and Triassic rocks of Scotland (Steel 1974; Watts 1976, 1978); in the Late Triassic and Jurassic of Connecticut and Massachusetts (Hubert 1977a, 1977b); in the late Cretaceous and early Tertiary of France (Freytet 1971, 1973); in the early Tertiary of France, England, Belgium, and the Netherlands (Buurman 1975); and the early Tertiary of California (Peterson and Abbott 1979). Fossil soils developed on limestone with karst topography have been found in the Middle Devonian of western Canada (Maiklem 1971; Wardlaw and Reinson 1971); in the Carboniferous of England (Walkden 1974), Kentucky (Walls, Harris, and Nunan 1975), and Missouri (Keller, Wescott, and Bledsoe 1954); in the Permian of New Mexico (Dunham 1969; Estaban and Pray 1977); in the Triassic of Italy (Bosellini and Rossi 1974); in the Jurassic of Italy (Bernoulli and Wagner 1971); in the Cretaceous of Greece (Faugeres and Robert 1969); in the Cretaceous and early Tertiary of France (Freytet 1971); and in the Eocene of Spain (Estaban 1972). Weathered zones at unconformities have also been reported on pre-Pennsylvanian surfaces in Colorado (Hubert 1960; Power 1969); within the Permian of New South Wales (Loughnan 1975); within the Jurassic of Italy (Folk and McBride 1976); and on a pre-Oligocene surface in a deep drill hole in the Ross Sea, Antarctica (Ford and Barrett 1975).

Forests would have had a greater stabilizing effect on the landscape than preexisting kinds of vegetation. Even today, forests have not achieved total cover of the landscape, but they were probably much less effective in controlling upland erosion during the Devonian and Carboniferous. Schumm (1968) has pointed out that the Euramerican Carboniferous coal measures have more and thicker clastic partings than the spectacularly thick early Tertiary coals of North America, Germany, and southeastern Australia. He suggested that this is due to greater erosion of less vegetated uplands during the Paleozoic. Further study of woodland and other fossil soils in sedimentary basins should refine this hypothesis considerably.

Tertiary Emergence of Grassland Soils

The development of savanna, steppe, prairie, and pampas vegetation on the plains, and of grassy vegetation above the snowline in alpine regions, also had a major effect on landscapes of the world. On the plains, new kinds of soils formed under the grassy swards, mollisol (of the U.S. Dept. of Agriculture), or chernozem, prairie soil, black earth, rendzina, and wiesenboden of older nomenclature. Evidence from fossil plants indicates that monocotyledonous angiosperms probably evolved during the early Cretaceous (Doyle 1973), but true grasses do not appear until the early Tertiary (Litke 1968). The best known megafossil record of grasses is in the Miocene to present sediments of the Great Plains of North America (Elias 1942; Thomassen 1979). Other than this the fossil record of grasses is generally poor. The emergence of grasslands within the interior of all the major continents at various times during the Tertiary is better indicated by other fossil plant remains and fossil mammals. In particular, the high crowned (hypsidont) teeth of grazing mammals indicate that coarse grassy fodder was widely available. On such grounds, savanna or pampas may have appeared in Argentina as early as the Eocene (Patterson and Pascual 1972). In Africa, there were probably considerable areas under savanna vegetation during the Oligocene, and it was probably more extensive during the Miocene and Pliocene (Tanner 1978; Axelrod and Raven 1978). In North America, savanna began to emerge as a vegetation type during the Oligocene, with steadily decreasing numbers of trees culminating in prairies as extensive as those of today by Pliocene times (Webb 1977). Savanna and steppe of central Asia appears to have become widespread during the Miocene, expanding into western Europe and China by the Late Miocene (Osborn 1910). In Australia, savanna may have been present during the Pliocene, but there is little evidence of savanna and grassland until the Pleistocene (Kemp 1978; Martin 1978).

Evidence from fossil soils is likely to give a much clearer idea of the age and nature of the early savanna and prairie communities and also of the coevolution of mammals and plants in these environments. David L. Dilcher and I have recently initiated a project with this exact aim, based on the Oligocene succession exposed in the Badlands National Monument of South Dakota. This is one of the richest fossiliferous areas in the world for the remains of extinct mammals, whose teeth and limbs appear adapted initially to forest and woodland and later to more open savanna or prairie conditions (Webb 1977). Apart from endocarps of hackberry (*Celtis*), possibly cached by rodents, almost all the leaves, trunks, and pollen of this vegetation appear to have decayed away long ago (Clark, Beerbower, and Kietkze 1967; Bjork and Leopold, personal communication). Our preliminary mapping in the area indicates that there are at least 87 successive fossil soils in the succession exposed in the Pinnacles area of the Badlands National Monument (Fig. 3.12). Laboratory examination of these is not complete, but some conclusions can be made from field observations. The thick fossil soil developed on the erosional unconformity between the latest Eocene to Oligocene Chadron Formation and latest Cretaceous marine rocks (Wanless 1923; Pettyjohn 1966) and most of the paleosols excavated in the Chadron Formation, have leached A horizons and reddish B horizons and numerous thick and deep root mottles (Fig. 3.13A). These fossil soils probably developed under forests and woodlands. In the overlying Scenic Member of the Brule Formation, such soils are only found in close association with sandy levee and channel deposits, indicating that gallery woodlands lined watercourses. Fossil soils of the floodplain at this level have much sparser large root mottles, abundant fine rootlets, and less pronounced B horizons (Fig. 3.13B), and probably were formed under savanna vegetation. Similar paleosols have also been recognized in the Orella Member of the Brule Formation in nearby Nebraska (Schultz, Tanner, and Harvey 1955; Schultz and Stout 1955; Harvey 1960). The whitewashed appearance of outcrops of the Poleslide Member of the Brule Formation, higher in the Badlands succession, is largely due to abundant carbonate nodules. Although there is some overlap of these from higher into lower paleosols, these nodules are most common in the lower portions of the paleosols (Fig. 3.13C). Some of the rare reduced root mottles of these paleosols have also been found in the nodules, and are evidence that they are caliche nodules in place. Caliche is also common in many younger Tertiary formations of the Great Plains of North America (Swineford, Leonard, and Frye 1958; Reeves 1970). It probably indicates increasingly warm and semiarid climate. Higher in the Poleslide Member there are some fossil soils of this kind in which I have not seen any of the large reduced root mottles over considerable lengths of these extensive outcrops (as in Fig. 3.13D). At the level of the Rockyford Ash Member of the Sharps Formation, a thick stream channel deposit, largely of

FIGURE 3.12. The Badlands National Monument of South Dakota, near the Pinnacles, an area with about 100 m of topographical relief. The late Cretaceous marine rocks (runneled lower slope), are capped by thick well-differentiated paleosols (light and dark bands), overlain by the latest Eocene to early Oligocene Chadron Formation (smooth gentle slopes), mid-Oligocene Scenic Member of the Brule Formation (light and dark banded unit in lower cliffs), mid to late Oligocene Poleslide Member of the Brule Formation (less strongly banded unit), and late Oligocene Sharps Formation (light colored rocks of far mountaintop).

resorted ash, has incised 10 m into floodplain claystones. In this area of the Badlands, it is apparent that small tracts of prairie emerged during the later Oligocene as the grassy portions of savanna expanded at the expense of trees. Increasing aridity, lowered water tables, and coarser ashy substrate appear to have accompanied these changes. Fire was probably also important, although not in evidence.

Probable savanna or pampas paleosols have also been reported by Andreis (1972) and Spalletti and Mazzoni (1978) from the Eocene to Oligocene Sarmiento Group in Chubut Province, Argentina. These paleosols have many characteristic soil microstructures and are associated with numerous fossil boli of dung beetles, diverse fossil mammal remains, and phytoliths (cited as evidence of grasses).

Continuing studies of fossil soils such as these may provide evidence for the origin of a number of different kinds of plant communities which are poorly represented in the fossil record, such as savanna, prairie, desert, and chaparral vegetation.

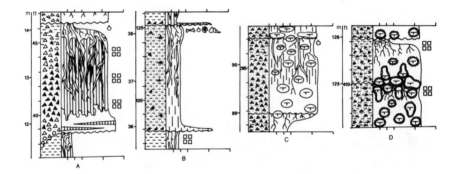

FIGURE 3.13. Oligocene paleosols of the Pinnacles area of the Badlands National Monument, South Dakota: **A,** well-differentiated paleosol of the Chadron Formation. **B,** weakly differentiated paleosol, with sparse gray mottles, in the Scenic Member of the Brule Formation. **C,** weakly differentiated caliche-bearing paleosol, with sparse gray mottles, in the Poleslide Member of the Brule Formation. **D,** weakly differentiated caliche-bearing paleosol, without larger gray mottles, in the Sharps Formation. Scale measurements refer to a measured section in the Pinnacles area in which the uppermost non-redeposited Cretaceous marine rocks are at about 8.3 m. Lithological key as for Figure 3.11.

The Impact of Humans on the World's Land Surfaces

Even if the species *Homo sapiens* soon becomes a diagnostic fossil of one of the briefest biostratigraphical zones in geological history, its effect on soils of the world is already conspicuous and irreversible. Modern cities, dams, parking lots, and highways are reshaping the landscape. Plowing, chemical fertilizers, forestry, irrigation, flood mitigation works, waste disposal, acid rain, and introduced animals and plants are altering the nature of soils, usually to our detriment. These problems are not new. More than 2,300 years ago, Plato lamented the spread of rocky, barren wastes in the Greece of his day, compared to the fertile soils that had been cleared of forest and cultivated by his ancestors (Glacken 1956). About 4,000 years ago much of the mighty cedar forests of Lebanon had been cut for Phoenician ships, towns, and export, and farmers terraced the steep cultivated slopes in an unsuccessful attempt to prevent more serious soil erosion (Lowdermilk 1943). Until about 5,000 years ago parts of the Sahara Desert were far less forbidding wastes than they have been since. Neolithic nomadic tribesmen have left numerous rock drawings which indicate that elephant, rhinoceros, lion, panther, giraffe, antelope, cattle, ram, and ostrich once lived there (Huzayyin 1956).

Much has been learned about the effects of ancient clearing and civilizations through the study of Quarternary fossil soils (see, e.g., Ložek

1967; Hardan 1971; Conry and Mitchell 1971). More could be done, particularly with older fossil soils associated with Miocene, Pliocene, and Pleistocene hominoid fossils. Spectacular new finds of such fossils are changing concepts of our own evolution as a species (Johanson and Taieb 1976; Leakey et al. 1976; Bishop 1978), but many questions remain. How and when was the evolution of *Homo sapiens* related to forest, savanna, and prairie environments? To what extent can the spread of grasslands be attributed to the use of fire by hominoids? Did the giant beasts of the Pleistocene become extinct because of overkill by hominoids, because of their effect on the ancient environments or because of other environmental changes? Detailed studies of fossil soils addressing these questions have not yet been forthcoming, but enough is now known of the geological occurrence of early hominoid fossils to indicate their potential. In the Middle Silts and Gravels Member of the Kapthurin Formation of Kenya, between 700,000 and 230,000 years old, Tallon (1978) reported hominoid remains (probably *Homo erectus*) and stone artifacts scattered over the surface of a fossil soil, which had a calcrete 2 m below the surface. This occupation site was evidently on lakeside flats just south of the nose of a trachyte flow, which was used to quarry the artifacts. Further studies are needed to establish the nature of the calcrete and the different kinds of lakeside vegetation and soils. A variety of fossil soils have also been found in association with hominoid remains, perhaps up to 2 million years old, in the Chesowanga area of the northern Rift Valley of Kenya (Bishop, Hill, and Pickford 1978), and also in association with hominoid remains 9 to 12 million years old (mid-Miocene) in the central Kenyan Rift Valley (Pickford 1978). Paleosols may also be useful in evaluating the habitats of Miocene hominoids from the Siwalik deposits of Pakistan (Pilbeam et al. 1977a, 1977b; Behrensmeyer, personal communication 1979).

CONCLUSIONS

The study of fossil soils is just beginning. Compared to other branches of earth sciences there are still few researchers, although their ranks are growing. There are innumerable projects unattempted, many involving major aspects of the evolution of terrestrial ecosystems. Undoubtedly, more will be revealed as work progresses.

Although useful in stratigraphical mapping, fossil soils also provide evidence for interpretation of ancient terrestrial environments. These interpretations are particularly effective when integrated with existing paleontological and geological studies. Such an approach promises to become an important additional way of understanding the past.

ACKNOWLEDGMENTS

I thank J. W. Schopf (University of California, Los Angeles), E. S. Barghoorn (Harvard University, Cambridge), A. K. Behrensmeyer (Yale University, New Haven), P. Bjork (South Dakota School of Mines, Rapid City), E. Leopold (University of Washington, Seattle), J. D. Grierson (State University of New York, Binghampton), R. L. Folk (University of Texas, Austin), D. L. Dilcher, J. F. Basinger, and S. R. Manchester (Indiana University, Bloomington) for help with the various interpretations presented in this paper. I also thank E. Ripley (Indiana University, Bloomington) for use of his facilities in taking the photomicrographs.

Work was funded by National Science Grant EAR9700898.

REFERENCES

Abbott, P. L., Minch, J. A., and Peterson, G. L. 1976. Pre-Eocene paleosol south of Tijuana, Baja California, Mexico. *J. Sediment. Petrol.* 46:355–61.

Allen, J. R. L. 1973. Compressional structures (patterned ground) in Devonian pedogenic limestones. *Nature, Phys. Sci.* 243:84–86.

———. 1974a. Sedimentology of the Old Red Sandstone (Siluro-Devonian) in the Clee Hill area, Shropshire, England. *Sediment. Geol.* 12:73–167.

———. 1974b. Studies in fluviatile sedimentation: implications of pedogenic carbonate units in the lower Old Red Sandstone, Anglo-Welsh outcrop. *Geol. J.* 9:181–208.

———. 1974c. Geomorphology of Siluro-Devonian alluvial plains. *Nature, Phys. Sci.* 249:644–45.

Allen, P. 1959. The Wealden environment Anglo-Paris Basin. *Phil. Trans. R. Soc.* (Lond.) B242:283–346.

———. 1976. Wealden of the Weald: a new model. *Proc. Geol. Assoc.* 86:389–436.

American Commission on Stratigraphic Nomenclature 1961. Code of stratigraphic Nomenclature. *Bull. Am. Ass. Petrol. Geol.* 45:645–60.

Anderson, J. G. C. 1965. The Precambrian of the British Isles. In *The Precambrian* (K. Rankama, ed.). New York: Interscience. Vol. 1, pp. 25–111.

Andreis, R. R. 1972. Paleosuelos de la formación Musters (Eoceno medio), Laguna del Mate, Prov. de Chubut, Rep. Argentina. *Revta Asoc. Min. Petr. Sed. Argent.* 3:91–98.

Axelrod, D. I., and Raven, P. H. 1978. Late Cretaceous and Tertiary vegetation history of Africa. In *Biogeography and Ecology of Southern Africa* (M. J. A. Werger and A. C. van Bruggen, eds.). Hague: Junk, pp. 77–130.

Baas-Becking, L. G. M., Kaplan, I. R., and Moore, D. 1960. Limits of the natural environment in terms of pH and oxidation-reduction potentials. *J. Geol.* 68:243–84.

Baldwin, E. M. 1976. *Geology of Oregon.* Dubuque: Kendall/Hunt.

Banks, H. P., 1966. Devonian floras of New York State. *Empire State Geogram* 4:1–24.

———. 1968. The early history of land plants. In *Evolution and Environment* (E. T. Drake, ed.). New Haven: Yale University Press.

———. 1975a: The oldest vascular plants: a note of caution. *Rev. Palaeobot. Palynol.* 20:13–25.

———. 1975b. Early vascular land plants: proof and conjecture. *Bioscience* 25:730–37.

Barbour, E. H. 1897. Nature, structure and phylogeny of *Daemonelix*. *Bull. Geol. Soc. Am.* 8:305–14.

Barghoorn, E. S., and Darrah, W. C. 1938. *Horneophyton*, a necessary change of name for *Hornea*. *Harvard Univ. Bot. Mus. Leafl.* 6:142–44.

Basinger, J. F., and Rothwell, G. W. 1977. Anatomically preserved plants from the Middle Eocene (Allenby Formation) of British Columbia. *Canad. J. Bot.* 55:1984–90.

Batten, D. J. 1973. Palynology of Early Cretaceous soil beds and associated strata. *Palaeontology* 16:399–424.

Beck, C. B. 1971. Problems of generic delimitation in paleobotany. *Proc. Nth. Am. Paleont. Conv.* 1:173–93.

Berkner, L. V., and Marshall, L. C. 1965. History of major atmosphere components. *Proc. U.S. Nat. Acad. Sci.* 53:1215–26.

Bernoulli, D., and Wagner, L. W. 1971. Subaerial diagenesis and fossil caliche deposits in the Calcare Massico Formation (Lower Jurassic, central Appenines, Italy). *Neues Jahrb. Geol. Paläont. Abh.* 138:135–49.

Bishop, W. W. 1978. *Geological Background to Fossil Man*. Edinburgh: Scottish Academic Press.

———. Hill, A., and Pickford, M. 1978. Chesowanja: a revised geological interpretation. In *Geological Background to Fossil Man* (W. W. Bishop, ed.). Edinburgh: Scottish Academic Press, pp. 309–27.

Blades, E. L., and Bickford, M. E. 1976. Volcanic ash-flows and volcaniclastic sedimentary rocks at Johnson Shut-ins, Reynolds Co., Missouri. *Abstr. Prog. Geol. Soc. Am.* 8:6.

Blank, H. R. 1978. Fossil laterite on bedrock in Brooklyn, New York. *Geology* 6:21–24.

Bloomfield, C. 1964. Mobilization and immobilization phenomena in soils. In *Problems in Palaeoclimatology* (A. E. M. Nairn, ed.). New York: Interscience, pp. 661–73.

Bonamo, P. M. 1977. *Rellimia thomsonii* (Progymnospermopsida) from the Middle Devonian. New York State. *Am. J. Bot.* 64:1272–85.

Booth, W. E. 1941. Algae as pioneers in plant succession and their importance in erosion control. *Ecology* 22:38–46.

Bosellini, A., and Rossi, D. 1974. Triassic carbonate buildups of the Dolomites, northern Italy. In *Reefs in Time and Space* (L. F. Laporte, ed.). *Spec. Publ. Soc. Econ. Paleont. Miner. Tulsa 18*, pp. 209–33.

Boucot, A. J., Dewey, J. F., Dineley, D. L., Fletcher, R., Fyson, W. K., Griffin, J. G., Hickox, C. F., McKerrow, W. S., and Ziegler, A. M. 1974. Geology of the Arisaig area, Antigonish County, Nova Scotia. *Spec. Pap. Geol. Soc. Am.* 139.

Brewer, R. 1964. *Fabric and Mineral Analysis of Soils.* New York: Wiley.

———, Crook, K. A. W., and Speight, J. G. 1970. Proposal for soil stratigraphic units in the Australian Stratigraphic Code. *J. Geol. Soc. Aust.* 17:103–9.

Buurman, P. 1975. Possibilities of palaeopedology. *Sedimentology* 22:289–98.

Campbell, S. E. 1979. Soil stabilization by a prokaryotic desert crust: implications for a Precambrian land biota. *Origins of Life* 9:335–48.

Chalyshev, V. I. 1969. A discovery of fossil soils in the Permo-Triassic. *Dokl. Acad. Sci. U.S.S.R., Earth Sci.* 182:53–56.

Clark, J., Beerbower, J. R., and Kietzke, K. K. 1967. Oligocene sedimentation, stratigraphy, paleoecology and paleoclimatology in the Big Badlands of South Dakota. *Fieldiana Geol. Mem.* 5.

Cloud, P. E. 1976. Beginnings of biospheric evolution and their biochemical consequences. *Paleobiology* 2:351–87.

Collins, W. H. 1925. North shore of Lake Huron. *Mem. Geol. Surv. Canada* 143.

Conry, M. J., and Mitchell, G. F. 1971. The age of Irish plaggen soils. In *Paleopedology; Origin, Nature and Dating of Paleosols* (D. H. Yaalon, ed.). Jerusalem: Int. Soc. Soil Sci. and Israel University Press, pp. 129–37.

Cox, B. F. 1979. Early Paleogene laterite and debris flow deposits, El Paso Mountain, California. *Abstr. Prog. Geol. Soc. Am.* 11:73–74.

Danilov, I. S. 1968. The nature and geochemical conditions of formation of variegated red Triassic and Permian rocks of the western Donetz Basin. *Lithol. Miner. Resources* 3:612–18.

Davidson, C. F. 1965. Geochemical aspects of atmospheric evolution. *Proc. U.S. Nat. Acad. Sci.* 53:1194–1204.

Degens, E. T. 1965. *Geochemistry of Sediments: A Brief Survey.* Englewood Cliffs, New Jersey: Prentice-Hall.

Donaldson, J. A. 1969. Descriptive notes (with particular reference to the late Proterozoic Dubawnt Group) to accompany a geological map of central Thelon Plain, Districts of Keewatin and Mackenzie. *Pap. Geol. Surv. Canad.* 68–49.

Dorf, E. 1964. The petrified forests of Yellowstone Park. *Sci. Am.* 210:107–13.

Douglas, J. G. 1969. The Mesozoic flora of Victoria. *Mem. Geol. Surv. Vict.* 28.

Doyle, J. A. 1973. Fossil evidence on the early evolution of monocotyledons. *Q. Rev. Biol.* 48:399–413.

Duchafour, P. 1978. *Ecological Atlas of Soils of the World* (translated by G. R. Mehnys, C. R. de Kimpe, and Y. A. Martel). New York: Masson.

Dunham, R. J. 1969. Vadose pisolites in the Capitan reef (Permian), New Mexico and Texas. In *Depositional Environments in Carbonate Rocks* (G. M. Friedman, ed.). *Spec. Pub. Soc. Econ. Paleont. Miner. Tulsa* 14:182–91.

Dury, G. H., and Haberman, G. M. 1978. Australian silcretes and northern hemisphere correlatives. In *Silcrete in Australia* (T. Langford Smith, ed.). Armidale: University of New England, Australia, pp. 223–59.

Eaton, T. H. 1942. Effect of submergence on a podzol soil profile in the Adirondack forest. *Soil Sci.* 53:383–97.

Edwards, D., Bassett, M. G., and Rogerson, C. W. 1979. The earliest land plants: continuing the search for proof. *Lethaia* 12:313–24.

Elias, M. K. 1942. Tertiary prairie grasses and other herbs from the High Plains. *Spec. Pap. Geol. Soc. Am.* 41.

Eskola, P. 1963. The Precambrian of Finland. In *The Precambrian* (K. Rankama, ed.). New York: Interscience. Vol. 1, pp. 145–203.

Estaban, M. 1972. The presence of fossil caliche at the base of the Eocene of the Catalonia Mountains, Tarragona, Barcelona, Spain. *Acta Geol. Hisp.* 7:164–68.

—— and Pray, L. C. 1977. Origin of the pisolitic facies of the shelf crest. In *Upper Guadalupian Facies, Permian Reef Complex, Guadalupe Mountains, New Mexico and Texas. Publ. Permian Basin Sect. Soc. Econ. Paleont. Miner. Midland* 77–16:479–84.

Fairchild, T. R., Schopf, J. W., and Folk, R. L. 1973. Filamentous algal microfossils from the Caballos Novaculite, Devonian of Texas. *J. Paleont.* 47:946–52.

Faugères, L., and R. P. 1969. Précisions nouvelles sur les altérations contenues dans le Série du Chaînon de Viglia (Kozani, Macedonie, Grèce). *C. R. Soc. Geol. Fr.* 3 3:97–98.

Feofilova, A. P. 1977. Paleopedology and its significance for the reconstruction of ancient landscapes. *Lithol. Miner. Resources* 12:650–55.

Fischer, A. G. 1965. Fossils, early life and atmospheric history. *Proc. U.S. Nat. Acad. Sci.* 53:1205–13.

Folk, R. L., and McBride, E. F. 1976. Possible pedogenic origin of Ligurian ophicalcite: a Mesozoic calichified serpentinite. *Geology* 4:327–32.

Ford, A. B., and Barrett, P. J. 1975. Basement rocks of the south central Ross Sea, site 270, D.S.D.P. Leg 28. *Init. Rep. Deep Sea Drill. Proj.* 28:861–68.

Frarey, M. J., and Roscoe, S. M. 1970. The Huronian Supergroup north of Lake Huron. In *Symposium on Basins and Geosynclines of the Canadian Shield*, (A. J. Baer, ed.). *Pap. Geol. Surv. Canada* 70–40:143–57.

Fraser, J. A., Donaldson, J. A., Fahrig, W. F., and Tremblay, L. P. 1970. Helikian basins and geosynclines of the northwestern Canadian Shield. In *Symposium on Basins and Geosynclines of the Canadian Shield* (A. J. Baer, ed.). *Pap. Geol. Surv. Canada* 70–40:213–38.

Freytet, P. 1971. Paléosols résiduels et paléosols alluviaux hydromorphes associés aux dépôts fluviatiles dans le Crétacé supérieur et l'Éocène basal du Languedoc. *Rev. Geogr. Phys. Geol. Dynam.* 13:245–360.

——. 1973. Petrography and paleoenvironment of continental carbonate deposits, with particular reference to the Upper Cretaceous and Lower Eocene of Languedoc (southern France). *Sediment. Geol.* 10:25–60.

Friedman, G. M. 1958. Determination of sieve size distribution from thin section data for sedimentary petrological studies. *J. Geol.* 66:394–416.

——. 1962. Comparison of moment statistical parameters for sieving and thin section data in sedimentary petrologic studies. *J. Sediment. Petrol.* 32:15–25.

Friend, P. F., Harland, W. B., and Gilbert-Smith, A. 1970. Reddening and fissuring associated with the Caledonian unconformity in north-west Arran. *Proc. Geol. Assoc.* 81:75–85.

Fritz, N. J. 1979. Depositional environment of the Yellowstone fossil forests as realted to Eocene plant diversity. *Abstr. Prog. Geol. Soc. Am.* 11:428.

Gerasimov, I. P. 1971. Nature and originality of paleosols. In *Paleopedology: Origin, Nature and Dating of Paleosols* (D. H. Yaalon, ed.). Jerusalem: Int. Soc. Soil Sci. and Israel University Press, pp. 15–27.

Gibbs, H. S. 1971. Nature of paleosols in New Zealand and their classification. In

Paleopedology: Origin, Nature and Dating of Paleosols (D. H. Yaalon, ed.). Jerusalem: Int. Soc. Soil Sci. and Israel University Press, pp. 229–44.

Glacken, C. J. 1956. Changing ideas of the habitable world. In *Man's Role in Changing the Face of the Earth* (W. L. Thomas, ed.). Chicago: University Chicago Press, pp. 70–92.

Gorter, J. D. 1978. Triassic environments in the Canning Basin, Western Australia. *Bur. Miner. Resour. J. Aust. Geol. Geophys.* 3:25–33.

Granger, H. C., and Warren, C. G. 1978. Some speculations on the genetic geochemistry and hydrology of roll-type uranium deposits. *Guidebook Ann. Conf. Wyoming Geol. Assoc.* 30:349–61.

Gray, J., and Boucot, A. J. 1977. Early vascular land plants: proof and conjecture. *Lethaia* 10:145–74.

Grierson, J. D. 1976. *Leclerquia complexa* Lycopsida; Middle Devonian): its anatomy and the interpretation of pyrite petrifications. *Am. J. Bot.* 63:1184–1202.

Hallbauer, D. K., and van Warmelo, K. T. 1974. Fossilized plants in thucolite from Precambrian rocks of the Witwatersrand, South Africa. *Precambrian Res.* 1:199–212.

Hardan, A. 1971. Archaeological methods for dating of soil salinity in the Mesopotamian Plain. In *Paleopedology: Origin, Nature and Dating of Paleosols* (D. H. Yallon, ed.). Jerusalem: Int. Soc. Soil Sci. and Israel University Press, pp. 181–87.

Hargraves, R. B. 1976. Precambrian geologic history. *Science* 193:363–71.

Harvey, C. H. 1960. Stratigraphy, Sedimentation and Environment of the White River Group of Northern Sioux County, Nebraska. Ph.D. dissertation, University of Nebraska, Lincoln.

Hattin, D. E., Siemers, C. T., and Stewart, G. F. 1978. Guidebook: Upper Cretaceous stratigraphy and depositional environments of western Kansas. *Guidebook Series Geol. Surv. Kansas* 3.

Hoffman, P. F., Fraser, J. A., and McGlynn, J. C. 1970. The Coronation Geosyncline of Aphebian age, District of Mackenzie. In *Symposium on Basins and Geosynclines of the Canadian Shield* (A. J. Baer, ed.). *Pap. Geol. Surv. Canada* 70–40:201–12.

Hubert, J. F. 1960. Petrology of the Fountain and Lyons Formations, Front Range, Colorado. *Colo. Sch. Mines Q.* 55:1–242.

——. 1977a. Paleosol caliche in the New Haven Arkose, Newark Group, Connecticut. *Palaeogeogr. Palaeoclim. Palaeoec.* 24:151–168.

——. 1977b. Paleosol caliche in the New Haven Arkose, Connecticut: record of semiaridity in Late Triassic-Early Jurassic time. *Geology* 5:302–4.

Huddle, J. W., and Patterson, S. H. 1961. Origin of Pennsylvanian underclays and related seat rocks. *Bull. Geol. Soc. Am.* 72:1043–1660.

Hunt, C. B. 1972. *Geology of Soils.* San Francisco: Freeman.

Hunt, P. A., Mitchell, P. B., and Paton, T. R. 1977. "Laterite profiles" and "lateritic ironstones" of the Hawkesbury Sandstone, Australia. *Geoderma* 19:105–21.

Huzayyin, S. 1956. Changes in climate, vegetation and human adjustment in the Saharo-Arabian belt, with special reference to Africa. In *Man's Role in Changing the Face of the Earth* (W. L. Thomas, ed.). Chicago: University of

Chicago Press, pp. 304–23.

Jessup, R. W., and Norris, R. M. 1971. Cainozoic stratigraphy of the Lake Eyre Basin. *J. Geol. Soc. Aust.* 18:303–31.

Johanson, D. C., and Taieb, M. 1976. Plio/Pleistocene hominid discoveries in Hadar, Ethiopia. *Nature, Phys. Sci.* 260:293–97.

Johnson, H. S., and Heron, S. D. 1965. Slump features in the McBean Formation and younger beds, Riley Cut, Calhoun County, South Carolina. *Geol. Notes S. Carolina Devel. Board Div. Geol.* 9:37–44.

Kalliokosi, J. 1975. Chemistry and mineralogy of Precambrian paleosols in northern Michigan. *Bull. Geol. Soc. Am.* 86:371–76.

———. 1977. Chemistry and mineralogy of Precambrian paleosols in northern Michigan: reply. *Bull. Geol. Soc. Am.* 88:1376.

Kanno, I. 1962. A new classification system of rice soils in Japan. *Trans. Int. Soc. Soil Sci. Conf. N.Z.* 8:617–24.

Keller, W. D., Wescott, J. F., and Bledsoe, A. O. 1954. The origin of Missouri fire clays. *Clays and Clay Min.* 2:7–46.

Kemp, E. M. 1978. Tertiary climatic evolution and vegetation history in the southeast Indian Ocean region. *Palaeogeogr. Palaeoclim. Palaeoec.* 24:169–208.

Kidston, R., and Lang, W. H. 1921. On Old Red Sandstone plants showing structure from the Rhynie chert bed, Aberdeenshire. Part V. The thallophyta occurring in the peat bed; the succession of the plants through a vertical section of the bed and the conditions of accumulation and preservation of the deposit. *Trans. R. Soc. Edinb.* 52:855–902.

Klappa, C. F. 1978. Biolithogenesis of *Microcodium*: elucidation. *Sedimentology* 25:489–522.

Krumbein, W. C., and Garrels, R. M. 1952. Origin and classification of chemical sediments in terms of pH and oxidation-reduction potential. *J. Geol.* 60:1–33.

Langford-Smith, T. 1978. *Silcrete in Australia.* Armidale: University New England, Australia.

Leakey, M. D., Hay, R. L., Curtis, G. H., Drake, R. E., Jackes, M. K., and White, T. D. 1976: Fossil hominids from the Laetolil Beds, Tanzania. *Nature, Phys. Sci.* 262:460–65.

Leeder, M. R. 1976. Palaeogeographic significance of pedogenic carbonates in the topmost Upper Old Red Sandstone of the Scottish Border Basin. *Geol. J.* 11:21–28.

Lewan, M. D. 1977. Chemistry and mineralogy of Precambrian paleosols in northern Michigan: discussion. *Bull. Geol. Soc. Am.* 88:1375–76.

Litke, R. 1968. Über den Nachweis tertiärer Gramineen. *Sond. Mon. Deutsch Akad. Wiss. Berlin* 10:462–71.

Livingston, D. E., and Damon, P. E. 1968. The ages of stratified Precambrian rock sequences in central Arizona and northern Sonora. *Canad. J. Earth Sci.* 5:763–72.

Loughnan, F. C. 1975. Correlatives of the Greta Coal Measures in the Hunter Valley and Gunnedah Basin, New South Wales. *J. Geol. Soc. Aust.* 22:243–53.

Lowdermilk, W. C. 1943. Lessons from the Old World to the Americans in land use. *Smithsonian Rept. for 1943*, pp. 413–28.

Ložek, V. 1967. Climatic zones of Czechoslovakia during the Quaternary. In

Quaternary Paleoecology (E. J. Cushinga and H. E. Wright, eds.). New Haven: Yale University Press, pp. 381–92.

Maiklem, W. R. 1971. Evaporative drawdown—a mechanism for waterlevel lowering and diagenesis in the Elk Point Basin. *Bull. Canad. Petrol. Geol.* 19:487–503.

Martin, H. A. 1978. Evolution of the Australian flora and vegetation through the Tertiary: evidence from pollen. *Alcheringa* 2:181–202.

McBride, E. F. 1974. Significance of color in red, green, purple, olive, brown and gray beds of Difunta Group. *J. Sediment. Petrol.* 44:760–73.

―― and Folk, R. L. 1977. The Caballos Novaculite revisited. Part II. Chert and Shale Member and synthesis. *J. Sediment Petrol.* 47:1261–86.

McDonnell, K. L. 1974. Depositional environments of the Triassic Gosford Formation, Sydney Basin. *J. Geol. Soc. Aust.* 21:107–32.

McFarlane, M. J. 1976. *Laterite and Landscape.* New York: Academic Press.

McGowran, B. 1979. Comment on Early Tertiary tectonism and lateritization. *Geol. Mag.* 116:227–30.

McKee, E. D. 1969. Paleozoic rocks of the Grand Canyon. *Guidebook Field Conf. Four Corners Geol. Soc.* 5:78–90.

McPherson, J. G. 1979. Calcrete (caliche) palaeosols in fluvial redbeds of the Aztec Siltstone (Upper Devonian), southern Victoria Land, Antarctica. *Sediment. Geol.* 22:267–85.

Meyer, R. 1976. Continental sedimentation, soil genesis and marine transgression in the basal beds of the Cretaceous in the east of the Paris Basin. *Sedimentology* 23:235–53.

Miall, A. D. 1977. A review of the braided river depositional environment. *Earth Sci. Rev.* 13:1–62.

Millot, G. 1970. *Geology of Clays* (translated by W. R. Farrand and H. Paquet). New York: Springer-Verlag.

Morrison, R. B. 1968. Means of time-stratigraphic division and long distance correlation of Quaternary successions. In *Means of Correlation of Quaternary Successions*, (R. B. Morrison and H. E. Wright, eds.). *Proc. Congr. Int. Ass. Quat. Res.* 8:1–113.

Nicholas, J., and Bildgen, P. 1979. Relations between the location of the karst bauxites in the northern hemisphere, the global tectonics and the climatic variations during geological time. *Palaeogeogr. Palaeoclim. Palaeoec.* 29:205–39.

Nilsen, T. H. 1978. Lower Tertiary laterite on the Iceland-Faeroe Ridge and the Thulean land bridge. *Nature, Phys. Sci.* 274:786–88.

―― and Kerr, D. R. 1978. Paleoclimatic and paleogeographic implications of a lower Tertiary laterite (latosol) on the Iceland-Faeroe Ridge, North Atlantic region. *Geol. Mag.* 115:153–82.

Northcote, K. H. 1974. *A Factual Key for the Recognition of Australian Soils.* Adelaide: Rellim Technical Publications.

―― and Skene, J. K. M. 1972. Australian soils with saline and sodic properties. *Soil Publ. Commonw. Sci. Ind. Res. Org. Aust.* 27.

Olsen, P. E. 1978. On the use of the term Newark for Triassic and Early Jurassic rocks of eastern North America. *Newsl. Stratigr.* 7:90–95.

Ortlam, D. 1971. Paleosols and their significance in stratigraphy and applied geology in the Permian and Triassic of southern Germany. In *Paleopedology: Origin,*

Nature and Dating of Paleosols (D. H. Yaalon, ed.). Jerusalem: Int. Soc. Soil Sci. and Israel University Press, pp. 321–27.

Osborn, H. F. 1910. *The Age of Mammals in Europe, Asia and North America.* New York: Macmillan.

Paepe, R. 1971. Dating and position of fossil soils in the Belgian Pleistocene stratigraphy. In *Paleopedology: Origin, Nature and Dating of Paleosols* (D. H. Yaalon, ed.). Jerusalem: Int. Soc. Soil Sci. and Israel University Press, pp. 261–69.

Patel, I. M. 1977. Late Precambrian fossil soil horizon in southern New Brunswick and its stratigraphic significance. *Abstr. Prog. Geol. Soc. Am.* 9:308.

Paton, T. R., and Williams, M. A. J. 1972. The concept of laterite. *Ann. Ass. Am. Geogr.* 62:42–56.

Patterson, B., and Pascual, R. 1972. The fossil mammal fauna of South America. In *Evolution, Mammals and Southern Continents* (A. Keast, F. C. Erk, and B. Glass, eds.). Albany: State University of New York Press, pp. 247–309.

Peterson, G. L., and Abbott, P. L. 1979. Mid-Eocene climatic change in southwestern California and northwestern Baja California. *Palaeogeogr. Palaeoclim. Palaeoec.* 26:73–87.

Pettyjohn, W. A. 1966. Eocene paleosol in the northern Great Plains. *Prof. Pap. U.S. Geol. Surv.* 550C:61–65.

Phillips, T. L., Peppers, R. A., Avcin, M. J., and Laughnan, P. F. 1974. Fossil plants and coal: patterns of change in the Pennsylvanian coal swamps of the Illinois Basin. *Science* 184:1367–69.

Philobbos, E. R., and Hassan, K. El-D. K. 1975. The contribution of paleosoil to Egyptian lithostratigraphy. *Nature, Phys. Sci.* 253:33.

Pickford, M. H. L. 1978. Geology, palaeoenvironments and vertebrate fauna of the mid-Miocene Ngorora Formation, Kenya. In *Geological Background to Fossil Man* (W. W. Bishop, ed.). Edinburgh: Scottish Academic Press, pp. 237–62.

Pilbeam, D. R., Barry, J., Meyer, G. E., Shah, S. M. I., Pickford, M. H. L., Bishop, W. W., Thomas, H., and Jacobs, L. L. 1977a. Geology and palaeontology of the Neogene strata of Pakistan. *Nature* 270:684–89.

———, Meyer, G. E., Badgely, C., Rose, M. D., Pickford, M. H. L., Behrensmeyer, A. K., and Shah, S. M. I. 1977b. New hominoid primates from the Siwaliks of Pakistan and their bearing on hominoid evolution. *Nature* 270:689–95.

Pirozynski, K. A. 1976. Fossil fungi. *Ann. Rev. Phytopath.* 14:237–46.

Plumstead, E. P. 1964. Palaeobotany of Antarctica. In *Antarctic Geolgoy* (R. J. Adie, ed.). New York: Interscience, pp. 637–54.

Power P. E. 1969. Clay mineralogy and paleoclimatic significance of some red regoliths and associated rocks in western Colorado. *J. Sediment. Petrol.* 39:876–90.

Rankama, K. 1955. Geologic evidence of chemical composition of the Precambrian atmosphere. In *Crust of the Earth* (A. Poldervaart, ed.). *Spec. Pap. Geol. Soc. Am.* 62:651–64.

Reeves, C. C. 1970. Origin, classification and geologic history of caliche on the High Plains of Texas and eastern New Mexico. *J. Geol.* 78:352–62.

Retallack, G. J. 1977a. Triassic palaeosols in the upper Narrabeen Group of New South Wales. Part 1. Features of the palaeosols. *J. Geol. Soc. Aust.* 23:383–99.

———. 1977b. Triassic palaeosols in the upper Narrabeen Group of New South

Wales. Part II. Classification and reconstruction. *J. Geol. Soc. Aust.* 24:19–34.

———. 1977c. Reconstructing Triassic vegetation of eastern Australasia: a new approach for the biostratigraphy of Gondwanaland. *Alcheringa* 1:247–77.

———. 1978. Floral ecostratigraphy in practice. *Lethaia* 11:81–83.

———. 1979. Early Tertiary fossil soils in the Badlands National Monument, South Dakota. *Abstr. Prog. Geol. Soc. Am.* 11:502.

Roeschmann, G. 1971. Problems concerning investigations of paleosols in older sedimentary rocks, demonstrated by the example of wurzelböden of the Carboniferous System. In *Paleopedology: Origin, Nature and Dating of Paleosols* (D. H. Yaalon, ed.). Jerusalem: Int. Soc. Soil Sci. and Israel University Press, pp. 311–20.

Roscoe, S. M. 1968. Huronian rocks and uraniferous conglomerates in the Canadian Shield. *Pap. Geol. Surv. Canada* 68–40.

Ruhe, R. V. 1965. Quaternary paleopedology. In *The Quaternary of the United States* (H. E. Wright and D. G. Frey, eds.). Princeton: Princeton University Press, pp. 755–64.

———. 1970. Soils, paleosols and environment. In *Pleistocene and Recent Environments of the central Great Plains* (W. Dort and J. K. Jones, eds.). *Spec. Publ. Dept. Geol. Univ. Kansas* 3:37–52.

Runnegar, B. 1977. *Alcheringa* news item: panel of experts discuss evidence for Precambrian Eukaryota at the 25th International Geological Congress, Sydney, August 1976. *Alcheringa* 1:311–14.

Sagan, C. 1965. Is the early evolution of life related to the development of the earth's core? *Nature* 206:448.

Schopf, J. M. 1970. Petrified peat from a Permian coal bed in Antarctica. *Science* 169:274–77.

———. 1978. *Foerstia* and recent interpretations of early vascular land plants. *Lethaia* 11:139–43.

Schopf, J. W. 1975. Precambrian paleobiology: problems and perspectives. *Ann. Rev. Earth Planet. Sci.* 3:213–49.

———. 1978. The evolution of the earliest cells. *Sci. Am.* 239:110–38.

Schultz, C. B., and Stout, T. M. 1955. Classification of Oligocene sediements in Nebraska. *Bull. Univ. Nebraska State Mus.* 4:17–52.

———, Tanner, L. G., and Harvey, C. H. 1955. Paleosols of the Oligocene of Nebraska. *Bull. Univ. Nebraska State Mus.* 4:1–16.

Schumm, S. A. 1968. Speculations concerning the paleohydrologic control of terrestrial sedimentation. *Bull. Geol. Soc. Am.* 79:1573–88.

Scott, A. C. 1977. A review of the ecology of the Upper Carboniferous plant assemblages, with new data from Strathclyde. *Palaeontology* 20:447–73.

———. 1978. Sedimentological and ecological control of Westphalian B plant assemblages from west Yorkshire. *Proc. Yorks. Geol. Soc.* 41:461–508.

———. 1979. The ecology of coal measure floras from northern Britain. *Proc. Geol. Assoc.* 90:97–116.

Senior, B. R., and Mabbutt, J. A. 1979. A proposed method of defining deeply weathered rock units based on regional geological mapping in southeast Queensland. *J. Geol. Soc. Aust.* 26:237–54.

Sharp, R. P. 1940. The Ep-Archaean and Ep-Algonkian erosion surfaces, Grand Canyon, Arizona. *Bull. Geol. Soc. Am.* 51:1235–69.

Singer, A. 1975. A Cretaceous laterite in the Negev Desert, southern Israel. *Geol. Mag.* 112:151–62.

Skog, J. E., and Banks, H. P. 1973. *Ibyka amphikoma*, gen. et sp. n., a new protoarticulate precursor from the late Middle Devonian of New York State. *Am. J. Bot.* 60:366–80.

Soil Survey Staff 1951. Soil Survey Manual. *Hdbk U.S. Dept. Agr.* 18.

———. 1962. *Supplement to U.S.D.A. Handbook 18, Soil Survey Manual (replacing pp. 173–88)*. Washington: U.S. Govt. Printing Office.

———. 1975. Soil Taxonomy. *Hdbk U.S. Dept. Agr.* 436.

Spalletti, L. A., and Mazzoni, M. M. 1978. Sedimentologia del Grupo Sarmiento en un perfil ubicado al sudeste del Lago Colhue Huapi, Provincia de Chubut. *Obra Centen. Mus. La Plata* 4:261–83.

Stace, H. C. T., Hubble, G. D., Brewer, R., Northcote, K. H., Sleeman, J. R., Mulcahy, M. J., and Hallsworth, E. G. 1968. *A Handbook of Australian Soils*. Adelaide: Rellim Technical Publications.

Stanton, R. L. 1972. *Ore Petrology*. New York: McGraw-Hill.

Steel, R. J. 1974. Cornstone (fossil caliche)—its origin, stratigraphic and sedimentological importance in the New Red Sandstone, Scotland. *J. Geol.* 82:351–69.

Swineford, A., Leonard, A. B., and Frye, G. C. 1958. Petrology of the Pliocene pisolitic limestone in the Great Plains. *Bull. Geol. Surv. Kansas* 130.

Tallon, P. W. J. 1978. Geological setting of the hominoid fossils and Acheulian artifacts from the Kapthurin Formation, Baringo District, Kenya. In *Geological Background to Fossil Man* (W. W. Bishop, ed.). Edinburgh: Scottish Academic Press, pp. 361–73.

Tanner, L. G. 1978. Embrithopoda. In *Evolution of African Mammals* (V. J. Maglio and H. B. S. Cooke, eds.). Cambridge: Harvard University Press, pp. 279–83.

Teruggi, M. E., and Andreis, R. R. 1971. Micromorphological recognition of paleosolic features in sediments and sedimentary rocks. In *Paleopedology: Origin, Nature and Dating of Paleosols* (D. H. Yaalon, ed.). Jerusalem: Int. Soc. Soil Sci. and Israel University Press, pp. 161–72.

Thomassen, J. R. 1979. Late Cenozoic grasses and other angiosperms from Kansas, Nebraska and Colorado: biostratigraphy and relationships to living taxa. *Bull. Geol. Surv. Kansas* 218.

Thompson, G. R., Fields, R. W. and Alt, D. 1977. Paleoclimatic interpretation of paleosols in the northern Rockies. *Abstr. Prog. Geol. Soc. Am.* 9: 768.

Tidwell, W. D. 1967. Flora of the Manning Canyon Shale. Part 1. A lowermost Pennsylvanian flora from the Manning Canyon Shale, Utah, and its stratigraphic significance. *Stud. Geol. Brigham Young Univ.* 14:3–66.

Ting, F. T. C. 1972. Petrified peat from a Paleocene lignite in North Dakota. *Science* 177:165–66.

Tranter, C. E., and Petter, C. K. 1963. Lower Permian and Pennsylvanian stratigraphy of the northern Rocky Mountains. *Guidebk. Field Conf. Wyo. Geol. Assoc.—Billings Geol. Soc.* 1:45–53.

Turner, B. R. 1970. Facies analysis of the Molteno sedimentary cycle. *Proc. Int. Gondwana Symp.* 2:313–17.

Walker, T. R. 1974. Formation of redbeds in a moist tropical climate: a hypothesis. *Bull. Geol. Soc. Am.* 85:633–38.

Walkden, G. M. 1974. Palaeokarstic surfaces in upper Visean (Carboniferous) limestones of the Derbyshire block, England. *J. Sediment. Petrol.* 44:1232-47.

Walls, R. A., Harris, W. B., and Nunan, W. E. 1975. Calcareous crust (caliche) profiles and early subaerial exposure of Carboniferous carbonates, northeastern Kentucky. *Sedimentology* 22:417-40.

Wanless, H. R. 1923. The stratigraphy of the White River beds of South Dakota. *Proc. Am. Philos. Soc.* 62:190-269.

Wardlaw, N. C., and Reinson, G. E. 1971. Carbonate and evaporite deposition and diagenesis, Middle Devonian Winnepegosis and Prairie evaporite formations of south central Saskatchewan. *Bull. Am. Ass. Petrol. Geol.* 55:1759-89.

Watts, N. L. 1976. Palaeopedogenic palygorskyite from the basal Permo-Triassic of northwest Scotland. *Am. Mineral.* 61:299-302.

———. 1978. Displacive calcite: evidence from recent and ancient calcretes. *Geology* 6:699-703.

Webb, S. D. 1977. A history of savanna vertebrates in the New World. Part 1. North America. *Ann. Rev. Ecol. Syst.* 8:355-80.

Williams, G. E. 1968. Torridonian weathering and its bearing on Torridonian palaeoclimate and source. *Scott. J. Geol.* 4:164-84.

Williamson, I. A. 1967. *Coal Mining Geology.* Oxford: Oxford University Press.

Woodrow, D. L., and Fletcher, F. W. 1967. Late Devonian paleogeography in southeastern New York and northeastern Pennsylvania. In *International Symposium on the Devonian System* (D. H. Oswald, ed.). Calgary: Alberta Society of Petroleum Geologists. Vol. II, pp. 1327-34.

Woodrow, D. L., Fletcher, F. W., and Ahrnsbrak, W. F. 1973. Paleogeography and paleoclimate at the deposition sites of the Devonian Catskill and Old Red facies. *Bull. Geol. Soc. Am.* 84:3051-64.

Wycoff, R. W. G., Davidson, F. D., Schwab, K. W., Gottesfeld, A. S., Brown, T. L., and Busek, P. R. 1972. Preliminary research in the Triassic Chinle Formation. *Suppl. Bull. Mus. Nthn Arizona* (Flagstaff) 47.

Yaalon, D. H. 1971. Soil-forming processes in time and space. In *Paleopedology: Origin, Nature and Dating of Paleosols* (D. H. Yaalon, ed.). Jerusalem: Int. Soc. Soil Sci. and Israel University Press, pp. 29-39.

Zajic, J. E. 1969. *Microbial Biogeochemistry.* New York: Academic Press.

4

BIOCHEMICAL EVOLUTION
IN EARLY LAND PLANTS

Tony Swain and Gillian Cooper-Driver

AN OVERVIEW OF EVOLUTION

Introduction

There are two main views about the forces which direct the course of evolution. The first stresses the importance of rigorous and selective competition between organisms and variations in their fecundity (Dobzhansky et al. 1977). Usually, however, only relatively closely related species are considered and the possible effect of others (e.g., pathogens, which could have been of importance in ancient ecological systems) are ignored (Van Valen 1973). The second view regards evolution, at least at the molecular level, (e.g., a consideration of the changes in the primary structure of both proteins and nucleic acids), as being selectively neutral, any variation occurring purely by chance. Since all changes in the biochemistry, morphology, or anatomy of an organism must depend ultimately on those which take place in the structure of deoxyribonucleic acid (DNA) and the translated enzymes, this neutralist view has often been interpreted as indicating that selection itself is an unimportant artifact of evolution (Dobzhansky et al. 1977; Ayala 1976). However, very few comparative studies have been carried out on the variations in the molecular structure of cognate proteins and nucleic acids in extant organisms below the order level. Where this has been done, the changes show a higher frequency than would be expected on the basis of the neutralist hypothesis (Boulter et al. 1979), and cast doubt on its usefulness.

In our opinion, therefore, both views are too simplistic. Evolution is the result of a finely honed interplay between a multiplicity of different organisms occurring in any given ecosystem which is obviously determined by their DNA and tempered by mutational events at the molecular level. Some of the latter events may be neutral, some lethal, while a very few allow the organism to steal a biochemical march on its competitors. All may be affected by changes in climate or in edaphic factors. The overall variation may sometimes result in an easily discerned anatomical, physiological, or morphological change (e.g., due to an increase in the cellular control of certain growth hormones), while at other times change can only be detected by a close examination of the comparative biochemistry of proteins or other components in certain cells in the organisms in question.

In this chapter we present data on the probable biochemical changes which took place in plants as they became established on land in the late Silurian or early Devonian (Banks 1979; Chaloner and Sheerin 1979). We believe that these were important in determining the ultimate success of the land plants because they enabled them to withstand either their new physical conditions (e.g., increased dehydration or ultraviolet [UV] radiation) or the challenge of new land-based predators and pathogens. These changes thus greatly influenced the biochemical and geochemical nature of our world (Cloud 1974; Lovelock 1979).

We will start by considering the probable complexity of ancient ecosystems and the effect that this might have had on the elaboration of biochemical pathways in prokaryotes. We then consider the biochemistry of so-called secondary compounds in higher plants, ultimately examining the changes which we presume have taken place in cell walls, in terpenoids, and in flavonoids in land plants from the Devonian to the early Carboniferous.

The Complexity of Ancient Ecosystems

Because of the sparseness of the fossil record and of the difficulty in both dating and interpretation, there is a tendency to assume that Precambrian life was rather simple and generally uncomplicated by competition or predation. Of course it is difficult to reconstruct so ancient a paleoecological system with any degree of certainty. However, we might assume that from the primeval "soup" (Brooks and Shaw 1973; Aw 1977) several different living forms could have originated, all of which were constrained by the energetic parameters conforming to the limits of every living cell (Broda 1975). It is possible, for example, that the Archaebacteria, Eubacteria, and Proeukaryotes may have originated independently and have been engaged in direct competition almost since life began (Woese and Fox 1977). In present-day ecosystems, where mainly single-celled organisms are in direct competition: for example, the hind-gut of the termites (Margulis, Chase, and To

1979), the rumen of cattle (Lloyd, McDonald, and Crampton 1978), the soil (Gray and Williams 1971), or in cacao fermentation (Urquhart 1961), there is an immense variation in the succession of organisms as the quantities and varieties of nutrients change with time.

Similar situations must have prevailed almost as soon as the first living cells evolved. Any individual cell or protocell (Fox and Dose 1972) existing at the dawn of life must have been surrounded by large numbers of others competing for the supply of abiogenetically formed nutrients or the wastes from early living cells. It may be presumed that the majority of these competitors were like-cells, but some potential predators may also have been present.

This situation must have led, perhaps rather slowly, to the elaboration and selection of new biotypes. At first, competition probably gave rise to the development of new metabolic pathways which utilized the available nutrients to better advantage energetically. Next, there could have been the generation of specific membranes to enable cells to restrict the entry of "nonnutritious" compounds or to retain those that were needed. Much later, one might expect the origin of more complex protective devices against competitors and predators. For example, the production of antibiotics, the development of new modes of nutrition which were independent of external nutrients (e.g., anaerobic photosynthesis), and the development of more accurate methods for the exchange of nuclear information via conjugation and like processes (Brock 1979).

All in all, then, it would appear that the Archaen period may well have been about as "cutthroat" as any modern prokaryotic system. The weapons used were presumably mainly chemical, and this had important repercussions on the overall ecology of subsequent eras.

The Origins of Biochemical Change

If we accept that truly replicating organisms which were able to fix carbon dioxide into sugars and so on originated over 3 billion years ago (Reimer, Barghoorn, and Margulis 1979), then it follows that *all* the elements of common primary biochemical metabolism (Metzler 1977) must have been present at that time (Broda 1975). That is, the replication and transcription of DNA, protein and lipid synthesis, glycolysis, the citric acid cycle, and the electron transport pathway were present in similar form to that found in the most primitive of present-day prokaryotes (Brock 1979). Even if we add on a billion years or so for this to be perfected, we may still ask what has happened in biochemical evolution since the Precambrian? The answer seems quite plain! Biochemical evolution involves the production of *novel compounds or processes*. These enable the organism: (1) to resist predators or pathogens; (2) to detoxify xenobiotics present in the environment; (3) to attract other, usually mutualistic organisms for the exchange of genetic materials or needed metabolites; and (4) to aid in the dispersal of spores, pollen, and so on (Swain 1977; Scheline 1978; Rosenthal and Janzen 1979).

The compounds or reactions which are important in these respects are distinct from those found in primary metabolism, although they may be often closely related to them. The enzymes and pathways responsible presumably arose via an initial gene doubling followed by mutation (Ohno 1970). This sluggish process presumably resulted first in modified primary pathways. For example, the first polyketide antibiotics may well have arisen by the elimination of all or some of the normal reductive steps in the biosynthesis of C_{16} and C_{18} fatty acids. This would give rise to polyketides with the same number of carbon atoms, such as the C_{16} curvularin and the various tetracyclines (Turner 1971) (Fig. 4.1). Similarly, a few changes in the enzymes responsible for the synthesis of the aminopolysaccharides present in prokaryotic cell walls could have resulted in the production of the strepto-mycins and gentamicins (Meyers, Gawetz, and Goldfein 1974) (Fig. 4.1). The same trends have undoubtedly been repeated throughout evolution. Extensions or alterations in existing biochemical pathways have given rise to almost all the various classes of higher plant and animal defensive or signaling compounds (Harborne 1977; Swain 1977; Muller-Schwarze and Mozell 1977; Rockstein 1978). All the biosynthetic processes so far known fit into the idea that biochemical evolution is *the elaboration of, or changes in, general pathways of metabolism through the mutation of doubled genes which lead to the formation of novel biochemical processes or secondary metabolites which give ecological advantages to the organisms concerned and thus eventually lead to their greater selection.*

BIOCHEMICAL EVOLUTION IN EARLY LAND PLANTS

Early Life on Land

The first fossil evidence of vascular land plants comes from the late Silurian (*Cooksonia*, Banks 1979; Chaloner and Sheerin 1979). It is certain that many prokaryotes and protists preceded this invasion onto land (Campbell 1979) and indeed were prerequisite to it. It also seems probable that there must have been a preceding period during which multicellular algal progenitors of vascular plants (or "protovascular" plants) gradually encroached into "amphibious" environments (Swain 1974a, 1978). These would naturally have included first intertidal zones, then river and lake banks, swamps, and later perhaps upland marshes. Indeed, the first land habitats were presumably all of this general type (McKerrow 1978).

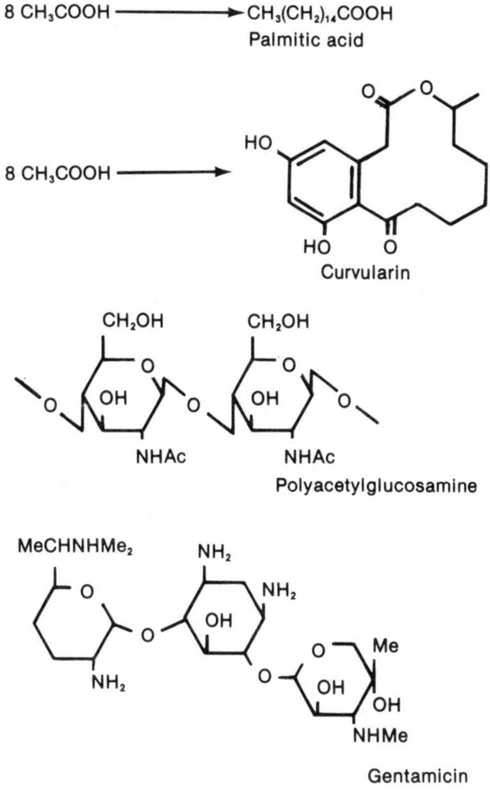

8 CH₃COOH ⟶ CH₃(CH₂)₁₄COOH
Palmitic acid

8 CH₃COOH ⟶

Curvularin

Polyacetylglucosamine

FIG. 4.1. Variations in primary pathways leading to secondary products. **A.** Fatty acid biosynthesis. **B.** Cell wall biosynthesis.

Gentamicin

The biochemical, morphological, and anatomical problems for any protovascular plant to adapt from a wholly aquatic to an amphibious environment were undoubtedly great. Unfortunately, there are no real intermediate forms, fossil or living, between the macroalgae and the land plants which might give us a clue to the evolution of vascular and other systems.

One of the first problems that land plants had to solve was that of water loss. Of course, many algae occupy intertidal zones today, and their water content may drop from 90 to 10 percent between tides (Carefoot 1977). They apparently cope with the problem in a similar way that land plants deal with freezing dehydration: that is, by concentrating soluble oligo- and polysaccharides in their cytoplasm. However, none of the algae possess water-conducting systems and thus usually cannot live for more than a day or so out of water.

To be possible to exist on land, plants needed to develop at least six new features: (1) the ability to conduct water and dilute salt solutions relatively quickly from one part to another—usually from the root or holdfast system to the aerial parts; (2) to reduce transpiration or other losses of water from cells exposed to the air and to control the ingress of water through the roots; (3) to ensure adequate exchange of both oxygen and carbon dioxide from the atmosphere to the plant; (4) to devise reproductive modes which do not require extreme water-rich environments; (5) to protect essential photosensitive compounds against the increase in both visible and ultraviolet light; and (6) to produce a variety of defensive compounds against the new predators and pathogens which were encountered on land.

The Silurian and early Devonian land environments colonized by plants must have initially been very hostile (McKerrow 1978). Probably they were similar to the salt flats or deserts of the southwestern United States with large diurnal variations in temperature, insolation and wind, and irregular amounts of rainfall (Cloudsley-Thompson 1975; Campbell 1979). Macrocellular living organisms could not have established themselves in such rigorous conditions without an association with nitrogen-fixers, detritus-decomposers, and so on. In fact, one might explain that the long period between the report of the first land plants in the Silurian and their rather rapid divergence in the late Devonian was due to the necessity to develop a whole complex of ecosystems, involving a number of mutualistic symbioses. However, we cannot be sure whether any multicellular animals were present in the very first land habitats. While there is reasonable evidence that most of the marine invertebrate phyla had developed by the mid-Silurian (McKerrow 1978), there is no real data that any land forms associated with plants arose until the mid-Devonian (Kevan, Chaloner, and Savile 1974; Chaloner and Sheerin 1979).

Remains of spider-like mites (arachnids) and detrital-feeding primitive myriapods are found in the plants of the Rhynie chert (Kevan, Chaloner, and Savile 1974; Swain 1978). Most of these were probably carnivores, but there is evidence that some may also have been facultative herbivores consuming both plant spores and sap. The obvious lesions made in the early plant fossils by the bites of primitive arthropods could have been the entry point for fungal saprophytes, the hypha of which are plainly seen in *Rhynia* (Kevan, Chaloner, and Savile 1974).

It seems probable that potential viral or bacterial pathogens could also have entered the plants in the same way, although there is no evidence of this. The Silurian-Devonian ecosystem, while thus being simpler than those found today, was obviously sufficiently diverse to exert quite severe selective pressures on the phyla present. Kevan, Chaloner, and Savile (1974) and

Chaloner and Sheerin (1979) have proposed that, as a result of predation by insect herbivores or fungal pathogens, early land plants evolved a number of protective devices, including larger and crenellated spores, spiny stems, and, finally, aborescent forms, which occur in the successive stages of the Devonian plant fossil record.

All such changes imply, of course, some variation in the molecular processes controlling development. However, there were undoubtedly other biochemical changes of equal importance, and these form the substance of the remaining part of this chapter.

Biochemical Variations in Cell Walls

Introduction

Unlike animals, the majority of plants, fungi, algal protists, and prokaryotes possess rather tough external cell walls. There are marked differences in the chemical structures of these walls in the four kingdoms, although they presumably serve the same biochemical and physiological purpose.

Excluding the mycobacteria (which have no walls), the most "primitive" cell walls are presumably those of the Archaebacteria and Eubacteria, which both contain net-like, although slightly different, peptidoglycans. These consist of a large number of parallel aminopolysaccharide chains which are cross-linked by 6- or 7-member polypeptides (Brock 1979; Balch et al. 1979). These are not really simple structures and, coupled with the even greater complexity of the outer sheaths of most bacteria, show that "cell-wall" integrity played a more important part in the evolution of primitive prokaryotes than is generally recognized. The cell walls of algae, plants, and fungi, on the other hand, consist of a number of discrete layers of usually different polysaccharides, arranged in parallel fibrils, which are usually laid over each other at angles to give a rough "weave-like" character. Except in vascular plants, there does not seem to be any covalent bonding or cross-linking, either between fibrils or the separate layers by the interaction of other cell-wall components.

Fungal Cell Walls

In the majority of fungi, the most important cell-wall polymer is chitin (1,4-poly-N-acetyl-D-glucosamine), which is also found in many lower animals (Jeuniaux 1971; Swain 1974a). It can be regarded as being an analog of the glycan chain in most prokaryotes (Fig. 4.1). Other polysaccharide components present in fungal cell walls include 1,3-glucans, mannans, galactomannans, and up to 30 percent polypeptides. There is, as stated previously, no cross-linking between the various components as occurs in the chitinized skeletons of invertebrates (Rockstein 1978). Obviously, in terms of their cell wall, fungi are a "half-way house" between prokaryotes and invertebrates and plants (Swain 1974a).

It should be noted that the Oomycetes, which are normally classified as fungi and probably were among the first to accommpany plants onto land, do not contain chitin in their cell wall. Instead, like many algae and all higher plants, their main wall constituent is cellulose. The Oomycetes also differ from other fungi in their mode of biosynthesis of lysine and of tryptophan (Swain 1974a) and as a result may be best regarded as achlorous algae (Ainsworth and Bisby 1971). It is of interest that there are many Oomycetes which are pathogenic to plants (e.g., *Pythium*) and they appear to be more susceptible to inhibition by higher plant defensive compounds than most other fungi. This could indicate that the Oomycetes have different permeability or other mechanisms to combat toxins than do other fungi (Cooper-Driver, Shintani, and Marchant 1980).

Algal and Plant Cell Walls

The central matrix of cell walls of the majority of algae and higher plants contain two or more layers of cellulose fibrils oriented at about 45° to each other. These are surrounded by a matrix of other polysaccharides, collectively called pectins or hemicelluloses (Preston 1979). The cell walls of red and brown algae contain many sulfated galactans and related polymers (McCandless and Craigie 1979). The varying hemicellulose polysaccharide chains can assume helical structures, especially in higher plants, and this leads to "a delicately balanced entity with specific functions essential to the continuing existence of the [plant] cell" (Preston 1979).

Changes in Cell Walls in Devonian Land Plants

Before we examine the importance of the previous findings to Devonian land plants, we need to consider three other features of higher plant cell-wall polysaccharides: (1) their acylation with both aliphatic and aromatic organic acids; (2) the encrusting of cell walls with lignins; and (3) their association in epidermal cells with lipid and the mixed lipid-lignin polymers, cutin, and suberin (McCandless and Craigie 1979; Preston 1979; Swain 1979; Kolattu-kudy 1980).

While sulfuric acid acylation of cell-wall polysaccharides, as mentioned earlier, is a relatively constant feature of certain algae, the formation of aromatic acid esters appears to be restricted to land plants (Swain 1974a). The main acids involved are ferulic acid (Fig. 4.2a) with lesser amounts of *p*-coumaric acid (Fig. 4.2b) and the corresponding benzoic acids. It is known that such acylations are an ancient feature in plants (Swain 1979; Friend

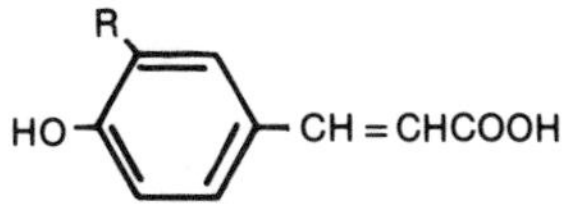

FIGURE 4.2. **A**. R = H *p*-Coumaric acid. **B**. R = OCH$_3$
Ferulic acid.

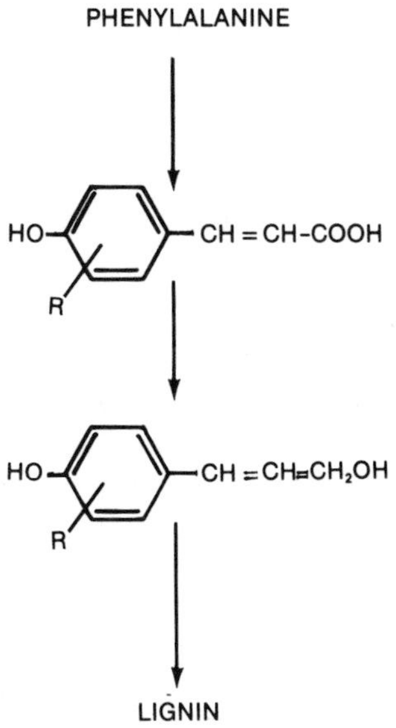

FIG. 4.3. Biosynthesis of lignins. R = 3 or 3,5- di-
methoxy.

1979) and the resulting esterified polysaccharides are more resistant to hydrolysis (Swain 1974a). It seems also probable that such acylation led eventually to the formation of lignins (Swain 1979; Preston 1979) (Fig. 4.3). Undoubtedly, these features gave both chemical and physical strength to plant cell walls, thus enabling early land plants to both withstand pathogens and to increase their size.

Perhaps more important, at least when plants first came onto land, was their ability to produce cutin and suberin and the associated water-impervious coatings of higher plants (Kolattukudy 1977, 1980) (Fig. 4.4). Again, the biosynthesis of these polymers involved only a slight diversion from the normal pathways of primary metabolism. The production of the dihydroxylated C$_{16}$ and C$_{18}$ fatty acids needed requires only ω-hydroxylation as a new feature, since the introduction of mid-chain hydroxyl groups at C$_9$ or C$_{10}$ follows from normal dehydration mechanisms (Mann 1978). Cutin, which covers the epidermal layers of leaves and stems of all land plants, differs from suberin, which is present on the surface of roots and wound tissue, in that it contains no protolignin units. A study of the chemistry of

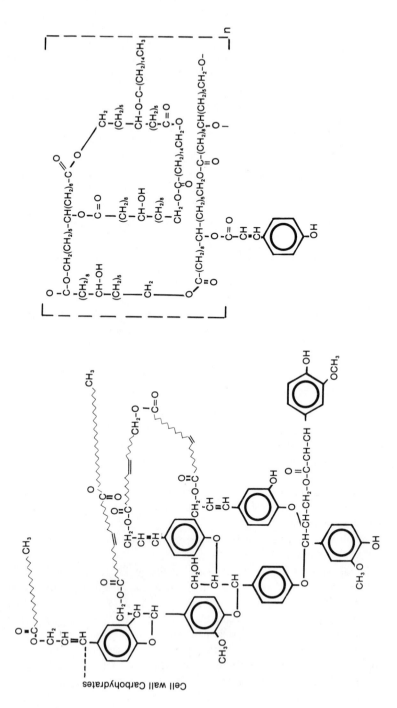

FIG 4.4. The structure of suberin and cutin.

Devonian fossils shows that dihydroxy fatty acid fragments expected to be produced by diagenesis of both cutin and suberin are only present in those remains which can be definitely ascribed to vascular plants and are not present in those from the algae (Niklas 1979, 1980).

The fact that suberin, which must have been present in the roots of Psilophytina (Kolattukudy 1978, 1980), has a part lignin-like structure, and the acylation of cell walls in polysaccharides by hydroxycinnamic acids is equally primitive, suggests that the biosynthetic route to the lignins themselves may have been derived secondarily as woody plants evolved during the Devonian. Again, Niklas (1979, 1980) and his colleagues have shown that aromatic acids and related compounds presumably produced from lignin and its precursors are present in Devonian tracheophyte fossils. It thus seems probable that polysaccharide acylation by ferulate may have been the most ancient feature. This presumably led to the formation of diferulyl units on the cell walls by C-C coupling of the aromatic rings. This step again was probably not novel, since phenolic ring coupling occurs in primitive organisms. The linked diferuloyl moiety thus formed on the cell wall could then have acted as a building stone for the elaboration of lignin.

The next stage in lignin (and suberin) biosynthesis was presumably the elaboration of the two-stage pathway from the cinnamic acids to the corresponding alcohols (Fig. 4.3). The latter are readily polymerized to form lignins (or the oligomers of the suberins) in the presence of a suitable monooxygenase type system. It is interesting that the suberin is present only on root surfaces (or wound tissues) and this points to the importance of the lignin-like moieties as protective agents in these tissues.

Finally, it can be presumed that using the biosynthetic pathways already established, plants produced polymeric lignins cross-linking cellulose and other polysaccharide layers. This allowed the plants to develop arborescent forms and thus partially escape from predation of their immature spores by flightless insects (Swain 1978). Undoubtedly, it also made stem penetration and leaf biting by such insects more difficult. This presumably was the selective force which led to the development of the primitive paleodictyopteridan sucking insects in the Carboniferous (Kukalova-Peck 1978). However, it should be remembered that the protection of cell walls in lignified and suberized tissues must also have had serious consequences on both the pathogenic and the detrital organisms of the early Paleozoic. These chemical defenses had to be destroyed before the various organisms could invade the underlying nutritious tissues. Indeed, it seems that the only *readily* available plant material for putative herbivores in the late Devonian were the germling spores or prothalli and various detrital components or associated saprophytes once their defenses had been overcome. For higher animals, this was poor fare, and is probably one reason why insect evolution took off mainly via carnivores in the early Carboniferous.

Conclusions

It seems highly probable that the earliest land plants showed little change in the basic structure of their cell walls from their presumed algal ancestors (Preston 1979). However, the ability of early land plants to hydroxylate normal fatty acids and polymerize the products to the water-impervious cutin, which was deposited along with waxes and other components on the outer side of their epidermal cells (Kolattukudy 1977, 1980), must have been an important determinant in their success. Such hydrophobic components are completely different and much more efficient at retaining water than the polysaccharide epidermal coats which are found in littoral algae (McCandless and Craigie 1979).

The second important change in Devonian land plants in respect to their cell walls was their ability to acylate the polysaccharide matrices with hydroxy aromatic acids, especially ferulic acid. With time, this led to the development of dimers and ultimately to protolignins. This made the cell walls much less susceptible to breakdown by the carbohydrases of invading microorganisms. Ultimately, the protolignins were found to be useful because of their incorporation into cutin-like epidermal constituents of roots and wound tissue (suberin) and finally to act as a *three*-dimensional cement between polysaccharide layers, rendering cells even more impervious both to attack by invading microorganisms and to loss of water. The advantage of this lignification process was finally seen in the structural strength it imparted to plants, enabling them in the middle Devonian to grow in height and girth into trees, and thus withstand many adverse physical conditions (Kevan, Chaloner, and Savile 1974; Swain 1978). As we shall see, these early trees suffered from one drawback: their inability to protect the cells of their inert highly lignified cores (heartwoods) from fungal attack. However, this depended also on the evolution of suitable fungi (or bacteria) to degrade lignin. The relatively rapid development of trees and shrubs in the late Devonian indicates that the fungi did not solve this problem immediately. However, the demise of some of the early arborescent lycopods and others in the Carboniferous perhaps indicates that wood-rotting fungi had evolved by that time and that to survive trees had to produce new defenses. We will return to this problem later.

The Biochemical Evolution of Terpenoids

Introduction

Terpenoid compounds are by far the most structurally diverse, widely distributed, and functionally variable class of secondary products in nature

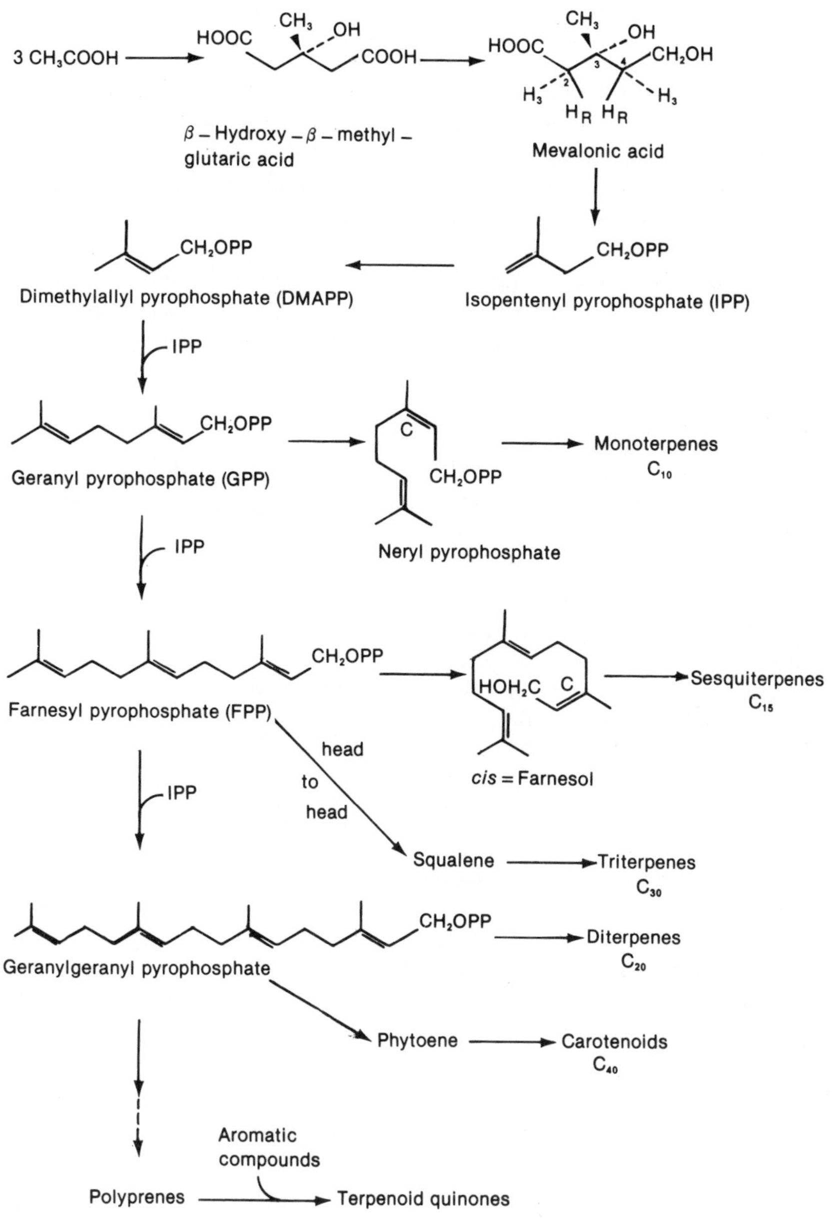

FIG. 4.5. Biosynthesis of terpenoids.

(Swain 1974a). All terpenoids contain two or more of the five carbon branched chain isoprene units joined together, mainly head-to-tail (Fig. 4.5), and most have one or more double bonds and/or ring systems per C_5 unit (Mann 1978; Goodwin 1979). The majority of terpenoids contain only C, H, and O, but halogenated derivatives occur in the red and brown algae (Faulkner and Fenical 1977), and nitrogen-containing terpenoid alkaloids are common in higher plants (Pelletier 1970). The simplest compounds of the class are the monoterpenes (C_{10}), which contain two isoprene units, and these are followed by sesquiterpenes (C_{15}), and diterpenes (C_{20}). The triterpenes (C_{30} and less) comprise a variety of different types of compounds from simple hydrocarbons to complex oxygenated saponins and cardiac glycosides and a number of alkaloids. By far the most biologically important triterpenoid group, however, are the tetracyclic (C_{21}-C_{29}) sterols, which play diverse roles in various organisms. The only important class of tetraterpenes (C_{40}) are the carotenoids, which are the coloring matters and auxiliary photosynthetic pigments of both pro- and eukaryotes. Higher terpenoids are also known, ranging from the widespread side-chains (6–10 isoprene units) of ubiquinones, which are present in all classes of organisms, to the high-molecular-weight polymers of rubber and gutta-percha (> 500 isoprene units), which are found only in angiosperms. Other groups of terpenoids with different numbers of isoprene units are known, but are relatively rare.

All classes of various terpenoids arise by the initial condensation of the two biological isoprene units, dimethylallyl pyrophosphate (DMAPP) and isopentenyl pyrophosphate (IPP) (Fig. 4.5), which are enzymically interconvertible and are formed from three molecules of acetic acid via mevalonic acid (Mann 1978). DMAPP acts as a starter for the biosynthesis of all terpenoids, and the subsequent addition of one, two, or three IPP units gives rise to geranyl (C_{10}) (GPP), farnesyl (C_{15}) (FPP), and geranylgeranyl (C_{20}) (GGPP) pyrophosphates, respectively. Most monoterpenes are formed by rearrangements of GPP, the sesquiterpenes from FPP, and the diterpenes from GGPP. Triterpenoids (C_{30}), including sterols, are *not* synthesized by the addition of two more IPP units to GGPP, but by a *head-to-head* condensation of two molecules of the C_{15} moiety, FPP, via an intermediate which has a "flexible" single bond between the two C_{15} halves, and this allows for the subsequent folding of the molecule to give either a tetra- or pentacyclic C_{30} triterpenoid (Mann 1978; Godwin 1979). The C_{40} tetraterpenes are similarly formed by the *head-to-head* condensation of two molecules of the C_{20} compound GGPP. However, in this case, the first formed intermediate has a *double bond* between its two halves that prevents cyclization of the central portion. This eventually gives rise to the conjugated central branched carbon chain found in most carotenoids. The polyisoprenes (ubiquinones, plastoquinones, rubber, etc.) are all head-to-tail condensations of DMAPP with successive IPP units (Mann 1978).

Distribution of Terpenoids in Plants

The distribution of the terpenoids in the plant kingdom is evolutionarily assymmetrical. By this, we mean that only the more complex molecules (ubiquinones, carotenoids, and triterpenes) are found in present-day members of the more ancient prokaryotes, while all these classes together with the structurally simpler mono-, sesqui-, and diterpenes are present in the more advanced eukaryotes. We have drawn attention to this situation previously (Swain 1974a), and suggest that it arose because the biosynthesis of the terpenoids originally involved an enzyme complex with an isoprene carrier protein (ICP) similar to that of the fatty acid synthetase. The latter, it will be recalled, catalyzes the production of C_{16} and C_{18} fatty acids from acetyl-CoA, with no simpler intermediates (e.g., butyric, octanoic acids, etc.) generally being formed. The evolutionarily most primitive terpenoid biosynthetic systems in prokaryotes were thus directed toward *higher* polymers, such as bactoprenols (C_{35}), which act as carriers in prokaryote wall synthesis (Brock 1979), ubiquinones which have terpenoid side chains up to C_{40} necessary for the generation of a proton flux to generate adenosine triphosphate (ATP) (Harold 1977, Trebst 1974), and the C_{15} or C_{20} side chains of the bacteriochlorophylls (Swain 1974a). The control mechanisms necessary for the production of the latter coupled with head-to-head synthetases could presumably then lead to the production of squalene or hopane triterpenoids (C_{30}) for stabilizing internal membranes (Ourisson, Rohmer, and Anton 1979; Balch et al. 1979) and to the carotenoids (C_{40}). The latter compounds might first have been produced in early prokaryotes because of their ability to protect bacterial chlorophylls against singlet oxygen photodestruction (Brock 1979); later, by polymerization, they could have given rise to one of the components of sporopollenin which enables spores to resist dehydration and so on (Brooks and Shaw 1973; Swain 1974a); finally they might then be used as auxiliary light receptors in photosynthesis (Brock 1979) or other light-driven responses (e.g., photodetection, etc.).

As mentioned earlier, no mono-, sesqui-, or diterpenes have been reported from prokaryotes. Furthermore, the structures of the complements of tri- and tetraterpenoids found in both Archaebacteria and Eubacteria are somewhat different from that found in eukaryotes. Thus, the Archaebacteria contain the acyclic triterpene precursor squalene (Fig. 4.6) in their membranes; the Eubacteria, including the cyanophytes, have the hopanoid-like triterpenes (e.g., diploterol [Fig. 4.7] and tetrahymanol [Fig. 4.8]), while the membranes of eukaryotes contain the ubiquitous 3-hydroxy containing sterols, for example, sitosterol (Fig. 4.9). Similarly, the carotenoids found in both classes of bacteria (including the blue-green algae) are usually hydrocarbons or open chain alcohols; the ubiquitous oxygenated carotenoid of higher protists and plants, for example, violaxanthin (Fig. 4.10) are absent.

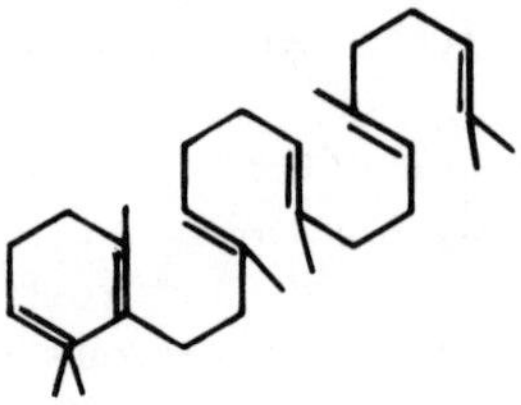

FIGURE 4.6. Squalene.

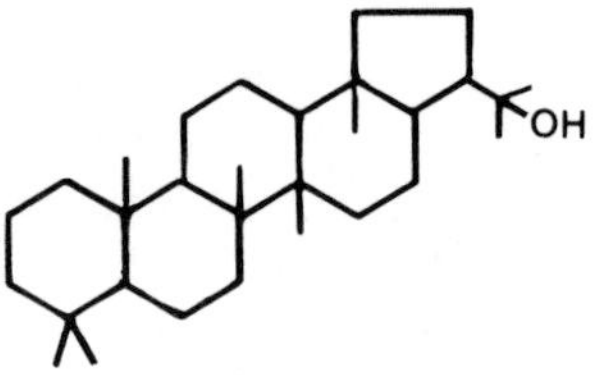

FIGURE 4.7. Diplopterol.

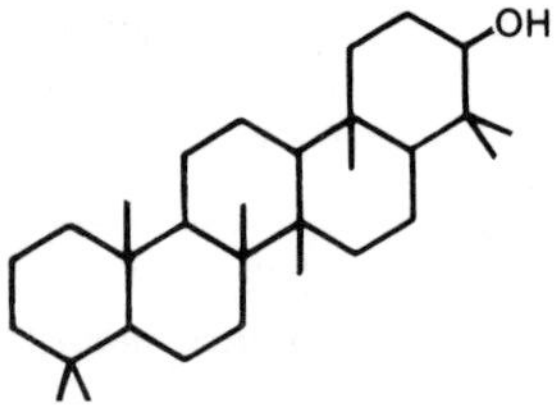

FIGURE 4.8. Tetrahymanol.

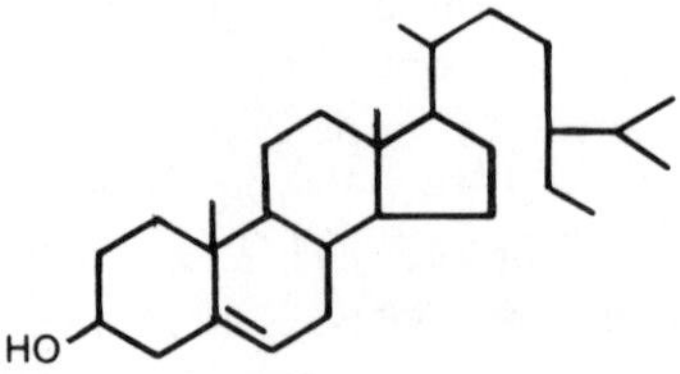

FIGURE 4.9. Sitosterol.

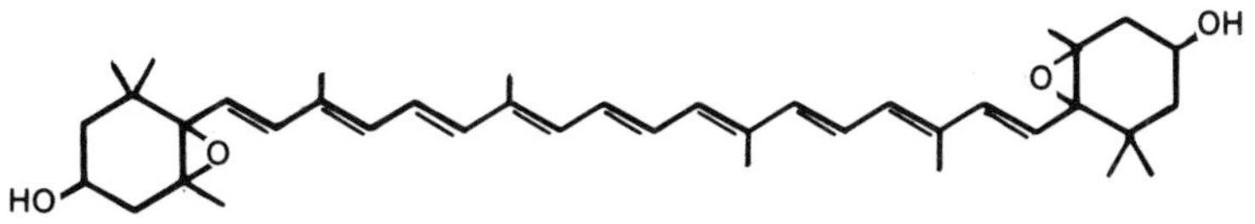

FIGURE 4.10. Violaxanthin.

The Evolution of the Terpenoids

It should be noted that the cyclization of squalene to sterols or the conversion of phytoene to xanthophylls both require oxygen. Thus, the differential distribution of uncyclized *hydrocarbons* of both tri- and tetra-terpenoids in the early prokaryotes and the cyclized alcohols or epoxides of both classes in the eukaryotes suggests that the most primitive organisms developed their biosynthetic pathways to the terpenoids in a system more anoxic that that prevailing at present.

Also as mentioned previously, prokaryotes lack mono-, sesqui-, and diterpenes, and it seems likely therefore that the biosynthetic routes to C_{30} or C_{40} terpenoids were the major targets which were only modified to release the needed FPP or GGPP monomers after the final evolution of the eukaryotes. These processes presumably involved a series of gene duplications and subsequent mutations (Ohno 1970), which may have been selected because the sesqui- and diterpenes produced interfered with the action of the biosynthesis of tri- or tetraterpenes in competitors or predators, or detrimentally changed the permeability of their membranes. In other words, the sesqui- and diterpenes found in protists, fungi, and plants (Turner 1971; Scheuer 1973; Runeckles and Mabry 1973; Ragan and Chapman 1978) may well have been originally selected for their ability to act as defensive agents. This certainly seems true in both algae (Faulkner and Fenical 1977) and higher plants (Harborne 1977).

The monoterpenes, on the other hand, undoubtedly had a different evolutionary history. Whereas one can postulate the release of either FPP or GGPP from an early inescapable "head-to-head" dimerization reaction, there is no biosynthetic equivalent for the monoterpenes. That is, there are no common C_{20} terpenes formed by a "head-to-head" dimerization. It is not surprising, therefore, that monoterpenes are absent from fungi (Turner 1971), and very rare in algae (Faulkner and Fenical 1977), the bryophytes (Markham and Porter 1978), and lower vascular plants (Swain 1974a). These volatile, pleasantly smelling compounds occur in largest amounts in the gymnosperms and certain families of angiosperms where they apparently act against insect herbivores as camouflage agents rather than as repellents. That is, they *mask* or interfere with the chemical communication systems of the insects, thus causing them to congregate in the wrong places, flee from no real enemy, or attempt to mate at the wrong time.

The Importance of Terpenoids in Devonian Land Plants

It can be seen from the outline given previously that the earliest land plants most probably had the capacity to synthesize a wide variety of terpenoids. This is confirmed in part by the finding of branched chain acids and sterane derivatives in the fossil remains of Devonian plants (Niklas and Gensel 1978; Niklas 1980). Of course, the branched chain hydrocarbons phytane and pristane have both been long known from early Precambrian cherts and their presence has been adduced as evidence for early photosynthesis, since it is believed that they were derived from the C_{20} phytol side-chain of chlorophylls. However, it seems possible that they could have equally well arisen from other early terpenoids such as primitive ubiquinones (Swain 1974a).

There is little evidence of a vast diversity of mono-, sesqui-, or diterpenoid biosynthesis in lower land plants today except for the bryophytes (Markham and Porter 1978). It is intriguing that the stereochemistry of the majority of the sesqui- and diterpenes isolated from these nonvascular plants has the opposite configuration *(enantio)* to the equivalent compounds found in algae, gymnosperms, and angiosperms. In this they resemble the fungi, suggesting that the bryophytes may have originated separately from the vascular plants. The biosynthetic capacity of the liverworts to produce sesquiterpenes is considerable, and some of these have been shown to be feeding deterrents against insects (Markham and Porter 1978; Mabry and Gill 1979).

For early vascular plants, however, probably the most important class of terpenoids were the sesqui- and diterpenoid plant growth hormones (abscisic acid and the gibberellins), the triterpenoid analogues of insect molting hormones (the phytoecdysones), and the sesquiterpenoid equivalents of insect juvenile hormones (the plant juvenoids) (Mabry and Gill 1979; Slama 1979). Abscisic acid (Fig. 4.11) is present in all classes of higher plants except liverworts (Hepaticae), and is involved in control of their winter dormancy in temperate regions. Obviously, the ability for plants to drastically reduce their metabolism during periods when the temperature, day length, and light intensity are all low was (and is) a great advantage. From its structure, abscisic acid was early believed to be formed as a breakdown product from carotenoids (e.g., violaxanthin [Fig. 4.10]) while some conversion appears possible, the main route of biosynthesis appears to be directly from FPP.

The gibberellins (e.g., GA_3 [Fig. 4.12]) are mainly responsible for increases in the growth of plants, especially stem elongation and leaf size. Again, one can see the obvious advantages in being able to control such

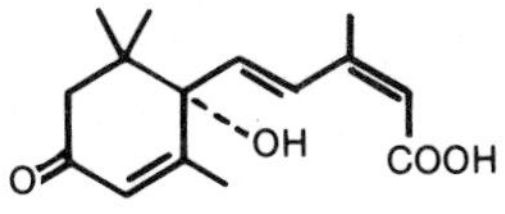

FIGURE 4.11. Abscisic acid.

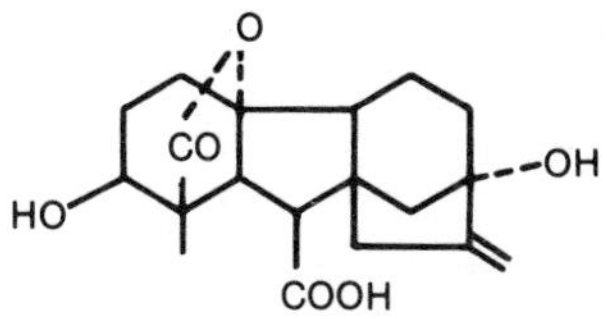

FIGURE 4.12. Gibberellic acid.

growth and development by a relatively simple hormonal system. One presumes that the development of the larger aborescent forms in the late Devonian must have been one consequence of the ability to synthesize such hormones. The gibberellins all arise from a GGPP precursor via the diterpenoid copalyl pyrophosphate and kaurene. Similar diterpenes to copalol are present in brown algae (Faulkner and Fenical 1977) so that only relatively small changes in the biosynthetic pathways were perhaps needed to elaborate the necessary pathways to GA_3 in early land plants. It may be noted that many of the related diterpenoids are toxic to other organisms (Mabry and Gill 1979).

The phytoecdysones (molting hormone [MH]) and plant juvenoids (JH) are a different "kettle of fish," for they represent the production of terpenoid compounds whose sole purpose appears to be to act as defensive compounds against insect herbivores (Slama 1979). In both cases, their production in plants apparently follows an extension of normal biosynthetic routes to other sesqui- and diterpenoids. Thus, the sesquiterpenoid insect juvenoids closely resemble the farnesyl side chains of bacterial chlorophylls; indeed, farnesol itself shows insect juvenile hormone (JH) activity; that is, it selectively inhibits metamorphosis to adult stages during early ecdyses, and thus ensures that the next instar is still "juvenile." In most insects the capacity to synthesize JH is reduced to zero prior to the last molt before the adult stage. However, if the hormone (or its analogs) is given to such insects they produce another sexually immature juvenile instar. Thus, plant juvenoids act by increasing the time that insect herbivores take to reach adulthood and thus reduce the number of eggs laid and juveniles occurring in the next generation (Slama 1979).

The steroidal (C_{27}) ecdysones of insects control the onset of ecdysis in both insects and crustacea. That is, they determine the time at which the process of shedding the hardened outer integument of one growth stage (instar) takes place, and thus how soon the animal reaches reproductive maturity (Slama 1979). However, these compounds (e.g, α-ecdysone [Fig. 4.13]) and their structural homologs accumulate in ferns and gymnosperms in concentrations of the order of 10^4 to 10^5 times greater than those found in insects. It is thus tempting to postulate that they were present in these plants as defenses against insect herbivores whose hormonal balance would perhaps be upset by ingesting large amounts of such substances. This hypothesis is reinforced by the fact that insects cannot synthesize any sterols (or their precursors) and depend on getting them from their diet. However, the evidence that phytoedysones affect modern herbivorous insects is equivocal (Slama 1979). Nevertheless, we believe that the accumulation of these compounds in ancient plant species indicates the possibility that they might well have been active against Devonian insects. Indeed, production of JH and MH analogs by Devonian and Carboniferous plants, especially the presumably terpenoid-rich ferns and protogymnosperms, may have been partially instrumental in leading to the giant flying insects of the mid-Paleozoic. The advantage to these plants could have been that on nutritional grounds such large insect forms would almost necessarily have had to be carnivorous!

Conclusions

The success of Devonian and early Carboniferous land plants undoubtedly depended in part on their ability to produce new physiologically active terpenoids both to control their growth and to defend them against herbivores. We have only discussed a few classes which appear to have been important in this respect. Many more plant terpenoids undoubtedly had deleterious effects on Devonian herbivores pathogens (Mabry and Gill 1979). It will never by known with certainty the importance of terpenoids to plant evolution, but we believe that without such components as part of *secondary* metabolism, the struggle between plants and their predators might well have shown a quite different turn.

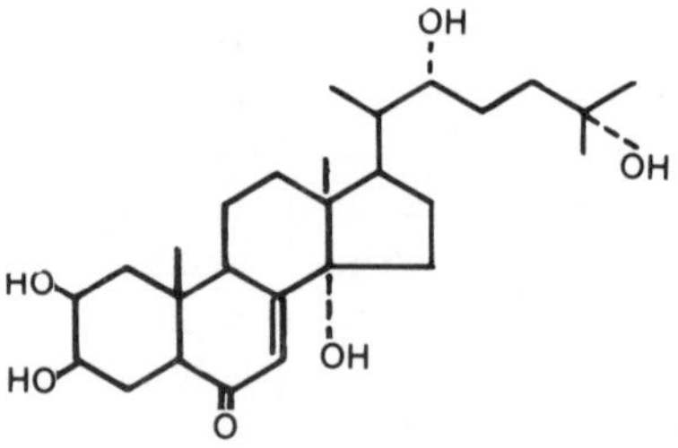

FIGURE 4.13.   α -Ecdysone.

The Biochemical Evolution of Flavonoids

Introduction

All higher plants accumulate at least one, and usually many, glycosides of the class of phenolic compounds known as flavonoids (e.g., apigenin [Fig. 4.14a]; quercetin [Fig. 4.14e]; cyanidin [Fig. 4.15]), and most woody plants contain oligomeric and polymeric derivatives of them, the proanthocyanidins (Fig. 4.16). Flavonoids are absent from prokaryotes, animals, and almost all fungi and algae, so they can be regarded as characteristic of land plants and presumably evolved mainly during and since the Devonian.

The flavonoids, unlike most other natural products, are formed biosynthetically by a combination of two distinct pathways. One part of the flavonoid molecule, the six carbons of ring A, arise from the polyketide route (the condensation of three acetyl-CoA residues) while the other part (ring B and the three carbons of the heterocyclic ring: $C_{2,3}$ and C_4) comes from the shikimate or phenylalanine pathway (Mann 1978; Hahlbrock and Grisebach 1979). The final precursor for most of the common flavonoids is the flavanone naringenin (Fig. 4.17), which, through subsequent oxidation (or reduction) of the central heterocyclic ring and by a series of hydroxyla-

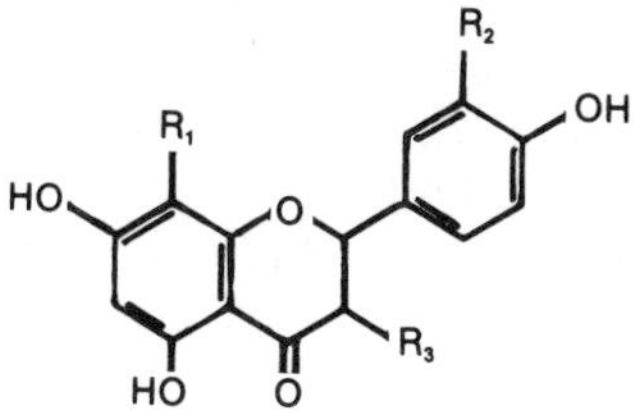

FIGURE 4.14. a $R_1 = R_2 = R_3 = H$; Apigenin
b $R_2 = R_3 = H$, $R_1 = $ glucose, vitexin
c $R_1 = R_3 = H$ $R_2 = OH$, Luteolin
d $R_1 = R_2 = OH$, $R_3 = H$, 8-Hydroxyluteolin
e $R_1 = H$, $R_2 = R_3 = OH$, Quercetin
f $R_1 = H$, $R_2 = OH$, $R_3 = $ glucose, Isoquercitrin

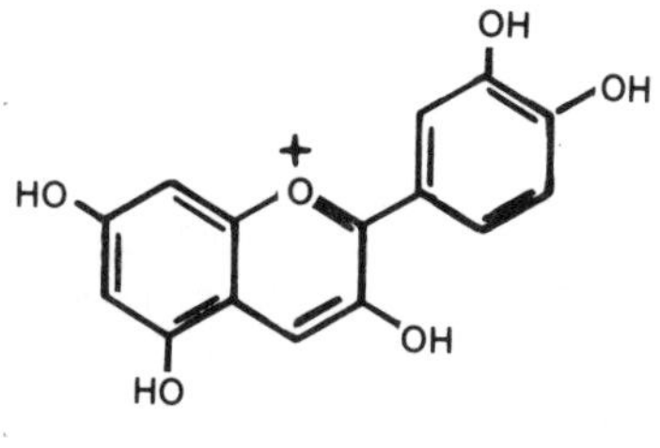

FIGURE 4.15. Cyanidin.

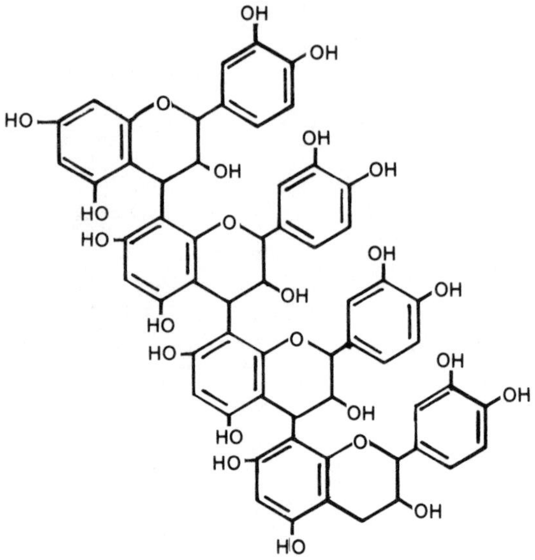

FIGURE 4.16. Procyanidin A; tetramer.

tions, $O =$ and C-methylations and glycosylations, gives rise to the different classes and types of flavonoids (Hahlbrock and Grisebach 1979).

The biochemical evolution of flavonoids virtually parallels increases in their structural complexity. Thus, only the simplest molecules (e.g., apigenin-C-glycosides [Fig. 4.14b]) are found in the most primitive organisms, while a variety of more highly oxidized compounds occur in the more advanced vascular plants (Swain 1974b). Interestingly, many of the more highly advanced members of the angiosperms show a reversal of this trend and accumulate flavones and their derivatives similar to those found in the most primitive plants (Harborne 1978). Another anomaly are the bryophytes: while most contain only simple flavones and their derivatives, the Hepaticae possess a variety of flavonols (e.g., quercetin), which are normally found in more advanced phyla; also, an aurone has been isolated from *Marchantia* (Markham and Porter 1978), a class of flavonoid common only to angiosperms.

Since the ability to produce and elaborate flavonoid compounds had obviously been selected during the course of early plant evolution, one may ask for what reason? The total absence of such compounds in prokaryotes tells against any original primary function in contrast to the terpenoids discussed earlier.

The most easily comprehensible ecological role of the flavonoids is that they are coloring matters which serve to attract flower pollinators or seed dispersal agents in numerous angiosperms (Harborne 1977). Their role here is adequately documented and any variation in their structure which results

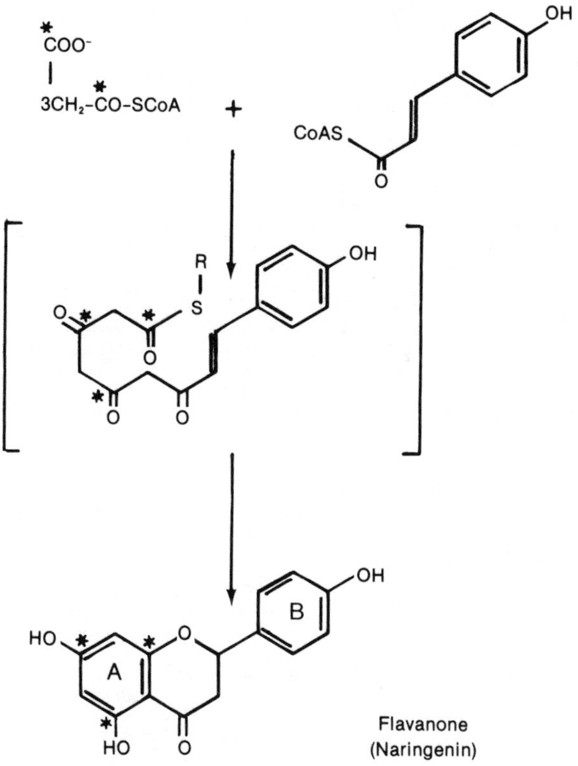

FIGURE 4.17. Flavonoid biosynthesis.

in a change of visible (or ultraviolet) light adsorption has been shown to be important in determining the guilds of animals which are attracted. However, it should be noted that flavonoids often occur in higher concentrations and in greater structural diversity in the leaves and stems of plants than in the flowers or fruit skins of the seed-bearing phyla. Obviously, their role in the leaves must be different from that in flowers and fruits, and indicates why they were important in Devonian plants.

The Distribution of Flavonoids in Plants

The most primitive organisms which contain flavonoids are two genera of the Characeae, *Chara* and *Nitella* (Swain 1974b). Both these algae grow in shallow fresh or brackish waters and show considerable morphological differentiation. They have a long fossil record, and possess characteristics (e.g., resistant spores, mitotic divisions, specific enzymes like glycolate oxidase) which point to their being closely related to land plants (Stewart and Mattox 1975; Pickett-Heaps 1975; Banks 1979). They both contain one or more apigenin-6- or 8-*C*-glycosides (Fig. 4.14b). We may thus regard these compounds as the primitive "target" of flavonoid biosynthesis. The formation of *C*-glycosides, rather than *O*-glycosides (e.g., isoquercitrin [Fig. 4.14f]) which are found in almost all higher plants, is undoubtedly significant. Indeed, *C-C* linkages are a hallmark of almost all "primitive" flavonoids. For example, *C*-glycosides are not only common in mosses and liverworts (but see previous discussion concerning the advanced flavonoids found in the latter), but are found in all orders of lower vascular plants (Cooper-Driver 1980). The most primitive class of such plants, the Psilophytina, contain a member of another group of *C-C*–linked compounds, the biflavones (amentoflavone [Fig. 4.18]), which is formed by the linking of two apigenin moieties (Cooper-Driver 1977, 1980). However, they also are able to form *O*-glycosides of both apigenin and amentoflavone as well as *C*-glycosides of the former (Cooper-Driver 1980).

In the Lycophytina, the three subclasses each contain a distinctive pattern of flavonoid compounds (Cooper-Driver 1980). *Selaginella* follows *Psilotum* in possessing only biflavones, albeit in greater variety. *Lycopodium* contains simple flavone derivatives, but with a greater variety of *O*-glycosidation, some *O*-methylation, and the presence of compounds having either two (luteolin [Fig. 4.14c]) or three hydroxy groups in their B-ring; *Isoetes* is like *Lycopodium*, but contains, in addition, a 2'-hydroxy substituted B-ring flavone (isoetin) and has 6- and 8-hydroxylated luteolin derivatives. The biosynthetic progression here is marked and important, for each of the new components mentioned requires one or more modified step(s) in biosynthesis. For example, the production of 8-hydroxyluteolin (Fig. 4.14d) indicates that there are two extra (or substituted) steps in the pathway which lead from the "primitive" 8-*C*-glycosyl apigenin (vitexin [11b]), one to introduce an -OH group in the C_3' position and the second to substitute an -OH group for the *C*-glucosyl at C_8.

The Sphenophytina show a further and much more radical change in flavonoid biosynthesis, the ability to introduce a hydroxyl group at C_3 of the

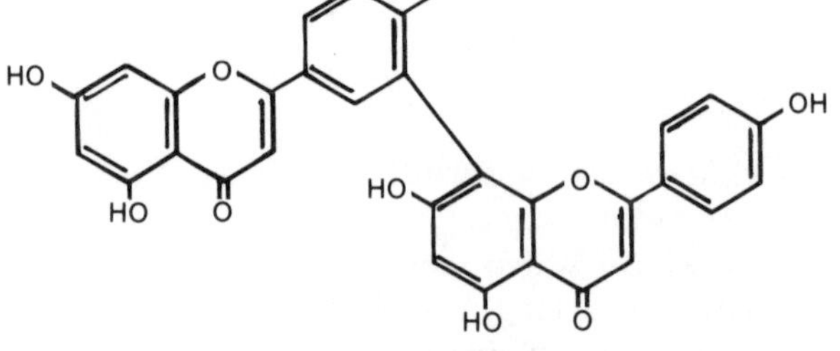

FIGURE 4.18. Amentoflavone.

heterocyclic ring. This leads to the flavonols (e.g., quercetin [Fig. 4.14e]) and, later, to the anthocyanidins (e.g., cyanidin [Fig. 4.15]). More importantly, it gave rise to the procyanidin tannins (Fig. 4.16) which were (and are) undoubtedly of even greater ecological importance (Cooper-Driver 1980).

The evolution of most other classes of flavonoids are shown in the Filicophytina where C- and O-methylation is relatively common and chalcones accumulate. Every order except the more recently evolved Ophioglossales contains procyanidins and prodelphinidins, in higher proportion than in any other class or subclass of land plants (Swain 1974b; Cooper-Driver 1980).

The formation of iso- and neoflavonoids seems to be restricted to the angiosperms (Swain 1974b; Harborne, Mabry, and Mabry 1975) and will not be further considered here. Nor will we discuss the formation of prenylated or other complex lignin-like flavonoid derivatives which appear to be also restricted to these higher categories of plants (Harborne, Mabry, and Mabry 1975).

The Evolution of the Flavonoids

As mentioned earlier, the "target" compound for flavonoid biosynthesis can be regarded as the flavone apigenin (Fig. 4.14a). Substitution at C_8 (or C_6) by either a C-linked glucose (see Fig. 4.14b) a second molecule of apigenin (e.g., amentoflavone [Fig. 4.18]), an -OH group, or a -CH_3 group can be regarded as being part of the series of biosynthetic advances which lead to the present (and presumably past) distribution of the flavonoids in the Psilophytina and Lycophytina.

The ability to hydroxylate the flavanone precursor of apigenin (naringenin, Fig. 4.17) at C_3 to produce a dihydroflavonol (aromadendrin) and thus flavonols and proanthocyanidins perhaps did not arise until the evolution of Sphenopsida, Pteropsida, and Protogymnospermopsida in the Upper Devonian (Chaloner and Sheerin 1979). If the phylogeny outlined by Chaloner and Sheerin (1979) is correct, we have to assume that the capacity to synthesize dihydroflavonols perhaps arose more than once during this period. However, the progression of complexity in the structure of many classes of secondary compounds (Swain 1974a) suggests that the order of *appearance* (not phylogeny) of the three phyla is as given previously, and only one original Trimerophytalean ancestor acquired the ability to form aromadendrin.

But what is the point of the increase in the structural diversity of the flavonoids? We suggested previously that the role of flavonoids in the Characeae was solely to act as screens against the deleterious effects of UV light (Swain 1974a, 1978). Their ability to do this is because they have maximum light adsorption peaks at 250–260 nm and 330–340 nm; the first can thus protect DNA against thymidine dimerization, while the second reduces the effect of longer wave UV on nicotinamide adenine dinucleotides. (NAD). In spite of the fact that the UV flux is now highly attenuated by the ozone layer, there appears to be still a need for plants to reduce the possibilities of damage from this source. This could be the reason why all angiosperm chloroplasts so far examined contain relatively high concentrations of flavonoid compounds (McClure 1975). This feature is also interesting in view of the endosymbiant theory of the origin of eukaryotic chloroplasts from a cyanophyte prokaryote (Whatley, John, and Whatley 1979), for it suggests that modifications in the biochemistry of the organelle must have continued as plants evolved on land, and must have involved changes in nuclear DNA to control the biosynthesis and transport of chloroplast-specific flavonoids (McClure 1975). The further elaboration and selection of flavonoids was most probably mainly due to their efficacy as protective agents against herbivores and pathogens, although the increase in *ortho* or vicinal hydroxylation patterns would have conferred on the resulting compounds a more efficient antioxidant and metal chelating role which may have been important in reducing intracellular damage by superoxides (Swain 1974a).

The Importance of Flavonoids in Devonian Land Plants

Obviously, the ability of the simple flavone derivatives to act as UV screens, antioxidants, and metal chelators was instrumental in determining their original selection in the advanced algae, and continued to play an important contribution to the success of early land plants. As mentioned earlier, increases in hydroxylation in either the A or the B rings (e.g., 8-hydroxyluteotin [Fig. 4.14d]) undoubtedly added to their protective roles in these respects.

However, we can see that the production of other flavone-based derivatives (e.g. biflavones, *O*-glycosides, *O*-methyl compounds) in the Psilophytina and Lycophytina point to new and different roles in these phyla. Obviously, one can only speculate what these might have been. Undoubtedly, the success of the early land plyla must have attracted a variety of predators: herbivores (mainly arthropods, but also other primitive multicellular animals) (Kevan, Chaloner, and Savile 1974), fungal saprophytes (including some pathogens), and a vast number of prokaryotes and protists, all of which could exploit the nutrients produced by these plants, either living or dead (Swain 1978). We know that flavonoid compounds influence all these associations between equivalent phyla today (Friend and Threlfall 1976; Chapman and Bernays 1978; Swain 1978; Rosenthal and Janzen 1979). We may presume, therefore, that the flavonoids were similarly active in the earliest land plants. That is, the more complex *O*-glycosides, *O*-methyl ethers of the flavonoids were involved as deterrents to predators of one sort or another in the early Rhynales, Zosterophyllales, and Trimerophytales.

Undoubtedly, the most dramatic step in flavonoid biosynthesis occurred in the Sphenophytina; that is, their ability to produce 3-hydroxylation in the flavonoids and hence the 3,4-dihydroxyflavan moieties which are the backbone of the proanthocyanidin (condensed) tannins (Fig. 4.16). These phenolic polymers must be regarded as the most important all-around protective agents "invented" by plants against herbivores and pathogens. They have stood the test of time and are still of enormous importance (Swain 1979). Their action is relatively simple. Their multiple phenolic hydroxyls form a sufficient number of hydrogen bonds to other groups in a variety of biologically important polymers, especially proteins, to form cross-links and so greatly reduce the degradability of these substances by enzymes. Hence, they are rendered almost nonavailable nutritionally to herbivores or saprophytes.

These condensed tannins, along with related phenolics, are of great importance in protecting the heartwoods of modern tree species against attack by saprophytes of one sort or another (Hillis 1977). We can presume that they must have played a similar role in the more successful Devonian trees. It seems highly likely as mentioned earlier that the development of lignification necessary for the generation of arborescent forms preceded the ability of the species to produce tannins and related phenolic fungicides which could protect the inner highly lignified dead cells against degradation by predators. Thus, the giant tree-like lycopods (e.g., *Cyclostigma*) presumably lacked such protection and as a result succumbed to saprophytes in the early Carboniferous. On the other hand, equally large protogymnosperms (e.g., *Archaeopteris*) most probably possessed proanthocyanidins, and this was an important factor in their persistence. Besides protecting such phyla against saprophytes in the virtually dead heartwoods, the proanthocyanidins would of course be effective deterrents against pathogenic fungi, bacteria, and viruses, as well as insect and other herbivores in leaves, fruits, and flowers. The early Sphenophytina may have represented an intermediate stage since condensed tannins are not present in all modern species of *Equistum*. In other words, the tree-like forms of the Sphenopsida in the Carboniferous may have arisen from a tannin-free line and thus died out early. However, we feel that the success of arborescent forms of almost all phyla in the Carboniferous must in part be due to their possession of condensed tannins. Their demise was possibly a result of their form of reproduction which involved a tannin-free haploid thalloid form (as found in most modern ferns, Cooper-Driver 1980). This would then be subject to more extensive predation perhaps as the Permian reptiles evolved.

The production of other flavonoids by late Devonian plants, such as flavonol *O*-glycosides, perhaps reflects the importance of these compounds as feeding deterrents (Swain 1977). However, in view of the fact that some of these substances have been shown to induce mutations in bacteria (Hardi-gree and Epler 1978), their role in combating pathogens should not be overlooked (Cooper-Driver, Shintani, and Marchant 1980).

CONCLUSIONS

We have discussed the probable importance of three major biochemical features which apparently changed as plants came onto land and, in our opinion, determined their success in the Devonian. Undoubtedly there were a number of other biochemical changes which were of like significance. In general, however, we believe that there is at present insufficient evidence to evaluate their evolutionary and ecological influence. We would like to stress that no single group of compounds (or other characters) really determines the ability of a given phyla to overcome the multiplicity of new challenges posed by predators, pathogens, or the environment. Every ecological system since the dawn of life has been complex, and no organism could survive without having evolved a large number of chemical defenses. Nevertheless, because there is a continuity in the development of antidotes to such defenses, biochemical evolution has proceeded and has led to the present complexity of plant secondary products. Undoubtedly, this will continue as the present group of defenses becomes obsolete. We can postulate that if there are say 10,000 secondary compounds unique to the angiosperms (undoubtedly a gross underestimate), then new or modified biosynthetic pathways arise on average every 10,000 years or so. A faster rate than protein evolution (Ayala 1976)! So we can expect there will be equally dramatic chemical change in the next 50 million years as happened in the Devonian when plants and associated organisms conquered the land.

ACKNOWLEDGMENTS

We wish to thank K. Niklas for his invitation to write this chapter in honor of Harlan Banks. It is a pleasure to acknowledge that Harlan Banks's contributions first stimulated our interest in paleobotany. We also wish to thank numerous colleagues for discussions, especially F. Carpenter and M. Douglas on insect-plant coevolution, and N. Larsen for helping in the production of this work.

REFERENCES

Ainsworth, G. C., and F. Bisby. 1971. *Dictionary of the Fungi.* 6th ed. London: Commonwealth Mycological Institute.

Aw, S. E. 1977. *Chemical Evolution*. Singapore: University Education Press.Ayala, F. J. (ed.). 1976. *Molecular Evolution*. Sunderland, Mass.: Sinauer, pp. x–277.

Balch, W. E., G. E. Fox, L. J. Magrum, C. R. Woese, and R. S. Wolfe. 1979. Methanogens: re-evaluation of a unique biological group. *Microbiol. Rev.* 43:260–96.

Banks, H. P. 1979. Floral assemblage zones in Siluro-early Devonian floras. In *Biostratigraphy of Fossil Plants* (D. Dilcher and T. N. Taylor, eds.). Stroudsburg, Pa.: Dowden, Hutchinson & Ross.

Boulter, D., D. Peacock, A. Guise, J. T. Cleaves, and G. Estabrook. 1979. Relationships between partial amino acid sequences of plastocyanin from members of ten families of flowering plants. *Phytochemistry* 18:603–8.

Brock, T. D. 1979. *Biology of Microorganisms*. 3rd ed. Englewood Cliffs, N.J.: Prentice-Hall, pp. xiv–802.

Broda, E. 1975. *The Evolution of the Bioenergetic Processes*. Oxford: Pergamon Press.

Brooks, J., and G. Shaw. 1973. *Origin and Development of Living Systems*. London: Academic Press, pp. xi–412.

Campbell, S. 1979. Soil stabilization by a prokaryotic desert crust; implications for pre-Cambrian land biota. *Origin of Life* 9:335–45.

Carefoot, T. 1977. *Pacific Seashores*. Vancouver, British Columbia: Douglas.

Chaloner, W. G., and A. S. Sheerin. 1979. *Devonian Macrofloras. Special Papers in Palaeontology*, No. 23, London: Palaeontological Society, pp. 145–61.

Chapman, R. F., and E. A. Bernays (eds.). 1978. Insect and host plant. *Ent. Exp. & Appl.* 24:201–766.

Cloud, P. E. 1974. The evolution of ecosystems. *Amer. Sci.*. 62:54–56.

Cloudsley-Thompson, J. L. 1975. *Terrestrial Environments*. London: Croom & Helm.

Cooper-Driver, G. A. 1977. Chemical evidence for separating the Psilotaceae from the Filicales. *Science* 198:1260–1.

———. 1980. The role of flavonoids and related compounds in fern systematics. *Bull. Torrey Bot. Club* (in press).

Cooper-Driver, G. A., J. Shintani, and C. Marchant. 1980. Anti-microbial activity in ferns and its role in the enthnobotany of New Guinea (in preparation).

Dobzhansky, T., F. J. Ayala, G. L. Stebbins, and J. W. Valentine. 1977. *Evolution*. San Francisco: Freeman, pp. xi–572.

Faulkner, D. J., and W. H. Fenical (eds.). 1977. *Marine Natural Products Chemistry*. New York: Plenum.

Fox, S. W., and K. Dose. 1972. *Molecular Evolution and the Origin of Life*. San Francisco: Freeman.

Friend, J. 1979. Phenolic substances and plant disease. *Rec. Adv. Phytochem.* 12:557–88.

Friend, J., and D. R. Threlfall. 1976. *Biochemical Aspects of Plant-Parasite Relationships*. London: Academic Press.

Goodwin, T. W. 1979. Biosynthesis of terpenoids. *Ann. Rev. Plant Physiol.* 30:369–404.

Gray, T. R. G., and S. T. Williams. 1971. *Soil Microorganisms*. Edinburgh: Oliver and Boyd.

Hahlbrock, K., and H. Grisebach. 1979. Enzymic controls in the biosynthesis of lignin and flavonoids. *Ann. Rev. Plant Physiol.* 30:105–30.

Harborne, J. B. 1977. *Introduction to Ecological Biochemistry.* London: Academic Press, pp. ix–243.

———. 1978. The evolution of flavonoids in the flowering plants. *Pure Appl. Chem.* 39.

Harborne, J. B., T. J. Mabry, and H. Mabry. 1975. *The Flavonoids.* London: Chapman & Hall.

Hardigree, A. A., and J. L. Epler. 1978. Comparative mutagenesis of plant flavonoids in microbial systems. *Mut. Res.* 58:231–39.

Harold, F. M. 1977. Ion current and physiological function in microorganisms. *Ann. Rev. Microbiol.* 30:181–203.

Hillis, W. E. 1977. Secondary changes in wood. *Rec. Adv. Phytochem.* 11:247–310.

Jeuniaux, C. 1971. Biochemical aspects of regressive evolution in animals. In *Moleclular Evolution* (E. Schoffeniels, ed.). Vol. 2. Amsterdam: North-Holland, pp. 304–13.

Kevan, P. G., W. G. Chaloner, and D. B. O. Savile. 1974. Evolution of early land plants. *Palaeontology* 18:391–405.

Kolattukudy, P. E. 1977. Lipid polymers and associated phenols. *Rec. Adv. Phytochem.* 11:185–246.

———. 1980. Biopolyester membranes in plants; cutin and suberin. *Science* (in press).

Kukalova-Peck, J. 1978. Origin and evolution of insect wings. *J. Insect Morphol.* 156:53–126.

Lloyd, L. E., B. E. McDonald, and E. W. Crampton. 1978. *Fundamentals of Nutrition.* 2nd ed. San Francisco: Freeman.

Lovelock, J. E. 1979. *Gaia.* Fair Lawn, N.J.: Oxford University Press, pp. ix–157.

Mabry, T. J., and J. E. Gill. 1979. Sesquiterpene lactones and other terpenoids. In *Herbivores* (G. A. Rosenthal and D. H. Janzen, eds.). New York: Academic Press, pp. 502–38.

Mann, J. 1978. *Secondary Metabolism.* Oxford: Clarendon Press.

Margulis, L., D. Chase, and L. P. To. 1979. Possible evolutionary significance of spirochactes. *Proc. R. Soc. (Lond.)* B204:189–98.

Markham, K. R., and L. J. Porter. 1978. Chemical constituents of the bryophytes. *Prog. in Phytochem.* 5:181–272.

McCandless, E. L., and J. S. Craigie. 1979. Sulfated polysaccharides in red and brown algae. *Ann. Rev. Plant Physiol.* 30:27–40.

McClure, J. W. 1975. Physiology and functions of flavonoids. In *The Flavonoids* (J. B. Harborne, T. J. Mabry, and H. Mabry, eds.). London: Academic Press. pp. 970–1055.

McKerrow, W. S. (ed.). 1978. *The Ecology of Fossils.* Cambridge, Mass.: M.I.T. Press.

Metzler, D. E. 1977. *Biochemistry.* New York: Academic Press.

Meyers, F. H., E. Jawetz, and A. Goldfein. 1974. *Review of Medical Pharamacology.* 4th ed. Los Altos, California: Lange.

Muller-Schwarze, D. and M. M. Mozell. 1977. *Chemical Signals in Vertebrates.* New

York: Plenum.

Niklas, K. 1979. An assessment of chemical features for the classification of plant fossils. *Taxon.* 28:505-16.

———. 1980. Paleobiochemical techniques and their applications to paleobotany. *Prog. Phytochem.* 6:143-82.

Niklas, K. J., and P. G. Gensel. 1978. Chemotaxonomy of some paleozoic vascular plants, Part III. *Brittonia* 30:216.

Ohno, S. 1970. *Evolution by Gene Duplication.* New York: Springer.

Ourisson, G., M. Rohmer, and R. Anton. 1979. From terpenes to sterols: macroevolution to microevolution. *Rec. Adv. Phytochem.* 13:131-62.

Pelletier, S. W. 1970. *Chemistry of the Alkaloids.* New York: Van Nostrand.

Pickett-Heaps, J. D. 1975. *The Green Algae.* Sunderland, Mass.: Sinauer.

Preston, R. D. 1979. Polysaccharide conformation and cell wall function. *Ann. Rev. Plant Physiol.* 30:55-78.

Ragan, M. A., and D. J. Chapman. 1978. *A Biochemical Phylogeny of the Protists.* New York: Academic Press, pp. x-317.

Reimer, T. O., E. S. Barghoorn, and L. Margulis. 1979. Primary productivity in an early Archean microbial system. *Precamb. Res.* 9:93-104.

Rockstein, M. (ed.). 1978. *Biochemistry of Insects.* New York: Academic Press.

Rosenthal, G. A., and D. H. Janzen. 1979. *Herbivores: Their Interaction with Secondary Metabolites.* New York: Academic Press.

Runeckles, V. C., and T. J. Mabry. 1973. Terpenoids: structure, biogenesis and distribution. (Rec. Adv. Phytochem. 6.) New York: Academic Press.

Scheline, R. R. 1978. *Mammalian Metabolism of Plant Xenobiotics.* London: Academic Press.

Scheuer, P. 1973. *Chemistry of Marine Natural Products.* New York: Academic Press.

Slama, K. 1979. Insect hormones and antihormones in plants. In *Herbivores* (G. A. Rosenthal and D. H. Janzen, eds.). New York: Academic Press, pp. 683-704.

Stewart, K. D., and K. R. Mattox. 1975. Comparative cytology, evolution and classification of the green algae. *Bot. Rev.* 41:104-35.

Swain, T. 1974a. Biochemical evolution in plants In *Comparative Biochemistry* (M. Florkin and E. Stotz eds.). Amsterdam: Elsevier, pp. 125-302.

———. 1974b. Flavonoids as evolutionary markers in primitive tracheophytes. In *Chemistry in Botanical Classification* (G. Bendz and J. Santesson, eds.). Stockholm: Nobel Foundation, pp. 81-92.

———. 1977. Secondary compounds as protective agents. *Ann. Rev. Plant. Physiol.* 28:479-501.

———. 1978. Plant-animal co-evolution: A synoptic view of the Paleozoic and Mesozoic. In *Biochemical Aspects of Plant and Animal Co-evolution* (J. B. Harborne, ed.). London: Academic Press, pp. 1-19.

———. 1979. Tannins and lignins. In *Herbivores* (G. A. Rosenthal and D. H. Janzen, eds.). New York: Academic Press, pp. 657-81.

Trebst, A. 1974. Energy conservation in the photosynthetic electron transport of chloroplasts. *Ann. Rev. Plant Physiol.* 24:423-58.

Turner, W. B. 1971. *Fungal Metabolites.* New York: Academic Press.

Urquhart, D. M. 1961. *Cocoa*. 2nd ed. New York: Wiley.

Whatley, J., P. John, and F. R. Whatley. 1979. The establishment of mitochondria and chloroplasts. *Proc. R. Soc. (Lond.)* B204:165–87.

Van Valen, L. 1973. A new evolutionary law. *Evol. Theory* 1:1–30.

Woese, C. R., and G. E. Fox. 1977. The concept of cellular evolution. *J. Mol. Evol.* 10:1–6.

EVIDENCE FROM FINDINGS
OF MOLECULAR BIOLOGY WITH REGARD
TO THE RAPIDITY OF GENOMIC CHANGE:
IMPLICATIONS FOR SPECIES DURATIONS

Thomas J. M. Schopf

INTRODUCTION

> *It seemed unlikely that bacteria could be as smart as molecular biologists,*
> *but apparently they are.*
>
> A comment on the use of restriction enzymes as molecular scalpels
> (Roberts 1978).
>
> *I have tried to show that the deeper we penetrate as we study genetic*
> *exchange the more we discover a multitude of mechanisms either acting as*
> *promoters of exchange or acting to set limits to it, and some do both*
> (Arber 1979).

Work in molecular biology has revealed extraordinary new ways in which mutations occur (in the broad sense of the creation of new hereditary types), and has illustrated a wider range of application of older methods than was previously known. I discuss here split genes, gene duplication and pseudogenes, legitimate recombination and gene conversion, illegitimate recombination and transposable elements, and heterochromatin. Knowledge of the molecular aspects of these topics is largely a product of the 1970s. Taken in total, these methods provide several ways of rapidly creating new genotypes, and could resolve the problem of how to account for rapid adaptation and rapid speciation. Average species durations might be on the order of 10^4 to 10^5 years instead of the conventional paleontological 10^6 to 10^7 years. The probability of persistence of "primitive" types may be far lower than the probability of convergence.[1]

The traditional paleontological description of speciation is as an *event*, and species durations customarily are considered to be 10^6 to 10^7 years. Average species durations for invertebrates are often given as 5 to 15 m.y. (million years), and 11 m.y. is a recent estimate (Raup 1978). Vertebrate species durations are considered shorter, on the order of 1 m.y. (see Schopf, 1977a, p. 559). I prefer to consider speciation as a *process* (instead of as an event) and I would consider support for that point of view any evidence which might lower traditional species "durations" to 10^3 to 10^4 years.

What I wish to contrast is mutation on the one hand, homeostatic mechanisms on the other hand, and their dual effect on change in deoxyribonucleic acid (DNA). In the broad sense, "mutation" is, by definition, "the origin of new hereditary types," as the well-known population geneticists Bodmer and Cavalli-Sforze (1976, p. 139) have used the term. (For example, Ravin [1956] included transformation, and Magni and Sora [1969] specifically cited the insertions and deletions of normal recombination as part of what can be generally considered chromosomal "mutation.")

The traditional paleontological view is that most species have long periods of genomic stasis. This contrasts with the view that the amount of genomic change is large, and periods of genomic stasis are short, as judged over paleontological time scales.

The need to know the rate and mechanism for genomic change is most evident in evolutionary studies, as indicated in two practical paleobotanical examples:

1. Henry Andrews, one of the most distinguished living paleobotanists, commented in his "Studies" (1961) that *Psilotum*, "a living plant that presents some similarity with [Devonian] *Rhynia* . . . has been the subject of much discussion as to whether it is primitive or reduced." If one does *not* see any differences of importance between *Psilotum* and *Rhynia*, then the next question is, *should* one see differences? Knowledge of the molecular mechanisms of change provides a framework in which to understand whether the chances of observing change would be, say, of 1 in a hundred or 1 in a million. If the process of change of characters is a very slow one, then the persistence of "primitive" types is to be expected; alternatively, if the process of change is a very rapid one, then the persistence of "primitive" types becomes a real puzzle, and demands either an explanation in and of itself as a special macroevolutionary phenomenon, or it demands an explanation such as saying it is "reduced," that is, an example of convergence on a simple morphology. In other words, different views of microevolution carry with them different answers to major "macroevolutionary" questions.

2. On another page, Andrews (1961) remarked that "fragmentary remains of many strange plants that are not satisfactorily decipherable suggest unique groups about which we may one day know more." In order to account for the evolutionary brevity of these strange plants, one might

surmise at the simplest level, as has been done in studies of animals over the past century, that these strange organisms didn't have the capability for genetic change (for recent sxpositions of this view see Bretsky and Lorenz 1970 or Gaemers 1976). On the other hand, this "racial senescence" interpretation could not apply—or at least not apply with anywhere near the force it might otherwise—if it were clear that all organisms have multitudinous factors which maintain and promote genetic change. In such a case, the search for good and poor risks might transfer from the genetic properties to some other factor, such as the ecological conditions in the part of the world in which the plants lived.

These two paleobotanical examples of the need to know the true rate of genomic change are based on an *implied understanding* of the rate and mechanism of creating genetic change. However the need for this information is not limited to paleobiology. Even in such an abiological topic as correlating the relative age of sequences of rocks, assumptions are made about the extent of genetic similarity of the taxa used for correlation. In terms of biogeographical patterns, or even of the *description* of morphological change through time, studies include assumptions about the rate and amount of change *expected* over distances and through time. Thus it is extremely important to consider whether paleontological "species" have approximately the same meaning as neontological species.

The concern of paleontologists for understanding genetics is not new. The National Research Council, Committee on Common Problems of Genetics, Paleontology and Systematics, held a famous conference at Princeton in 1946, resulting in the book edited by Jepsen, Simpson, and Mayr, "Genetics, Paleontology and Evolution," published in 1949. One motivation for the conference was that 5 years earlier, Muller (1941) had summarized at the Cold Spring Harbor Symposium the then recent discovery of x-ray–induced genetic changes, which led him to seek to distinguish "minute rearrangements" from "mutations."

Despite the Princeton meeting, genetics was not often appreciated in paleontology. For example, as late as the 1955 Brookhaven Symposium on mutation, Muller (1956) wrote, "I am reminded here of the taunts long ago hurled at *Drosophila* workers by some paleontologists and other biologists in nongenetic fields. They stressed the pathological character of the mutants and their obvious unfitness to live. They used this unfitness as an argument against their being representatives of the changes out of which evolution was built, forgetting that it is just the sort of thing to be expected of the more conspicuous changes if their direction has been unplanned and if selection of mutations has played the guiding role in adaptation." Many paleontologists today do not yet appreciate Muller's point.

If genetics was of importance in understanding evolution in the 1940s, it can hardly be less important today. Consider the change since 1946. From the double helix in 1953, to recombinant DNA in 1973, to the present biochemical investigation of those "minute rearrangements," there is excellent reason for paleontologists to consider the paleontological implications of genetic information.[2] Indeed, in November 1980 the Field Museum sponsored a conference on macroevolution, the purpose of which was again to consider the interplay of genetics and paleontology (Schopf 1980c).

TRACKING THE ENVIRONMENT

Paleontologists have long contended that changes through time in both environments and biotas are correlated (as will be dealt with by others in this book). This is by definition *adaptation*, where "adaptation" is a purely descriptive term for a historical sequence of events to indicate that environmental change and organism change are seemingly related at some level. The purpose of this section is to indicate that organisms genotypically track the environment, that is, genotypically "adapt." At any given moment in time, this genetic change is adaptation *within* a species; seen through time, these genetic changes become the substance of transformation *between* species.

True genotypic changes in populations over ecologic time (seasons to years) in response to ecologic perturbation have been inferred in several investigations. These include reports of (1) esterase loci of olive fruit flies (*Dacus oleae*) in fields sprayed with organophosphate insecticides (Krimbas and Tsakas 1971); (2) nickel tolerance of fresh-water protozoans (*Tetrahymena sonneborni*) from streams in the vicinity of the mine tailings of Sudbury, Ontario (Nyberg and Bishop 1979; D. Nyberg, personal communication); (3) lead and/or zinc tolerance of various plants (*Anthoxanthum odoratum*, *Festuca ovina*, and *Agrostis canina*) growing on metal-rich soils adjacent to mines in North Wales, or beneath galvanized (zinc-coated) fences (Antonovics 1971); and (4) leucine amino peptidase and glutamate oxylate transaminase loci of bryozoans (*Schizoporella errata*) in warm shallow-water areas contrasted with populations in adjacent cooler waters of the open coast (Schopf 1977b). One may also cite the extreme reduction of eye size in cave fish in as few as 100 generations because of regulatory genes that affect relative growth rate (T. Poulson, personal communication), and the Pleistocene origin of freshwater fish (*Lucifuga spelacotes*) of marine ancestry which occur in grottos of the Bahamas (Campbell 1978). In these and in other better publicized cases (e.g., industrial melanism in the moth *Biston betularia* documented by Kettlewell [Ford 1979]), the genotypic adaptations indicate that in *ecologic time*, correlations between changes in species and in environment are not merely haphazard correlations between time series. The point I wish to emphasize is the *rapidity* with which genetic adaptations can and do occur.

Using adaptation as a descriptive term, there may be nothing special about the taxa in question except that they were in the right place at the right time and managed to survive. A statement like "present day bacteria possess enzymes which are the end products of millions of years of evolution" (Betz et al. 1974) becomes a truism, and may represent "survival of the fittest" only because those which survive are *defined* as being fit (discussed in detail by Schopf 1979).

The preceding paragraphs dealt with case histories which are most dramatically seen when species are chemically or physically challenged by sharp, human-caused perturbations of the environment. More "natural" causes of genetic adaptation are also numerous, but are not as readily discovered in the field. Similar adaptations can be evoked by changes in temperature, as has been observed in flowering plants (Fincham 1973, p. 196), and in *Drosophila* (Plough 1941). Fungi and a variety of plants, such as bracken fern, produce strong mutagens which induce bladder tumors in cows (reviewed by Nagao, Sugimura, and Matsushima 1978), and which presumably function as a chemical defense against predators. The technical ability to detect and assay for mutagens in natural populations, and the DNA repair systems to counteract the mutagen, are just now becoming available. The production of mutagens may be yet another way in which organisms are primed to respond genetically to their environment.

PROMOTION OF NEW HEREDITARY TYPES AND SPECIATION

I could summarize what follows by the statement that the 1981 view of mutation is that organisms are known now to have recognized that mutation is far too important to be left to nature; they have taken its control "into their own hands." I should add right away that this is not a restated version of vitalism.[3] Mutation is merely a series of molecular mechanisms for doing what we see on a macroscopic scale—that is, yet another go at adaptation.

I will focus on five aspects of mutation (recalling that I use the term mutation in the broad sense of the origin of new hereditary types). This subdivision is to some extent arbitrary. The historical accident of the way workers entered different aspects of the study of mutation has meant that similar phenomena have been attacked and described in different ways, and in different literature.[4]

Evolution is organismal change ("adaptation") set within the context of environmental change. Although there is probably a continuum of effects, it is useful to try to consider the relative level of different genetic ways by which adaptation occurs. The purpose of this section is to present information on the discoveries of the past decade which have led to the conclusion that the genome is in a constant state of turmoil (McClintock 1978, 1980, and earlier).

Split Genes

Prior to 1977, a "gene" consisted of continuously coding DNA, and this resulted in a strict colinearity between the DNA base sequence and the protein amino acid sequence. This colinearity still appears to be true for prokaryotes. However, in eukaryotes, the DNA of most genes is transcribed initially into a precursor messenger RNA (mRNA), and some segments of the precursor mRNA are then excised; thus, the mature mRNA is spliced together like parts along on assembly line (Crick 1979; Dugaiczyk, Woo and O'Malley 1979). Accordingly, many eukaryotic genes are composed of two parts: expressed DNA segments called exons and unexpressed DNA sequences called introns (or intervening sequences). (Although splicing may be a prerequisite for stable mRNA formation in most cases [Hamer and Leder 1979], in at least 1 species [*Drosophila melanogaster*] ribosomal RNA genes with intervening sequences are *not* expressed [Long and Dawid 1979].)

The ovalbumin gene has at least 7 exon fragments (Kourilsky and Chambon 1978; Lai et al. 1979) and the conalbumin gene (an egg white protein) has at least 17 exons, beautifully shown in mRNA-DNA heteroduplex electron microscope photographs (Cochet et al. 1979). One of the collagen genes has more than 50 exons (see Solomon 1980). In all cases, splicing of the precursor mRNA to mature RNA seems confined to the nucleus (Piper, Wardale, and Crew 1979). Gilbert (1978) projected that the amount of DNA in the unexpressed intron portions will be 5 to 10 times the amount in the expressed exon portions.

The immediate evolutionary question is what are the implications if genes come in parts. Both Doolittle (1978) and Darnell (1978) argued that split genes arose at an early stage in eukaryote evolution. Nuclear RNA splicing may be a process which becomes possible once a division into nuclear and cytoplasmic compartments was evolved (Crick 1979). Splicing could also be the molecular mechanism whereby genes which are duplicated (see section on gene duplication and pseudogenes) can be expressed without having any of the sequences adjacent to the duplication also being expressed (Sakano et al. 1979a). In any event, the possibility of internally altering the act of assembly has two clear implications for living species.

1. Proteins can, in principle, be assembled in combinatorial fashion by exon shuffling (Gilbert 1978, 1979; Stein et al. 1980). The middle exon in the globin gene codes for a heme binding group (Craik, Buchman and Beychok 1980) and has been suggested to have had its origin at another place in the genome (Gilbert 1979). Evolution of proteins by the modulus method, each

of whose parts was itself functional, also has been hypothesized to have arisen in families of genes coding for the recognition of membranes (Schilling et al. 1980), in the ovomucoid gene in bird egg whites (Stein et al. 1980), and in various gene segments of the immunoglobulin system (Sakano et al. 1979b; Weigert et al. 1980). Introns may also evolve as modules; the first completely sequenced yeast mitochondrial intron revealed striking terminal inverted repeats which "may suggest a mitochondrial transposable element" (Dujon 1980). This combinatorial mode of evolution, for both exons and introns, is in accord with the principle that where the evolution of proteins is concerned, the "ability to perform a new function is unlikely to be associated with great novelty of structure" (Watts and Watts 1968).

2. As Chambon remarked in his 1978 summary of the Cold Spring Harbor Symposium, "Obviously the transcribed intervening sequences are good candidates for . . . sites of regulation of eukaryotic gene expression" (p. 1212). Split genes present the possibility of what one might call trojan horse evolution in that the control of the expression of each gene partly resides within the gene itself rather than solely with regulatory loci located elsewhere in the genome. Mutations in the unexpressed introns of the mitochondrial gene for cytochrome b (with at least five exons) have pleiotropic effects on the expression of cytochrome oxidase (Church, Slonimski, and Gilbert 1979; Dujon 1979). A second example of developmental control over exon expression is the evolution of secreted proteins from membrane-bound proteins by the addition of polyadenylation sites from the intron adjacent to the expressed exon; thus two mRNAs can be produced from a single gene by alternative RNA processing pathways (Early et al. 1980). In general, the evolution of regulatory control is important because the evolution of new morphological patterns may be altered by regulatory processes (see, e.g., Wilson, Carlson, and White 1977, pp. 620–25; Lande 1980b).

Protein coding sequences (exons) appear to evolve slowly, and mainly by point mutations, as in genes for ovalbumin (Heilig et al. 1980), vitellogenin, the precursor of yolk protein (Wahli et al. 1980), β-globin (van Ooyen et al. 1979; Efstratiadis et al. 1980), and preproinsulin (Perler et al. 1980). In contrast, in these same four examples, the noncoding sequences (introns) have evolved much more rapidly, and by deletions and insertions of various sizes, even to the point of intron excision in preproinsulin (also see remarks below on transposable elements).

Gene Duplication and Pseudogenes

In 1935, Bridges wrote, "In my first report on duplications at the 1918 meetings of the A.A.A.S. I emphasized the point that the main interest in duplications lay in their offering a method for evolutionary increase in lengths of chromosomes with identical genes which could subsequently mutate separately and diversify their effects." Bridges's explanation (developed for the bar eye-shape locus in *Drosophila melanogaster* by Sturtevant [1925], and then presented to account for "pseudoallelism" by Lewis [1951]) has now become standard. As MacIntyre (1976, p. 451) put it, ". . . the prima facie reason why gene duplications are important in evolution appears to be that they provide genetic raw material for adaptation."

One specific way in which adaptation can occur, and for which clear documentation exists, is for gene duplication to vary gene dosage (Alt et al. 1978; Herman, Madl, and Kari 1979). In *Salmonella*, duplication frequency of the four rRNA (rrn) loci was 3×10^{-2} per chromosomal site for broth-grown cells. The richer the broth, the higher the rate of growth and the higher the rate of duplication. Anderson and Roth (1979) suggested that an increase in the *rrn* genes was adaptive because growth rate in rich medium was limited by the supply of ribosomes. In higher eukaryotes (mouse cells), the number of gene copies is also proportional to the challenge (genes for dihydrofolate reductase in medium with increasing amounts of methotrexate); and, as with the *Salmonella* work, the number of gene copies generally decreases when the challenge is removed (Schimke et al. 1978). In general, gene duplications "tend to be selected when the amount of substrate for the enzyme is abnormally low or when the population is presented with a novel and heretofore nonmetabilizable substrate" (MacIntyre, 1976, p. 454; see also Hegeman and Rosenberg 1970). Adaptations in local populations owing to gene duplication is one among many types of adaptation which, is not readily discernible in portions of the phenotype available to paleontologists.

Of particular interest in the context of this chapter is the case cited earlier (see section Tracking the Environment) of esterase duplication in olive fruit flies following insecticide application, and a more recent case of another example of esterase duplication in the peach-potato aphid *Myzus persicae* following insecticide application (Devonshire and Sawicki 1979). For these aphids (and other cases, Anderson and Roth, 1977, p. 483; Schimke et al. 1978; Alt et al. 1978), loss of the additional activity provided by the additional locus occurs when the environmental challenge is removed.

Gene duplication may also be responsible for the large number of segments in some split genes. For the conalbumin gene with 17 exons, the suggestion of Cochet et al. (1979) is that this represents a duplication of an ancestral gene which had 7 or 8 exons (the related but distinct ovalbumin gene has 8 exons and the ovomucoid gene has at least 7 exons).

In sum, there are a very large number of examples of gene duplication recorded in the literature, and the number is increasing annually (Ohno 1970; Doolittle 1979 [but literature coverage ceasing about 1973]; Zipkas and Riley 1975; MacIntrye 1976; Ferris and Whitt 1979; phage and bacterial duplications reviewed by Anderson and Roth 1977; Starlinger 1977a). Examples of gene duplication include genes for the immunoglobulins (Edelman and Gally 1967; Hood and Talmage 1970; Seidman et al. 1978; Sakano et al. 1979a), ovalbumin (Royal et al. 1979; Heilig et al. 1980), various hormones (Martial et al. 1979), fibrinogen (Doolittle et al. 1979), subunits of hemoglobin and other globins and of lactate dehydrogenase (Markert, Shaklee, and Whitt 1975), globins (Efstratiadis et al. 1980; Jeffreys et al. 1980), preproinsulin (Perler et al. 1980), vitellogenin (Wahli et al. 1980), ovomucoid (Stein et al. 1980), glutamate tRNA (Hosbach, Silberklang, and McCarthy, 1980), collagen (Solomon, 1980), and probably histones (Hereford et al. 1979); MacIntyre (1976) reviewed 17 well-studied systems of gene duplication. The documentation of gene duplication as an adaptational and evolutionary process is now widespread.

In addition to duplications for genes present in one or a few copies, duplications also occur in tandem-repeated genes of thousands to millions of copies. This is known in ribosomal genes for 5S, 18S and 28S RNA (see Swift 1974, p. 969; Tartoff 1975; Boncinelli and Furia 1979), and in genes for histones (Chernyshev et al. 1980).

When genes are duplicated there is no necessary reason why both copies will be maintained. Indeed DNA sequences of genes and adjacent regions have revealed nontranscribed *pseudogenes*—defined as "a region of DNA that displays significant homology to a functional gene but has mutations that prevent its expression" (Proudfoot 1980). These have now been described from genes for 5S RNA, globin, and others. Pseudogenes appear to be relics of a duplication from times past, and thus now are "relics of evolution" (Jacq, Miller, and Brownlee 1977; Fedoroff and Brown 1978; Lacy and Maniatis 1980; Proudfoot 1980). Since pseudogenes are no longer active, they accumulate replacement bases at a far higher rate than do active genes (Proudfoot and Maniatis 1980).

The major cytological mechanism envisaged by Sturtevant (1925), and nearly a half century later by Ohno (1970), to cause gene duplication was unequal crossing over between sister chromatids. Tartof (1974, 1975) and MacIntyre (1976) reviewed subsequent literature and again concluded that unequal crossing over in mitotically dividing cells was probably a prominent mechanism of causing gene duplication. Kurnit (1979) also emphasized mitotic crossing over in heterochromatic duplications. Sister chromatid exchange presumably occurs during DNA synthesis whereas meiotic recombination occurs after semiconservative DNA synthesis is complete (Latt and Schreck 1980), and thus these are different processes as also shown by genetic analysis (Gatti, Pimpinelli, and Baker 1980). Unequal meiotic recombination has been conclusively demonstrated in yeast tandem gene clusters for ribosomal RNA (Petes 1980).

There is increasing evidence at the molecular level that gene duplication is mediated by short sequences of bases located at the boundaries of genes (see Schopf 1980a). These sequences are like (and may be) satellite DNA sequences, and occur adjacent to genes, as for dihydrofolate reductase (Bostock and Clark 1980) or in the Balbiani rings of salivary glands of the midge *Chironomus* (Wobus et al. 1980); similarly, repeated individual globin genes were found to be flanked by inverted repeats of 140 to 400 bp and sets of repeated globin genes were flanked by inverted repeats of 1400 bp (Fritsch, Lawn, and Maniatis 1980). In this fashion, whole blocks of genes can evolve as a unit, a process termed "coincidental evolution" (Hood, Campbell, and Elgin 1975; Lauer, Shen, and Maniatis 1980), later modified to "concerted evolution" (Zimmer et al. 1980). In bacteria, DNA fragments with genes can circularize if they have redundant terminal sequences, and these fragments may then recombine with the bacterial chromosome (Schmid and Roth 1980); perhaps the "free rDNA copies" involved in the magnification of rDNA in *Drosophila* evolved in a similar fashion (Boncinelli and Furia 1979). These molecular mechanisms of gene duplication and gene amplification are like some of the mechanisms involving the movement of transposable elements (MacHattie and Jackowski 1977; Anderson and Roth 1977, p. 501; Meyer and Iida 1979; and see later section on transposable elements).

In summary, during the past five years gene duplication has been found by molecular biologists to be very widespread in both prokaryotes and eukaryotes. It is conceivable that different processes mediate the duplication of a gene from one to several copies, versus the production of some thousand or more copies. The historical evolutionary remnants of some gene duplication are seen in pseudogenes, which are not now transcribed but which have a base pair sequence very similar to an adjacent functional gene. The recognition of pseudogenes adjacent to genes gives the impression of a continuous, dynamic changing genome.

Legitimate Recombination and Gene Conversion

Legitimate (or general) recombination commonly results in a mismatch between adjacent base pairs in the region which is recombined (i.e., a heteroduplex is formed) (see Goodenough 1978 or Radding 1978). What gives evolutionary importance to this topic is the apparent high frequency with which novel strands can be generated by recombination, given the fact that recombination in general may speed the substitution of advantageous mutants (Felsenstein and Yokoyama 1976).

In bacteria, special genes have been found to control and promote recombination (designated *rec A, rec B*, and so on), and genes enhancing recombination also occur in phage (Miller, Mozola, and Friedman 1980) and in eukaryotes. For example, in the nematode *Caenorhabditis elegans* the mutant *rec-1* increases the recombination frequency for genes on 3 different chromosomes "at least three fold higher than that found in the wild type" (Rose and Baillie 1979). In general, recombination does not occur with an equal probability at all places along a chromosome, and there are "hot spots" for legitimate recombination near special sites known as Chi sites (Stahl 1979a, 1979b). Chi sites occur in phage, in bacteria, and in yeast (see Stahl et al. 1980). Legitimate recombination may be initiated at places with DNA sequences having inverted complementary repeats, which would serve as places of recognition between adjacent strands (Wagner and Radman 1975).

Once legitimate recombination has occurred, the resulting gene products (or other phenotypes) should appear in equal abundance if further replication is true. In fungi, where the eight products of DNA replication can be identified after meiosis and mitosis, the expected Mendelian ratio is 4:4 (the protocol is most clearly presented by Fogel et al. 1979). In fact, numerous cases of 6:2 or 2:6 have been scored. These non-Mendelian ratios result during strand replication from the conversion of one of the mismatched bases to the appropriate other base in a process known as mismatch repair (Wildenberg and Meselson 1975).

Gene conversion is the term applied to the formation of these instances of non-Mendelian ratios. The term "gene conversion" was first used by Winkler in 1930 (but in a different sense than used today [namely, he used it as an alternative to chromosome interchange; see Stern 1971, p. 24]). Gene conversion is a molecular response to maintain a stable DNA configuration, and thus has more in common with DNA repair than any other topic in this chapter. (The *rec A* protein, e.g., is involved both in recombination and in repairing mutagenic damage [Craig and Roberts 1980].)

Gene conversion can occur in mitosis or meiosis but, as with recombination in general, it is 1,000 to 10,000 times more frequent in meiosis (Fogel, Hurst, and Mortimer 1971). In a sample of 80 mutants in the fungi *Ascobolus immersus*, the frequency of gene conversion from gene to gene varied by a factor of 100 (Nicolas 1979). In the evolutionary context, the importance is that "gene conversion in hybrids occurs at frequencies orders of magnitude greater than spontaneous mutation of homozygotes" (Esposito and Esposito 1977, p. 65; further documentation provided by Watt 1972).

Indeed, in fungi, and possibly in all eukaryotes, recombination within a gene "is most often due to gene conversion rather than classical reciprocal recombination" (Esposito and Esposito 1977, p. 67). Gene conversion by itself can only convert a base to another preexisting base and does not result in new base substitutions in DNA. (For example, gene conversion is involved in determination of yeast mating type [Haber, Rogers, and McCusker 1980; Klar et al. 1980]). In two allele crosses, however, hybrid DNA may contain two mismatched base pairs at different places in the DNA within a single locus. Independent repair of mismatches can generate new recombinants and in this way "gene conversion could be important in generating new alleles" (Holliday et al. 1979).

Mitotic gene conversion is also a feasible mechanism whereby an individual heterozygous for a base pair mutation can in one stroke become homozygous. In homozygous condition, the mutation stands an enormously greater chance of spreading in the population as a whole. Some experimental evidence suggests that gene conversion has this evolutionary (adaptational) signficance (Esposito 1981).

In summary of legitimate recombination and gene conversion, new discoveries have emphasized that these processes occur at higher frequencies than was previously known, but more importantly that the formation of new genotypes is enhanced by specific molecular mechanisms.

Illegitimate Recombination and Transposable Elements

"Illegitimate recombination" is the joining of DNA segments which were not previously associated and which lack appreciable homologous nucleotide sequences (a nucleotide is a base and its attached sugar and phosphate groups, each gene consisting on the order of 3×10^3 nucleotide pairs) (Weisberg and Adhya 1977; Franklin 1978; Low and Porter 1978). Recombination genes (such as *rec A*) are not required for illegitimate recombination. Transposable elements, as will be discussed, can be responsible for illegitimate recombination. (Illegitimate recombination has also included what is called "site-specific recombination" because the recombination depends on the existence of *specific* sites in one or both DNA molecules.)

Forty years ago in premolecular biology days, McClintock (1941) described spontaneous aberrations in chromosome size and form in *Zea mays* as including "reciprocal translocations, inversions, deficiencies, ring-chromosomes, a duplication, fragments, and a secondary trisome." Moreover, in some cases the modifications occurred in only some tissues, and arose during the development of individual plants. Some features of De Vries' famous *Oenothera*, the evening primrose, also fit this pattern (Goldschmidt 1958). As late as 1974, these spontaneous aberrations were attributed to the action of a "controlling element" which became integrated into a gene, and then was excised from the gene and reintegrated on yet another chromosome (Fincham and Sastry 1974, p. 17).

This "controlling element" of maize is now considered to be a eukaryotic example of a class of specific DNA segments known as transposable elements (Calos and Miller 1980; Cohen and Shapiro 1980; Shapiro 1981; Scott et al. 1980; Bukhari, Shapiro, and Adhya 1977; McClintock 1978, 1980; and especially see Movable Genetic Elements, Cold Spring Harbor

Symposium, Vol. 45, 1981). Because transposable elements move to new sites on chromosomes, they have been loosely referred to as jumping genes.

In bacteria, where transposable elements are best characterized, they are described as "a new pathway for the evolution of prokaryotic genomes" because they "obviously offer selective advantages to organisms like bacteria which are subject to rapid change in environmental pressures" (Shapiro, Adhya, and Bukhari 1977). However, on some scale, for *every* organism, there is always some environmental phenomenon that can be said to cause a "rapid change in environmental pressure." Thus, the need to cope with a rapidly changing environment is not limited to bacteria, and neither are transposable elements.

Transposable elements mediate DNA rearrangements (Dawid and Botchan 1977; Campbell, Benedik, and Heffernan 1979; Gehring, in McKay 1979). These rearrangements include gene duplication (Rasmuson, Green, and Karlsson 1974; Anderson and Roth 1977, p. 501; Meyer and Iida 1979), and they have been implicated as the original mechanism involved in joining antibody genes (Sakano et al. 1979a), and in generating immunoglobulin gene diversity (Seidman, Max, and Leder 1979; Davis, Kim and Hood 1980). At least one transposable element (IS2) carries a promoter which is capable of turning on genes distal to it (Saedler 1977; Nisen and Shapiro 1979). In sum, many and perhaps all spontaneous mutations in bacteria result from transposable elements (Shapiro 1981; W. Arber personal communication) and the same is now being suggested for eukaryotes (see papers in Movable Genetic Elements, Cold Spring Harbor Symposium, Vol. 45, 1981).

Among eukaryotes other than maize, circumstantial evidence exists for insertion mutations in *Drosophila melanogaster* where mutable eye color genes revert at "inordinately" high frequencies of 10^{-3} to 10^{-4} per gamete (Green 1977, 1980; Rasmuson et al. 1980; see also Gehring, in McKay 1979). Male recombination (Mr) factors in *D. melanogaster* as well as hybrid dysgenesis (Sved 1976) are also attributed to movable genetic elements (Thompson and Woodruff 1980; Kidwell, Kidwell, and Sved 1977). (The relationship of transposable elements to middle repetitive DNA is considered in the following section on heterochromatin, but suffice it to say here that the two appear to be functionally identical (Dunsmuir et al. 1980), at least as far as certain repeated sequence families [copia, 412 and 297, see Rubin et al. 1980]). In yeast, site-specific transposable elements are strongly implicated in expression of the mating-type locus, where they function to ensure the existence of the genetic adaptability accorded to diploids (Hicks, Strathern, and Klar 1979; Klar 1980). Other yeast transposable elements are now being described (Greer and Fink 1979; Chaleff and Fink 1980; Roeder and Fink 1980), but their biologic function is not clear. Also, in yeast, transposable elements have been discovered in mitochondria (Dujon 1980). A developmental process similar to that which controls the alternate expression of the yeast mating-type locus may be responsible for alternate gene expression in flagellar antigens of the enteric bacterium *Salmonella* (Zieg et al. 1977). Covalently closed circular DNAs of Cyanobacteria (blue-green algae) also appear to have the general distribution of transposable elements (Lau, Sapienza, and Doolittle 1980). Most recently, retroviruses (i.e., the former RNA tumor viruses) are considered to have evolved from transposable elements (Temin 1980, and Movable Genetic Elements, Cold Spring Harbor Symposium, Vol. 45, 1981). These viruses have the same type of molecular organization as do transposable elements. "Defective" endogenous retroviruses occur in 20 to 50 copies in the mouse genome (Keshet et al. 1980). Thus movable genetic elements occur in many subdivisions of the biotic world, and in many fucntions in different taxa, and appear to strongly influence organism evolution.

The introduction of rapid methods to sequence DNA has allowed for understanding the mechanisms whereby transposable elements are transferred. Almost always, the sequences of base pairs at the ends of the transposable elements are inverted repeats (or inverted repeats at the end of direct repeats) (Calos and Miller 1980; Shapiro 1981). These inverted repeats presumably serve as recognition sites for proteins involved in transposition. In the transposable element Tn 3, the terminal inverted repeats are required for transposition (Heffron et al. 1979), which occurs at specific sites in the recipient genome (Tu and Cohen 1980). Other transposable elements are not as specific in their site of insertion, although "hot spots" for insertion commonly occur (reviewed in Calos and Miller 1980). Subsequent to selection of the site for transposition into the host chromosome, replication of the transposable element occurs (perhaps according to the model of Shapiro 1979; see also Cohen and Shapiro 1980). This mechanism can account for illegitimate, site-specific recombination, as occurs in bacteria (Ghosal and Saedler 1979) and in yeast (Gaillard, Strauss, and Bernardi 1980).

(1) From studies most extensively carried out in prokaryotes, three types of transposable elements are defined (Campbell et al. 1979); they form a transitional series, possibly all having descended from the same ancestor (Grinsted et al. 1980); also see chapter in Movable Genetic Elements, Cold Spring Harbor Symposium, Vol. 45, 1981).

Simple insertion sequences (IS elements) contain no known genes unrelated to insertion function and are generally shorter than 2 kilobases (kb). IS elements by themselves have no known phenotypic expression, but "insertion of an IS element into a gene abolishes the function of the gene and thus causes a mutation" (Starlinger 1977b, p. 25). The presence of an IS element in a locus is reported to stimulate the deletion of adjacent genetic material "by as much as a thousand-fold" over spontaneous background levels (Shapiro 1977). When IS elements are connected with other genes into larger units (see item 3), they are responsible for the transfer between bacteria of the *Escherichia coli* fertility factor F, and of antibiotic resistant plasmids to the bacterial chromosome.

(2) Transposons (Tn elements) often contain two copies of an IS element and are generally larger than 2 kb, and include additional genes related to functions other than insertion. Approximately 25 transposons are now known, and each of them has a specific phenotype, such as conferring antibiotic resistance. In considering transposons in his Nobel lecture, Arber (1979) wrote that "In principle, there is no limit set for genes to be picked up at one time or another on a transposable element, since the elements flanking a transposon can also transpose independently and thus by chance give rise to the formation of new transposons." This would allow for parallel evolution if the same gene were picked up by different flanking sequences (IS elements). This has occurred in Tn5, coding for Kanamycin resistance (Yamamoto and Yokoto 1980).

(3) Episomes are complex, self-replicating elements, often containing IS and Tn elements (for recent literature see Starlinger 1977a). Episomes have long been considered of importance in bacterial evolution in aiding bacterial adaptation (Campbell 1972). At least some episomes integrate at specific sites on the host chromosome by legitimate recombination (examples include bacteriophage λ [47,000 base pairs and 50 genes], and the F [fertility] plasmid of *E. coli*; see Radding [1978, p. 858]. Stahl [1979a], and Landy et al. [1979] for discussion of genes responsible for recombination). Lambda chiefly integrates at one chromosomal site, which has a 15 base pair homology with the attachment site. Some episomes integrate by illegitimate recombination (e.g., the bacteriophage *mu* [for mutation]. *Mu* is unique [to date] in that it seemingly is integrated at random into the host DNA.)

In summary of illegitimate recombination and transposable elements, their importance for evolution is that not only do they provide a mechanism for creating new hereditary types, but that this is done at a much higher frequency of occurrence than simple base substitutions of classical "mutation." The full impact of insertion elements on evolution is yet to be determined. In his Nobel address, Arber (1979, p. 364) wrote that "it remains largely unknown how many different IS elements are carried" even in the most commonly studied bacterial strain *E. coli* K12. In principle, and seemingly in practice, IS elements can mobilize any gene, or portion of a gene, and transfer it to somewhere else in the genome, thus causing insertions, deletions, rearrangements of regulatory and coding sequences, and causing duplications and amplification, with attendant implications for adaptation and evolution (Shapiro 1981).

Heterochromatin and Speciation

A chromosome consists of two types of material, which a half century ago Emil Heitz (1928; Passarge 1979) designated euchromatin ("true chromatin") and heterochromatin ("mixed chromatin"), according to whether the chromatin stained lightly (euchromatin) or heavily (heterochromatin) in karyotype preparations (chromatin being portions of the nucleus that stain with basic dyes [see Swift 1977]). Today, heterochromatin is typically characterized by the existence of very long sequences of DNA that are not (for the most part) translated into protein. This is in contrast to the situation in euchromatin, which consists of sequences of genes, significant portions of which are translated into proteins. Species with larger amounts of heterochromatin tend to have larger amounts of euchromatin (Rees and Narayan 1977), and longer chromosomes (Schmid 1980) than species with lesser amounts of heterochromatin. Different types of heterochromatin are distinguished according to its amount and placement along chromosomes, according to its time and extent of activity (Steinemann 1980), and according to the nature of its DNA. Several excellent reviews of heterochromatin and repetitive DNA have appeared, including those of Cooper 1959; Walker 1971a, 1971b; Bostock 1971; Yunis and Yasmineh 1971; Pardue 1975; Back 1976; Skinner 1977; Peacock et al. 1977; John and Miklos 1979; Miklos and John 1979; Brutlag 1980; Long and Dawid 1980).

In contrast to the previous sections—on split genes, gene duplication, legitimate recombination and gene conversion, and illegitimate recombination and transposable elements—the topic of heterochromatin includes a very large descriptive literature. The principal purpose of this literature has been to document the occurrences of heterochromatin in a wide variety of species. This documentation occurs in karyotypic analyses, and, for more than a decade now, in reports on density gradient centrifugation in CsCl solutions (Peacock et al. 1974), and on the extent and speed of reassociation of DNA at different temperatures (Britten and Kohne 1968; Wilson and Thomas 1974). The purpose of these two physical methods has been to determine the number and size of DNA sequences which comprise chromosomes in general. A 1971 review indicated the occurrence of repetitive DNA in more than 100 species of plants and animals, from *Euglena* to the binturong to humans (Bostock 1971), although there is a large variation in the amount of heterochromatin from species to species (Fox 1972).

Heterochromatin was discovered to constitute from less than 1 percent to more than 80 percent of the total DNA of various species. According to the nature of the heterochromatic DNA, heterochromatin consists of two general types: highly repetitive and intermediate repetitive. The highly repetitive DNA occurs in large blocks often adjacent to centromeres or at the ends of chromosomes, whereas the intermediate repetitive DNA is intercolated between genes along the chromosome. Typically, the highly repetitive DNA is characterized by thousands to millions of copies of a DNA sequence which itself is usually only 2 to 12 base pairs in length (often called simple sequence DNA, or satellite DNA, because it occurs in bands adjacent to or satellite to the main band of DNA in a CsCl density gradient centrifugation). As an example from plants, approximately 75 percent of wheat DNA consists of highly repeated sequences in heterochromatin (Bendich and McCarthy 1970; Flavell and Smith 1975; Peacock et al. 1978). Long strings of tandemly arranged, simple sequence DNA may be terminated with a segment with a different sequence, and this whole unit may then be repeated many times over, thus producing a two-tier pattern of tandem organization (Tartof 1975, p. 359; Bedbrook, O'Dell, and Flavell 1980; Dennis, Dunsmuir, and Peacock 1980). The length of repeat units of repetitive DNA appears to be modulated by chromosomal structure (owing to nucleosome spacing; Musich, Brown, and Maio 1980, and earlier).

The intermediate (or "middle") repetitive DNA typically consists of 20 to 50 different "families," each with several hundred copies of the same DNA sequence, which itself is on the order of a few or several hundred nucleotides long (Bouchard and Swift 1977). The repetitive DNA itself is transcribed (Varley, Macgregor, and Erba 1980), but is far too simple to code for any proteins (data summarized by Swift 1974), although some genes (specifically histone genes) are included in the heterochromatic region.

In the past few years, the DNA of these tandem repeats, and of other portions of heterochromatin, has been sequenced, and this has lent support to a major idea about the evolutionary significance of heterochromatin.[5] The idea is that a substantial fraction of intermediate repetitive DNA includes transposable elements. Specifically, several papers in the past 3 years have demonstrated that elements of repeated gene families of repetitive DNA occur in tens to hundreds of chromosomal positions, and in different places from one laboratory stock or natural population to the next in yeast (Cameron, Loh, and Davis 1979) and in *Drosophila* (Yoon and Richardson 1976a; Perlman, Phillips, and Bishop 1976; Finnegan et al. 1978; Potter et al. 1979; Wensink, Tabata, and Pachl 1979; Young 1979; Kidd and Glover 1980). Human karyotypic polymorphism also occurs at sites where satellite DNA is found (Ferguson-Smith 1973). And in some boid and colubrid snakes, larger chromosomes are inferred to have evolved from smaller chromosomes by the addition of heterochromatin (Mengden and Stock 1980). Presumably in yeast, *Drosopophila*, and *Homo sapiens*, the individual repetitive DNA element could function as a "plumbing connector," so to speak, providing the link that permits a gene duplication, chromosomal inversion, or deletion, crossing over, etc., and in these ways facilitate recombination (Bonner and Wu 1973). By this scenario, terminal sequences of transposable elements act as the recognition points for proteins which could move them to and from different chromosomal sites.

In *Drosophila*, Yoon and Richardson (1976b, 1978, p. 483) observed that "the first break of a chromosome associated with an inversion was accompanied by the occurrence of intercalary heterochromatin if there was none there previously." In many cases, chromosome breaks preferentially occur at the euchromatic-heterochromatic boundary (Gatti 1979). Lee (1975) presented additional evidence that repetitious DNA provides homologous regions for joining broken chromosomes. Most importantly, sister chromatid exchange is located at the junction between eucromatin and heterochromatin (Latt and Schreck 1980). Other case histories have been cited in which "developmental rates, mating behavior and viability all may be affected by a single change in the location of a block of heterochromatin" (see also Lucchesi and Suzuki 1968; Rees and Dale 1974; Bingham 1980).

If this molecular explanation for middle repetitive DNA is correct, it would account for the observation that the occurrence and amount of heterochromatin is highly correlated with the incidence of recombination *outside* of the heterochromatic region. This correlation between heterochromatin and extraheterochromatic recombination has been demonstrated both experimentally and in the field (extensively reviewed by John and Miklos 1979; Miklos and John 1979; Yamamoto and Miklos 1978; Miklos and Nankivell 1976; Rick 1971; Wolf and Wolf 1969; Becker 1969; Walen 1964).

There is one additional observation concerning heterochromatin that seems of prime evolutionary interest. That observation is that "no two species have yet been found that share all of their highly repetitive DNA fractions. The common finding is that extremely closely related species share some, but not all, of their satellite DNA" (Cseko et al. 1979, p. 478; similar observations have been made in many other taxa as reported by Holmquist 1975; King 1980; John and King 1980; Rice and Straus 1973; Mizuno and Macgregor 1974; Hennig, Hennig, and Stein 1970; Rimpau, Smith, and Flavell 1978). In one type of satellite DNA only 4 out of 101 *Drosophila* species had the same sequence, and in these 4 species the amounts differed greatly (Cseko et al. 1979).

In extreme cases, fixed differences in heterochromatin may be the only distinguishing chromosomal feature in Hawaiian *Drosophila* with otherwise identical chromosomal banding patterns. As White (1973, p. 198) put it, "The discovery that the satellite DNA's of closely related species may be very different forces us to the view that structural rearrangements involving duplications and deletions of this material must have occurred on a scale that has been quite unappreciated in the past." In fact, it has been noted that differences in heterochromatin content are easier to distinguish in some *Drosophila* than are the external morphological features (reviewed by John and Miklos 1979, p. 25; Holmquist 1975). In the kangaroo rat, *Dipodomys*, the amount of satellite DNA per species is correlated directly with the number of recognized subspecies (Mazrimas and Hatch 1972) It is also significant that the enormous differences in *amount* of simple sequence DNA between species could easily arise in fewer than 100 generations by nonhomologous crossing over (MacIntyre 1976, p. 448; Smith 1974, 1976; Southern 1975; see also section on gene duplication).

The small number of different sequences in satellite DNAs led to the "library" hypothesis by which the same DNAs were suggested to occur in a wide variety of species (Salser et al. 1976; Appels and Peacock 1978). Since the sequences generally are not long, there is a finite number of possible sequences. There are on the order of 10^6 living species and so by chance some species will share a sequence (tables of probabilities computed by Gall and Atherton 1974). (In a somewhat analogous fashion, many popular songs over a several-year period will tend to sound the same.) For satellite DNA this "chance" of cooccurrence is probably higher the more closely related are the species. As noted in the preceding paragraph, some sequences are the same in different *Drosophila* species. In addition, *Drosophila melanogaster* and its sibling *D. simulans* share at least 7 highly repeated DNAs (Peacock et al. 1978). Four species from the three major rodent suborders share one type of repeated sequence (Fry and Salser 1977). For this reason, Peacock et al. (1978) emphasized that the length of the tandem arrays of a repeat (rather than the nucleotide sequence itself) may be particularly variable in evolution. It does appear that heterochromatin is capable of very sudden amplification (Burns and Gerstel 1973). This would then be followed by chromosomal changes (as discussed in the broad survey of vertebrates by Fredga [1977], and in a very large invertebrate literature, much of it appearing in the journal *Chromosoma*, some reviewed by White [1973, 1978]).

By the general view considered in this paper, heterochromatin may serve as a major general influence on mediating eukaryotic, chromosomal, and genomic variability, and through that, to organismal adaptation. As such, variation in heterochromatin types and/or amount would be an early (the earliest?) genetic marker for adaptationally isolated populations.

Variation in heterochromatin seems to provide a clear causal explanation at the molecular level as to why incipient species and species groups can often be characterized by karyotypic changes (a very large number of data exist, including information on considerable geographical differentiation within a species; much information has been reviewed by White 1968, 1973, 1975, 1978; Shaw 1976; see also Wilson et al. 1975; Wilson 1975; Wilson, Carlson, and White 1977; Bush et al. 1977). Heterochromatin influences genomic variability and the arrangement of chromatin in the nucleus (Comings 1980). There is a reasonable (but controversial) literature that differing amounts of heterochromatin in different individuals is significant for (1) proper chromatin binding (Mayfield and Ellison 1975); (2) "strength" of centromere adherence at meiosis (Lindsley and Novitski 1958; (3) both normal chromosome pairing and ectopic or nonhomologous pairing (for example, Macgregor and Kezer 1971; Barr and Ellison 1972; Yoon 1980); and especially (4) general meiotic pairing (see, for example, White 1973, pp. 565, 775), and hence for the ease of sexual reproduction.

The role of heterochromatin in proper meiotic pairing was first indicated by Gershenson in 1933 in experiments with *Drosophila* using an X chromosome with a deficiency for part of its heterochromatin. Twenty years later, Sandler and Braver (1954) provided further evidence in *Drosophila* that the amount of disjunction (that is, the separation of chromosomes at mitosis and meiosis) is a function of the amount and distribution of heterochromatin. In particular, ". . . normal disjunction is dependent upon the pairing of heterochromatic regions." And some 20 years after that, Peacock, Miklos, and Goodchild (1975; Peacock 1965) attributed male nondisjunction to improper pairing during meiosis. Sperm dysfunction was attributed to the failure of normal meiotic pairing of the sex chromosomes (hence, leading to meiotic drive) (Peacock and Miklos 1973). And in an analysis of recombination, Hawley (1980) suggested yet again that "one function of constrictions, and thus of intercalary heterochromatin, is the establishment of proper chromosomal associations for meiotic recombination." Another observation in agreement with the idea that heterochromatin adjacent to the centromere is important in pairing is in the important phenomenon known as "affinity." In crosses of different subspecies and species of mice, centromeres of the same parental origins have an "affinity" for each other as though there is recognition of like and dislike centromeric regions (Mitchie 1953, 1956; Wallace 1953, 1958).

Notwithstanding the evidence implicating heterochromatin in pairing, there is no question but that heterochromatin is not *necessary* for pairing (John 1976). In laboratory experiments with specially constructed chromosomes which have the normal heterochromatin reduced or totally missing, chromosomes have been observed to pair quite well (John and Miklos 1979). Therefore, the presence of recognition sites carried by heterochromatin may in these instances be *sufficient* to aid in pairing, but is not a necessity.

Supernumerary heterochromatin occurs in separate long segments, especially in what are called B chromosomes (Hewitt 1973; Carlson 1978), perhaps most extensively studied in maize (Rhoades 1978). Data from several species (John and Miklos 1979, p. 58) supported the view that "the supernumerary heterochromatin is capable of generating an array of genotypes among the gametes different from that produced in individuals of the same population which lack such supernumerary systems." In corn, B chromosomes increase recombination rates in normal or A chromosomes, alter the timing of the mitotic cycle, and influence a system of unequal distribution of sister chromatids (or nondisjunction) in the pollen; this provides a method for varying A chromosome dosage (Carlson 1978). This B control of nondisjunction in laboratory material has allowed the placement of new mutations on specific chromosome arms, which requires only one generation of mating. The general consensus is that the occurrence of B chromosomes in the corn plant leads to novel genotypes, and similar results obtain for grasshoppers (Nomacho, Carballo, and Cabrero 1980). Altogether B's thus far have been described from several hundred insect species and from about one percent of the caryotypically studied mammalian species (Volobujev 1980), in addition to their extensive occurrence in plants. Thus, the existence of B's may be a significant factor in generating variability of evolutionary importance.

If meiotic pairing is important in reproduction, then the ease of developing reproductive isolation might be influenced considerably by the variation in the amount of heterochromatin over the range of a species, other things being equal. Yamamoto and Miklos (1978, p. 71) wrote that "There is likely to be *continuous* variation in the amount of satellite DNA between individuals of a species." Spatial variability exists in type and amount of heterochromatin over the geographic range of several species (reviewed for grasshoppers, humans, and other species by John and King 1977; Kurnit 1979; Craig-Holmes, Moore, and Shaw 1973; Angell and Jacobs 1975; Shaw and Knowles 1976; Shaw, Webb, and Wilkinson 1976; Hennig and Walker 1970; Forejt 1973; Hewitt 1972; Keyl 1965; Britten et al. 1979). In *Drosophila robusta* clines occur in geographic variation in recombination (Carson 1955), but it is not known how this compares with changes in heterochromatin (L. Throckmorton, personal communication).

The amount of heterochromatin also appreciably influences the length of time of the cell cycle (Sved and Verlin 1980; G. Dover, personal communication, 1980). Thus populational variation in amount of hetero-chromatin seemingly could form an incipient isolating mechanism both with regard to ease of pairing, and/or with regard to length of time of DNA synthesis of different chromosomal strands.

This view of speciation at a subkaryotypic level has developed essen-tially during the past decade. Where cytological evidence was available, it seemed the natural course of events that each species was karyotypically distinct from all others. So prevalent was this view that as recently as 1967 it was considered important enough to publish in the *Proceedings of the National Academy of Sciences* the conclusion that "it is possible for speciation and evolution to be based entirely on mutational changes occurring at the submicroscopic level. Chromosomal changes, when they occur interspecifically, appear to be incidental accompaniments of specia-tion" (Carson, Clayton, and Stalker 1967).

In summary of heterochromatin, it appears that (1) the amount and type of DNA in heterochromatin is involved in influencing genomic variabil-ity, especially through recombination, but also through many types of mutations; (2) the amount and type of DNA in heterochromatin may be related to the ease of meiotic pairing; (3) because of these two factors, individually or together, the amount and type of heterochromatin is a significant factor in adaptation and in the development of reproductive isolation as part of the speciation process; and (4) this may account for the observation that the type and amount of DNA in heterochromatin is a more sensitive indication of species formation than are chromosome karyotypes or external morphology; moreover (5) changes in the type and amount of heterochromatin are rapid in ecologic time, and likely instantaneous in geologic time; thus (6) speciation may be rapid in ecologic time, and instantaneous in geologic time.

On balance, for the reasons reviewed in the past several paragraphs, it seems reasonable for Brutlag et al. (1978, p. 1137) to have concluded that "variations in satellite DNA could lead to speciation" (as suggested previously in somewhat different ways by Yunis and Yasmineh 1971; Corneo 1976; Hatch et al. 1976; Fry and Salser 1977).

DELAYING OF NEW HEREDITARY TYPES

If the genome is in a "constant state of turmoil," what keeps it from being a "run-away" system? When does adaptation become injurious, and when is repair required? In terms of the preceding several pages, when do split genes become "too split"? When is gene duplication a liability? How often does gene conversion "convert" to the "wrong" gene? Can karyotypic and other chromosomal changes, which are mediated by transposable elements, be too extreme?

The only aspect of "repair" that has been studied in any detail is the repair of incorrect matching of bases. In *E. coli* K-12, 12 genes were known as of 1976 which cause 1 to 3 base pair changes at a frequency as much as 10^5 times greater than background (Cox 1976; Sevastopoulos and Glaser 1977; mechanism of gene action summarized by Radman et al. 1979). In molecular terms, mutation rates of base pairs are a trade-off between the rate of polymerization of nucleotides in DNA replication (Muzyczka, Poland, and Bessman 1972; Speyer, Karam, and Lenny 1966) and the accuracy of proofreading (Kornberg 1974, p. 89; Drake and Baltz 1976, p. 32). (Similarly, any other factor which distorts normal DNA replication, such as Mn^{2+} in place of Mg^{2+} [Kornberg 1974, p. 108] can change the mutation rate.) There are "a plethora of potential mispairs" as illustrated by Drake and Baltz (1976, p. 20).

What follows is a brief discussion of the two main types of systems concerned with base pair correction (although other types have been named [Lieberman 1976; Witkin 1975; Hanawalt 1975; and especially thoroughly considered by Kondo 1975]). The study of repair systems inevitably lags behind the study of mutational systems, since change has to be identified before one even knows that repair can begin. Knowledge of repair systems is further confused by the large number of ways in which it is studied—from cell cultures of different sorts, to phage and bacteria. An indication of this confusion is that of the 50 or so independent genes in *E. coli* K-12 which affect responses to DNA damage, several were described under more than one name (Hanawalt et al. 1979, Table 1).

One way in which DNA repair mechanisms seem to work is that recombination itself is a repair mechanism (Cox 1978; Howard-Flanders 1978). Another way that DNA "repair" occurs is by the expression of genes carried by plasmids, which have been taken up by the host (Hofemeister, Köhler, and Filippov 1979). Even mismatch repair (discussed later) is called upon for the "generation of diversity" (Seidman et al. 1978). To cite these three mechanisms as repair mechanisms is the same as saying that to create stability one uses mechanisms normally considered to lead to change, and refers back to the quotation by Arber (1979) with which this chapter began.

DNA Proofreading System

In bacteria and phage, a proofreading system acts on normal replication of DNA. This involves an enzyme which recognizes and corrects a non–base-paired terminus (Kornberg 1974, pp. 85, 87). When DNA is injured, either chemically or photochemically, the injured part can be excised, the gap filled by new DNA, and the pieces of DNA ligated. Special enzymes are either known or postulated to mediate these repair processes. It has been estimated that the proofreading system reduced errors in DNA replication to approximately 10^{-10} per base pair replication (Cox 1976, p. 150; Loeb et al. 1979).

In replication of DNA, eukaryotes are reported to be as error free as prokaryotes, even though eukaryotes (other than fungi) seem to lack the specific bacterial proofreading enzyme activity (Cox 1976, p. 150). Achievement of a low rate of error in DNA replication in eukaryotes is yet to be understood.

DNA Repair Systems

Two general systems (and many variants) are concerned with DNA repair once damage has occurred. Many aspects have been considered (see, e.g., Wolstenholme and O'Connor 1969; Beers, Herriott, and Tilghman 1972; Altmann 1972; Hanawalt and Setlow 1975; and Hanawalt, Friedberg, and Fox 1978). First, major DNA damage is caused by ultraviolet (UV) light; this source of energy "fuses" dimers between adjacent (instead of opposite) bases (Hanawalt 1975). The photoreactivation repair system for UV damage requires normal light for dimer splitting and is considered "the simplest and most general" (Kondo 1974) of any of the repair systems (Painter 1974; Lieberman 1976; Sutherland 1978). Photoreactivation is the direct reversal of the dimer configuration (Hanawalt et al. 1979, p. 784).

The presence of UV repair systems is sometimes cited (Kondo 1974) as being an evolutionary relic of a response to primitive atmospheres which presumably had a UV level much higher than the present day. Photoreactivation repair genes (e.g., the *phr* gene of the present-day *E. coli*) are considered to be the direct lineal descendent of its ancestor some 3.5 b. y. BP (billion years before the present). This evolutionary scenario seems most unlikely to me. For one thing, there is no positive evidence for it. Secondly, numerous experiments involving specific genes (see the section on Gene Duplication and Pseudogenes) or levels of genetic variability in the whole genome indicate a rather short "memory" for earlier, environmental conditions. Rather, I would imagine that the current existence of the *phr* gene is because it serves today to repair UV damage. The human hereditary disease xeroderma pigmentosum is, for example, induced by sunlight. For many species of aquatic organisms, tolerance to UV exposure and natural levels of exposure appear to be in close balance, as though in equilibrium (Calkins and Thordardottir 1980).

Second, other than photoreactivation, all other types of DNA repair are removals of lesions in DNA and thus fall under the general rubric of excision (or dark) repair (Hanawalt et al. 1979). Excision repair does not seem to be present in plants (Painter 1974). In principle, the mechanism of excision repair is quite simple. Damaged nucleotides are cut by an endonuclease which introduces a nick in the damaged DNA; the nucleotides are released by an exonuclease which cuts and releases the damaged segment (Waldstein 1978). A prominent cause of lesions requiring excision repair is heat. Heat is calculated to induce on the order of 100 base pair mismatches per diploid cell per day in the human genome (Drake and Baltz 1976). This is so significant that Drake and Baltz (1976, p. 25) consider that "efficient repair systems must exist to protect large genomes against heat mutagenesis." Most of the current study of DNA repair is of one or another variant of excision repair.

RATE OF MUTATION AND RATE OF GENOMIC CHANGE

The historical sense of "mutation rate" refers to base pair substitution. "Mutation rate" is given in many different units depending on the type of change one is considering (i.e., per cell, per gene, per gamete, per base pair, per cell division, per 1000 codons, per locus, per radiation unit [rad], and in paulings—per 10^9 amino acid sites per year—, etc.). When radiation-induced mutation rates are converted from per rad per locus to the amount of DNA per nucleus, the normalized mutation rates appear to be proportional to the total genome size (Abrahamson et al. 1973; Wolff et al. 1974).

A myriad of data exist on "mutation rate," but for present purposes six types of changes are mentioned: base substitutions, single loci, duplications, deletions, recombination, and quantitative morphologic characters.

1. Base substitutions per amino acid site per generation are 1 in 10^8 bases (Kimura and Ohta 1973). Neutral base substitutions per amino acid site per year are 1 in 10^9 bases (Kimura and Ohta 1973). However, considering all *tolerable* mutations (a much bigger class than the lethals), the base substitutions per site per generation is on the order of 1 in 10^4 genes (Ohno 1970, for larger genes specifying a polypeptide chain which contains many functionally less critical sites). The mutation rate of the immunoglobulin G molecule is about 10^{-5} per cell per cell cycle, which for a typical adult human amounts to about 200 mutant genes per day (Adetugbo, Milstein, and Secher 1977).

2. Mildly deleterious single locus mutations per generation in *Drosophila* are on the order of 1 in 6×10^5 loci (Simmons and Crow 1977) to 5×10^6 loci (Voelker, Schaffer and Mukai 1980) and lethal single locus mutations per generation are on the order of 1 in 10^6 loci (Simmons and Crow 1977; Lande 1980b). Sometimes these figures are also given as per chromosome if one has an estimate of the number of loci per chromosome.

3. Duplications per gene occur at a rate of 1 in 10^3 to 10^5 genes (Starlinger 1977a; Anderson and Roth 1977, p. 484), or at a rate of 1 in 10^5 to 10^8 cells (MacIntyre 1976). In *Salmonella*, the peak rate is cited as one duplication every 3×10^2 cells (Anderson and Roth 1979).

4. Deletions per cell in *E. coli* are on the order of 1 in 10^6 to 10^9 cells (Starlinger 1977a); deletions caused by insertion elements cover an enormous range, on the order of 1 in 10^3 to 10^8 cells (Reif and Saedler 1977; Arber 1979), and deletions caused by certain transposons under special conditions are on the order of 1 in 10 cells (MacHattie and Jackowski 1977).

5. Nonreciprocal intragenic recombination per locus is in the range of 10^{-4} to 10^{-5} (Watt 1972). The minimum estimate of the frequency of unequal crossovers at the rRNA tandem in *Drosophila* is estimated to be 2.8×10^{-4} changes per gamete per generation (Frankham, Briscoe, and Nurthen 1980).

6. For quantitative characters, Lande (1980b) cited the rate of mutation as 10^{-2} per gamete per character per generation, with abundant pleiotropy. The rate of reversion of stable mutants to wild type in *Drosophila melanogaster*, per gamete, is on the order of 1 in 10^5 to 10^6 gametes (Green 1977), whereas unstable mutants (possibly related to transposons) revert to wild type at a rate on the order of 1 in 10^3 to 10^4 gametes (Green 1977).

If mutation rates are as high as indicated, then, in classical terms, this imposes a large "genetic load" (Simmons and Crow 1977). The concept of genetic load has undergone an enormous change as well as the data on which it was originally based) (Knudson 1979). The traditional view, epitomized by Muller's term "load," connotes something to be avoided—as indeed was the motivation for the term in the case of changes brought about by radiation and other mutagens unleashed by human beings. However, the natural "load" (in the sense of natural genomic variability within a single population or species) appears to be so high that one has rather to figure out why this should be so. An answer is that heterozygosity passes from being a curse to providing a population "with the variation in individual Darwinian fitness that is needed in order that the population might cull itself under times of stress. Genetic load, then, is an essential component of adaptedness or of high population fitness where *persistence through time* (that is, *non-extinction*) is of utmost importance (Thoday 1953; Slobodkin 1968)" (Wallace 1977, emphasis his). In short, Wallace (1978) concluded that "a genetic load, rather than being a burden on a population, is essential for the persistence of the population through time in a variable environment," as emphasized in many places in the present chapter.

The rate of genomic change can be estimated by comparing the genetic differences between two species whose time of splitting is known. A meaningful comparison cannot be made on a locus by locus basis—there are both too many loci, and a good part of the genome does not consist of typical "loci." However, one can make a comparison for the different types of DNA—highly repetitive, moderately repetitive, and unique. The comparison for repetitive DNA can be made by measuring the degree of reassociation of DNA within each class, within and between species, using standard methods (Britten and Kohne 1968; Wilson and Thomas 1974; Salser 1978). The degree of reassociation is a function of the identity of the DNA being compared, as measured by the change in temperature necessary to permit reannealing. (However, valid comparisons between species are very sensitive to the length of time since divergence. For example, Appels and Peacock [1978] calculated expected degree of divergence between two *Drosophila* species [*D. simulans* and *D. melanogaster*] based on a time of divergence "approximately 10^6 years ago." The observed divergence was much greater than anticipated; therefore, selection was invoked by the authors to account for the difference. However, if one takes the observed difference and works the equation backward, one obtains a time of divergence for these two species of 4×10^5 years. It seems to me that the evidence for the ancestor of these species of *Drosophila* would not allow one to distinguish 4×10^5 from 10^6 years.)

There is to my knowledge no systematic study of the *rate* of genomic change involving several species whose lineages are clearly known. Apparently, the extent of similarity of highly repetitive DNA can vary markedly depending on the taxa being considered (e.g., order of magnitude differences comparing within rodents versus within primates; Rice 1972). The rate of addition of repeated DNA to the genome seems to amount in some cases "to several percent of the total DNA per million years" (Britten 1972). For highly repetitive DNA in rodents, Southern (1974) estimated the rate of change to be on the order of 1 percent of the bases per 10^6 years. The determination of genomic change for unique DNA has been made by comparing the percentage loci held in common, for a sampling of loci. Increasing species divergence reveals increasing genetic distance (see Ayala 1976).

Results of a decade ago indicated a "total mutation rate" for prokaryotes on the order of 0.2 percent per organism per replication (Drake 1970). A well-integrated study of the rate of total genomic change for eukaryotes is now technically feasible.

CAVEATS AND REASONABLE DOUBTS

How General Are These Mechanisms?

Most of the molecular genetics summarized thus far has been demonstrated to occur only in a few taxa, usually prokaryotes, or if in eukaryotes in yeast, or at the most also in *Drosophila* and maize. (And universality does not occur—heat shock genes of *Drosophila* as well as histone genes, for example, lack introns.) The relevance of these few organisms to the rest of the biotic world must be in some doubt, especially now that even the genetic code has been found to be nonconservative—that is, the same triplet of base pairs has been shown in two instances to code for different amino acids in mitochondrial DNA compared to nuclear DNA (UGA is used as a tryptophan codon and not as a termination codon, and AUA may code for methionine and not isoleucine [Barrell, Bankier, and Drouin 1979]). In setting aside the natural termination codon UGA, a "readthrough protein" is created, as in overlapping genes which occur in several phages (Shaw and Murialdo 1980). A readthrough protein has the same effect as does gene splicing in that two distinct coding regions are thus linked together (Geller and Rich 1980).

Is the Potential Realized?

It is not at all clear that all of the potential for change actually results in change. Even if the mechanisms outlined above do apply broadly in the biological world (and thus one is forbidden to make the claim that organisms do not have the capacity for change), it may be a considerable step to say then that the capacity for change also means that this capacity is used in the manner proposed. Nevertheless even though one may wonder how general these mechanisms are, I am in agreement with Allan Campbell (1979, p. 259) when he wrote, ". . . any event frequent enough to be observable in the laboratory probably happens in nature as well."

Paradox of Species Stability

Too rapid genomic change introduces the paradox of how to account for the seeming stability of species. The chief evidence for species stability is the fossil record (discussed later), and the reasonable geographical stability of abundant species of living organisms. One wonders, however, in the absence of a fossil record, but knowing the age of the earth, would anyone have guessed that the average duration of an invertebrate species is 11 m.y.?

In support of taking the fossil record seriously and literally, Starlinger (1977a) suggested that certain combinations of genes are much more stable than others, and instabilities may be quickly cast out. This is the view of "good mixing genes." In support of this general view of genomic stability is the apparent fact that some proteins have not changed appreciably for hundreds of millions of years (Wilson, Carlson, and White 1977), although recent data show that base changes in the "silent" third codon position are much more extensive than the amino acid sequence indicated. There could hardly be the concept of molecular clocks unless genomic stability was sufficiently conservative for many proteins to have changed at a recognizable rate. (Again, however, the rate of fixation of replacement substitutions is much more rapid in the third position than in the first two positions [Efstratiadis et al. 1980]). In addition, the band-for-band identity in chromosomes of several species of *Drosophila* argues for stability of at least those parts of the genome in those species.

Paradox of Taxonomic Equilibrium

If rates of speciation and species durations are as rapid as, say, 10^4 years, then, in the long run, so must be the average rates of extinction, or else one factor would soon overwhelm the other, as was pointed out to me by D. M. Raup. This suggests that pronounced negative feedback mechanisms must exist to control speciation and extinction. If so, these feedback mechanisms have not been clearly identified to work on that short a time scale.

In summary of caveats and reasonable doubts, there is plenty of evidence to suggest that if rates of speciation and species durations were as rapid as 10^4 years, then this presents its own series of problems.

WHAT ALL OF THIS MIGHT MEAN: A VIEW OF SPECIES DURATIONS

If rates of mutation and genetic adaptation can be rapid, then what lines of evidence support the view that this adaptation is translated into speciation? Let us first consider the level of whole biotas.

Enormous changes have occurred in the areal extent of both tropical rain forests and coral reefs during the past few thousand years, and changes in areal extent are correlated with changes in diversity. During the Pleistocene, tropical rain forests went from a third their present extent during the dry intervals to twice their present extent during wet periods (Shackleton 1977; see also Flenley 1979). Species diversity is certainly importantly and perhaps primarily a function of habitable area (Flessa and Sepkoski 1978; Connor and McCoy 1979). Because of this relationship, and because tropical rain forests are extraordinarily speciose, changes in areal coverage of tropical rain forests by a factor of 6 were probably accompanied by considerable speciation and extinction.

Similarly, the areal coverage of reefs (as well as their correlated diversity) has enormously expanded during the past 4,000 years when sea level has been at approximately its present position. There is a comparatively meager record of reefs from about 13,000 to 4,000 years ago when sea level rapidly rose from approximately 150 m below its present level. The modern expansion of reefs is *not* just the historical continuation of an older, equally diverse and equally expansive coral reef tract, but instead is the result of the present pause in the rise of sea level. Similar major environmental changes occur over time scales of hundreds to several thousands of years in river discharge (Riehl and Meitín 1979), submarine slumps (Woodcock 1979), and lakes, and these changes must also affect major biotas.

The common metaphor of tracking the environment is the adaptive landscape with static valleys and peaks, generally as seen looking out of the window of an airplane. I think this still-life image gives quite the wrong impression. Instead, I would imagine looking out of the window over the ocean—or Lake Michigan—and watching the intersecting wave trains that rise and fall over short time scales and short distances. The evidence cited previously (see section on Tracking the Environment) is consistent with the view that, from an organism's point of view, tracking the environment requires *constant* adjustment, flexibility, and adaptation.

I believe that the strongest evidence consistent with the view of constant genetic readjustment is that taxa in the deep sea, in as homogeneous and as uniform an environment as exists on earth, have just as high a level of heterozygosity as terrestrial forms (Gooch and Schopf 1973). Moreover, the deep sea has as high a level of species diversity (Sanders and Hessler 1969) and of complexity of morphologic specialization (Schopf 1973) as exists in any biota on earth. Thus these organisms did not "retire," or declare a moratorium on evolution, and in this "constant" environment achieve "genetic perfection" in a particular homozygous state. Rather, adaptation has continued, seemingly (to our eyes) independent of *major* environmental differences.

This high degree of variability in deep-sea species at the genetic level, and of species diversity at the external morphological level, only presents a problem in understanding adaptation if one has a world view that conceives of a "best" way to do things. Perhaps there is no "best" way. Perhaps the world (from an organism's point of view) is filled with many different vectors, along each of which there is an adaptational gradient. (Graphical analysis involving ergonomics shows that specialization will appear to be optimized along all environmental gradients that are sufficiently uniform that organisms can specialize upon them [Schopf 1972].) In the real world, both the vectors, and the gradients along each vector, are always changing. The remarks of geneticists predicated with statements like "In the absence of selection, that is, in a predictable environment" (Cox 1976, p. 152) give utterly the wrong impression of how the biotic world operates. (Parenthetically, the process of tracking the environment makes no statement about *which* taxa expand or contract; those processes may well be able to be described in stochastic terms in the sense that there is no *a priori* reason for expansion of some taxa relative to others. In retrospect, of course, the particular species which are present will *appear* to be there for deterministic reasons, but the inevitability of those being the species which survive is purely a *retrospective* judgment [discussed in detail by Schopf 1979].)

Thus, at the level of changing biotas, considerable speciation and extinction has most probably occurred over a few thousand years. This degree of change seems entirely consistent in terms of the known mechanisms for creating genomic differentiation.

Even though the reader may grant that many environments change rapidly, one could argue that the Pleistocene is unique. Thus the newly documented potential for genetic change is merely for the maintenance of typical "within species" variation. By this view, these adaptations are small-scale phenomena and the metaphor of intersecting wave trains on a body of water is simply "noise" in the signal (which might be the whole body of water itself). Populations might adapt to each little wave crest, but the species itself remains constant. Is this likely?

Dollo's law of the impossibility of returning exactly to the same set of characteristics (Gould 1970) applies to the genome as a whole. Changes in the genome, and attendant physiological and morphological features, may map out random walks through time. Owing to the fact that the habitat is forever changing, specialization is never "complete." Genome change is inevitable. There is no perfect mousetrap and it is an illusion to expect that one would have evolved. Stochastic disruption of habitats by variation in the physical, chemical and biological world (e.g., rainfall, runoff, food, temperature, etc., Schopf 1980b) guarantees that even for the species, the adaptive topography is more like a seascape with multiple intersecting, rising and falling wave trains than like a static mountain and valley landscape. Even if the physical or chemical world appears relatively uniform, the biotic component of the environment is always changing. Many genetic mechanisms (some of which are reviewed in this chapter) dictate rapid and continuous biochemical, physiological, and morphological adaptation to changing environments, and thus allow the capability of rapid and continuous speciation.

Lande (1980a) has analyzed the quantitative aspects of changes in morphologic traits during incipient speciation. He showed "that even completely isolated populations with effective sizes on the order of a hundred individuals can maintain enough genetic variability to undergo substantial and geologically rapid phenotypic evolution. . . . These processes occurring in small populations are below the spatial and temporal resolution of the fossil record of most organisms, but are too slow to be easily detected in living populations except by comparative methods." I would only add that since the microevolutionary process is continuous and recurring, as the environment continually changes, then prolonged periods of stasis (on the order of 11 m.y., the *average* duration of an invertebrate "species") are likely to be an illusion (Schopf and Dutton 1976, p. 263).

Even if one grants that (1) the environment rapidly shifts, and (2) genomic change proceeds along enough different vectors distributed among enough different planes through time so that populations that actually or potentially cannot interbreed are *likely* to develop over, say, 10^4 years, then what does one do with a fossil record that records an average species duration 10^6 to 10^7 years?

The crux of the matter may be the recognition of "species" over geologic time. One begins by inferring by analogy with morphologic degrees of difference between modern taxa when it is that reproductive isolation is likely to be found. It was Haldane's (1949, p. 406) assessment that ". . . it has taken about half a million years for a change [to occur which is] large enough for zoologists to give it a name with full certainty."

For at least four reasons, the geologic record per se may not be trustworthy in yielding a biologically meaningful number for rates of speciation or for species duration. These and other factors are discussed by Schopf (1981).

1. *Bias of recognizing short-lived species.* If species first include only a few individuals—whether arising sympatrically or allopatrically or by whatever chromosomal or other mechanism one wants to envisage—then the probability of extinction of those first few individuals must be considerably higher than the probability of their persistence. As a first approximation, it seems reasonable to assume some sort of exponential decay for the probability of extinction. If so, most species may not be recognized even by neontologists. And of those recognized by neontologists, most certainly would not be seen by paleontologists. Hence any "average" duration is significantly biased towards the record of longer-lived species. Figure 5.1 illustrates two views of possible frequency distribution of the duration of

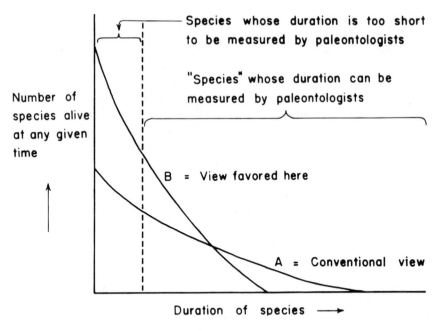

FIGURE 5.1. Two possible frequency distributions of duration of number of species alive at any given moment in time. One view (A) is the conventional view; the other view (B) is the one supported here. The conventional view has many more long-lived species, and many fewer short-lived species, than the view favored here.

species alive at any given moment. These views differ in recognizing different numbers of short-lived and long-lived species. Van Valen (1973; see also Raup 1975) suggested that for that part of the curve of Figure 5.1 which is seen by paleontologists, the rate of extinction is uniform for a given group in a particular adaptive zone.

2. *Bias of paleontologists having to recognize species in hard parts.* Species formation initially is not strongly reflected in external morphology, and it takes even longer before changes occur in the few hard parts which are customarily available to paleontologists. One need only think of all of the various species of invertebrates which lack hard parts, or of those like *Drosophila* with only a few, or even those like salamanders with several to realize that speciation and changes in hard parts are two quite distinct topics. Of course when a species has hard parts, like a clam, one uses these for convenience. But one need also recall the discovery of deep-sea bivalves whose complicated digestive tracts and other soft parts are quite distinctive (seen through semitransparent shells) but whose very simplified shells and hinge lines reveal little of phylogenetic significance (Allen and Sanders 1973, p. 304). For the bivalve specialist in particular, this makes one realize how

easily one was and can be misled by considering only hard parts—as a paleontologist must.

For taxonomists, the 1970s could be called the decade of sibling species (distinct species which are morphologically difficult for humans to distinguish though the animals themselves may have no difficulty). Owing to the widespread use of electrophoresis as a way to distinguish genomes, and of the wider application of karyotypic methods, nearly every major group of organisms has been discovered to have extensive complexes of sibling species. One example is the Hydrobiidae, a family of freshwater snails of world wide distribution. Assignment of the 11 genera and 92 species resisted correct assignment owing to "convergence in shell, radula, penis, and operculum" (Davis 1979). Only characters of the female reproductive system proved to be reliable and confirmed by electrophoretic analysis of various taxa (G. M. Davis, personal communication 1980). The same decoupling of morphological and biochemical changes was emphasized in a study of restriction enzyme fragments of DNA from two species of nematodes of the genus *Coenorhabditis* which are "morphologically indistinguishable" (Emmons, Klass, and Hirsh 1979; Hirsh et al. 1979). And in another recent study, this one on a fiddler crab, Salmon et al. (1979, p. 190) concluded that "available evidence suggests that speciation in most of the other North American fiddler crabs has proceeded without significant morphological divergence." What one finds at the molecular level may provide for rapid adaptation, and what one finds at the gross morphological level may be much more constrained by a variety of factors (e.g., structural design). Sibling species are of course invisible in most paleontological materials with the result that taxa separate in space and in time are simply lumped together.

Mayr (1963) noted that sibling species are rare in mammals, accounting for only approximately 5 percent of the species. Other groups of comparable diversity may have 20 percent of the species as sibling. If on the average 10 percent of any group consists of sibling species, and if such species are, as many have documented, on the order of 10^3 to 10^4 years old, and if there is a steady state in world diversity, then all of the world's fauna would turn over in only 10^4 to 10^5 years.

Perhaps the strongest question to ask is what proportion of random mutations affect hard parts versus soft parts. In a series of experiments at the Oak Ridge National Laboratory, mouse spermatogonia were exposed to gamma radiation and 2,646 male progeny then were scored for dominant mutation in skeletal features. The BEIR III Report (1980) records that "the effects found consisted mostly of the following changes: too few or too many bones, major changes in the shapes of bones . . . fusions of bones, and changes in the relative position of bones." The important point is not the extent of morphologic change in the skeletal system, but amount relative to the whole organism. By comparison with the total number of body systems, and recognizing the pleiotropic nature of dominant mutations, the conclusion was then reached that these skeletal mutations only represent "about 10% of total dominant mutations" (Selby 1979; BEIR III Report 1980, p. 509). A similar figure of 10 percent as an estimate of dominant skeletal mutations (compared with total dominant mutations) applies to humans (also in the BEIR III Report). If mutation is random with respect to skeletal and nonskeletal features, then, over geological time, taxa may record only about 10 percent of the total number of major mutations. Significant skeletal change may under-represent true taxonomic change by about a factor of 10, and this of course will make durations of species in the fossil record appear much longer than they really were.

3. *Bias of morphological complexity.* Many have pondered and remarked on how to compare organisms of different external morphological complexity (see Cherry, Case, and Wilson 1978; Schopf et al. 1975; Schopf 1979). Cell biologists have also considered this question. Miklos and John (1979, p. 269), for example, wrote: "At first sight it may seem that an organism as simple as a fly would be unlikely to reveal anything of relevance concerning the heterochromatin and satellite DNAs of man, primarily because of the extreme biological differences between them. It is worth emphasizing, therefore, that the level of morphological and physiological complexity of the phenotype bears no constant relationship to the level of biochemical complexity of the satellite DNAs within the chromosome."

A comparison of internal and external modification can also be made in bacteria. There certainly is no evidence that *E. coli* has a long fossil record—or any fossil record—although some rods and spheres are well preserved. However, the sophisticated chemotactic behavior and large number of chemotactic bacterial genes (Parkinson 1977) and other data in a recent book on mechanisms of bacterial adaptation (Sokatch and Ornston 1979) hardly suggest that bacteria are simple. A lot of changes occur inside rods and spheres.

There are strikingly different rates of change in gross morphological features (recall the paleontological dictum that "only complicated organisms evolve" because "uncomplicated" organisms do not have enough features for one to see any change). So too there are vastly different rates of change in protein evolution. Rates of amino acid substitution in the heme pocket are 3 to 10 times slower than on the outside of the heme molecule (Kimura and Ohta 1973), and there is a 100-fold difference in rates of evolution among proteins in general (Wilson, Carlson, and White 1977, p. 609). The rate of change of the mitochondrial genome exceeds that of the single copy fraction of the nuclear genome by approximately "a factor of ten" (Brown, George, and Wilson 1979; Brown and Goodman 1979). As Wilson, Carlson, and White (1977, p. 616) emphatically state, ". . . we must face the fact that sequence evolution and phenotypic evolution can proceed at independent rates." I would add, in neither the case of morphology nor of proteins does the rate of change have any necessary connection with the rate of change of a third factor, namely, reproductive isolation and speciation. These three different levels and types of organization have often *appeared* to be related, since changes in each of them can be *correlated* with time.

In sum, as has been known for many years (but not emphasized), adaptational change often, even usually, is not discernible in the part of the phenotype available to a paleontologist. Only a small amount of the total genotype has an external expression, and an even smaller part of that genotype is reflected in the very small part of the organism actually preserved as a fossil. Indeed, the term "trace fossil," restricted in paleontological literature for tracks and trails, is a misnomer since *all* fossils are trace fossils.

4. *Bias of methods to estimate durations of taxa.* One might infer from an "average duration" of 11 m.y. that certain morphological forms in fact persist uniformly through deposits for 11 m.y. In fact, most species appear to be known only from one geographical region and one series of outcrops; on that basis, the species typically is assigned to a particular geological stage. In tabulations, the duration of the species is then given as the length of the stage; since, on the average, the duration of a geological stage is on the order of 10 m.y., it is no accident the average duration of a species comes out to be near to 10 m.y. The fact that durations of species are given in terms of stage lengths has been shown to influence strongly the shape of survivorship curves based on "species durations" (Sepkoski 1975).

Even "rapid" rates of speciation in paleozoological terms are likely to be biased toward the slow side. Consider the case of "best possible" resolution of speciation. In deep-sea sediments, rates of sedimentation are on the order of a cm/10^3 years. Bioturbation, however, mixes layers, perhaps to 10 cm, and thus reduces resolution to 10^4 years. Over time spans of 10^4 years, erosion, mixing caused by slumps (turbidites), and changing ocean currents occur, so that resolution of discrete events is further reduced to $\simeq 10^5$ years. The most rapid rate of species evolution observed in morphological types is from oceanic plankton, and this rate is on the order of 2 or 3 × 10^5 years. So-called continuous geological sections are just "relatively continuous." At the November, 1979 Paleontological Society meeting, for example, a speaker referred to a Tertiary section as continuous—and by that she then said she meant that the biggest gap in the record was no more than 5 or 6 million years. The record of continuous sedimentation is even poorer in shallow water sediments than it is in deep-sea sediments.

At present the most widely cited general estimate of species durations in invertebrates is from Raup (1978). This figure of mean 11.1 m.y. and median of 7.7 m.y. is a backward calculation from data on generic durations, as derived from the "cohort method." The value of the cohort method for genera is that there are a lot of genera that could be used (12,000); the difficulty is that the first census point is after 90 percent of each cohort is no longer existing. This is not a direct measure of generic survivorship, let alone species survivorship. Other difficulties arise with direct methods of calculating species survivorship.

One might argue that genetic changes occur in a lineage through time, and thus the main impact of the views presented here is on the "arbitrary" phyletic subdivision of a gradual transitional lineage (i.e., anagenesis). In fact, evidence for rapid genomic change also implies that phyletic splitting (i.e., cladogenesis) often should occur—that is, lineages need be "separated" only for short periods of time (a few thousand years) in order to achieve reproductive isolation (see, for example, the discussion of speciation in sea stars and other marine invertebrates in the Cape Cod region in Schopf and Murphy [1973]). Thus, both phyletic transformation *and* phyletic splitting may occur far more often than has been generally recognized.

Indeed, the genetic changes that occur between two or more dividing *species* reveal a pattern of continuously diverging genomes. The evidence for this statement is based on percentages of alleles held in common by species in different stages of evolution in both plants (Gottlieb 1976) and animals (Avise 1976) and percentage similarity of repetitive sequences of DNA (Mizuno and Macgregor 1974, p. 292). In both the single copy DNA and the repetitive DNA, genomes of species diverge gradually from each other, but seemingly over a short time scale.

The process of speciation may be instantaneous geologically. If so, and if speciation is a *continuous* process, then geologic recognition of species *durations* may be chiefly controlled by geological rather than biological events. A question such as the relative importance of species multiplication *versus* species transition within a single lineage (the so-called punctuated equilibria versus phyletic gradualism, Gould and Eldredge 1977) cannot, I believe, be resolved in the fossil record. Studies of fossil lineages from that point of view may say more about patterns of sedimentation than about any biological process.

SUMMARY

Speciation as a process may be far faster than is normally acknowledged. Speciation as an event may be so instantaneous geologically that many such events might well occur within the best possible resolution of the fossil record. Both the genotypic tracking of the environment and the origin of reproductive isolation occur without any significant change in structural design in hard parts. These ideas may be much more acceptable to paleobotanists, who follow the views of Levin (1979) on the plasticity of plant species, than to many zoologists. However, several examples occur in marine invertebrates where species seem to have evolved in approximately 10^4 years (Schopf and Murphy 1973). I am not alone in considering that these discoveries of the past decade in molecular biology lead to the view that there has been unprecedented genomic change over short intervals of time (Reanney 1978, p. 2). Kondo (1977) has even contended that these mechanisms may provide the genetic basis for the driving force in a Goldschmidtian view (1952) of macroevolution.

Recall the Andrews (1961) quotation on comparison of modern *Psilotum* and Devonian *Rhynia*. If rates of genomic change are anywhere near as high as I have suggested, I think it is most unlikely that *Psilotum* is primitive in anything like the sense of having retained these characters for 300 million years.

This recalls the popular notion of a "living fossil" in the sense of an organism that "has not changed in over 200 million years" (a typical caption to a picture of the horseshoe crab, *Limulus polyphemus*, this time in the 1979 Earthwatch catalog). In fact there is not a single fossil specimen of the modern horseshoe crab *Limulus polyphemus* despite millions of live specimens; the family to which it is assigned only extends back into the Miocene [Størmer 1955]. Remarks such as *Limulus polyphemus* having an "immense antiquity," and "a half billion years of evolution" [Goldberg et al. 1975] are totally incorrect (except in the trivial sense that every species lineage has an immense antiquity.)

With regard to the evolutionary significance of the "strange plants" also discussed by Andrews (1961), the new genetic information lends support to their being viewed chiefly as random forays into the realm of morphological possibilities. Their lack of persistence was not for lack of innate capability for adaptation—or at least there is no evidence for that.

Let us again refer back to 1941 when Demerec, the director of the Cold Spring Harbor Laboratory, was referring to the discovery of X-ray–induced mutability, and wrote, "The evidence has accumulated indicating that changes in genes occur with an appreciably higher frequency than it had earlier been assumed; moreover it has been found that this frequency may be different in different genes, and that it may be affected by various hereditary factors." How much data on the origin of new hereditary types have accumulated since then! Many more mechanisms of change have been found, and this has evolutionary significance. We are closer than was Demerec but do not yet have an unbiased sampling of change of the entire genome—an unbiased sampling of adaptive capability, so to speak. There is a very great need for putting together all of the different mechanisms and estimating the rate of genomic change for individuals of natural populations.

The basic point I have tried to make is that the origin of new hereditary types is far from being a passive response to external ecological factors. A typical geological argument about mutation is that, as a highly regarded petrologist at Chicago recently put it to me, chlorine released by Mt. St. Helens rises to deplete the ozone layer which thus unleashes UV radiation, and this is hypothesized to cause a spate of mutation. In light of the several mechanisms whereby mutation already is known to arise naturally, sometimes from genes specifically for the purpose of *causing* mutation (in the broad sense), one is led to believe that organisms have taken the introduction of new hereditary types "into their own hands." In one sense, mutation was much too important to be left to chance. I am reminded of the quote with which I began: "It seemed unlikely that bacteria could be as smart as molecular biologists, but apparently they are" (Roberts, 1978). In fact, bacteria got there first.

NOTES

1. This chapter makes good my own commitment to a topic which I have been concerned about for more than a decade (chiefly in work at Woods Hole), and concerning which I wrote some 4 years ago, that "the results of work in molecular evolution should provide a strong indication of the extent to which the palaeontologists' morphological species in fact represents a good approximation of changes in the underlying genome. This has vitally important consequences for the model of speciation which one brings to the fossil record" (Schopf 1977a, p. 561).

2. The greatest initial difficulty for a paleontologist [trying] to appreciate this work is likely to be the terminology, much of which can be overcome with a reasonable specialized dictionary (e.g., Rieger, Michaelis, and Green 1976), or a modern genetics text (e.g., Goodenough 1978).

3. The essence of *vitalism* is an independent "force" or influence which is not mechanistic, and which cannot be reduced to simpler terms, and which is displayed in the life and evolution of organisms.

4. For example, reports on recombination are published distinct from the literature on the morphology of chromosomes, and this topic in turn forms a literature which is separate from that on the occurrence of transposable elements. Partly for these reasons of shifting emphasis, some topics which would have been covered 5 years ago are now superseded. For example, in *Drosophila*, situations which 8 years ago were (Green 1973) (or would have been) ascribed to independent "mutator genes" are now considered examples of insertion elements (Rasmuson, Green, and Karlsson 1974; Green 1977, 1978; Bregliano et al. 1980). Not covered here is the role of viruses in general, and retroviruses in particular, as a mechanism to allow for "rapid mutation and rearrangement of genes and for transfer of genetic information between cells," what Bishop (1978, p. 79) called the " 'molecular paleontology' of endogenous viral genes."

5. The principal purpose of this discussion is to consider the possible evolutionary significance of work in heterochromatin. Accordingly, an attempt has been made to tie together various observations instead of providing a listing of disparate data.

ACKNOWLEDGMENTS

This chapter was written to honor Harlan Banks on the occasion of his retirement from regular teaching at Cornell University; and most particularly to acknowledge the esteem and long-time friendship which his friend and fellow paleobotanist (and my father), James M. Schopf (1911–78), felt for him, and to record appreciation for the help which he has given my brother, J. William Schopf, also a paleobotanist. For very helpful reviews of an earlier draft of this work, I thank those whose special knowledge is in genetics and molecular biology, J. Spofford, B. McClintock, H. Swift, N. Cozzarelli, T. Petes, and R. Haselkorn, and in evolutionary biology and paleontology, D. Raup, and R. Lande.

REFERENCES

Abrahamson, S., M. A., Bender, A. D. Conger, and S. Wolff. 1973. Uniformity of radiation-induced mutation rates among different species. *Nature* 245:460–62.

Adetugbo, K., C. Milstein, and D. S. Secher. 1977. Molecular analysis of spontaneous somatic mutants. *Nature* 265:299–304.

Allen, J. A., and H. L. Sanders. 1973. Studies on deep-sea protobranchia (Bivalvia); the families Siliculidae and Lametilidae. *Mus. Comp. Zool. Bull.* 145:263–310.

Alt, F. W., R. E., Kellems, J. R. Bertino, and R. T. Schimke. 1978. Selective multiplication of dihydrofolate reductase genes in methotrexate-resistant variants of cultured murine cells. *J. Biol. Chem.* 253:1357–70.

Altmann, H. (ed.). 1972. DNA-Repair Mechanisms. *Symposia Medica Hoechst.* Stuttgart: F. K. Schattauer Verlag.

Anderson, R. P., and J. R. Roth. 1977. Tandem genetic duplications in phage and bacteria. *Ann. Rev. Microbiol.* 31:473–505.

———. 1979. Gene duplication in bacteria: alteration of gene dosage by sister-chromosome exchanges. *Cold Spring Harbor Symposia on Quantitative Biology* 43:1083–87.

Andrews, H. N., Jr. 1961. *Studies in Paleobotany.* New York: Wiley.

Angell, R. R., and P. A. Jacobs. 1975. Lateral asymmetry in human constitutive heterochromatin. *Chromosoma* 51:301–10.

Antonovics, J. 1971. The effects of a heterogeneous environment on the genetics of natural populations. *Am. Sci.* 59:593–99.

Appels, R., and W. J. Peacock. 1978. The arrangement and evolution of highly repeated (satellite) DNA sequences with special reference to *Drosophila. Inter. Rev. Cytol.* (Suppl.) 8:69–126.

Arber, W. 1979. Promotion and limitation of genetic exchange. *Science* 205:361–65.

Avise, J. C. 1976. Genetic differentiation during speciation. In *Molecular Evolution* (F. J. Ayala, ed.). Sunderland, Mass.: Sinauer, pp. 106–22.

Ayala, F. J. (ed.). 1976. *Molecular Evolution.* Sunderland, Mass.: Sinauer.

Back, F. 1976. The variable condition of euchromatin and heterochromatin. *Inter. Rev. Cytol.* 45:25–64.

Barr, H. J., and J. R. Ellison. 1972. Ectopic pairing of chromosome regions containing chemically similar DNA. *Chromosoma* 39:53–61.

Barrell, B. G., A. T. Bankier, and J. Drouin. 1979. A different genetic code in human mitochondria. *Nature* 282:189–94.

Becker, H. J. 1969. The influence of heterochromatin, inversion-heterozygosity and somatic pairing on X-ray induced mitotic recombination in *Drosophila melanogaster*. *Mol. Gen. Genet.* 105:203–18.

Bedbrook, J. R., M. O'Dell, and R. B. Flavell. 1980. Amplification of rearranged repeated DNA sequences in cereal plants. *Nature* 288:134–137.

Beers, R. F., Jr., R. M. Herriott, and R. C. Tilghman. 1972. Molecular and cellular repair processes. *The Johns Hopkins Med. J.* Suppl. No. 1.

BEIR III Report. 1980. The effects on populations of exposure to low levels of ionizing radiation. Report of the Advisory Committee on the Biological Effects of Ionizing Radiations. Washington, D.C.: National Academy Press (See Chapter on Genetic Effects, pp. 71–134).

Bendich, A. J., and B. J. McCarthy. 1970. DNA comparisons among barley, oats, rye, and wheat. *Genetics* 65:545–65.

Betz, J. L., P. R. Brown, M. J., Smyth, and P. H. Clarke. 1974. Evolution in action. *Nature* 247:261–64.

Bingham, P. M. 1980. The regulation of white locus expression: a dominant mutant allele at the white locus of *Drosophila melanogaster*. *Genetics* 95:341–353.

Bishop, J. M. 1978. Retroviruses. *Ann. Rev. Biochem.* 47:35–88.

Bodmer, W. F., and L. L. Cavalli-Sforza. 1976. *Genetics, Evolution and Man*. San Francisco: Freeman.

Boncinelli, E., and M. Furia. 1979. Patterns of reversion to *bobbed* condition of magnified *bobbed* loci in *D. melanogaster*. *Mol. Gen. Genet.* 176:81–85.

Bonner, J., and J. R. Wu. 1973. A proposal for the structure of the *Drosophila* genome. *Proc. Nat. Acad. Sci.* 70:535–37.

Bostock, C. J. 1971. Repetitious DNA. *Adv. Cell Biol.* 2:153–223.

Bostock, C. J. and E. M. Clark. 1980. Satellite DNA in large marker chromosomes of methotrexate-resistant mouse cells. *Cell* 19:709–715.

Bouchard, R. A., and H. Swift. 1977. Nature of the heterogeneity in mispairing of reannealed middle-repetitive fern DNA. *Chromosoma* 61:317–33.

Bregliano, J. C., G. Picard, A. Bucheton, A. Pelisson, J. M. Lavige, and P. L'Heritier. 1980. Hybrid dysgenesis in *Drosophila melanogaster*. *Science* 207:606–11.

Bretsky, P. W., and D. M. Lorenz. 1970. An essay on genetic-adaptive strategies and mass extinctions. *Geol. Soc. Am. Bull.* 81:2449–56.

Bridges, C. B. 1935. Salivary chromosome maps. *J. Hered.* 26:60–64.

Britten, R. J. 1972. DNA Sequence interspersion and a speculation about evolution. In *Evolution of Genetic Systems* (H. H. Smith, ed.). New York: Gordon and Breach, pp. 80–94.

Britten, R. J., and D. E. Kohne. 1968. Repeated sequences in DNA. *Science* 161:529–40.

Britten, R. J., T. J. Hall, Z. Lev, G. P. Moore, A. S. Lee, T. L. Thomas, and E. H. Davidson. 1979. Examples of evolution and expression in the sea urchin genome. In *Eucaryote Gene Regulation* (R. Axel, T. Maniatis, and C. F. Fox, eds.). *ICN-UCLA Symposium on Molecular and Cellular Biology.* 14:219–27.

Brown, W. M., M. George, Jr., and A. C. Wilson. 1979. Rapid evolution of animal mitochondrial DNA. *Proc. Nat. Acad. Sci.* 76:1967–71.

Brown, W. M., and H. M. Goodman. 1979. Quantitation of intrapopulation variation by restriction endonuclease analysis of human mitochondrial DNA. In *Extrachromosomal DNA* (D. J. Cummings, P. Borst, I. B. Dawid, S. M. Weissman, and C. F. Fox, eds.) *ICN-UCLA Symposium on Molecular and Cellular Biology* 15:485–99.

Brutlag, D. L. 1980. Molecular arrangement and evolution of heterochromatic DNA. *Ann. Rev. Genet.* 14:121–44.

Brutlag, D., M. Carlson, K. Fry, and T. S. Hsieh. 1978. DNA sequence organization in *Drosophila* heterochromatin. Cold Spring Harbor Symposia on Quantitative Biology 42:1137–46.

Bukhari, A. I., J. A. Shapiro, and S. L. Adhya (eds.). 1977. *DNA Insertion Elements, Plasmids, and Episomes.* Cold Spring Harbor Laboratory.

Burns, J. A., and D. U. Gerstel. 1973. Formation of megachromosomes from heterochromatic blocks of *Nicotiana tomentosiformis*. *Genetics* 75:497–502.

Bush, G. L., S. M. Case, A. C. Wilson, and J. L. Patton. 1977. Rapid speciation and chromosomal evolution in mammals. *Proc. Nat. Acad. Sci.* 74:3942–46.

Calkins, J., and T. Thordardottir. 1980. The ecological significance of solar UV radiation on aquatic organisms. *Nature* 283:563–66.

Calos, M. P. and J. H. Miller. 1980. Transposable elements. *Cell* 20:579–95.

Camacho, J. P. M., A. R. Carballo, and J. Carbero. 1980. The B-chromosome system of the grasshopper *Eyprepocnemis plorans* subsp. *plorans* (Charpentier). *Chromosoma* 80:163–76.

Cameron, J. R., E. Y. Loh, and R. W. Davis. 1979. Evidence for transposition of dispersed repetitive DNA families in yeast. *Cell* 16:739–51.

Campbell, A. 1972. Episomes in evolution. In *Evolution of Genetic Systems* (H. H. Smith, ed.) New York: Gordon and Breach, pp. 534–62.

Campbell, A. 1979. The virus concept and its applicability to slow transmissible agents of disease. In *Slow Transmissible Diseases of the Nervous System.* (S. B. Prusiner) Vol. 2, pp. 253–69. New York: Academic Press.

Campbell, A., M. Benedik, and L. Heffernan. 1979. Viruses and inserting elements in chromosomal evolution. In *Concepts of the Structure and Function of DNA, Chromatin and Chromosomes* (A. S. Dion, ed.). Symposia Specialists, Inc., pp. 51–79.

Campbell, A., D. E. Berg, D. Botstein, E. M. Lederberg, R. P. Novick, P. Starlinger, and W. Szybalski. 1979. Nomenclature of transposable elements in prokaryotes. *Gene* 5:197–206.

Campbell, D. G. 1978. *The Ephemeral Islands. A Natural History of the Bahamas.* New York: Macmillan.

Carlson, W. R. 1978. The B chromosome of corn. *Ann. Rev. Genet.* 16:5–23.

Carson, H. L. 1955. Variation in genetic recombination in natural populations. *J. Cell. Comp. Physiol.* 45:221–36.

Carson, H. L., F. E. Clayton, and H. D. Stalker. 1967. Karyotypic stability and speciation in Hawaiian *Drosophila. Proc. Nat. Acad. Sci.* 57:1280–85.

Chaleff, D. T., and G. R. Fink. 1980. Genetic events associated with an insertion mutation in yeast. *Cell* 21:227–37.

Chambon, P. 1978. Summary: the molecular biology of the eukaryotic genome is coming of age. *Cold Spring Harbor Symposia on Quantitative Biology* 42:1209–34.

Chernyshev, A. I., V. N. Bashkirov, B. A. Leibovitch, and R. B. Khesin. 1980. Increase in the number of histone genes in case of their deficiency in *Drosophila melanogaster*. *Mol. Gen. Genet.* 178:663–68.

Cherry, L.M., S.M. Case, and A. C. Wilson. 1978. Frog perspective on the morphological difference between humans and chimpanzees. *Science* 200:209–11.

Church, G. M., P. P. Slonimski, and W. Gilbert. 1979. Pleiotropic mutations within two yeast mitochondrial cytochrome genes block mRNA processing. *Cell* 18:1209–15.

Cochet, M., F. Gannon, R. Hen, L. Maroteaux, F. Perrin, and P. Chambon. 1979. Organisation and sequence studies of the 17-piece chicken conalbumin gene. *Nature* 282:567–74.

Cohen, S. N., and J. A. Shapiro. 1980. Transposable genetic elements. *Sci. Am.* 242:40–49.

Comings, D. E. 1980. Arrangement of chromatin in the nucleus. *Hum. Genet.* 53:131–43.

Connor, E. F., and E. D. McCoy. 1979. The statistics and biology of the species-area relationship. *Am. Nat.* 113:791–833.

Cooper, K. W. 1959. Cytogenetic analysis of major heterochromatic elements (especially Xh and Y) in *Drosophila melanogaster* and the theory of "heterochromatin." *Chromosoma* 10:535–88.

Corneo, G. 1976. Do satellite DNA's function as sterility barriers in eukaryotes? *Evol. Theory* 1:261–65.

Cox, B. S. 1978. Recombination and repair in simple eukaryotes. In *DNA Repair Mechanisms*. (P. C. Hanawalt, E. C. Friedberg, and C. F. Fox, eds.). *ICN-UCLA Symposia on Molecular and Cellular Biology* 9:429–35.

Cox, E. C. 1976. Bacterial mutator genes and the control of spontaneous mutation. *Ann. Rev. Genet.* 10:135–56.

Craig, N. L., and J. W. Roberts. 1980. *E. coli* recA protein-directed cleavage of phage λ repressor requires polynucleotide. *Nature* 283:26–30.

Craig-Holmes, A. P., F. B. Moore, and M. W. Shaw, 1973. Polymorphism of human C-band heterochromatin. I. Frequency of variants. *Am. J. Hum. Genet.* 25:181–92.

Craik, C. S., S. R. Buchman, and S. Beychok. 1980. Characterization of globin domains: Heme binding to the central exon product. *Proc. Natl. Acad. Sci. USA* 77:1384–88.

Crick, F. 1979. Split genes and RNA splicing. *Science* 204:264–71.

Cseko, Y. M. T., N. A. Dower, P. Minoo, L. Lowenstein, G. R. Smith, J. Stone, and R. Sederoff. 1979. Evolution of polypyrimidines in *Drosophila*. *Genetics* 92:459–84.

Darnell, J. E., Jr. 1978. Implications of RNA-RNA splicing in evolution of eukaryotic cells. *Science* 202:1257–60.

Davis, G. M. 1979. The origin and evolution of the gastropod family Pomatiopsidae, with emphasis on the Mekong River Triculinae. *Acad. Natural Sci. of Phila.* Monograph 20.

Davis, M. M., S. K. Kim, and L. Hood. 1980. Immunoglobulin class switching: developmentally regulated DNA rearrangements during differentiation. *Cell* 22:1–2.

Dawid, I. B., and P. Botchan. 1977. Sequences homologous to ribosomal insertions occur in the *Drosophila* genome outside the nucleolus organizer. *Proc. Nat. Acad. Sci.* 74:4233–37.

Demerec, M. 1941. Unstable genes in *Drosophila. Cold Spring Harbor Symposia on Quantitative Biology* 9:145–50.

Dennis, E. S., P. Dunsmuir, and W. J. Peacock. Segmental amplification in a satellite DNA: restriction enzyme analysis of the major satellite of *Macropus rufogriseus. Chromosoma* 79:179–98.

Devonshire, A. L., and R. M. Sawicki. 1979. Insecticide-resistant *Myzus persicae* as an example of evolution by gene duplication. *Nature* 280:140–41.

Doolittle, R. F. 1978. Genes in pieces: were they ever together? *Nature* 272:581–82.

———. 1979. Protein evolution. In *The Proteins* (H. Neurath and R. L. Hill, eds.) 3rd ed., Vol. IV. New York: Academic Press, pp. 1–118.

Doolittle, R. F., K. W. K. Watt, B. A., Cottrell, D. D. Strong, and M. Riley. 1979. The amino acid sequence of the α-chain of human fibrinogen. *Nature* 280:464–68.

Drake, J. W. 1970. *The Molecular Basis of Mutation.* San Francisco: Holden-Day.

Drake, J. W., and R. H. Baltz. 1976. The biochemistry of mutagenesis. *Ann. Rev. Biochem.* 45:11–37.

Dugaiczyk, A., S. L. C. Woo, and B. W. O'Malley. 1979. Genes-in-pieces. In *Ontogeny of Receptors and Reproductive Hormone Action* (T. H. Hamilton, J. H. Clark, and W. A. Sadler, eds.). New York: Raven Press, pp. 1–11.

Dujon, B. 1979. Mutants in a mosaic gene reveal functions for introns. *Nature* 282:20–27.

———. 1980. Sequence of the intron and flanking exons of the mitochondrial 21S rRNA gene of yeast strains having different alleles at the ω and rib-1 loci. *Cell* 20:185–97.

Dunsmuir, P., W. J. Brorein, Jr., M. A. Simon, and G. M. Rubin. 1980. Insertion of the *Drosophila* transposable element *copia* generates a 5 base pair duplication. *Cell* 21:575–79.

Early, P., J. Rogers, M. Davis, K. Calame, M. Bond, R. Wall, and L. Hood. 1980. Two mRNAs can be produced from a single immunoglobulin μ gene by alternative RNA processing pathways. *Cell* 20:313–19.

Edelman, G. M., and J. A. Gally. 1967. Somatic recombination of duplicated genes: an hypothesis on the origin of antibody diversity *Proc. Nat. Acad. Sci.* 57:353–58.

Efstratiadis, A., J. W. Posakony, T. Maniatis, R. M. Lawn, C. O'Connell, R. A. Spritz, J. K. DeRiel, B. G. Forget, S. M. Weissman, J. L. Slightom, A. E. Blechl, O. Smithies, F. E. Baralle, C. C. Shoulders, and N. J. Proudfoot. 1980. The structure and evolution of the human β-globin gene family. *Cell* 21:653–68.

Emmons, S. W., M. R. Klass, and D. Hirsh. 1979. Analysis of the constancy of DNA sequences during development and evolution of the nematode *Caenorhabditis elegans. Proc. Nat. Acad. Sci.* 76:1333–37.

Esposito, M. S. 1981. Mutation and recombination in diploid cells: a unifying hypothesis. In preparation.

Esposito, M. S., and R. E. Esposito. 1977. Gene conversion, paramutation, and controlling elements: a treasure of exceptions. In *Cell Biology* (D. M. Prescott and L. Goldstein, eds.). Vol. 1. New York: Academic Press, pp. 59–92.

Fedoroff, N. V., and D. D. Brown. 1978. The nucleotide sequence of the repeating unit in the oocyte 5S ribosomal DNA of *Xenopus laevis. Cold Spring Harbor Symposia on Quantitative Biology* 42:1195–1200.

Felsenstein, J. and S. Yokoyama. 1976. The evolutionary advantage of recombination. II. Individual selection for recombination. *Genetics* 83:845–59.

Ferguson-Smith, M. A. 1973. Human autosomal polymorphism and the nonrandom involvement of chromosomes in translocations. *Chromosomes Today* 4:235–46.

Ferris, S. D., and G. S. Whitt. 1979. Evolution of the differential regulation of duplicate genes after polyploidization. *J. Mol. Evol.* 12:267–317.

Fincham, J. R. S. 1973. Localized instabilities in plants—a review and some speculations. *Genetics* (Suppl.) 73:195–205.

Fincham, J. R. S., and G. R. K. Sastry. 1974. Controlling elements in maize. *Ann. Rev. Genet.* 8:15–50.

Finnegan, D. J., G. M. Rubin, M. W., Young, and D. S. Hogness. 1978. Repeated gene families in *Drosophila melanogaster. Cold Spring Harbor Symposia on Quantitative Biology* 42:1053–63.

Flavell, R. B., and D. B. Smith. 1975. Genome organization in higher plants. *Stadler Genetics Symposia* 7:47–69.

Flenley, J. 1979. *The Equatorial Rain Forest: A Geological History.* London: Butterworths.

Flessa, K. W., and J. J. Sepkoski, Jr. 1978. On the relationship between Phanerozoic diversity and changes in habitable area. *Paleobiology* 4:359–66.

Fogel, S., D. D. Hurst, and R. K. Mortimer. 1971. Gene conversion in unselected tetrads from multipoint crosses. *Stadler Genetics Symposia* 1/2:89–110.

Fogel, S., R. K. Mortimer, K. Lusnak, and F. Tavares. 1979. Meiotic gene conversion: a signal of the basic recombination event in yeast. *Cold Spring Harbor Symposia on Quantitative Biology* 43:1325–41.

Ford, E. B. 1979. H. B. D. Kettlewell. *Nature* 281:166.

Forejt, J. 1973. Centromeric heterochromatin polymorphism in the house mouse. *Chromosoma* 43:187–201.

Fox, D. P. 1972. DNA content of related species. *Chromosomes Today* 3:32–37.

Frankham, R., D. A. Briscoe, and R. K. Nurthen. 1980. Unequal crossing over at the rRNA tandon as a source of quantitative genetic variation in *Drosophila. Genetics* 95:727–42.

Franklin, N. C. 1978. Genetic fusions for operon analysis. *Ann. Rev. Genet.* 12:193–221.

Fredga, K. 1977. Chromosomal changes in vertebrate evolution. *Proc. Royal Soc. London.* Series B. 199:377–97.

Fritsch, E. F., R. M. Lawn, and T. Maniatis. Molecular cloning and characterization of the human β-like globin gene cluster. *Cell* 19:959–72.

Fry, K., and W. Salser. 1977. Nucleotide sequences of HS-α satellite DNA from kangaroo rat *Dipodomys ordii* and characterization of similar sequences in other rodents. *Cell* 12:1069–84.

Gaemers, P. A. M. 1976. New concepts in the evolution of the Gadidae (Vertebrata, Pisces), based on their otoliths. *Mededelingen Werkgroep Tertiaire en Kwartaire Geologie* 13:3–32.

Gaillard, C., F. Strauss, and G. Bernardi. 1980. Excision sequences in the mitochondrial genome of yeast. *Nature* 283:218–20.

Gall, J. G., and D. D. Atherton. 1974. Satellite DNA sequences in *Drosophila virilis*. *J. Mol. Biol.* 85:633–64.

Gatti, M. 1979. Genetic control of chromosome breakage and rejoining in *Drosophila melanogaster*: spontaneous chromosome aberrations in X-linked mutants defective in DNA metabolism. *Proc. Nat. Acad. Sci.* 76:1377–81.

Gatti, M., S. Pimpinelli, and B. S. Baker. 1980. Relationships among chromatid interchanges, sister chromatid exchanges, and meiotic recombination in *Drosophila melanogaster*. *Proc. Natl. Acad. Sci.* 77:1575–79.

Geller, A. I., and A. Rich. 1980. A UGA termination supression tRNA^{Trp} active in rabbit reticulocytes. *Nature* 283:41–46.

Gershenson, S. 1933. Studies on the genetically inert region of the X-chromosome of *Drosophila*. *J. Genet.* 28:297–313.

Ghosal, D., and H. Saedler, 1979. IS2-61 and IS2-611 arise by illegitimate recombination from IS2-6. *Mol. Gen. Genet.* 176:233–38.

Gilbert, W. 1978. Why genes in pieces? *Nature* 271:501.

———. 1979. Introns and exons: playgrounds of evolution. In *Eucaryote Gene Regulation* (R. Axel, T. Maniatis, and D. F. Fox, eds.). *ICN-UCLA Symposia on Molecular and Cellular Biology* 14:1–12.

Goldberg, R. B., W. R. Crain, J. V. Ruderman, G. P. Moore, T. R. Barnett, R. C. Higgins, R. A. Gelfand, G. A. Galau, R. J. Britten, and E. H. Davidson. 1975. DNA sequence organization in the genomes of five marine invertebrates. *Chromosoma* 51:225–51.

Goldschmidt, R. B. 1952. Evolution, as viewed by one geneticist. *Am. Sci.* 40:84–98.

———. 1958. Genic conversion in *Oenothera*? *Am. Nat.* 92:93–104.

Gooch, J. L., and T. J. M. Schopf. 1973. Genetic variability in the deep sea: relation to environmental variability. *Evolution* 26:545–52.

Goodenough, U. 1978. *Genetics*. New York. 2nd ed. Holt, Rinehart and Winston.

Gottlieb, L. D. 1976. Biochemical consequences of speciation in plants. In *Molecular Evolution* (F. J. Ayala, ed.). Sunderland, Mass.: Sinauer, pp. 123–40.

Gould, S. J. 1970. Dollo on Dollo's Law: irreversibility and the status of evolutionary laws. *J. Hist. Biol.* 3:189–212.

Gould, S. J., and N. Eldredge. 1977. Punctuated equilibria: the tempo and mode of evolution reconsidered. *Paleobiology* 3:115–51.

Green, M. M. 1973. Some observations and comments on mutable and mutator genes in *Drosophila*. *Genetics* (Suppl.) 73:187–94.

———. 1977. The case for DNA insertion mutations in *Drosophila*. In DNA *Insertion Elements, Plasmids, and Episomes* (A. I. Bukhari, J. A. Shapiro, and S. L. Adhya, eds.). Cold Spring Harbor Laboratory, pp. 437–45.

———. 1978. The genetic control of mutation in *Drosophila*. *Stadler Genetics Symposia* 10:95–104.

———. 1980. Transposable elements in *Drosophila* and other diptera. *Ann. Rev. Genet.* 14:109–20.

Greer, H., and G. R. Fink. 1979. Unstable transpositions of *his4* in yeast. *Proc. Nat. Acad. Sci.* 76:4006–10.

Grinsted, J., C.-L. Choi, P. M. Bennet, R. Schmitt, and M. H. Richmond. 1980. On the evolution of transposable elements. Abstract for paper for 192nd meeting of The Genetical Society, March 31-April 2, 1980 at Univ. of Leeds. *Heredity* 45:137–57.

Haber, J. E., D. T. Rogers, and J. H. McCusker. 1980. Homothallic conversions of yeast mating-type genes occur by intrachromosomal recombination. *Cell* 22:277–89.

Haldane, J. B. S. 1949. Human evolution: past and future. In *Genetics, Paleontology and Evolution* (G. L. Jepsen, G. G. Simpson, and E. Mayr, eds.). Princeton N.J.: Princeton University Press, pp. 405–18.

Hamer, D. H., and P. Leder, 1979. Splicing and the formation of stable RNA. *Cell* 18:1299–1302.

Hanawalt, P. C. 1975. Molecular mechanisms involved in DNA repair. *Genetics* 79:179–97.

Hanawalt, P. C., P. K. Cooper, A. K. Ganesan, and C. A. Smith. 1979. DNA repair in bacteria and mammalian cells. *Ann. Rev. Biochem.* 48:783–836.

Hanawalt, P. C., E. C. Friedberg, and C. F. Fox. (eds.) 1978. *DNA Repair Mechanisms. ICN-UCLA Symposia on Molecular and Cellular Biology* 9:1–813.

Hanawalt, P. C., and R. B. Setlow (eds.). 1975. *Molecular Mechanisms for Repair of DNA.* New York: Plenum Press.

Hatch, F. T., A. J. Bodner, J. A. Mazrimas, and D. H. Moore, II. 1976. Satellite DNA and cytogenetic evolution. *Chromosoma* 58:155–68.

Hawley, R. S. 1980. Chromosomal sites necessary for normal levels of meiotic recombination in *Drosophila melanogaster*. I. Evidence for and mapping of the sites. *Genetics* 94:625–46.

Heffron, F., B. J. McCarthy, H. Ohtsubo, and E. Ohtsubo, 1979. DNA sequence analysis of the transposon Tn3: three genes and three sites involved in transposition of Tn3. *Cell* 18:1153–63.

Hegeman, G. D., and S. L. Rosenberg. 1970. The evolution of bacterial enzyme systems. *Ann. Rev. Microbiol.* 24:429–62.

Heitz, E. 1928. Das Heterochromatin der Moose I. *Jahrbücher für wissenschaftliche Botanik.* 69:762–819.

Heilig, R., F. Perrin, F. Gannon, J. L. Mandel, and P. Chambon. 1980. The ovalbumin gene family: structure of the X gene and evolution of duplicated split genes. *Cell* 20:625–37.

Hennig, W., I. Hennig, and H. Stein. 1970. Repeated sequences in the DNA of *Drosophila* and their localization in giant chromosomes. *Chromosoma* 32:31–63.

Hennig, W., and P. M. B. Walker. 1970. Variations in the DNA from two rodent families (Cricetidae and Muridae). *Nature* 225:915–19.

Hereford, L., K. Fahrner, J. Woolford, Jr., M. Rosbash, and D. B. Kaback. 1979. Isolation of yeast histone genes H2A and H2B. *Cell* 18:1261–71.

Herman, R. K., J. E. Madl, and C. K. Kari. 1979. Duplications in *Caenorhabditis elegans. Genetics* 92:419–35.

Hewitt, G. 1972. The structure and role of B-chromosomes in the mottled grasshopper. *Chromosomes Today* 3:208–22.

———. 1973. Evolution and maintenance of B Chromosomes. *Chromosomes Today* 4:351–69.

Hicks, J., J. N. Strathern, and A. J. S. Klar. 1979. Transposable mating type genes in *Saccharomyces cerevisiae*. *Nature* 282:478–83.

Hirsh, D., S. W. Emmons, J. G. Files, and M. R. Klass. 1979. Stability of the *C. elegans* genome during development and evolution. In *Eucaryote Gene Regulation* (R. Axel, T. Maniatis, and C. F. Fox, eds.), *ICN-UCLA Symposia on Molecular and Cellular Biology* 14:204–18.

Hofemeister, J., H. Köhler, and V. D. Filippov. 1979. DNA repair in *Proteus mirabilis*. VI. Plasmid (R46-) mediated recovery and UV mutagenesis. *Mol. Gen. Genet.* 176:265–73.

Holliday, R., P. J. Pukkila, J. M. Dickson, A. Spanos, and V. Murray. 1979. Relationships between the correction of mismatched bases in DNA and mutability. *Cold Spring Harbor Symposia on Quantitative Biology* 43:1317–23.

Holmquist, G. 1975. Organisation and evolution of *Drosophila virilis* heterochromatin. *Nature* 257:503–6.

Hood, L., J. H. Campbell, and S. C. R. Elgin. 1975. The organization, expression, and evolution of antibody genes and other multigene families. *Ann. Rev. Genetics*. 9:305–54.

Hood, L., and D. W. Talmage, 1970. Mechanism of antibody diversity: germ line basis for variability. *Science* 168:325–34.

Hosbach, H. A., M. Silberklang, and B. J. McCarthy. 1980. Evolution of a *D. melanogaster* glutamate tRNA gene cluster. *Cell* 21:169–78.

Howard-Flanders, P. 1978. Historical perspectives and keynotes on DNA repair. In *DNA Repair Mechanisms* (P. C. Hanawalt, E. C. Friedberg, and C. F. Fox, eds.). *ICN-UCLA Symposia on Molecular and Cellular Biology* 9:105–11.

Jacq, C., J. R. Miller, G. G. Brownlee. 1977. A pseudogene structure in 5S DNA of *Xenopus laevis*. *Cell* 12:109–20.

Jeffreys, A. J., V. Wilson, D. Wood, J. P. Simons, R. M. Kay, and J. G. Williams. 1980. Linkage of adult α- and β-globin genes in *X. laevis* and gene duplication by tetraploidization. *Cell* 21:555–64.

Jepsen, G. L., G. G. Simpson, and E. Mayr (eds.). 1949. *Genetics, Paleontology and Evolution*. Princeton, N.J.: Princeton University Press.

John B., and M. King. 1980. Heterochromatin variation in *Cryptobothrus chrysophorus*. III. Synthetic hybrids. *Chromosoma* 78:165–86.

John, B., and G. L. G. Miklos, 1979. Functional aspects of satellite DNA and heterochromatin. *Internat. Rev. Cytol.* 58:1–114.

Keshet, E., Y. Shaul, J. Kaminchik, and H. Aviv. 1980. Heterogeneity of "virus-like" genes encoding retrovirus-associated 30S RNA and their organization within the mouse genome. *Cell* 20:431–39.

Keyl, G.-G. 1965. A demonstrable local and geometric increase in the chromosomal DNA of *Chironomus*. *Experientia* 21:191–93.

Kidd, S. J., and D. M. Glover, 1980. A DNA segment from *D. melanogaster* which contains five tandemly repeating units homologous to the major rDNA insertion. *Cell* 19:103–19.

Kidwell, M. G., J. F. Kidwell, and J. Sved. 1977. Hybrid dysgenesis in *Drosophila melanogaster*: a syndrome of aberrant traits including mutation, sterility and male recombination. *Genetics* 86:813–33.

Kimura, M., and T. Ohta, 1973. Mutation and evolution at the molecular level. *Genetics* (Suppl.) 73:19–35.

King, M. 1980. C-banding studies on Australian hylid frogs: secondary constriction structure and the concept of euchromatin transformation. *Chromosoma* 80:191–217.

Klar, A. J. S. 1980. Interconversion of yeast cell types by transposable genes. *Genetics* 95:631–48.

Klar, A. J. S., J. McIndoo, J. N. Strathern, and J. B. Hicks. 1980. Evidence for a physical interaction between the transposed and the substituted sequences during mating type gene transposition in yeast. *Cell* 22:291

Knudson, A. G., Jr. 1979. Our load of mutations and its burden of disease. *Am. J. Hum. Genet.* 31:401–13.

Kondo, S. 1974. Radiation genetics in microorganisms and evolutionary considerations. *Genetics* 78:149–61.

———. 1975. DNA repair and evolutionary considerations. *Adv. Biophys.* 7:91–162.

———. 1977. Evolutionary considerations on DNA repair and mutagenesis. In *Molecular Evolution and Polymorphism* (M. Kimura, ed.). Proceedings of 2nd Taniguchi International Symposium on Biophysics. National Institute of Genetics, Mishima, Japan, pp. 313–31.

Kornberg, A. 1974. *DNA Synthesis*. San Francisco: Freeman.

Kourilsky, P., and P. Chambon. 1978. The ovalbumin gene: an amazing gene in eight pieces. *Trends Biochem. Sci.* 3:244–47.

Krimbas, C. B., and S. Tsakas. 1971. The genetics of *Dacus oleae*. V. Changes of esterase polymorphism in a natural population following insecticide control— selection or drift? *Evolution* 25:454–60.

Kurnit, D. M. 1979. Satellite DNA and heterochromatin variants: the case for unequal mitotic crossing over. *Human Genetics* 47:169–86.

Lacy, E., and T. Maniatis. 1980. The nuclotide sequence of a rabbit β-globin pseudogene. *Cell* 21:545–53.

Lai, E.C., S. L. C. Woo, A. Dugaiczyk, and B. W. O'Malley, 1979. The ovalbumin gene: alleles created by mutations in the intervening sequences of the natural gene. *Cell* 16:201–11.

Lande, R. 1980a. Genetic variation and phenotypic evolution during allopatric speciation. *Am. Nat.* 114:463–79.

———. 1980b. What nature makes of variation. Review of: Macroevolution: Pattern and Process, by S. M. Stanley. *Paleobiology* 6:233–238.

Landy, A., R. H. Hoess, K. Bidwell, and W. Ross. 1979. Site-specific recombination in bacteriophage λ: structural features of recombining sites. Cold Spring Harbor Symposia on Quantitative Biology 43:1089–97.

Latt, S. A., and R. R. Schreck. 1980. Sister chromatid exchange analysis. *Am. J. Human Genet.* 32:297–313.

Lau, R. H., C. Sapienza, and W. F. Doolittle. 1980. Cyanobacterial plasmids: their widespread occurrence, and the existence of regions of homology between plasmids in the same and different species. *Molec. Gen. Genet.* 178:203–11.

Lauer, J., C-K. J. Shen, and T. Maniatis. 1980. The chromosomal arrangement of human α-like globin genes: sequence homology and α-globin gene deletions. *Cell* 20:119–30.

Lee, C. S. 1975. A possible role of repetitious DNA in recombinatory joining during chromosome rearrangement in *Drosophila melanogaster*. *Genetics* 79:467–70.

Levin, D. A. 1979. The nature of plant species. *Science* 204:381–84.

Lewis, E. B. 1951. Pseudoallelism and gene evolution. *Cold Spring Harbor Symposia on Quantitative Biology* 16:159–74.

Lieberman, M. W. 1976. Approaches to the analysis of fidelity of DNA repair in mammalian cells. *Internat. Rev. Cytol.* 45:1–23.

Lindsley, D. L., and E. Novitski. 1958. Localization of the genetic factors responsible for the kinetic activity of X chromosomes of *Drosophila melanogaster*. *Genetics* 43:790–98.

Loeb, L. A., L. A. Weymouth, T. A. Kunkel, K. P. Gopinathan, R. A. Beckman, and D. K. Dube. 1979. On the fidelity of DNA replication. *Cold Spring Harbor Symposia on Quantitative Biology* 43:921–27.

Long, E. O., and I. B. Dawid. 1979. Expression of ribosomal DNA insertions in *Drosophila melanogaster*. *Cell* 18:1185–96.

——. 1980. Repeated genes in eukaryotes. *Ann. Rev. of Biochem.* 49:727–66.

Low, K. B., and D. D. Porter. 1978. Modes of gene transfer and recombination in bacteria. *Ann. Rev. Genet.* 12:249–87.

Lucchesi, J. C., and D. T. Suzuki. 1968. The interchromsomal control of recombination. *Ann. Rev. Genet.* 2:53–86.

Macgregor, H. C., and J. Kezer. 1971. The chromosomal localization of a heavy satellite DNA in the testis of *Plethodon c. cinereus*. *Chromosoma* 33:167–82.

MacHattie, L. A., and J. B. Jackowski, 1977. Physical structure and deletion effects of the chloramphenicol resistance element Tn9 in phage lambda. In *DNA Insertion Elements, Plasmids, and Episomes.* (A. I. Bukhari, J. A. Shapiro, and S. L. Adhya, eds.). Cold Spring Harbor Laboratory, pp. 219–28.

MacIntyre, R. J. 1976. Evolution and ecological value of duplicate genes. *Ann. Rev. Ecol. Systemat.* 7:421–68.

Magni, G. E., and S. Sora. 1969. Relationships between recombination and mutation. In *Mutation as Cellular Process* (G. E. W. Wolstenholme and M. O'Connor, eds.). London: J. and A. Churchill, pp. 186–98.

Markert, C. L., J. B. Shaklee, and G. S. Whitt. 1975. Evolution of a gene. *Science* 189:102–14.

Martial, J. A., R. A. Hallewell, J. D. Baxter, and H. M. Goodman. 1979. Human growth hormone: complementary DNA cloning and expression in bacteria. *Science* 205:602–7.

Mayfield, J. E., and J. R. Ellison. 1975. The organization of interphase chromatin in Drosophilidae. *Chromosoma* 52:37–48.

Mayr, E. 1963. Animal Species and Evolution. Cambridge, Mass: Belknap Press of Harvard University Press.

Mazrimas, J. A., and F. T. Hatch. 1972. A possible relationship between satellite DNA and the evolution of Kangaroo Rat species (genus *Dipodomys*). *Nat. New Biol.* 240:102–5.

McClintock, B. 1941. Spontaneous alterations in chromosome size and form in *Zea mays. Cold Spring Harbor Symposia on Quantitative Biology* 9:72–81.

——. 1978. Mechanisms that rapidly reorganize the genome. *Stadler Genetics Symposia.* 10:25–47.

——. 1980. Modified gene expressions induced by transposable elements. In *Mobilization and Reassembly of Genetic Information* (W. A. Scott, R. Werner, D. R. Joseph, and J. Schultz, eds.). New York: Academic Press, pp. 11–19.

McKay, R. 1979. Probing eukaryotic gene control. *Nature* 282:556–57.

Mengden, G. A., and A. D. Stock. 1980. Chromosomal evolution in serpents: a comparison of G and C chromosomes banding patterns of some colubrid and boid genera. *Chromosoma* 79:53–64.

Meyer, J., and S. Iida. 1979. Amplification of chloramphenicol resistance transposons carried by phage P1Cm in *Escherichia coli*. *Mol. Gen. Genet.* 176:209–19.

Miklos, G. L. G., and B. John. 1979. Heterochromatin and satellite DNA in man: properties and prospects. *Am. J. Hum. Genet.* 31:264–80.

———. and R. N. Nankivell. 1976. Telomeric satellite DNA functions in regulating recombination. *Chromosoma* 56:143–67.

Miller, H. I., M. A. Mozola, and D. I. Friedman. 1980. *int*-h3: an *int* mutation of phage λ that enhances site-specific recombination. *Cell* 20:721–29.

Mitchie, D. 1953. Affinity: a new genetic phenomenon in the house mouse. Evidence from distant crosses. *Nature.* 171:26–27.

———. 1956. "Affinity." Proc. R. Soc. (Lond.) Series B—*Biol. Sci.* 144:241–59.

Mizuno, S., and H. C. Macgregor, 1974. Chromosomes, DNA sequences, and evolution in salamanders of the genus *Plethodon*. *Chromosoma* 48:239–96.

Muller, H. J. 1941. Induced mutations in *Drosophila*. *Cold Spring Harbor Symposia on Quantitative Biology* 9:151–67.

———. 1956. On the relation between chromosome changes and gene mutations. *Brookhaven Symposia in Biology.* No. 8. Mutation, pp. 126–47.

Musich, P. R., F. L. Brown, and J. J. Maio. 1980. Highly repetitive component a and related alphoid DNAs in man and monkeys. *Chromosoma* 80:331–48.

Muzyczka, N., R. L. Poland, and M. J. Bessman. 1972. Studies on the biochemical basis of spontaneous mutation. I. A comparison of the deoxyribonucleic acid polymerases of mutator, antimutator, and wild type strains of bacteriophage T4. *J. Biol. Chem.* 247:7116–22.

Nagao, M., T. Sugimura, and T. Matsushima. 1978. Environmental mutagens and carcinogens. *Ann. Rev. Genet.* 12:117–59.

Nicolas, A. 1979. Variation of gene conversion and intragenic recombination frequencies in the genome of *Ascobolus immersus*. *Mol. Gen. Genet.* 176:129–38.

Nisen, P., and L. Shapiro. 1979. *E. coli* ribosomal RNA contains sequences homologous to insertion sequences IS1 and IS2. *Nature* 282:872–74.

Nyberg, D., and P. Bishop. 1979. Nickel tolerance inheritance in *Tetrahymena sonneborni*. *Genetics* 91:s89.

Ohno, S. 1970. *Evolution by Gene Duplication*. New York: Springer-Verlag.

Painter, R. B. 1974. DNA damage and repair in eukaryotic cells. *Genetics* 78:139–48.

Pardue, M. L. 1975. Repeated DNA sequences in the chromosomes of higher organisms. *Genetics* 79:159–70.

Parkinson, J. S. 1977. Behavioral genetics in bacteria. *Ann. Rev. Genet.* 11:397–414.

Passarge, E. 1979. Emil Heitz and the concept of heterochromatin: longitudinal chromosome differentiation was recognized fifty years ago. *Am. J. Hum. Genet.* 31:106–15.

Peacock, W. J. 1965. Nonrandom segregation of chromosomes in *Drosophila* males. *Genetics* 51:573–83.

Peacock, W. J., R. Appels, P. Dunsmuir, A. R. Lohe, and W. L. Gerlach. 1977. Highly repeated DNA sequences: chromosomal localization and evolutionary conservatism. In *International Cell Biology, 1976–1977* (B. R. Brinkley and K. R. Porter, eds.). New York: Rockefeller University Press, pp. 494–506.

Peacock, W. J., D. Brutlag, E. Goldring, R. Appels, C. W. Hinton, and D. L. Lindsley. 1974. The organization of highly repeated DNA sequences in *Drosophila melanogaster* chromosomes. *Cold Spring Harbor Symposia on Quantitative Biology* 38:405–16.

Peacock, W. J., A. R. Lohe, W. L. Gerlach, P. Dunsmuir, E. S. Dennis, and R. Appels. 1978. Fine structure and evolution of DNA in heterochromatin. *Cold Spring Harbor Symposia on Quantitative Biology* 42:1121–35.

Peacock, W. J., and G. L. G. Miklos. 1973. Meiotic drive in *Drosophila*: new interpretations of the segregation distorter and sex chromosome systems. *Adv. Genet.* 17:361–409.

Peacock, W. J., G. L. G. Miklos, and D. J. Goodchild. 1975. Sex chromosome meiotic drive in *Drosophila melanogaster*. *Genetics* 79:613–34.

Perler, F., A. Efstratiadis, P. Lomedico, W. Gilbert, R. Kolodner, and J. Dodgson. 1980. The evolution of genes: the chicken preproinsulin gene. *Cell* 20:555–66.

Perlman, S., C. Phillips, and J. O. Bishop. 1976. A study of foldback DNA. *Cell* 8:33–42.

Petes, T. D. 1980. Unequal meiotic recombination within tandem arrays of yeast ribosomal DNA genes. *Cell* 19:765–74.

Piper, P., J. Wardale, and F. Crew. 1979. Splicing of the late mRNAs of polyoma virus does not occur in the cytoplasm of the infected cell. *Nature* 282:686–91.

Plough, H. H. 1941. Spontaneous mutability in *Drosophila*. *Cold Spring Harbor Symposia on Quantitative Biology* 9:127–37.

Potter, S. S., W. J. Brorein, Jr., P. Dunsmuir, and G. M. Rubin. 1979. Transposition of elements of the *412, copia* and *297* dispersed repeated gene families in *Drosophila*. *Cell* 17:415–27.

Proudfoot, N. J. 1980. Pseudogenes. *Nature* 286:840–41.

———. and T. Maniatis. 1980. The structure of a human α-globin pseudogene and its relationship to α-globin duplication. *Cell* 21:537–44.

Radding, C. M. 1978. Genetic recombination: strand transfer and mismatch repair. *Ann. Rev. Biochem.* 47:847–80.

Radman, M., G. Villani, S. Boiteux, A. R. Kinsella, B. W. Glickman, and S. Spadari. 1979. Replicational fidelity: mechanisms of mutation avoidance and mutation fixation. *Cold Spring Harbor Symposia on Quantitative Biology* 43:937–46.

Rasmuson, B., M. M. Green, and B. M. Karlsson. 1974. Genetic instability in *Drosophila melanogaster*. *Mol. Gen. Genet.* 133:237–47.

Rasmuson, B., I. Montell, A. Rasmuson, H. Svahlin, and B-M. Westerberg. 1980. Genetic instability in *Drosophila melanogaster*. *Molec. Gen. Genet.* 177:567–70.

Raup, D. M. 1975. Taxonomic survivorship curves and Van Valen's Law. *Paleobiology* 1:82–96.

———. 1978. Cohort analysis of generic survivorship. *Paleobiology* 4:1–15.

Ravin, A. W. 1956. The properties of bacterial transforming systems. *Brookhaven Symposia in Biology*. No. 8. Mutation, pp. 33–49.

Reanney, D. C. 1978. Coupled evolution: adaptive interactions among the genomes of plasmids, viruses, and cells. *Internat. Rev. Cytol.* (Suppl.) 8:1–68.

Rees, H., and P. J. Dale. 1974. Chiasmata and variability in *Lolium* and *Festuca* populations. *Chromosoma* 47:335–51.

Rees, H., and R. K. J. Narayan. 1977. Evolutionary DNA variation in *Lathyrus*. *Chromosomes Today* 6:131–39.

Reif, H.-J., and H. Saedler. 1977. Chromosomal rearrangements in the *gal* region of *E. coli* K12 after integration IS1. In *DNA Insertion Elements, Plasmids, and Episomes*. (A. I. Bukhari, J. A. Shapiro, and S. L. Adhya, eds.). Cold Spring Harbor Laboratory, pp. 81–91.

Rhoades, M. M. 1978. Genetic effects of heterochromatin in maize. In *Maize Breeding and Genetics* (D. B. Walden, ed.). New York: Wiley, pp. 641–71.

Rice, N. R. 1972. Change in repeated DNA in evolution. In *Evolution of Genetic Systems* (H. H. Smith, ed.). New York: Gordon and Breach, pp. 44–79.

Rice, N. R., and N. A. Straus. 1973. Relatedness of mouse satellite deoxyribonucleic acid to deoxyribonucleic acid of various *Mus* species. *Proc. Nat. Acad. Sci.* 70:3546–50.

Rick, C. M. 1971. Some cytogenetic features of the genome in diploid plant species. *Stadler Genetics Symposia* 1/2:153–74.

Rieger, R., A. Michaelis, and M. M. Green. 1976. *Glossary of Genetics and Cytogenetics*. 4th ed. Berlin: Springer-Verlag.

Riehl, H., and J. Meitín, 1979. Discharge of the Nile River: a barometer of short-period climate variation. *Science* 206:1178–79.

Rimpau, J., D. Smith, and R. Flavell. 1978. Sequence organisation analysis of the wheat and rye genomes by interspecies DNA/DNA hybridisation. *J. Mol. Biol.* 123:327–59.

Roberts, R. J. 1978. Restriction endonucleases: a new role *in vivo*? *Nature* 271:502.

Roeder, G. S., and G. R. Fink. 1980. DNA rearrangements associated with a transposable element in yeast. *Cell* 21:239–49.

Rose, A. M., and D. L. Baillie. 1979. A mutation in *Caenorhabditis elegans* that increases recombination frequency more than threefold. *Nature* 281:599–600.

Royal, A., A. Garapin, B. Cami, F. Perrin, J. L. Mandel, M. LeMeur, F. Brégégègre, F. Gannon, J. P. LePennec, P. Chambon, and P. Kourilsky. 1979. The ovalbumin gene region: common features in the organisation of three genes expressed in chicken oviduct under hormonal control. *Nature* 279:125–32.

Rubin, G. M., W. J. Brorein, Jr., P. Dunsmuir, R. Levis, S. S. Potter, E. Strobel, and E. Young. 1980. Transposable elements in the *Drosophila* genome. In *Mobilization and Reassembly of Genetic Information* (W. A. Scott, R. Werner, D. R. Joseph, and J. Schultz, eds.). New York: Academic Press, pp. 235–241.

Saedler, H. 1977. *IS1* and *IS2* in *E. coli*: implications for the evolution of the chromosome and some plasmids. In *DNA Insertion Elements, Plasmids and Episomes* (A. I. Bukhari, J. A. Shapiro, and S. L. Adhya, eds.). Cold Spring Harbor Laboratory. pp. 65–72.

Sakano, H., K. Hüppi, G. Heinrich, and S. Tonegawa. 1979a. Sequences at the somatic recombination sites of immunoglobulin light-chain genes. *Nature* 280:288–94.

Sakano, H., J. H. Rogers, K. Hüppi, C. Brack, A. Traunecker, R. Maki, R. Wall, and S. Tonegawa. 1979b. Domains and the hinge region of an immunoglobulin heavy chain are encoded in separate DNA segments. *Nature* 277:627–33.

Salmon, M., S. D. Ferris, D. Johnston, G. Hyatt, and G. S. Whitt. 1979. Behavioral and biochemical evidence for species distinctiveness in the fiddler crabs. *Evolution* 33:182–91.

Salser, W. 1978. Globin mRNA sequences: analysis of base pairing and evolutionary implications. *Cold Spring Harbor Symposia on Quantitative Biology* 42:985–1002.

Salser, W., S. Bowen, D. Browne, F. E. Adli, N. Fedoroff, K. Fry, H. Heindell, G. Paddock, R. Poon, B. Wallace, and P. Whitcome. 1976. Investigation of the organization of mammalian chromosomes at the DNA sequence level. *Fed. Proc.* 35:23–35.

Sanders, H. L., and R. R. Hessler. 1969. Ecology of the deep-sea benthos. *Science* 163:1419–24.

Sandler, L., and G. Braver. 1954. The meiotic loss of unpaired chromosomes in *Drosophila melanogaster. Genetics* 39:365–77.

Schilling, J., B. Clevinger, J. M. Davie, and L. Hood, 1980. Amino acid sequence of homogeneous antibodies to dextran and DNA rearrangements in heavy chain V-region gene segments. *Nature* 283:35–40.

Schimke, R. T., F. W. Alt, R. E. Kellems, R. J. Kaufman, and J. R. Bertino. 1978. Amplification of dihydrofolate reductase genes in methotrexate-resistant cultured mouse cells. *Cold Spring Harbor Symposia on Quantitative Biology* 42:649–57.

Schmid, M. 1980. Chromosome banding in amphibia. *Chromosoma* 80:69–96.

Schmid, M., and J. R. Roth. 1980. Circularization of transduced fragments: a mechanism for adding segments to the bacterial chromosome. *Genetics* 94:15–29.

Schopf, T. J. M. 1972. Varieties of paleobiologic experience. In *Models in Paleobiology* (T. J. M. Schopf, ed.). San Francisco: Freeman Cooper, pp. 8–25.

———. 1973. Ergonomics of polymorphism: its relation to the colony as the unit of natural selection in species of the Phylum Ectoprocta. In *Animal Colonies* (R. S. Boardman, A. H. Cheetham, and W. A. Oliver, Jr., eds.), pp. 247–94.

———. 1977a. Patterns of evolution: a summary and discussion. In *Patterns of Evolution* (A. Hallam, ed.). Amsterdam: Elsevier, pp. 547–61.

———. 1977b. Population genetics of bryozoans. In *Biology of Bryozoans* (R. Zimmer and R. Wollacott, eds.). New York: Academic Press, pp. 459–86.

———. 1979. Evolving paleontological views on deterministic and stochastic approaches. *Paleobiology* 5:337–52.

———. 1980a. The genome—1980 style. *Paleobiology* 6:143–45.

———. 1980b. *Paleoceanography.* Cambridge, Mass.: Harvard University Press.

———. 1980c. Macroevolution: the fifth dimension? *Paleobiology* 6:380–82.

———. 1981. Punctuated equilibria: where the issues now rest. *Paleobiology* 7:(In Press).

Schopf, T. J. M. and A. R. Dutton. 1976. Parallel clines in morphologic and genetic differentiation in a coastal zone marine invertebrate: the bryozoan *Schizoporella errata. Paleobiology* 2:255–64.

Schopf, T. J. M., and Murphy, L. S. 1973. Genetic similarity and a model for the evolution of the hybridizing seastars *Asterias forbesi* and *A. vulgaris. Biol. Bull.* 145:589–97.

Schopf, T. J. M., D. M. Raup, S. J. Gould, and D. S. Simberloff. 1975. Genomic vs.

morphologic rates of evolution: influence of morphologic complexity. *Paleobiology* 1:63–70.

Scott, W. A., R. Werner, D. R. Joseph, and J. Schultz, eds. 1980. *Mobilization and Reassembly of Genetic Information*. New York: Academic Press.

Seidman, J. G., A. Leder, M. Nau, B. Norman, and P. Leder. 1978. Antibody diversity. *Science* 202:11–17.

Seidman, J. G., E. E. Max, and P. Leder. 1979. A κ-immunoglobulin gene is formed by site-specific recombination without further somatic mutation. *Nature* 280:370–75.

Selby, P. B. 1979. Radiation-induced dominant skeletal mutations in mice: mutation rate, characteristics, and usefulness in estimating genetic hazard to humans from radiation. In *Radiation Research Proceedings of the 6th International Congress of Radiation Research, May 13–19, 1979*. Tokyo. (S. Okada, M. Imamura, T. Terashima, and H. Yamaguchi, eds.). Tokyo: Toppan Printing Co. pp. 537–44.

Sepkoski, J. J., Jr. 1975. Stratigraphic biases in the analysis of taxonomic survivorship. *Paleobiology* 1:343–55.

Sevastopoulos, C. G., and D. A. Glaser, 1977. Mutator action by *Escherichia coli* strains carrying *dnaE* mutations. *Proc. Nat. Acad. Sci.* 74:3947–50.

Shackleton, N. J. 1977. Carbon-13 in *Uvigerina*: tropical rainforest history and the equatorial Pacific carbonate dissolution cycles. In *The Fate of Fossil Fuel CO₂ in the Oceans* (N. R. Andersen and A. Malahoff, eds.). New York: Plenum Press, pp. 401–27.

Shapiro, J. A. 1977. DNA insertion elements and the evolution of chromosome primary structure. *Trends Biochem. Sci.* 2:176–80.

———. 1979. Molecular model for the transposition and replication of bacteriophage Mu and other transposable elements. *Proc. Nat. Acad. Sci.* 76:1933–37.

———. 1981. Changes in gene order and gene expression. In *Research Frontiers in Aging and Cancer*, 1st Internat'l Symposium, Washington, D. C. Edited by L. Thomas and J. Ultmann. National Cancer Institute Monograph, pp. 1–95.

Shapiro, J. A., S. L. Adhya, and A. I. Bukhari. 1977. Introduction: new pathways in the evolution of chromosome structure. In *DNA Insertion Elements, Plasmids, and Episomes* (A. I. Bukhari, J. A. Shapiro, and S. L. Adhya, eds.). Cold Spring Harbor Laboratory, pp. 3–11.

Shaw, D. D. 1976. Population cytogenetics of the genus *Caledia* (Orthoptera: Acridinae). I. Inter- and intraspecific karyotype diversity. *Chromosoma* 54:221–43.

Shaw, D. D., and G. R. Knowles. 1976. Comparative chiasma analysis using a computerised optical digitiser. *Chromosoma* 59:103–27.

Shaw, D. D., G. C. Webb, and P. Wilkinson. 1976. Population cytogenetics of the genus *Caledia* (Orthoptera: Acridinae). *Chromosoma* 56:169–90.

Shaw, J. E. and H. Murialdo. 1980. Morphogenetic genes C and Nu3 overlap in bacteriophage λ. *Nature* 283:30–35.

Simmons, M. J., and J. F. Crow. 1977. Mutations affecting fitness in *Drosophila* populations. *Ann. Rev. Genet.* 11:49–78.

Skinner, D. M. 1977. Satellite DNA's *BioScience* 27:790–96.

Slobodkin, L. B. 1968. Toward a predictive theory of evolution. In *Population Biology and Evolution* (R. C. Lewontin, ed.), pp. 187–205.

Smith, G. P. 1974. Unequal crossover and the evolution of multigene families. *Cold Spring Harbor Symposia on Quantitative Biology* 38:507–13.

———. 1976. Evolution of repeated DNA sequences by unequal crossover. *Science* 191:528–35.

Sokatch, J. R., and L. N. Ornston (eds.). 1979. *The Bacteria. Mechanisms of Adaptation*. Vol. 7. New York: Academic Press.

Solomon, E. 1980. The collagen gene family. *Nature* 286:656–57.

Southern, E. M. 1974. Eukaryotic DNA. In *MTP International Review of Science: Biochemistry Series*. 1(6): *Biochemistry of Nucleic Acids* (K. Burton, ed.). London: Butterworths, pp. 101–39.

———. 1975. Long range periodicities in mouse satellite DNA. *J. Mol. Biol.* 94:51–69.

Speyer, J. F., J. D. Karam, and A. B. Lenny. 1966. On the role of DNA polymerase in base selection. *Cold Spring Harbor Symposia on Quantitative Biology* 31:693–97.

Stahl, F. W. 1979a. Special sites in generalized recombination. *Ann. Rev. Genet.* 13:7–24.

———. 1979b. Summary. *Cold Spring Harbor Symposia on Quantitative Biology* 43:1353–56.

Stahl, F. W., M. M. Stahl, R. E. Malone, and J. M. Crasemann. 1980. Directionality and nonreciprocality of Chi-stimulated recombination in phage λ. *Genetics* 94:235–48.

Starlinger, P. 1977a. DNA rearrangements in procaryotes. *Ann. Rev. Genet.* 11:103–26.

———. 1977b. Mutations caused by the integration of IS*1* and IS*2* into the *gal* operon. In *DNA Insertion Elements, Plasmids, and Episomes* (A. I. Bukhari, J. A. Shapiro and S. L. Adhya, eds.). Cold Spring Harbor Laboratory, pp. 25–30.

Stein, J. P., J. F. Catterall, P. Kristo, A. R. Means, and B. W. O'Malley. 1980. Ovomucoid intervening sequences specify functional domains and generate protein polymorphism. *Cell* 21:681–87.

Steinemann, M. 1980. Chromosomal replication in *Drosophila virilis*. *Chromosoma* 78:211–23.

Stern, C. 1971. From crossing-over to developmental genetics. *Stadler Genetics Symposia* 1/2:21–28.

Størmer, L. 1955. Merostomata. In *Treatise on Invertebrate Paleontology* (R. C. Moore, ed.). Part P. Lawrence Kansas: Geological Society of America, pp. P4–P41.

Sturtevant, A. H. 1925. The effects of unequal crossing over at the bar locus in *Drosophila*. *Genetics* 10:117–47.

Sutherland, B. M. 1978. Photoreactivation in mammalian cells. *Internat. Rev. Cytol.* (Suppl.) 8:301–34.

Sved, J. A. 1976. Hybrid dysgenesis in *Drosophila melanogaster*: a possible explanation in terms of spatial organization of chromosomes. *Austr. J. Biol. Sci.* 29:375–88.

Sved, J. A., and D. Verlin. 1980. Similarity of centromeric heterochromatin in strains of *Drosophila melanogaster* which interact to produce hybrid dysgenesis.

Chromosoma 78:353–63.

Swift, H. 1974. The organization of genetic material in eukaryotes: progress and prospects. *Cold Spring Harbor Symposia on Quantitative Biology* 38:963–79.

———. 1977. Introductory remarks. In *International Cell Biology*, 1976–1977 (B. R. Brinkley and K. R. Porter, eds.). New York: Rockefeller University Press, pp. 489–93.

Tartof, K. D. 1974. Unequal mitotic sister chromatid exchange as the mechanism of ribosomal RNA gene magnification. *Proc. Nat. Acad. Sci.* 71:1272–76.

———. 1975. Redundant genes. *Ann. Rev. Genet.* 9:355–85.

———. 1979. Evolution of transcribed and spacer sequences in the ribosomal RNA genes of *Drosophila. Cell* 17:607–14.

Temin, H. M. 1980. Origin of retroviruses from cellular moveable genetic elements. *Cell* 21:599–600.

Thoday, J. M. 1953. Components of fitness. *Symposium of the Society for Experimental Biology* 7:96–113.

Thompson, J. N., Jr., and R. C. Woodruff. 1980. Increased mutation in crosses between geographically separated strains of *Drosophila melanogaster. Proc. Natl. Acad. Sci.* 77:1059–62.

Tu, C-P. D., and S. N. Cohen. 1980. Translocation specificity of the Tn3 element: characterization of sites of multiple insertions. *Cell* 19:151–60.

van Ooyen, A., J. van den Berg, N. Mantei, and C. Weissmann. 1979. Comparison of total sequence of a cloned rabbit β-globin gene and its flanking regions with a homologous mouse sequence. *Science* 206:337–44.

Van Valen, L. 1973. A new evolutionary law. *Evol. Theory* 1:1–30.

Varley, J. M., H. C. Macgregor, and H. P. Erba. 1980. Satellite DNA is transcribed on lampbrush chromosomes. *Nature* 283:686–88.

Voelker, R. A., H. E. Schaffer, and T. Mukai. 1980. Spontaneous allozyme mutations in *Drosophila melanogaster*: rate of occurrence and nature of the mutants. *Genetics* 94:961–68.

Volobujev, V. T. 1980. The B-chromosome system of mammals. *Genetica* 52/53:333–37.

Wagner, R. E., and Radman, M. 1975. A mechanism for initiation of genetic recombination. *Proc. Nat. Acad. Sci.* 72:3619–22.

Wahli, W., I. B. Dawid, T. Wyler, R. Weber, and G. U. Ryffel. 1980. Comparative analysis of the structural organization of two closely related vitellogenin genes in *X. laevis. Cell* 20:107–17.

Waldstein, E. 1978. Enzymology of nucleotide excision repair. In *DNA Repair Mechanisms* (P. C. Hanawalt, E. C. Friedberg, and C. F. Fox, eds.). *ICN-UCLA Symposia on Molecular and Cellular Biology* 9:219–24.

Walen, K. H. 1964. Somatic crossing over in relationship to heterochromatin in *Drosophila melanogaster. Genetics* 49:905–23.

Walker, P. M. B. 1971a. Origin of satellite DNA. *Nature* 229:306–8.

———. 1971b. "Repetitive" DNA in higher organisms. *Prog. Biophys.* 23:147–90.

Wallace, B. 1977. Recent thoughts on gene control and the fitness of populations. *Genetika* 9:323–34.

———. 1978. Population size, environment, and the maintenance of laboratory cultures of *Drosophila melanogaster. Genetika* 10:9–16.

Wallace, M. E. 1953. Affinity: a new genetic phenomenon in the house mouse. Evidence from within laboratory stocks. *Nature* 171:27–28.

———. 1958. Experimental evidence for a new genetic phenomenon. *Philos. Trans. R. Soc.* (Lond.) (Series B) 241:211–53.

Watt, W. B. 1972. Intragenic recombination as a source of population genetic variability. *Am. Nat.* 106:737–53.

Watts, R. L., and D. C. Watts, 1968. The implications for molecular evolution of possible mechanisms of primary gene duplication. *J. Theoret. Biol.* 20:227–44.

Weigert, M., R. Perry, D. Kelley, T. Hunkapiller, J. Schilling, and L. Hood. 1980. The joining of V and J gene segments creates antibody diversity. *Nature* 283:497–99.

Weisberg, R. A., and S. Adhya. 1977. Illegitimate recombination in bacteria and bacteriophage. *Ann. Rev. Genet.* 11:451–73.

Wensink, P. C., S. Tabata, and C. Pachl. 1979. The clustered and scrambled arrangement of moderately repetitive elements in *Drosophila* DNA. *Cell* 18:1231–46.

White, M. J. D. 1968. Models of speciation. *Science* 159:1065–70.

———. 1973. *Animal Cytology and Evolution.* 3rd ed. Cambridge, Mass.: Cambridge University Press.

———. 1975. Chromosomal repatterning—regularities and restrictions. *Genetics* 79:63–72.

———. 1978. *Modes of Speciation.* San Francisco: Freeman.

Wildenberg, J., and M. Meselson. 1975. Mismatch repair in heteroduplex DNA. Proc. Nat. Acad. *Sci.* 72:2202–6.

Wilson, A. C. 1975. Evolutionary importance of gene regulation. *Stadler Genetics Symposia* 7:117–33.

Wilson, A. C., G. L. Bush, S. M. Case, and M.-C. King. 1975. Social structuring of mammalian populations and rate of chromosomal evolution. *Proc. Nat. Acad. Sci.* 72:5061–65.

Wilson, A. C., S. S. Carlson, and T. J. White. 1977. Biochemical evolution. *Ann. Rev. Biochem.* 46:573–639.

Wilson, D. A., and C. A. Thomas, Jr. 1974. Palindromes in chromosomes. *J. Mol. Biol.* 84:115–44.

Winkler, H. 1930. *Die Konversion der Gene.* Jena: Fischer.

Witkin, E. M. 1975. Elevated mutability of *polA* and *uvrA polA* derivatives of *Escherichia coli* B/r at sublethal doses of ultraviolet light: evidence for an inducible error-prone repair system ("SOS Repair") and its anomalous expression in these strains. *Genetics* 79:199–213.

Wobus, U., H. Baumlein, R. Panitz, and E. Serfling. 1980. Periodicities and tandem repeats in a Balbiani ring gene. *Cell* 22:127–35.

Wolf, B. E., and E. Wolf. 1969. Adaptive value and interaction between alpha-heterochromatin and autosomal polymorphism in *Phryne cincta. Chromsomes Today* 2:44–55.

Wolff, S., S. Abrahamson, M. A. Bender, and A. D. Conger. 1974. The uniformity of normalized radiation-induced mutation rates among different species. *Genetics* 78:133–34.

Wolstenholme, G. E. W., and M. O'Connor (eds.). 1969. *Mutation as Cellular*

Process. London: J. and A. Churchill.

Woodcock, N. H. 1979. Sizes of submarine slides and their significance. *J. Struct. Geol.* 1:137–42.

Yamamoto, M., and G. L. G. Miklos. 1978. Genetic studies on heterochromatin in *Drosophila melanogaster* and their implications for the functions of satellite DNA. *Chromosoma* 66:71–98.

Yamamoto, T. and T. Yokota. 1980. Construction of a physical map of a kanamycin (Km) transposon, Tn5, and a comparison to another Km transposon, Tn903. *Molec. gen. Genet.* 178:77–83.

Yoon, J. S. 1980. Mechanisms of chromosome evolution in Hawaiian *Drosophila. Abstracts of the Second International Congress of Systematic and Evolutionary Biology*, p. 111.

Yoon, J. S., and Richardson, R. H. 1976a. A model for genome change: pseudo-chromocenter hypothesis. *Genetics* 83:s85.

———. 1976b. Evolution of Hawaiian drosophilidae. II. Patterns and rates of chromosome evolution in an antopocerus phylogeny. *Genetics* 83:827–43.

———. 1978. Evolution in Hawaiian drosophilidae. III. The microchromsome and heterochromatin of *Drosophila. Evolution* 32:475–84.

Young, M. W. 1979. Middle repetititive DNA: a fluid component of the *Drosophila* genome. *Proc. Nat. Acad. Sci.* 76:6274–78.

Yunis, J. J., and W. G. Yasmineh. 1971. Heterochromatin, satellite DNA, and cell function. *Science* 174:1200–9.

Zieg, J., M. Silverman, M. Hilmen, and M. Simon. 1977. Recombinational switch for gene expression. *Science* 196:170–72.

Zimmer, E. A., S. L. Martin, S. M. Beverley, Y. W. Kan, and A. C. Wilson. 1980. Rapid duplication and loss of genes coding for the α chains of hemoglobin. *Proc. Nat. Acad. Sci.* 77:2158–62.

Zipkas, D., and Riley, M. 1975. Proposal concerning mechanism of evolution of the genome of *Escherichia coli.* Proc. Nat. Acad. Sci. 72:1354–58.

6

ARCHAEOPTERIS AND ITS ROLE
IN VASCULAR PLANT EVOLUTION

Charles B. Beck

INTRODUCTION

The Givetian (Middle Devonian) to Tournaisian (Lower Mississippian) progymnosperm, *Archaeopteris* (including *Callixylon*), is characterized geographically, morphologically, and anatomically. Its possible evolutionary relationships to *Cordaites*, lebachiacean conifers, and the pteridophytic Noeggerathiopsida are considered and two hypotheses are proposed: (1) Cordaitales and Lebachiaceae represent independent lines of evolution originating from *Archaeopteris* or some closely related, similar progymnosperm; and (2) the Noeggerathiopsida represent a direct extension of the progymnosperm line (in particular, the archaeopterid line) of evolution through the Carboniferous. The latter proposal is supported by new information from fertile material and a restoration of the strobilus of *Archaeopteris macilenta*.

As the dominant element in the flora of the late Devonian, *Archaeopteris* was clearly a plant of great importance. Its significance today is related directly to the fact that, among Devonian plants, *Archaeopteris* is by far the best known both in terms of the extent of our knowledge of the entire plant and the details of its morphology and anatomy. Indeed, it is one of the most intensively and completely studied of fossil plants. As is true of most extinct plants, however, there is still much to learn, especially about variation within and among species. Our concept of the genus is clouded not only by difficulties of species delimitation, but also by difficulties in selecting objective bases for establishing genera. As I have previously suggested (Beck 1969, 1970), *Archaeopteris* may encompass several genera.

This very important group of plants had a circumglobal distribution during late Devonian and into early Mississippian times as judged from fossil remains of foliage and structurally preserved axis fragments (*Callixylon*[1]; see Beck 1960a, 1960b). Whereas *Archaeopteris* lived on land masses (continental plates) that were located in tropical to subtropical latitudes (see Ziegler and Bambach, Chapter 7, this volume), fossil specimens have been collected from Ellesmere Island (Andrews, Phillips, and Radforth 1965; Nathorst 1904) and Bear Island (Nathorst 1902) in the Arctic; Timan, Siberia (Petrosyan 1976), the Donetz Basin (Zalessky 1911; Petrosyan 1967), and Kazakhstan (Lepekhina 1963; Petrosyan 1967; Iurina and Lemoigne 1979) in the U.S.S.R.; central Europe (Kräusel and Weyland 1929, 1937; Marcelle 1957); Ireland (Johnson 1911, 1914); eastern Canada (Arnold 1939); western Canada (Scheckler 1978); northeastern U.S.A. (Arnold 1930a, 1931, 1936, 1939; Beck 1960a, 1960b, 1962b, 1964a, 1970, 1971, 1979; Carluccio, Hueber, and Banks 1966; Hoskins and Cross 1951; Kräusel and Weyland 1941; Phillips, Andrews, and Gensel 1972); southwestern U.S.A. (Arnold 1934; Bennett 1959); and China (Lee and Tsai 1978). For pre-1900 literature, see the references cited previously, and Boureau (1970, pp. 405–56).

The great abundance of its fossil remains in some sediments strongly suggests that *Archaeopteris* formed extensive forests (Beck 1964a), and it is very likely that this arborescent plant (Beck 1962a, 1964b) played a significant role in the ecology of late Devonian plant communities. Whereas any attempt to define its ecological role would involve almost total speculation, its role in vascular plant evolution seems to be less speculative, and it is this latter topic which I shall discuss in this chapter. Since the discovery that the organ genus *Callixylon* represents the anatomically preserved stems and roots of *Archaeopteris* (Beck 1960a, 1960b) and the establishment of the Progymnospermopsida (Beck 1960b) in which it is included, *Archaeopteris* has become prominent in discussions of the origin of seed plants.

It is important to consider the evolutionary role of *Archaeopteris* because it existed just prior to and during the early part of a major period of adaptive radiation—perhaps the second major wave of vascular plant diversification. As Banks (1968) has emphasized, the first adaptive radiation of vascular plants, beginning in the Silurian, resulted in the delimitation of at least two major lines of evolution represented by the zosterophyllophytes, and the rhyniophytes and trimerophytes. Evolution within the Rhyniophytina seems to have led to the progymnosperms in which the second major adaptive radiation may very well have had its origins, having been stimulated by the origin of the seed habit during the Upper Devonian. According to Chaloner and Sheerin (1979) the predominance of homosporous reproduction during the early evolution of land plants may have facilitated the wide distribution of a relatively few similar types of plants. As diversity in the kinds of habitats increased during late Devonian times, vascular plants must have been able to capitalize on the increase in genotypical diversity resulting from heterospory and its consequent outbreeding, thus accounting in part for the great diversification of vascular plants during late Devonian and early Carboniferous times.

Archaeopteris seems to encompass the characteristics of a group from which several different lines of vascular plants—both pteridophytes and seed plants—might have evolved (Beck 1971, 1976; Meeuse 1963). There is evidence to support a possible close relationship between *Archaeopteris* and several other major groups: two groups of seed plants, the Cordaitaceae and the Lebachiaceae, and a group of pteridophytes, the Noeggerathiopsida. Before discussing these possible relationships, we shall review the morphology and anatomy of *Archaeopteris* as they are currently understood.

MORPHOLOGY AND ANATOMY OF *ARCHAEOPTERIS*

There is ample evidence to indicate that at least some species of *Archaeopteris* attained the stature of large trees (Arnold 1931; Beck 1962a, 1964b) (Fig. 6.1). The discovery of large logs several feet in diameter and up to 28 feet in length in the Upper Devonian New Albany shale of Indiana and the Caballos chert of Texas, and a stump with a diameter at the base of about 5 feet in the Woodford chert (Lower Mississippian) of Oklahoma attest to this fact (see Beck 1964b). A knowledge of branching within the crown of the tree is, however, lacking, and the restoration by Beck (1962a) (Fig. 6.1) is partly speculative, being based on the assumption that branching in *Archaeopteris* might have been similar to that of a modern coniferophyte. The clear knowledge that branching in *Archaeopteris* was pseudomonopodial (Beck 1971; Scheckler 1978) has implications which must be considered in any reassessment of the habit of the plant. Lateral branch systems which may have been deciduous, much as in the case of the modern conifers *Taxodium*, *Sequoia*, *Metasequoia*, etc.,[2] (Beck 1971) were apparently typically plagiotropic, that is, flattened in one plane (Fig. 6.2). In other words, the ultimate branches were distichous. However, Scheckler (1978) provided anatomical evidence of some irregularity in this pattern. The pseudomonopodial branching in *Archaeopteris* is reflected in the fact that ultimate branches and leaves on the main axes of lateral branch systems developed in the same ontogenetic spiral (Beck 1971; Scheckler 1978) (Figs. 6.3, 6.5). Whereas leaves on the main axes of lateral branch systems were helically arranged (Carluccio, Hueber, and Banks 1966; Beck 1971) (Fig. 6.5), those on ultimate branches were decussate, at least in several species (Beck 1971). Nevertheless, all vegetative leaves in lateral branch systems are thought to have become developmentally oriented in essentially one plane (Fig. 6.2), apparently in response to the photosynthetic function of the leaves (Beck

FIGURE 6.1. Restoration of *Archaeopteris*. (From Beck [1962a], by permission.)

FIGURE 6.2. Restoration of plagiotropic lateral branch system of *Archaeopteris macilenta*. (From Beck [1971], by permission.)

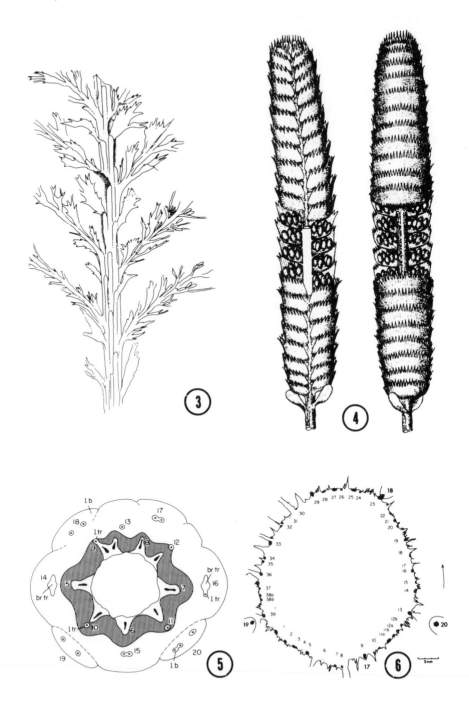

1971). The leaves, which were decurrent on the axes bearing them, flared from a narrow base to become flabellate and rounded distally, and varied from nearly entire to deeply dissected (Figs. 6.3, 6.14, 6.28). Leaves, typically about 1.5 to 5 cm in length, decreased in size from near the base of the lateral branch systems toward the tips, and from the bases of ultimate branches toward their tips (Beck 1971) (Fig 6.2). Leaves have been observed attached to an axis bearing lateral branch systems (Beck 1960b, 1962a), and it had been assumed that leaves were borne on all orders of branching, at least during early developmental stages. Recently, however, Beck (1979) has suggested that lateral branch systems only might have been produced in some regions of the plant since he was not able to find any anatomical evidence of leaf traces in several axes of *Callixylon* whose primary vascular systems he studied.

Some lateral branch systems were fertile. In these, some to most of the ultimate branches—commonly those located centrally within the lateral branch system—produced fertile leaves on the adaxial surface of which were borne sporangia (Figs. 6.13, 6.15, 6.16, 6.31). These ultimate fertile shoots were morphologically similar to the vegetative shoots except that the central ultimate appendages functioned as sporophylls, whereas some basal and apical ultimate appendages functioned primarily as photosynthetic organs. As I shall demonstrate later, the sporophylls were oriented in planes at opposing angles to that in which the axes of the ultimate branches lay in contrast to the photosynthetic appendages which were oriented in planes more or less parallel to that of the axis bearing them. Individual sporophylls tended to be more highly dissected than the vegetative leaves, but the degree of dissection apparently varied with the species (Beck 1971; Andrews, Phillips, and Radforth 1965; Phillips, Andrews, and Gensel 1972). Furthermore, there was an intergradation in form between typical vegetative leaves and typical sporophylls.

Several species have been demonstrated to be heterosporous (Arnold 1939; Pettitt 1965; Phillips, Andrews, and Gensel 1972); and these are characterized by sporangia of two slightly different morphologies. The microsporangia are relatively long and slender compared with the somewhat shorter and broader megasporangia. Microspores are about 40 μm in diameter, and megaspores about eight times larger (see Phillips, Andrews,

FIGURES 6.3–6.6. **6.3.** *Archaeopteris macilenta.* Part of lateral branch system showing helical pattern of leaves on penultimate axis. Note also that ultimate branches and leaves on the penultimate axis occur in the same parastichies. (From Beck [1971], by permission.) **6.4.** Restoration of *Noeggerathiostrobus bohemicus.* (From Halle [1954], by permission.) **6.5.** Restoration of transverse section of the penultimate axis of a lateral branch system of *Archaeopteris.* Traces to leaves and lateral branches occur in the same ontogenetic spiral. (From Beck [1971], by permission.) **6.6.** *Callixylon brownii.* Camera lucida drawing of primary vascular system in transverse view. (From Beck [1979], by permission.)

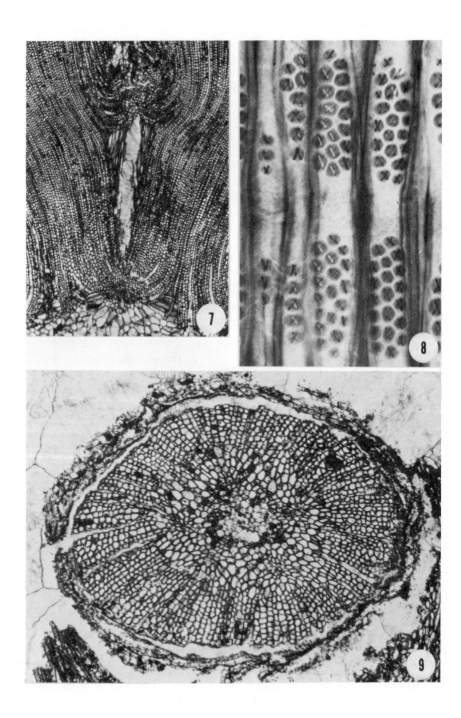

and Gensel 1972). The trilete microspores are characterized by finely ornamented, granulate or psilate exines (Phillips, Andrews, and Gensel 1972) and can be assigned to the dispersed spore genus *Cyclogranisporites* (Pettitt 1965; Phillips, Andrews, and Gensel 1972). The megaspores are trilete with raised laesurae extending to the equator. Megaspore exines are characterized by dense arrays of cones and rods that may fuse into ridges and crests, giving a somewhat reticulate or rugulate appearance (Phillips, Andrews, and Gensel, 1972). They resemble closely the dispersed spore genus *Biharisporites* (Pettitt 1965; Phillips, Andrews, and Gensel 1972). Both microspores and megaspores may be characterized by an inner body or mesosporium. No species differences have been detected in either microspores or megaspores (Phillips, Andrews, and Gensel 1972).

Main stems are characterized by a large parenchymatous pith (Fig. 6.6) containing, in some species, a few scattered tracheid-like cells with reticulate wall sculpturing (Arnold 1930a). Mesarch strands of primary xylem occur at the periphery of the pith, typically in contact with secondary xylem (Figs. 6.6, 6.7), but sometimes separated by a few parenchyma cells from the secondary xylem. These parenchyma cells may have been part of the primary xylem. The nature of the primary phloem, and whether or not it was associated with primary xylem in vascular bundles, are unknown. The three-dimensional architecture of the system of primary xylem strands is not understood in detail. Although individual strands may bifurcate, or fuse with an adjacent strand, many seem to extend longitudinally over a distance of 4 cm or more without bifurcating or fusing in a specimen of *Callixylon brownii* (Beck 1979). Both leaf traces and branch traces diverge radially from bundles of the stele (Arnold 1930a; Beck 1979; Scheckler 1978) (Figs. 6.6, 6.7). In some parts of the plant, both leaf traces and the somewhat larger branch traces developed in main stems (Scheckler 1978), whereas in others, branch traces only seem to have been produced (Beck 1979).

The lateral branch systems were apparently relatively determinate (Beck 1971; Scheckler 1978), and this is reflected in their anatomy. The middle region of the main axis of lateral branch systems, between the base and apex, resembles main stems in having a pith and primary xylem strands that may be separate from one another (Beck 1971; Carluccio, Hueber, and Banks 1966; Scheckler 1978) (Fig. 6.5). Individual xylem strands are triangular in transverse section (Fig. 6.5), differing from the circular to tangentially elongate strands (as seen in transverse section) of the main stem (Figs. 6.6, 6.7). Like those of the main stem, however, each has a single protoxylem

FIGURES 6.7–6.9. **6.7.** *C. zalesskyi.* Transverse section showing radial divergence of trace to lateral appendage. × 22. (From Beck [1979], by permission.) **6.8.** Radial section of *C. newberryi.* × 280. (From Beck [1970], by permission.) **6.9.** Transverse section of embedded axis with characteristics of the base of penultimate axis of a lateral branch system of *Archaeopteris.* × 48. (From Beck [1979], by permission.)

strand that divides along a radial plane prior to radial trace departure (Fig. 6.5). In basal and apical regions of the main axis of the lateral branch systems, at least in *Archaeopteris macilenta*, the bundles are continuous, forming a cylinder and, judging from the protoxylem strands, are fewer in number than in the midregion (Scheckler 1978). During development, the vascular bundles increased in number and became progressively more discrete from the base toward the midregion. Similar changes occurred in reverse from the midregion distally as development gradually slowed, and ceased. A similar pattern characterized the ultimate branches of the lateral branch systems except that in these the vascular bundles never became completely discrete, and in apical, and presumably also, basal, regions, the primary xylem was protostelic (Scheckler 1978). These changes are consistent with those of other branch or shoot systems characterized by relatively determinate growth (Beck 1969; Eggert 1961; Scheckler 1978).

In all orders of branching, traces diverged radially. This is atypical among plants with eusteles, and probably reflects the origin of the *Archaeopteris* eustele directly from a protostele (Beck 1979).

Secondary wood is remarkable in its close resemblance to that of modern conifers, but it is much more highly variable in character extremes (Beck 1969). The wood consists of tracheids and rays, with no evidence of axial parenchyma (Figs. 6.7–6.12). Tracheids are storied and are characterized by tapered to fairly blunt ends. Bordered pits on the radial walls of tracheids are either uniseriate (*Callixylon arnoldii*; see Beck 1962b) or multiseriate (Figs. 6.8, 6.12) and occur in groups which, in cells derived from the same cambial initial, are arranged in radial bands (Figs. 6.8, 6.12). Tracheids near the boundaries of growth layers in some species are characterized by bordered pits on tangential walls (Beck 1970). These tangential pits are smaller than those of the radial walls and are distributed randomly. Pit borders may be circular or angular (Fig. 6.8). Apertures vary from circular (in *C. arnoldii*; Beck and Coy 1981) to narrowly elliptical or lenticular, and if not circular, are crossed in a pit pair (Fig. 6.8). The pit membrane seems to be homogeneous and of uniform thickness in *C. newberryi* (Schmid 1967), whereas in *C. arnoldii* and an unnamed species the membrane is characterized by central circular and peripheral regions quite distinct from each other (Beck and Coy 1981). Whether or not the central region represents a torus is unclear.

Vascular rays vary from uniseriate to multiseriate and from very low to very high. Whereas uniseriate rays may predominate in the wood of some species, such as *C. erianum* (Arnold 1930a; Beck 1970) and *C. arnoldii* (Beck 1962b), some biseriation—commonly only partial biseriation—also usually occurs (Fig. 6.10). In *C. newberryi*, a species with conspicuous, high, multiseriate rays, there is an intermixture of abundant low, uniseriate rays. The wood of *C. whiteanum* is characterized by an approximately equal

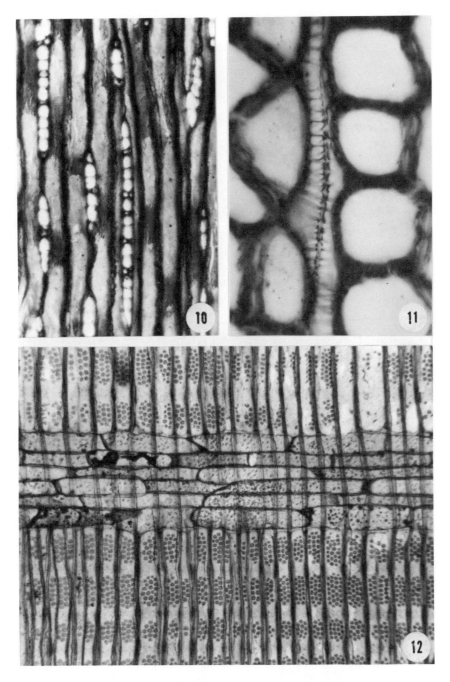

FIGURES 6.10–6.12.   6.10. Secondary wood of *C. erianum* in tangential view. × 95. **6.11.** Ray tracheids in *C. erianum* as seen in transverse section. × 470. **6.12.** Radial section of *C. newberryi*. × 100. (All from Beck [1970], by permission.)

FIGURE 6.13. *Archaeopteris.* Parts of two fertile lateral branch systems. × 1.

intermixture of tall, biseriate and tall, uniseriate rays. Rays consist solely of parenchyma cells in some species, but in others contain ray tracheids as well (Beck 1970). Ray tracheids are conspicuous and abundant in *C. erianum* (Arnold 1930a), occurring in long radial, sometimes biseriate, rows, both marginal and interspersed (Fig. 6.10). The ray tracheids of *C. erianum* are of interest, not only because of their distribution and abundance, but also because of the helical, inner secondary wall sculpturing (Fig. 6.11) that provides them with a structure essentially identical to that of the ray tracheids of the modern conifer *Sequoia* (see Beck 1970). In *C. zalesskyi* and *C. brownii* ray tracheids are less abundant and may occur in rows of varying lengths, sometimes as isolated, single ray tracheids (Beck 1970). Although Arnold (1931) reported ray tracheids in *C. newberryi*, I have not been able through my own extensive observations of both type and other material to confirm their presence in this species. Proof of ray tracheids consists of the demonstration of bordered pits in their walls. This can be accomplished with certainty only by repeated observations of crossed apertures in bordered pit pairs between two ray cells or between a ray cell and a contiguous axial tracheid; or even better, by observing such bordered pit pairs in sectional view (Fig. 6.11). It is clear that the nature of the rays and the distribution of various ray types demonstrate a considerable diversity and may provide a clue to the taxonomic ranks of established categories.

Archaeopteris and other progymnosperms were unique among woody Devonian plants in producing secondary phloem as well as secondary xylem. Indeed, this characteristic distinguishes them from most other Paleozoic woody plants, except the gymnosperms; because as Scheckler and Banks (1971) emphasize, "cambial activity does not produce any secondary phloem in woody ferns, lycopods and calamites." On the basis of unpublished observations on a root fragment, tentatively identified as *C. zalesskyi*, and the early report by Arnold (1930b), the secondary phloem of *Archaeopteris* can be described as being comprised of alternating bands of two types of thin-walled cells, varying in size and form, and traversed by vascular rays. Cells nearest the cambium are irregularly rectangular in transverse view with average radial and tangential dimensions of about 40 μm. These cells, about 186 μm long, have transverse end walls and occur in superposed columns. Cells of the other type represented in the phloem have tangential and longitudinal dimensions similar to those of the cells adjacent to the cambium, but their radial dimension is much greater, on the average, 155 μm. Some cells in both regions contain dark contents, presumably products of cell metabolism. Sieve cells have not been identified.

Roots have not been found in organic connection with stems, but root fragments (collected from the same horizons as stems, and sometimes occurring in the same rock matrix as stems) have been identified as

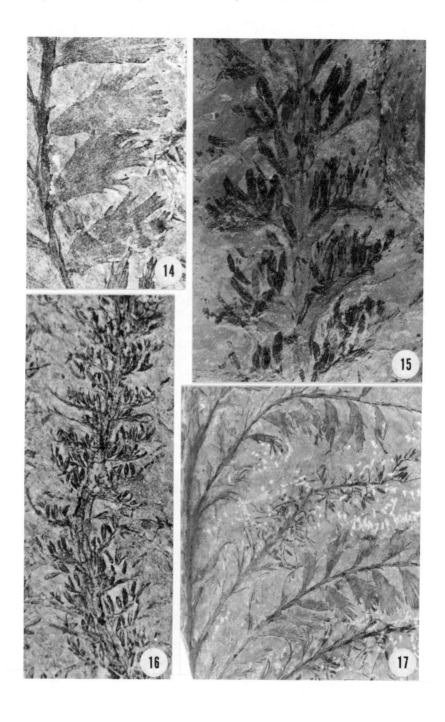

Archaeopteris (*Callixylon*) on the basis of secondary wood characteristics (including ray tracheids and radially aligned groups of circular bordered pits) (Beck 1953) (Fig. 6.18). Root primary xylem is protostelic, and comprises a four-ribbed column, each rib of which contains two exarch protoxylem strands. Secondary xylem seems to exhibit features essentially identical to those of the secondary wood of stems. Growth layers may be well defined and parenchymatous tissues surrounding the secondary xylem relatively well preserved (Fig. 6.18).

THE ROLE OF *ARCHAEOPTERIS* IN VASCULAR PLANT EVOLUTION

We know *Archaeopteris* essentially as an entire plant, and we have a tremendous amount of detailed information about it—much more than I have been able to convey in the preceding brief characterization. Indeed, it is only because we do know so much about *Archaeopteris* that we can make meaningful statements about its role in the evolution of vascular plants. Commonly, in paleobotany, evolutionary speculations are of necessity made on the basis of individual organs, or small groups of characters. This is, at best, dangerous since the most meaningful evolutionary conclusions will be made on the basis of the whole plant.

In attempting to determine the role of *Archaeopteris* in vascular plant evolution, our analyses are by the time-honored methodology of comparative morphology and anatomy wherein one determines similarities and differences. Proposals of evolutionary relationship are based on the assumption that the greater the similarity between two taxa, the closer the evolutionary relationship. In other words, one assumes that shared characteristics reflect a common gene pool. And when dealing with the fossil record, we have the added important element of time. So we can often know with confidence that a group which is considered ancestral existed earlier in time than its proposed descendants.

Archaeopteris exhibits the characteristics which make it a likely candidate from which several major groups of plants might have evolved. The suggestion of a relationship between *Archaeopteris* and the Noeggerathiopsida was made by Hirmer in 1940. I suggested a possible evolutionary relationship between *Archaeopteris* and the cordaites and the primitive

FIGURES 6.14–6.17. *Archaeopteris.* **6.14.** *A. macilenta.* × 3. (From Beck [1971], by permission.) **6.15.** Part of a strobilus showing decussate arrangement of sporophylls and large number of sporangia scattered over the adaxial surface of each sporophyll. × 5. **6.16.** Strobilus with sporophylls oriented at right angles to plane of the break and appearing to bear only a single row of sporangia. × 2. **6.17.** *A. macilenta,* demonstrating in this specimen a mixture of strobili and vegetative shoots borne on a penultimate axis. × 1.

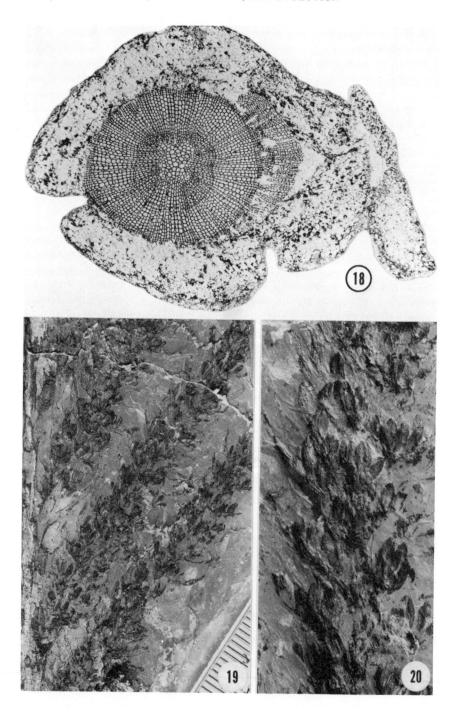

conifers in 1960, and homologies in reproductive structures were proposed by Meeuse in 1963. A possible relationship between *Archaeopteris* and *Archaeosperma* was suggested by Pettitt and Beck (1968) and expanded by Phillips, Andrews, and Gensel (1972).

Let us now consider in detail possible homologies in reproductive structures, and evolutionary relationships (Fig. 6.21) between *Archaeopteris* and the primitive coniferopsids (*Cordaites*, and Lebachiaceae) on the one hand and *Archaeopteris* and the Noeggerathiopsida on the other. For a discussion of the suggested relationship between *Archaeopteris* and *Archaeosperma*, the reader is referred to Pettitt and Beck (1968) and Phillips, Andrews, and Gensel (1972).

Archaeopteris, *Cordaites*, and Primitive Conifers

The similarities between *Archaeopteris, Cordaites*, and primitive lebachiacean conifers are so great that one cannot escape the conclusion that *Archaeopteris*, which occurs earliest in the fossil record, might very well be ancestral to the primitive coniferopsid seed plants. The *Archaeopteris* fertile branch system seems to be a structural type from which both the primitive conifer and cordaite fructifications could have evolved. The entire *Archaeopteris* lateral branch system, with its two orders of branching, seems to be homologous with the similarly constructed female cone of the Lebachiaceae. Likewise, it seems to be homologous with the entire female fertile branch system of *Cordaites* (Fig. 6.21). If we accept these possibilities, it follows then that ultimate fertile shoots of *Archaeopteris* would be homologous with the axillary fertile shoots in both the lebachiacean and cordaitalean female fructifications (Fig. 6.21). It is interesting that the axillary fertile shoots of both are characterized by basal sterile appendages followed by sporophylls just as in the ultimate fertile shoots of *Archaeopteris*.

As for the male fructifications, the entire *Archaeopteris* fertile branch system would seem to be homologous with the entire male fertile branch system of *Cordaites* which is organized exactly like the female fertile branch system. By contrast, however, only the ultimate fertile shoot of *Archaeopteris* seems to be homologous with the male cone of the Lebachiaceae (Fig. 6.21).

It is reasonable to suggest these possible homologies in reproductive structures not only because of morphologic similarity between them, but also because there are so many other features in anatomy and morphology common to these three groups that suggest a close genetic relationship. For

FIGURES 6.18–6.20. **6.18.** *Callixylon petryi.* Transverse section of root. ×19. **6.19–6.20.** *Archaeopteris* strobili. **6.19.** ×1.8. **6.20.** Enlargement of central part of the middle strobilus shown in 6.19. ×4.7.

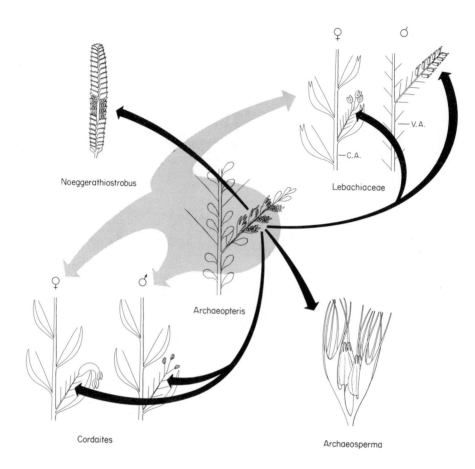

FIGURE 6.21. Suggested homologies in reproductive structures of *Archaeopteris*, *Noegger-athiostrobus*, *Lebachiaceae*, *Cordaites*, and *Archaeosperma*. Gray arrows indicate organs or specialized branch systems (the lebachiacean female cone, and both male and female fertile branch systems of *Cordaites*) considered to be homologous with the entire fertile branch system of *Archaeopteris*. Black arrows indicate organs considered homologous with the strobili (ultimate fertile shoots) of *Archaeopteris*. Drawings of *Archaeopteris*, Lebachiaceae, and *Cordaites* are diagrammatic and certain liberties have been taken for the sake of clarity. In particular, bract-axillary shoot units of the female cone of the Lebachiaceae are more widely separated than in life. Furthermore, they appear distichous in the diagram but were actually helically arranged. Leaves of the axillary shoots of male and female fertile branch systems of *Cordaites*, and leaves of the axillary shoots of the female lebachiacean cone were actually helically arranged. Leaves of the lebachiacean vegetative shoots bearing male strobili as well as the basal vegetative appendages and the microsporophylls of male strobili were also borne helically. Only about one-half of the vegetative leaves and sporophylls of *Archaeopteris* are included. (The restoration of *Noeggerathiostrobus* has been redrawn from Halle [1954], by permission; the restoration of *Archaeosperma* has been redrawn from Pettitt and Beck [1968], by permission.) C. A. = cone axis. V. A. = vegetative axis.

example: (1) all are characterized by a eustele enclosing a wide pith; (2) secondary xylem of all three is pycnoxylic and lacks axial wood parenchyma and resin canals; (3) in all three of these groups, pitting in the secondary wood is circular-bordered with elliptical apertures. Pitting is predominantly

FIGURE 6.22. Strobilus of *Archaeopteris*. For interpretation see Fig. 6.23. × 7.

FIGURE 6.23. Camera lucida drawing of strobilus shown in Fig. 6.22. Sporophylls are viewed from their abaxial sides. Some sporangia (shaded) extend beyond the broken margins of the sporophylls.

multiseriate, and occurs on radial walls only except in regions of late wood; (4) the vascular cambium produced secondary phloem as well as secondary xylem in all groups; and (5) leaves of all are simple with dichotomous venation[3] and supplied by a single leaf trace.

There are some conspicuous differences between *Archaeopteris* and the two groups of primitive coniferopsid seed plants, but many of these reflect advanced character states or conditions in the latter which are represented in *Archaeopteris* by a corresponding primitive character state. For example, branching in the primitive seed plants is axillary whereas it is pseudomonopodial in *Archaeopteris*; and traces to lateral appendages in primitive coniferopsids diverge initially in a tangential plane in contrast to the primitive radial divergence of traces in *Archaeopteris*. Most conspicuously, the seed habit characterizes reproduction in the cordaites and primitive conifers in contrast to heterosporous pteridophytic reproduction in *Archaeopteris*.

As for the evolutionary relationships between *Archaeopteris*, Cordaitales, and Lebachiaceae, there are only two logical alternatives. One is that *Archaeopteris*, Cordaitales, and Lebachiaceae comprise a single line of evolution. The other is that Cordaitales and the primitive conifers represent separate lines of evolution, both having originated from *Archaeopteris* or some related progymnosperm. The first alternative was suggested previously by Beck (1960b, 1962a, 1966) and Meeuse (1963), among others. The relationship between *Cordaites* and the Lebachiaceae was earlier proposed and supported by Rudolf Florin (see Florin [1951] for a summary and references to his original studies), largely on the basis that an evolutionary condensation of the lax female fertile branch system of *Cordaites* would result in a female cone similar to that of the Lebachiaceae. In other words, Florin believed that the cone scale with its ovules in modern conifers was derived by reduction from the axillary fertile shoot of the cordaite female fertile branch system. He supported this proposal by demonstrating intermediate forms of axillary fertile shoots in female conifer cones of the Lebachiaceae. These provide, indeed, convincing evidence of the evolution of the cone scale of the modern conifers. What is still not clear, however, is whether this evolutionary line originated with *Cordaites*. Wilde's (1944) interpretation of the evolution of the conifer male cone, based on her analysis of fertile branching systems in the Podocarpaceae, provided a logical hypothesis for the evolution of the simple male conifer cone from the compound male fertile branch system of *Cordaites*. Furthermore, *Archaeopteris* from the Upper Devonian and Lower Mississippian, *Cordaites* from the Pennsylvanian, and the Lebachiaceae from the Pennsylvanian and early Permian comprise a nearly unbroken fossil record from Upper Devonian into the Permian, but with a hiatus, at least in our knowledge, in the Mississippian.

On the other hand, there are some important differences between *Cordaites* and primitive conifers that seem to support the second alternative. (1) Branching in Lebachiaceae and *Cordaites* was strikingly different. In Lebachiaceae several lateral branches—perhaps as many as five or six—diverged from the main trunk at approximately the same level. These laterals were main axes of plagiotropic lateral branch systems. Branching in *Cordaites*, in contrast, was much more random, with the result that the habit was possibly deliquescent rather than excurrent. Importantly, no plagiotropic lateral branch systems were produced. (2) In both female and male fertile branch systems of *Cordaites* the axillary fertile shoots and their subtending bracts were arranged distichously (but note exception discussed later) whereas in the female lebachiacean cone the axillary shoots and subtending bracts were helically arranged. (3) The compound male fructifications of *Cordaites* were strikingly different from the simple male cones of the Lebachiaceae which were borne singly on vegetative shoots. (4) The leaves of *Cordaites* were consistently simple, linear, unforked, and very large, whereas the bracts of the female cones and the leaves on the trunk and on the main axes of lateral branch systems of the Lebachiaceae were relatively very small and commonly bifurcate.

Except for the first, the character states of *Cordaites* just listed do not

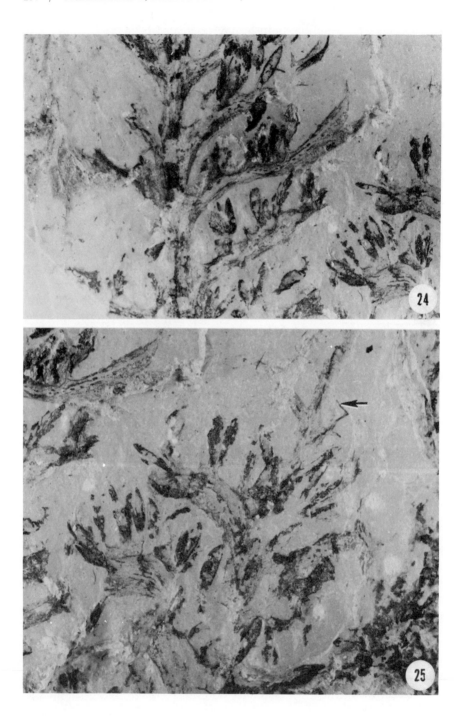

seem like reasonable intermediates between the comparable character states of *Archaeopteris* and the Lebachiaceae or primitive character states from which the conditions in the Lebachiaceae might have been derived. To the contrary, the listed character states of *Cordaites* seem, for the most part, to be advanced, even specialized, conditions that could have evolved independently and directly from *Archaeopteris*, or some comparable ancestor. In this regard, it seems especially important to consider in more detail the distinctive morphology of the fertile structures in both groups.

The compound fertile male branch system of *Cordaites* is clearly a specialized structure. Its main axis is distinctly smaller in size than other lateral branches in the crown of the tree. In no sense, however, is it simply a small, vegetative branch bearing simple male strobili. Instead, the male strobili occur in the axils of small, specialized bracts—very different from vegetative leaves—and they are generally considered to be arranged distichously along the main axis. In *Cordaianthus concinnus*, however, whereas the male strobili develop alternately on opposite sides of the primary axis of the fertile branch system, each successive pair is in a plane offset from that of the preceding pair by about 60°. Consequently, male strobili (axillary fertile shoots) are disposed in four ranks (Rothwell 1977). The axis on which they are borne as well as its stele is, nevertheless, consistently bilaterally symmetrical, a condition often characteristic of specialized axes among extant plants (Rothwell 1977). The specialized compound male branch system of *Cordaites* is, therefore, very different from the condition in the Lebachiaceae in which the simple male strobili are arranged singly and terminally on typical vegetative shoots (Florin 1951). The question that arises is whether or not this condition in the Lebachiaceae could have been derived from *Cordaites*.

Wilde (1944) demonstrated the remarkable similarity between the fertile branch systems of the extant Southern Hemisphere conifer, *Podocarpus*, and those of *Cordaites*. Both male and female branch systems of two species, *P. spicatus* and *P. andinus*, are compound, resembling comparable fertile branch systems of *Cordaites*. Interestingly, in both male and female branch systems of these species of *Podocarpus*, the arrangement of the bracts and their axillary fertile shoots is helical, a presumably more primitive pattern than the distichous arrangement in *Cordaites*.

Wilde (1944) found evidence from her comparative study of extant Podocarpaceae for a reduction in the fertile male branch systems by the

FIGURES 6.24–6.25. *Archaeopteris macilenta.* × 8. **6.24.** Median longitudinal view of part of a strobilus with sporophylls oriented at right angles to plane of the break. **6.25.** Sporophylls of a strobilus borne on the same axis and adjacent to that shown in Fig. 6.24. The break through the strobilus was tangential, providing a view of the adaxial surface of the sporophylls and sporangia attached thereto.

elimination of bracts and axillary male strobili and hypothesized that the majority of species characterized by simple male strobili occurring singly or in clusters evolved from species with primitive compound fertile branch systems. She believed that similar patterns of evolution could account for the presence of single male strobili in other conifers, including the primitive Paleozoic conifers. As she noted, however, there is no supporting fossil evidence. No new evidence to change the picture has been presented since 1944. Consequently, Wilde's proposal must remain largely hypothetical. Her interpretation of the morphologic nature of the fertile structures in the podocarps does, however, suggest the possibility of a polyphyletic nature of the Coniferales. Is it not possible that the Podocarpaceae might be descendants of the Cordaitales, whereas other conifers might be descendants of the Lebachiaceae? It is not within the realm of this chapter to pursue this hypothesis further, and any very meaningful analysis concerning it would require extensive comparative studies of the fructifications of many conifer families in combination with additional investigations on the nature of the fertile structures of Paleozoic conifers.

Finally, it should be noted that *Buriadia heterophylla*, a primitive conifer of the Gondwana flora, exhibits a distribution of seeds quite unlike that of better known members of the Lebachiaceae. According to Pant and Nautiyal (1967), the anatropous ovules are borne randomly on otherwise typical vegetative shoots, and each ovule, borne on a short stalk, replaces a vegetative leaf in the phyllotactic spiral. Pant and Nautiyal (1967) considered this to be a primitive condition from which the more compact cones of the Lebachiaceae might have evolved by reduction. Whereas a fertile branch system such as that of *Buriadia* might represent an intermediate stage between the *Archaeopteris* type of fertile branch system and the *Lebachia* type of cone, it seems very unlikely that it could have evolved from the apparently more specialized female fertile branch system of *Cordaites*.

On the basis of the differences between *Cordaites* and Lebachiaceae listed previously—in particular because there is no basis in the fossil record to account for the striking difference in morphology of the fertile male structures in the two groups, because of the possible primitive nature of the lebachiacean ovuliferous branch system as reflected in *Buriadia*, so different from that of any known cordaite, and because of the possibly significant absence of ray tracheids in *Cordaites*—I suggest that the Cordaitales might represent an evolutionary line quite distinct from that which resulted in the primitive conifers. The apparent discontinuity in the fossil record between the archaeopterids of the Lower Mississippian and the primitive conifers of the Upper Pennsylvanian poses a problem, but one which may be solved as we learn more about possible pteridophytic descendants of *Archaeopteris* in the Carboniferous.

I do not know which, if either, of the alternatives discussed above is the correct one, but I believe the preponderance of available evidence supports the latter. It should be seriously considered as a reasonable alternative to the older viewpoint encompassing the evolution of primitive conifers directly from *Cordaites*.

Archaeopteris and the Noeggerathiopsida

Finally, I wish to consider in some detail the possible relationship between *Archaeopteris* and the Noeggerathiopsida, a poorly known group of heterosporous pteridophytes that occurs in the fossil record throughout the Carboniferous and possibly extends into the Permian (see Boureau 1964). Included in the group are foliage genera such as *Noeggerathia, Palaeopteridium*, and *Saaropteris*, among others; and the fructifications, *Noeggerathiostrobus, Lacoea, Discinites*, and *Saarodiscites*. *Tingia* and *Tingiostachya* have also been included in the group (see Boureau 1964), but their taxonomic affinity is not clear. Foliage and fructifications have been assigned to the group largely on the basis of their sedimentary association (Hirmer 1940; Halle 1954; Boureau 1964). The discovery of *Noeggerathiostrobus* attached to a short axis bearing vegetative leaves identifiable as *Noeggerathia* (Stur 1878), however, provided generally accepted confirmation of the organic relationship of these genera. Any residual scepticism will have been erased by Šetlík's (1956) demonstration of the organic attachment of *Noeggerathia* and *Noeggerathiostrobus* to the same branch.

Noeggerathiopsid foliage is often characterized as consisting of pinnate (*Noeggerathia*) (Figs. 6.26, 6.27) or bipinnate fronds. *Palaeopteridium*, considered to be the foliage of the plant that bore *Discinites* (Němejc 1928; Hirmer 1940) and *Lacoea* (Leary and Pfefferkorn 1977), and *Saaropteris*, commonly associated with *Saarodiscites* (Hirmer 1940) are interpreted as bipinnate fronds in which second order (ultimate) branches are arranged alternately in two ranks. The apparent absence of rachial pinnules (Kidston 1923) supports this interpretation. *Noeggerathia*, by contrast, has been interpreted by several workers (Seward 1910; Němejc 1931; Halle 1954; Setlík 1956) as possibly a plagiotropic shoot bearing simple alternate leaves arranged distichously.

All plants considered to belong to this group bore strobili composed of laminate sporophylls, two-ranked in *Noeggerathiostrobus* (Stur 1878; Hirmer 1940; Remy and Remy 1956) and *Lacoea* (Leary 1973) (Figs. 6.4, 6.29B,C), and encircling the axis in *Discinites* (Fig. 6.29D) and *Saarodiscites* (Hirmer 1940). *Tingiostachya* is characterized by whorls of four sporophylls, each of which bore a single adaxial, tetralocular synangium (Browne 1933). Both megasporangia and microsporangia were borne adaxially on the same sporophyll (Němejc 1928; Remy and Remy 1956). Megaspores, about eight times larger than microspores and characterized by smooth exines, are

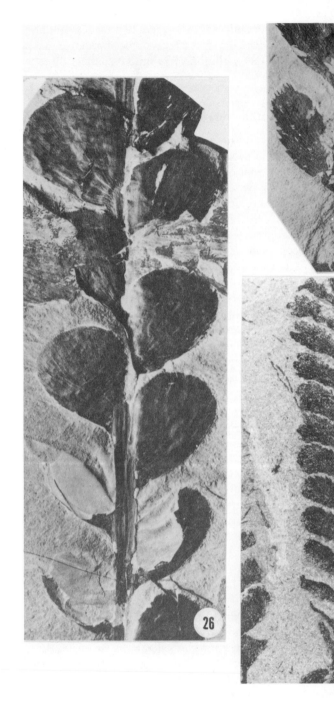

similar to *Calamospora*. Microspores of some species have been assigned to the dispersed spore genus *Cyclogranisporites*.

Taxonomically, the Noeggerathiopsida have been assigned to almost every major group, including ferns, gymnosperms, sphenophytes, and even the palms (for a general discussion see Halle 1954). Halle (1954) concluded that the safest course was "to regard the Noeggerathineae as an isolated group of pteridophyta *incertae sedis*." As early as 1940, however, Hirmer had very strongly emphasized the probable relationship between Noeggerathiopsida and *Archaeopteris*. This farsighted viewpoint has become more and more attractive as our knowledge of *Archaeopteris* has increased dramatically during the last several decades.

Archaeopteris-like foliage occurs from Upper Devonian throughout the Carboniferous (see Leary and Pfefferkorn 1977) (Fig. 6.30). Some genera, for example, *Palaeopteridium* (Kidston 1923), are so similar to *Archaeopteris* that many authors, including Kidston, had earlier identified it as *Archaeopteris*. Indeed, it is still not certain that *Palaeopteridium* and some species of *Anisopteris* and *Rhacopteris* are not the foliage of *Archaeopteris*, or its immediate descendants. The apparent absence of rachial pinnules on the main frond axes, and the presumption that the laminate photosynthetic organs were pinnules rather than simple leaves, weakens this argument. One must recall, however, that lateral branch systems of *Archaeopteris* were also interpreted as fronds prior to investigations of internal structure of the main axis, and careful studies of external morphology (Carluccio, Hueber, and Banks 1966; Beck 1971) which demonstrated them to be plagiotropic branch systems. Anatomical and additional morphological information is needed for a clearer understanding of the nature of this Carboniferous, *Archaeopteris*-like foliage. The fact that *Palaeopteridium* might be more frond-like than the lateral branch systems of *Archaeopteris*, however, does not necessarily negate the possibility of a close phylogenetic relationship between these genera. Indeed, as has been emphasized many times (Beck 1970, 1971; Banks 1970; Doyle 1978; Carluccio, Hueber, and Banks 1966; Matten 1968, etc.), compound fronds might have evolved from compound lateral branch systems; and the presence of a noeggerathiopsid foliage genus such as *Palaeopteridium*, similar in general aspect to *Archaeopteris* lateral branch systems and immediately following *Archaeopteris* in the geologic column (Leary and Pfefferkorn 1977), lends credence to this suggestion.

In some ways, *Noeggerathia* is more similar to *Archaeopteris* than is *Palaeopteridium*. Although differing from lateral branch systems of *Archae-*

FIGURES 6.26–6.28. *Noeggerathia foliosa.* × 2. **6.26.** Vegetative shoot showing axis bearing two rows of alternate leaves on its adaxial side. (From Šetlík [1956], by permission.) **6.27.** Abaxial view of vegetative shoot. (From Šetlík [1956], by permission.) **6.28.** Ultimate vegetative shoot of *Archaeopteris*. × 1.5.

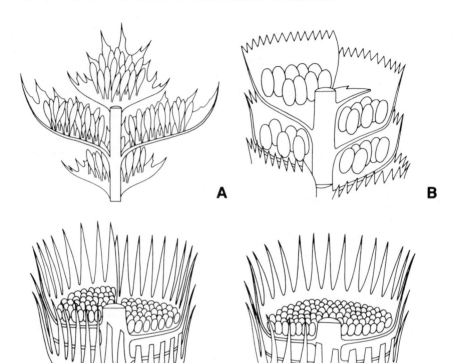

FIGURE 6.29. Possible sequence of stages in the evolution of the noeggerathialean strobilus as suggested by Leary and Pfefferkorn (1977). **6.29A.** *Archaeopteris.* **6.29B.** *Noeggerathiostrobus.* **6.29C.** *Lacoea.* **6.29D.** *Discinites.* (6.29B, C, D redrawn from Leary and Pfefferkorn [1977], by permission.) (6.29A. Original.)

opteris in consisting of only one branch order, *Noeggerathia* is now widely interpreted as a plagiotropic shoot (see references cited previously). Whereas the simple leaves have been usually considered to be arranged distichously (see Boureau 1964), Šetlík (1956) demonstrated a clear asymmetry in leaf arrangement, with alternate leaves characterized by decurrent bases like those of *Archaeopteris* (Beck 1971) arranged in two orthostichies on the adaxial side of the shoot axis (Fig. 6.26) and no leaves at all on the abaxial side (Fig. 6.27). The loss of two adjacent orthostichies of leaves from the ultimate branch of the *Archaeopteris* lateral branch system (characterized by decussate phyllotaxy) and a 45° rotation of the axis, or in the position of the orthostichies, would result in a condition like that in *Noeggerathia*.

A possible major difference in habit between *Noeggerathia* and *Archaeopteris* is reflected in the closely spaced helical arrangement of the leaf-

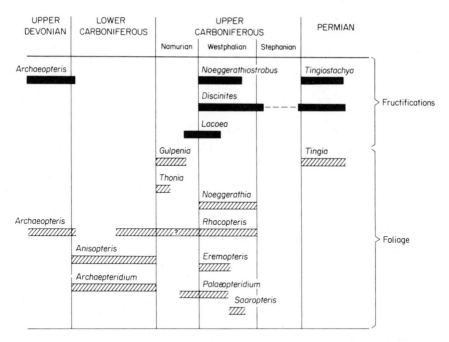

FIGURE 6.30. Known distribution in the geologic column of fructifications and foliage of *Archaeopteris*, noeggerathialeans, and similar forms. (From Leary and Pfefferkorn [1977], by permission.)

bearing shoots on large branches with a diameter of about 4 to 5 cm (Šetlík 1956). While this type of morphology—more reminiscent of a shrub than of a tree—neither detracts from nor supports a possible phylogenetic relationship between these groups, it does call attention to the possibility that Noeggerathiopsida as well as *Archaeopteris* might have been characterized by several different growth forms.

Arnold first demonstrated heterospory in *Archaeopteris* in 1939. Subsequent studies by Pettitt (1965) and Phillips, Andrews, and Gensel (1972) have shown that heterospory was common in the genus and probably characteristic of the entire group. As in Noeggerathiopsida, megasporangia and microsporangia were borne on the same sporophyll. Although spores of *Archaeopteris* are only about one-half as large as those of Noeggerathiopsida, the size ratio between megaspores and microspores is the same (about 8:1), and the spores are similar in general morphological features. *Archaeopteris* megaspores have sculptured exines and those of Noeggerathiopsida are smooth, but the microspores are so similar that those of some species of both groups have been assigned to the same dispersed spore genus, *Cyclogranisporites*.

As our understanding of the nature of the sporophylls of *Archaeopteris* has improved, largely through the work of Phillips, Andrews, and Gensel (1972), the possible close relationship of *Archaeopteris* and the noeggerathiopsids has gained credence. Phillips, Andrews, and Gensel (1972) demonstrated the laminate nature of the fertile ultimate appendages in *Archaeopteris macilenta*, and their planate, but much branched, nature in *A. halliana*. This morphology, in combination with the occurrence of an admixture of megasporangia and microsporangia on their adaxial surfaces, provide these sporophylls with a remarkably close resemblance to the sporophylls of noeggerathiopsids. Consequently, the placement of *Archaeopteris* at the base of a proposed evolutionary sequence of noeggerathiopsid strobili (Leary and Pfefferkorn 1977) (Fig. 6.29), which includes *Noeggerathiostrobus, Lacoea,* and *Discinites*, can now be rather strongly supported.[4] Strong additional support comes from recent studies in my laboratory and a resulting new reconstruction of the strobilus of *Archaeopteris macilenta*.

The Strobilus of *Archaeopteris macilenta*

In order to determine the three-dimensional morphology of the ultimate fertile shoots of *Archaeopteris*, fertile material collected from a road cut on the southeast side of state route #10, two miles northeast of the Cannonsville Reservoir dam, near Cannonsville, Delaware County, New York was studied. This material, from the Katsberg formation, of Frasnian (lower Upper Devonian) age, is on file under #64125 in the Paleobotanical Collections of the Museum of Paleontology, University of Michigan. In order to determine the arrangement of the ultimate fertile appendages, their morphology, and the arrangement of sporangia, 40 transfers were made, largely according to the method of Walton (see Lacey 1953). These supplemented observations on other specimens which underwent dégagement.

Several of these fertile specimens have been identified with certainty as *Archaeopteris macilenta* on the basis of vegetative leaf morphology (Figs. 6.14, 6.17, 6.24, 6.25). Since the fertile specimens are intermixed in the collection with a large number of solely vegetative specimens (see Beck 1971), all of which seem to have the characteristics of *A. macilenta*, and all of which were collected from the same shaly lens, one can only conclude that the fertile material probably also represents this species.

As previously reported by many workers, fertile lateral branch systems seem to be only partly fertile, the fertile ultimate shoots usually occupying the midregion (Fig. 6.13, right). Commonly, all ultimate shoots in such a region are fertile (Figs. 6.13 left, and 6.19), but occasionally there is an intermixture of fertile and vegetative ultimate shoots (Fig. 6.17). As reported by Beck (1971) and Phillips, Andrews, and Gensel (1972), there is a transition between solely fertile and solely vegetative shoots. The transitional shoots are characterized by a larger number of basal vegetative leaves, and by fertile ultimate appendages that become progressively more laminate and bear fewer scattered sporangia in the direction of the solely vegetative region (Fig. 6.13). This transition zone may include three or four ultimate shoots (Fig. 6.13). When observed on the surface of the split rock matrix (both part and counterpart), ultimate fertile shoots appear to bear two ranks of linear fertile ultimate appendages (Figs. 6.13 left, and 6.16), each of which bears a single row of sporangia (Fig. 6.16). More recent studies (Carluccio, Hueber, and Banks 1966; Beck 1971; Phillips, Andrews, and Gensel 1972), however, have begun to provide a different, more accurate picture.

Analysis of the transfers corroborates my earlier conclusion (Beck 1971) that the ultimate fertile appendages are decussately arranged (Fig. 6.15). They also show conclusively that, in *A. macilenta*, they are basally laminate and that they bear many sporangia scattered over the adaxial surfaces (Figs. 6.15, 6.20, 6.22–6.25).

It is now apparent that the ultimate fertile shoots of *Archaeopteris* exhibit the characteristics of strobili, and that the fertile ultimate appendages are sporophylls. The laminate nature of the sporophylls in *A. macilenta* is clearly demonstrated in several transfers and strongly suggested in several others. The outer surface of the strobilus (Figs. 6.22, 6.23) was exposed by interrupting the digestion process before the matrix had been completely removed. The sporophylls, viewed from their abaxial surfaces, are broadly laminate. Whereas some evidence of marginal (especially apical) dissection is visible, the distal parts of the sporophylls were largely broken off either in the transfer process or prior to preservation. Sporangia, or fragments of sporangia attached to the adaxial surfaces, can be observed extending beyond the distal edges of the sporophylls (Figs. 6.22, 6.23). The presence of many sporangia on the adaxial surface of sporophylls is clearly demonstrated in Figures 6.15 and 6.20, although in these the laminate nature of the sporophylls is not clear. The transfer illustrated in Figures 6.24 and 6.25 contains parts of two adjacent strobili, one (Fig. 6.24) broken along an essentially median longitudinal plane, the other (Fig. 6.25) broken tangentially. Consequently, both sectional (Fig. 6.24) and adaxial surface views of sporophylls of adjacent strobili are demonstrated. Whereas very careful observation of the sporophylls illustrated in sectional view (Fig. 6.24) might suggest that they were not simple, linear structures bearing a single row of adaxial sporangia, one could not possibly ascertain an accurate picture of the morphology of the sporophylls. By contrast, the adaxial surface view (Fig. 6.25) provides a remarkable, although not complete, picture of the sporophylls of this strobilus. They are broadly laminate, flaring from the base, and terminate in several irregularly toothed segments (Fig. 6.25). Each "tooth" seems to end in a slender spine-like projection (Fig. 6.25, arrow), a view expressed by Phillips, Andrews, and Gensel (1972), but this may be an artifact of preservation. The spine-like tip may represent the end of a vein which was more resistant to degradation than the enclosing lamina. Sporangia were attached singly or in small clusters to the adaxial surface extending nearly to the margins of the sporophylls. Many of the sporangia still attached to these sporophylls seem to be marginal. The more marginal sporangia which during compaction might have become oriented, essentially, in the plane of the sporophyll would be those most likely to be included in a transfer of a specimen exposed by a tangential break through the strobilus. Since more centrally located sporangia were not in contact with the adhesive (being separated from it by the lamina), they were apparently lost during the maceration procedure. It is clear that numerous sporangia were attached to the adaxial surfaces of the sporophylls, extending from near the base to within a distance from tips of the terminal segments of about one-half the total length of the sporophylls (Figs. 6.15, 6.20, 6.24). These observations corroborate those of Phillips, Andrews, and Gensel (1972) and provide the basis for a new reconstruction of the strobilus of *Archaeopteris macilenta* (Fig. 6.31).

Basally the strobilus bears vegetative leaves, arranged somewhat irregularly at first, but becoming decussate. These leaves intergrade through a short transition zone with decussately arranged sporophylls, the more basal of which seem to bear fewer sporangia and to be more completely laminate (i.e., less dissected) than more distal ones. Centrally located sporophylls are also conspicuously laminate, but are dissected apically, usually not beyond the approximate midpoint between base and apex. The strobilus may terminate in a few vegetative leaves that diminish in size and degree of dissection toward the tip.

Whereas the vegetative leaves on ultimate branches of *Archaeopteris* became developmentally oriented in parallel planes in relation to the prevailing light source, the sporophylls clearly did not. Instead, they were inserted in a plane intersecting that of the axis on which they were borne. This explains why they commonly appear as linear structures in compression specimens which, when exposed by breaking the rock matrix, present a largely median longitudinal view of the strobilus (Fig. 6.16). The strobili, therefore, were conspicuously three-dimensional and deviated from the general plagiotropic condition characteristic of other parts of the lateral branch systems. Indeed, it is no longer entirely clear to what extent the ultimate branches were distichously arranged since Scheckler (1978) has demonstrated ultimate branches deviating from this pattern.

Perhaps the most significant consequence of our better comprehension of the nature of the *Archaeopteris* strobilus is the recognition of its striking resemblance to the noeggerathiopsid strobilus (Figs. 6.4, 6.29B–D). In almost every feature—the basal vegetative leaves, the laminate sporophylls,

FIGURE 6.31. Restoration of a strobilus of *Archaeopteris macilenta* borne on a penultimate axis of a lateral branch system.

the numerous adaxial sporangia, the admixture of megasporangia and microsporangia on a sporophyll, the longitudinal dehiscence of sporangia, and the general similarity of the spores (microspores of both groups have been placed in the same dispersed spore genus)—these strobili are fundamentally similar. Differences in the number of rows and in the arrangement of the sporophylls, and minor details in morphology and size of strobilar components, are probably not significant. Indeed, when one now considers both vegetative and reproductive characteristics of the two groups, the evidence for a close evolutionary relationship between *Archaeopteris* and the Noeggerathiopsida seems quite compelling. I am willing to suggest that the Noeggerathiopsida might represent an extension of the progymnosperm line through the Carboniferous.

In this chapter I have suggested possible evolutionary relationships between *Archaeopteris* and the primitive coniferopsid seed plants, Cordaitales and Lebachiaceae, as well as between *Archaeopteris* and the pteridophytic Noeggerathiopsida. I wish to emphasize that these proposals are, at this stage, merely hypotheses. And they will remain so until we learn much more about the several groups involved. We need to know more about the anatomy of the primitive Paleozoic conifers and there is still much to learn about the cordaites. As for the Noeggerathiopsida, nothing is known about their anatomy, and almost nothing about branching patterns; and we can only guess about the affinities of the *Archaeopteris*-like foliage of the Carboniferous—some of which has been assigned to the Noeggerathiopsida. Finally, we must continue our investigations of *Archaeopteris* and other progymnosperms.

If this chapter has done nothing else, I hope it will have generated some interest which may lead to further research in these areas. And consequently, that future studies will contribute to our even clearer understanding of the role of *Archaeopteris* in vascular plant evolution.

NOTES

1. Although it is not certain that all secondary wood with radially aligned groups of pits (Callixylon) represents *Archaeopteris*, the bulk of the evidence supports the view that it does. I am not able to confirm the report of radially banded, grouped pits in the aneurophyte *Triloboxylon* (Scheckler and Banks 1971).

2. In these groups only the ultimate branches are deciduous.

3. Among conifers, dichotomous venation characterizes primitive taxa such as *Lebachia* (bifurcate leaves), *Buriadia,* and *Carpentieria* (Florin 1951).

4. On the basis of their known distribution in the geologic column (Fig. 6.30), it can be argued that *Lacoea* should precede *Noeggerathiostrobus* in this proposed evolutionary sequence. The placement of *Noeggerathiostrobus* before *Lacoea* (Leary and Pfefferkorn 1977) was based on the greater distance between sporophylls in *Noeggerathiostrobus*.

ACKNOWLEDGMENTS

Supported by NSF grants DEB 7514861 A01 and DEB 7811165.

I acknowledge with gratitude the art work of D. Bell and the assistance in photography of D. Bay and R. Lowry.

REFERENCES

Andrews, H. N., T. L. Phillips, and N. W. Radforth. 1965. Paleobotanical studies in arctic Canada. I. *Archaeopteris* from Ellesmere Island. *Can. J. Bot.* 3:545–56.

Arnold, C. A. 1930a. The genus *Callixylon* from the Upper Devonian of central and western New York. *Pap. Mich. Acad. Sci.* 11:1–50.

———. 1930b. Bark structure of *Callixylon. Bot. Gaz.* 90:427–31.

———. 1981. On *Callixylon newberryi* (Dawson) Elkins et Wieland. *Contr. Mus. Paleont. Univ. Michigan* 3:207–32.

———. 1934. *Callixylon whiteanum* sp. nov., from the Woodford chert of Oklahoma. *Bot. Gaz.* 96:180–85.

———. 1936. Observations on fossil plants from the Devonian of Eastern North America I. Plant remains from Scaumenac Bay, Quebec. *Contr. Mus. Paleont. Univ. Michigan* 5:37–48.

———. 1939. Observations on fossil plants from the Devonian of eastern North America. IV. Plant remains from the Catskill Delta deposits of northern Pennsylvania and southern New York. *Contrib. Mus. Paleontol. Univ. Mich.* 5:271–313.

Banks, H. P. 1968. The early history of land plants. In *Evolution and Environment* (E. T. Drake, ed.). New Haven: Yale University Press, pp. 73–106.

———. 1970. *Evolution and Plants of the Past.* Belmont, Calif.: Wadsworth.

Beck, C. B. 1953. A new root species of *Callixylon. Am. J. Bot.* 40:226–33.

———. 1960a. Connection between *Archaeopteris* and *Callixylon. Science* 131:1524–25.

———. 1960b. The identity of *Archaeopteris* and *Callixylon. Brittonia* 12:351–68.

———. 1962a. Reconstructions of *Archaeopteris*, and further consideration of its phylogenetic position. *Am. J. Bot.* 49:373–82.

———. 1962b. Plants of the New Albany Shale. II. *Callixylon arnoldii* sp. nov. *Brittonia* 14:322–37.

———. 1964a. Predominance of *Archaeopteris* in Upper Devonian flora of western Catskills and adjacent Pennsylvania. *Bot. Gaz.* 125:126–28.

———. 1964b. The woody, fern-like trees of the Devonian. *Mem. Torrey Bot. Club* 21:26–37.

———. 1966. On the origin of gymnosperms. *Taxon* 15:337–39.

———. 1969. Problems of generic delimitation in paleobotany. *Proc. N. A. Paleontol. Conv., Part C*, pp. 173–93.

———. 1970. The appearance of gymnospermous structure. *Biol. Rev. Camb. Philos. Soc.* 45:379–400.

———. 1971. On the anatomy and morphology of lateral branch systems of *Archaeopteris. Am. J. Bot.* 58:758–84.

———. 1976. Current status of the Progymnospermopsida. *Rev. Palaeobot. Palynol.* 21:5–23.

———. 1979. The primary vascular system of *Callixylon. Rev. Palaeobot. Palynol.* 28:103–15.

Beck, C. B., K. Coy, and R. Schmid. 1981. Observations on the fine structure of *Callixylon* wood. Amer. J. Bot. (In press).

Browne, I. 1933. The Noeggerathiae and the Tingiae. *New Phytol.* 32:344–58.

Carluccio, L. C., F. M. Hueber, and H. P. Banks. 1966. *Archaeopteris macilenta,* anatomy and morphology of its frond. *Am. J. Bot.* 53:719–30.

Chaloner, W. G., and A. Sheerin. 1979. Devonian macrofloras. The Devonian System. *Spec. Pap. Palaeontol.* 23:145–61.

Doyle, J. A. 1978. Fossil evidence on the evolutionary origin of tropical trees and forests. In *Tropical Trees as Living Systems* (P. B. Tomlinson and M. H. Zimmermann, eds.). Cambridge: Cambridge University Press, pp. 3–36.

Eggert, D. A. 1961. The ontogeny of Carboniferous arborescent Lycopsida. *Palaeontographica* 108B:43–92.

Florin, R. 1951. Evolution in cordaites and conifers. *Acta Horti Bergiani* 15:285–388.

Halle, T. G. 1954. Notes on the Noeggerathiineae. *Svensk Bot. Tidskr.* 48:368–80.

Hirmer, M. 1940. In M. Hirmer and P. Guthörl, Die Karbon-flora des Saargebietes. Abteilung 3: Filicales und Verwandte (Noeggerathiineae; *Rhacopteris*). *Palaeontographica* (Bot. Suppl.) 9:1–60.

Hoskins, J. H., and A. T. Cross. 1951. The structure and classification of four plants from the New Albany shale. *Am. Midl. Nat.* 46:684–716.

Iurina, A., and Y. Lemoigne. 1979. Sur la presence du *Callixylon newberryi* (Dawson) Elkins et Wieland 1814, en Kazakhstan (U.R.S.S.) au Devonien Superieur. *Palaeontographica* 170B:1–9.

Johnson, T. 1911. Is *Archaeopteris* a pteridosperm? *Sci. Proc. Roy. Dublin Soc.* (N.S.) 13:114–36.

———. 1914. *Ginkgophyllum* kiltorkense sp. nov. *Sci. Proc. Roy. Dublin Soc.* 14:169–78.

Kidston, R. 1923. Fossil plants of the Carboniferous rocks of Great Britain. *Mem. Geol. Surv. Gr. Brit., Palaeontology* 2:1–375.

Kräusel, R., and H. Weyland. 1929. Beiträge zur Kenntnis der Devonflora. III. Abh. Senckenberg. *Naturforsch. Ges.* 41:317–59.

———. 1937. Pflanzenreste aus dem Devon X. Zwei Pflanzenfunde in Oberdevon der Eifel. *Senckenbergiana* 19:338–55.

———. 1941. Pflanzenreste aus dem Devon von Nord-Amerika. II. Die Oberdevonischen Floren von Elkins, West-Virginien, und Perry, Maine, mit Berücksichtigung einiger Stücke von der Chaleur-Bai, Canada. *Palaeontographica* 83B:3–78.

Lacey, W. S. 1953. Methods in palaeobotany. *N.W. Nat.* 24:234–49.

Leary, R. L. 1973. *Lacoea,* a Lower Pennsylvanian noeggerathialean cone from Illinois. *Rev. Palaeobot. Palynol.* 15:43–50.

Leary, R. L., and H. W. Pfefferkorn. 1977. An early Pennsylvanian flora with *Megalopteris* and Noeggerathiales from west-central Illinois. *Ill. State Geol. Surv. Circ.* 500:1–77.

Lee, H. H., and C. Y. Tsai. 1978. Devonian floras of China. Papers for the International Symposium on the Devonian System, 1978, No. 3:1–15. Nanking Institute of Geology and Paleontology, Academia Sinica.

Lepekhina, V. G. 1963. New finds of cordaitean woods from upper Paleozoic of Kazakhstan. *J Palaeont.* 4:101–9.

Marcelle, H. 1957. *Callixylon velinense* nov. sp., un bois à structure conservée du Dévonien de Belgique Bull. *Acad. Roy. Belg.* 37:908–19.

Matten, L. C. 1968. *Actinoxylon banksii* gen. et sp. nov.: A progymnosperm from the Middle Devonian of New York. *Am. J. Bot.* 55:773–82.

Meeuse, A. D. J. 1963. From ovule to ovary: A contribution to the phylogeny of the megasporangium. *Acta Biotheor.* 16:127–82.

Nathorst, A. G. 1902. Zur Oberdevonischen Flora der Bären-Insel. *J. Svenska Ventenkaps-Akad. Handl.* 36:1–60.

———. 1904. Die oberdevonische Flora des Ellesmere-Landes. Rept. 2nd Norwegian Arctic Expedition in the Fram, 1898–1902, No. 1:1–22.

Němejc, F. 1928. A revision of the Carboniferous and Permian flora of the coal-districts in Central Bohemia. *Palaeont. Boh.* 12:41–82.

———. 1931. The morphology and systematic relations of the Carboniferous Noeggerathiae with regard to the "genera" *Tingia* and *Plagiozamites* of Eastern Asia. *Preslia* 10:111–14.

Pant, D. D., and D. D. Nautiyal. 1967. On the structure of *Buriadia heterophylla* (Feistmantel) Seward & Sahni and its fructification. *Phil. Trans. Roy. Soc.* (Lond.) 252B:27–48.

Petrosyan, N. M. 1967. Stratigraphic importance of the Devonian flora of the USSR. In *International Symposium on the Devonian System* (D. H. Oswald, ed.). Calgary: Alberta Society of Petroleum Geologists. 2:579–86.

Pettitt, J. M. 1965. Two heterosporous plants from the Upper Devonian of North America. *Bull. Br. Mus. Nat. Hist. (Geol.)* 10:83–92.

Pettitt, J. M., and C. B. Beck. 1968. *Archaeosperma arnoldii*—a cupulate seed from the Upper Devonian of North America. *Contr. Mus. Paleontol. Univ. Mich.* 22:139–54.

Phillips, T. L., H. N. Andrews, and P. G. Gensel. 1972. Two heterosporous species of *Archaeopteris* from the Upper Devonian of West Virginia. *Palaeontographica* 139B:47–71.

Remy, W., and R. Remy. 1956. *Noeggerathiostrobus vicinalis* E. Weiss und Bemerkungen zu ähnlichen Fruktifikationen. *Abh. Deutsch. Akad. Wiss. Berlin.* 1956(z):3–11.

Rothwell, G. W. 1977. The primary vasculature of *Cordaianthus concinnus*. *Am. J. Bot.* 64:1235–41.

Scheckler, S. E. 1978. Ontogeny of progymnosperms. II. Shoots of Upper Devonian Archaeopteridales. *Can. J. Bot.* 56:3136–70.

Scheckler, S. E., and H. P. Banks. 1971. Anatomy and relationships of some Devonian progymnosperms from New York. *Am. J. Bot.* 58:737–51.

Schmid, R. 1967. Electron microscopy of wood of *Callixylon* and *Cordaites*. *Amer. J. Bot.* 54:720–29.

Šetlík, J. 1956. Contribution a l'étude de *Noeggerathia foliosa* Sternberg. *Rospravy Ústředního Ústavu Geologického* 21:79–106.

Seward, A. C. 1910. *Fossil Plants.* Cambridge: Cambridge University Press. Vol. 2.

Stur, D. 1878. Zur Kenntnis der Fruktifikation der *Noeggerathia foliosa* Stbg. aus den Radnitzer Schichten des Oberen Carbon von Mittel-Böhmen. *Verhandl. K. K. Geologisch. Reichs-Anstalt* 15:329–36.

Wilde, M. H. 1944. A new interpretation of coniferous cones. I. Podocarpaceae (*Podocarpus*). *Ann. Bot.* (N.S.) 8:1–41.

Zalessky, M. D. 1911. Étude sur l'anatomie du *Dadoxylon tchihatcheffi* Goeppert. *Trudy. geol. Kom.* 68:18–29.

7

PALEOECOLOGY OF MIDDLE PENNSYLVANIAN AGE COAL SWAMPS IN SOUTHERN ILLINOIS/HERRIN COAL MEMBER AT SAHARA MINE NO. 6

Tom L. Phillips and William A. DiMichele

INTRODUCTION

Most of the morphological studies of late Desmoinesian age (late Westphalian D) coal-ball plants in the Euramerican floral province have utilized specimens from the Herrin (No. 6) Coal at the Sahara Coal Company Mine No. 6 in southern Illinois. The compiled coal-ball flora of 59 genera and 68 identified species is the largest known for a single mine in the Pennsylvanian. Quantitative analysis of coal-swamp vegetation from peat profiles from two sites with 12 to 15 coal-ball zones, 526 coal balls, and 31,555 cm² surface area of peels (biomass determinations) indicate that the seam is dominated by lycopods with 63 to 65 percent of the volume; ferns and pteridosperms are subdominants with 15 to 17 percent and 15 to 16 percent, respectively. Sphenopsids contributed 4 percent with cordaites ≤ 0.2 percent. The organ composition of the peat profiles is 35 to 47 percent for roots, 27 to 42 percent for stems, 17 to 18 percent foliage, and 6 to 9 percent fructifications. Lycopods and ferns are the major contributors of roots and fructifications; lycopod stems and pteridosperm foliage are the most abundant for those organs. On a seam basis the peat is largely composed of these genera: *Lepidophloios* (29 to 49 percent), *Lepidodendron* (13 to 27 percent), *Psaronius* (15 to 16 percent), and *Medullosa* (13 to 14 percent). The most complete vertical section of coal-ball zones indicates an oscillating series of swamp environments between strongly dominated *Lepidophloios* forests with low diversity and diverse forests with *Lepidodendron* or rarely *Sigillaria*, a lower story of *Psaronius* and/or *Medullosa*, and a ground story of small plants. Changes in vegetation occur in relationship to the five clastic partings in the seam. *Sigillaria-Paralycopodites* assemblages with the maximum fusain content for the profile occur between the most prominent pair of gray shale bands. Indications of two floods intervened by an extreme dry period are compared to the "blue band." *Lepidophloios* (prolonged standing water and net rising water table) and *Sigillaria* (driest habitat conditions) assemblages are the extremes in polar ordination of communities. *Lepidodendron-Medullosa* assemblages are variously intermediate in habitats and are diverse. *Psaronius* probably exhibits the broadest ecological amplitude. Dominance diversity curves of representative assemblages are illustrated. The paleoecology of the two sites differs significantly in thickness and number of coal-ball zones, relative abundances of aerial and root composition, and percent volume of *Lepidophloios* and *Lepidodendron scleroticum*. Beta-diversity values for the two sites are 2.4 to 3.1. The field relations of coal-ball zones, clastic bands, major fusain and pyrite occurrences, and the continuity and preservational qualities of the vegetation are consistent with independent coal-ball formation from the bottommost coal-ball zone upward in a recurrent series of permineralizing episodes.

The maximum development of Pennsylvanian age coal swamps in midcontinent United States occurred during the Desmoinesian Epoch, approximately the equivalent of Westphalian D in western Europe. This interval contains most of the minable coal reserves in the Interior Coal Province and most of the known coal-ball deposits from which peat stages of the coals can be studied. Two broadly different kinds of coal-swamp settings seemed to have prevailed successively in the early and late Desmoinesian. Lycopod trees, primarily *Lepidophloios* and *Lepidodendron*, dominated the vegetation on the whole, but they were subdominants (on a seam basis) where cordaitean seed plants dominated coastal mangrove-like swamps in the Western Region of the Interior Coal Province (Oklahoma, Kansas, Missouri, Iowa). In the lower delta plain environments of the Eastern Region or Illinois Basin Coal Field (Illinois and western portions of Indiana and Kentucky) the cordaites were concurrently subdominant. This "cordaitean interval" of swamp vegetation attained its zenith early in the Desmoinesian and ended with the Iron Post Coal Member of Oklahoma and with the Summum Coal Member of Illinois in the middle Desmoinesian.

In the late Desmoinesian swamps of the Illinois Basin Coal Field lycopod trees dominated with abundant tree ferns and seed ferns; cordaites were rare, constituting ≤ 0.5 percent of the coal-ball peats. This is the time interval during which the peats of the Herrin Coal were deposited. In the Desmoinesian-Missourian transition the principal lycopod trees of Desmoinesian swamps abruptly disappeared. Tree ferns dominated many of the Missourian coal-swamps with subdominant seed ferns (Phillips et al. 1974; Phillips and Peppers 1979).

The two most economically important coals of the late Desmoinesian of the Illinois Basin are the Springfield and Herrin Coal Members in the upper part of the Carbondale Formation of the Kewanee Group (Hopkins and Simon 1975). These two coals represent about 75 percent of the minable reserves in Illinois or about 120 billion tons. Most of these reserves are in the Herrin seam which is 4 to 10 feet thick over >10,000 square miles (Smith and Stall 1975).

Mining activities in the Herrin Coal have resulted in the discovery of coal balls in more than 18 mines in Illinois since the first such report by Cady (1937). Although there are more known coal-ball occurrences in the Herrin than in any other coal in the United States, most of the paleobotanical studies of coal-ball plants in the Herrin, and, in turn, in the late Desmoinesian, have been based on specimens from the Sahara Coal Company No. 6 Mine near Carrier Mills in southern Illinois. The mine has yielded the largest number of coal balls with well-preserved plants of any mine in Illinois although there are thicker and more massive occurrences locally at other mines in the southern part of the coalfield (Kosanke, Simon, and Smith 1958; DeMaris and Bauer 1978). The mine opened in 1936 and has been a continued source of permineralized peats since the late 1950s when the coal balls became known to the Illinois State Geological Survey. About 5,000 acres of the Herrin Coal have been mined there.

Because of the frequency of coal-ball deposits, locally occupying most of the seam thickness, and the good to excellent preservation of the peat, the Sahara mine was selected as an experimental site for the quantification and vegetational analysis of swamp peats in the Pennsylvanian by Phillips, Kunz, and Mickish (1977). The primary objectives of their study were to develop a botanical index to the constitution of coal, to determine specifically the vegetational changes that occurred within the temporal span of the swamp at various sites, to compare them, and to relate these botanical data to the geologic settings. They also established the feasibility of the kind of study initiated by Schopf (1939). Further work has been necessary to begin to interpret the paleoecology of the swamp from a natural assemblage or community approach. This has required intensive sampling at new sites with special attention to clastic and fusain bands in the coal and greater precision in extracting zones of coal balls. It was necessary to monograph the lycopods from coal-ball peats in order to develop a practical means of identifying the bulk of the vegetation at generic and specific levels. These and related studies on the lycopods were carried out by DiMichele (1979a, 1979b, 1979c, 1980), DiMichele, Mahaffy, and Phillips (1979), DiMichele and Phillips (in press), Phillips (1979), and Leisman and Phillips (1979).

It now seems possible to begin to deal with swamp communities on a quantitative basis and to attempt to determine some of the environmental parameters associated with different kinds of swamps and with successive environments within them. While numerous problems remain, we have attempted to emphasize what can now be determined about such an ancient coal swamp. To the extent that botanical constituents and swamp paleoecology are central to interrelating and predicting coal qualities, apart from rank, they have great potential application in the selective exploration and beneficiation of coal reserves. Swamp plants track environments and represent major sources of detailed information on plant morphology, reproductive biology, and evolution. Development of a paleoecological data base seems imperative for understanding these aspects of swamp plants as well as predicting the qualities of the derived coals.

ENVIRONMENTAL SETTING

The paleogeographic map of Westphalian C/D time by Ziegler et al. (1979) provides the general environmental setting for the Illinois Basin Coal Field and the Herrin swamp, located just south of the paleoequator (Fig. 7.1). The Sahara mine is located at the southernmost part of the U-shaped distribution of coal-ball occurrences in the Desmoinesian of the Illinois Basin. According to the climatic model used by Ziegler et al. (1979), the Herrin swamp was in the tropical rainy zone of the Prevailing Easterlies with the rising Appalachians as a potential orographic barrier to precipitation.

During the Pennsylvanian Period the Michigan River system (Pryor and Sable 1974) was the principal stream system into the Illinois Basin. It drained eastern parts of the Canadian Shield and northern extensions of the Appalachian Mountain belt, flowing westward then into the basin. It was the source of terrigenous deltaic sediments upon which the Herrin swamp developed and of channels contemporaneous with the swamp. The principal paleochannel of this system within the swamp is known as the Walshville (Johnson 1972). It has been traced along a continuous meandering course for 274 km (Nelson 1979) and its southernmost limit is about 45 km west of the Sahara mine (Fig. 7.2).

While the subsidence rates in the Illinois Basin are considered slow and gentle compared to those in the Appalachian region they were not uniform in the Herrin swamp (Wanless 1956). However, changes in water tables appear to have been relatively similar over much of the Herrin swamp during most of its existence. These could account for the marked similarity of the general kinds of vegetation in the swamp and of the kinds of changes that occurred. The data on the miospores of the two most abundant kinds of lower vascular plants, lycopods and ferns, provided by R. A. Peppers, Illinois State Geological Survey, indicate marked quantitative similarities over the regions sampled (Fig. 7.2). The known occurrences of coal balls and extensive profiles of coal-ball peats are more limited regionally and largely

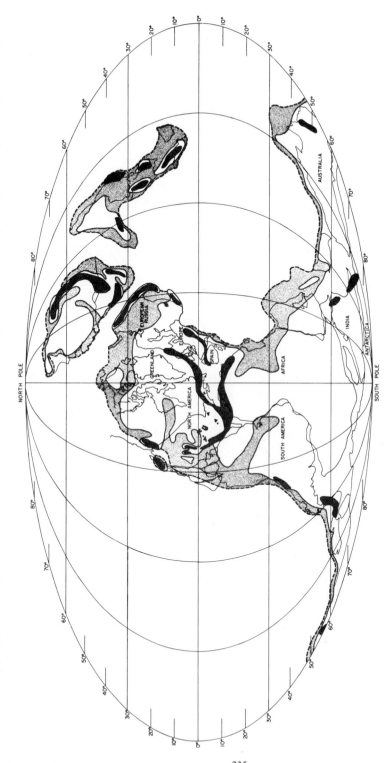

FIGURE 7.1. Coal-ball occurrences in the middle Pennsylvanian of Euramerica. The interval of time depicted by the paleogeographical reconstruction by Ziegler and Scotese (1979) is Westphalian C-D with coal-ball occurrences indicated by black dots in North America and European Russia. The Illinois Basin Coal Field is just south of the paleoequator and is outlined by a U-shaped series of black dots. Black shading = mountains; gray shading = shallow shelves which surround the lowlands indicated in white.

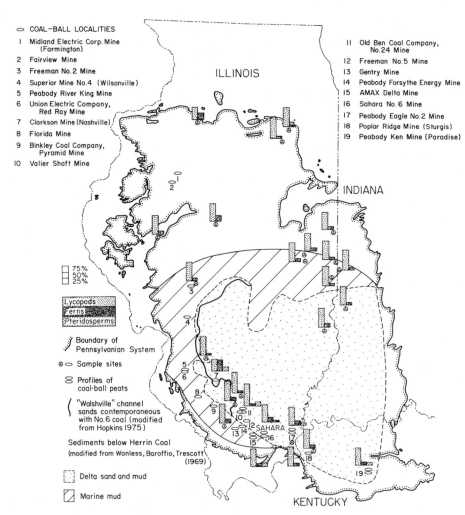

COAL—BALL LOCALITIES

1 Midland Electric Corp. Mine (Farmington)
2 Fairview Mine
3 Freeman No. 2 Mine
4 Superior Mine No. 4 (Wilsonville)
5 Peabody River King Mine
6 Union Electric Company, Red Ray Mine
7 Clarkson Mine (Nashville)
8 Florida Mine
9 Binkley Coal Company, Pyramid Mine
10 Valier Shaft Mine

11 Old Ben Coal Company, No. 24 Mine
12 Freeman No. 5 Mine
13 Gentry Mine
14 Peabody Forsythe Energy Mine
15 AMAX Delta Mine
16 Sahara No. 6 Mine
17 Peabody Eagle No. 2 Mine
18 Poplar Ridge Mine (Sturgis)
19 Peabody Ken Mine (Paradise)

ILLINOIS

INDIANA

75%
50%
25%

Lycopods
Ferns
Pteridosperms

Boundary of Pennsylvanian System

Sample sites

Profiles of coal-ball peats

"Walshville" channel sands contemporaneous with No. 6 coal (modified from Hopkins 1975)

Sediments below Herrin Coal (modified from Wanless, Baroffio, Trescott (1969)

Delta sand and mud

Marine mud

SAHARA

KENTUCKY

FIGURE 7.2. Peat and miospore abundances of major plant groups in the Herrin and Kentucky No. 11 Coal Member in the Illinois Basin Coal Field. The coal-ball localities occur along a continuous southern to northwestern arc across the coal field with the Sahara No. 6 Mine located near the southern extremity of the Herrin Coal in Illinois and to the east of the "Walshville" channel. Palynological data on the lycopods and ferns, provided by R. A. Peppers, Illinois State Geological Survey, indicate a relatively uniform vegetation over much of the swamp. For further explanation of peat data, see text. (Modified from DiMichele and Phillips [in press].)

fall along a geographic arc, roughly paralleling the southern and western portion of the basin. The geographic locations of coal-ball occurrences reflect both mining activities as well as similar kinds of geographic settings within the swamp, but thus far, no marked regional change in the swamp vegetation of the Herrin swamp has been detected. The lycopods were dominants of the seam vegetation with 72 to 75 percent of the biomass; ferns were usually second with 11 to 17 percent (Phillips, Kunz, and Mickish 1977). Pteridosperms were the most variable with 6 to 14 percent. Sphenopsids accounted for 1 to 4.5 percent and cordaites ≤ 0.5 percent.

Another widespread phenomenon in the Herrin Coal are shale partings, some of which extend over great distances. Correlative coals as far away as Kansas have been recognized with similar patterns of shale partings. The most prominent of these is called the "blue band."

COAL-BALL DISTRIBUTION AND COLLECTIONS

Despite the frequent occurrences of coal balls at the Sahara mine there has been no systematic mapping of locations over the past 20 years. However, the principal sites in the western portion of the mine (mining prior to 1966) were recorded and these are consistent with the approximate east-west trend of major coal-ball occurrences sampled in the eastern portion of the mine since 1971 (Fig. 7.3). Vertical sections (VS) 1 and 2 (Fig. 7.3) were used by Phillips, Kunz, and Mickish (1977) to experimentally establish adequate sampling of the peats. VS 5 was collected 1.6 km east of VS 2 and VS 4 is 0.6 km east of VS 5. Random samples and additional coal-ball profiles (VS 3, 6) were collected but are not included in this study.

The seam thickness averages 138 to 152 cm over most of the area except where massive coal-ball deposits occupy the entire seam thickness (VS 4). At VS 4 the thickness was 222 cm, of which 202 cm was coal-ball material. The thickness of the seam at VS 5 was 151 cm with 126 cm of coal-ball zones. The Anna Shale had been removed from both outcrops, perhaps with some top coal at VS 5, but the black roof shale was well exposed in proximity to all the coal-ball occurrences. The Anna Shale is the roof type over almost 90 percent of the Herrin Coal (Krausse et al. 1979).

The primary reference site for the study is VS 4 (Fig. 7.4). The zonation of coal balls was aided by the presence of numerous persistent shale partings, characteristic sizes of coal balls in some zones and distinct benches of coal. In sector 1 (VS 4) each of coal-ball zones was quite distinct except zones 14 and 15, a solid mass of permineralized peat which was arbitrarily subdivided. Certain of the coal-ball zones were laterally traceable over variable distances and, where possible, were collected in meter wide exposures. There were no coal balls in zone 0, VS 4, and such collections (A, B, sector 5) were

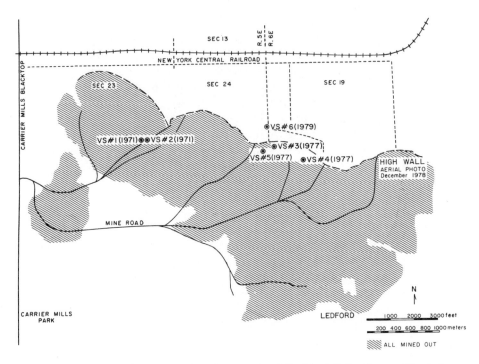

FIGURE 7.3. Map of the Sahara Coal Company Inc. Mine No. 6, Saline County, Illinois, in the Herrin (No. 6) Coal. The mine is located about 8 km (5 miles) southwest of Harrisburg. The locations and collection dates of the vertical sections of coal balls are shown along an east-west trend which coincides with coal-ball occurrences in the older (prior to 1966) mine area on the west side of the Carrier Mills Blacktop. (Prepared from an aerial photograph [December 1978] provided by Robert Gullic, Sahara Coal Company.)

obtained 9 m away in order to establish what was in the bottommost zone (mostly stigmarian root system). The details of sample sizes, thicknesses of zones, and some of the quantitative results are given in Figures 7.6 to 7.9.

The coal-ball collections from VS 4 (sector 1) bear the collection numbers 19,914–19,981 (zone 0) and 20,801–21,028; those of adjacent sectors are 21,029–21,100 and 21,401–21,406. Collections from VS 5 are numbered 20,501–20,696. All specimens and peels are housed in the Paleobotanical Collections (Davenport Hall), University of Illinois, Urbana. Spore slides from maceration 2545 of the Herrin Coal are located in the Coal Section, Illinois State Geological Survey, Urbana.

The coal-ball zones were color-coded with spray paint on the exposed

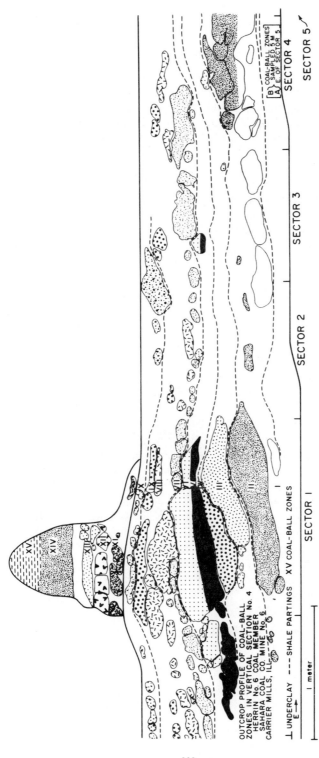

FIGURE 7.4. Outcrop profile of coal-ball zones in vertical section 4 in the Herrin (No. 6) Coal Member, Sahara Coal Co. Mine No. 6, near Carrier Mills, Illinois. The shading or symbols for each coal-ball zone correspond to those at the top of Figure 7.6. For further explanation, see text. (Prepared by the authors.)

sides and then on the tops for orientation after extraction. Coal-ball zones are not necessarily identical to natural vegetational zones; consequently, the orientation of coal balls is necessary for potential separation or merger of vegetational zones within one coal-ball zone or several. Several profiles from a given area allow examination of vegetational breaks from different coal-ball zonations, as well as detection of local variability in the peat layers and vegetational sequences.

QUANTIFICATION AND DATA MANIPULATION

The coal balls from each zone were cut into slices about 2.5 cm thick, transversely to the stratification of peat layers. The peels from all the faces were examined to aid in identification of contents of the middle peel and to determine if the peat of the coal ball was markedly different, requiring two peels for representative sampling. The middle peel usually constituted the maximum cross-sectional area and the botanical constituents were identified within cm² grids by taxa, organ, tissue, preservational states (pyritic, fusinized), and according to type of gametophyte for heterosporous fructifications. The identified plant material by cm² area is treated as a measure of volume or biomass. Data were sorted according to taxa, organs, and tissues by zone and with weighted zone thicknesses by seam profile for percent volume and percent number of the botanical categories. Calculations were made with all botanical categories with and without unidentifiable material. The unidentifiable portion of the coal-ball on a cm² area basis is simply termed "unidentified" and is given for each of the profiles. Thereafter, all the data used in peat profile plots and importance values in community analysis (aerial portions only) are normalized to 100 percent identified plant material. The quantitative components of the "unidentified" portion of the Herrin peats have been given in detail by Phillips, Kunz, and Mickish (1977) and are not included herein. The percent of the "unidentified" categories is markedly smaller than given by Phillips, Kunz, and Mickish (1977) who determined as precisely as possible how much area was not botanically identifiable. With that determined for numerous Herrin sites we have emphasized whatever is identifiable in grid areas.

The dominant and largest kinds of trees in the swamps were lycopods which have similar root systems, known as *Stigmaria*, and it is often not possible to directly relate the amount of root material contributed by each species to the peat. *Sigillaria* is an exception (Eggert 1972). Similarly, there are various amounts of leaf and stem tissue which could not be definitely assigned to one of the *Lepidodendron* species or to any particular arborescent lycopod. In order to arrive at approximate total biomass contributions by each of these lycopod trees (Table 7.5), the remaining uncertain percent volumes were determined for species based on ratios proportional to identifiable aerial tissues of the plants. This is generally satisfactory except for the fructifications of *Lepidodendron*. *Achlamydocarpon varius* is closely associated with *L. dicentricum*, and it may also have been a disseminule of *L. scleroticum*; therefore, it is listed separately in total biomass contributions. *Achlamydocarpon takhtajanii* occurred rarely, but there was no evidence of its putative parent plant, *Lepidodendron serratum* (Leisman and Rivers 1974). In the cases of *Psaronius* and *Medullosa* assemblages, the percent volume of each is summarized at the generic level.

It should be emphasized that the practical basis for dividing the peat profiles into vegetation zones are the sedimentological breaks of coal-ball zones. The techniques of community analysis are outlined by Whittaker (1975). The alpha-diversity (within a coal-ball zone or habitat) patterns are assessed on the percent volume of taxa within a zone. Importance values of taxa within each zone are based on the percent volume of aerial remains to reduce biases of introduced root material from subsequent assemblages above. *Psaronius* root mantle was the only exception with all inner root mantle and 50 percent of the outer roots counted in the aerial portion. Tabulated percent volumes (importance values) of aerial portions of each taxon were normalized to a 100 percent total per zone, allowing comparisons among zones. A possible bias here is in zones with very abundant root material and perhaps an insufficient aerial composition, such as zone 0, VS 4.

Taxa were grouped to form assemblages of natural affinity and to reduce the combined effect of form taxa increasing taxonomic diversity and reducing abundances of natural species or genera. The organ affinities of the lycopod taxa are indicated in the floral list (Table 7.1). As mentioned previously, *Achlamydocarpon varius* was somewhat of a problem and was included with *Lepidodendron dicentricum* if *L. scleroticum* was not present in the zone. *Psaronius* included all the appropriate assemblage except where several species are represented. *Psaronius* cf. *chasei* (Morgan 1959) and *Scolecopteris* of the *S. minor* group (Millay 1979) are the most abundant and were treated as one species. Where *Psaronius melandrus* occurs rarely along with *Scolecopteris* of the *S. latifolia* group, these were treated separately as a second species. *Medullosa* assemblages were tabulated separately from associated form foliage for percentage similarity analysis. *Alethopteris* cf. *lesquereuxii* was the most abundant foliage form. In calculations involving presence and absence data, species of form foliage were used to determine medullosan diversity. Form taxa problems were not significant in other groups.

Beta-diversity is measured in several ways and these procedures were used. Direct measurement of the beta-diversity of an entire profile (a single number) is obtained by:

$$\text{Beta-diversity} = \frac{Sc}{\bar{S}}$$

where, Sc =total number of species in the vertical profile (each only counted once regardless of total number of occurrences) and $\bar{S}$ = the average number of species per coal-ball zone of the profile. The higher the resultant number the larger the variability in species composition among the zones of a profile. Measurement of the similarity of zones within a profile is calculated by comparing each zone with every other zone (Table 7.8).

$$\text{Community coefficient} = \frac{2S\ ab}{Sa + Sb}$$

The community coefficient is a measure of the degree of compositional (floristic) similarity of two zones based on presence-absence of taxa, where Sab = number of taxa common to zones a and b; Sa + Sb is the sum of the number of taxa in zones a and b. Percentage similarity of two zones is a quantitative measure of the compositional (percent volume = biomass) similarity of two zones. It is calculated as the sum of smaller relative importance values in a species by species comparison of zones.

The compositional dissimilarity (1-percentage similarity) of zones of a profile can be quantitatively displayed in a polar ordination (Bray-Curtis ordination). Two axis ordinations were used to evaluate the zones in VS 4 (Fig. 7.11) and VS 5. Percentage dissimilarity data were used to compute Pythagorean distances of zones along x- and y-axes defined by the chosen end points (highly dissimilar vegetational zones), which are discussed with the results.

In polar ordination the most important factor in ordinating vegetation zones (based on coal-ball zones) is choice of suitable end points to define the axes. The end points must be sufficiently different to separate the other vegetation zones into groups with similar composition and structure. Ideally, this will allow some quantitative recognition of environmental gradients which may be deduced from other data. End points were chosen in VS 4 and 5 by comparing compositional data (both floristic and biomass) for zones of the profiles. Community coefficients were not useful for distinguishing most zones. The first pair of end points (x-axis) was selected on the basis of the great dissimilarity from each other and from as many other vegetation zones of the profile as possible. The second set (y-axis) was chosen primarily to separate those zones grouped in the center of the single axis plot.

SAHARA COAL-BALL FLORA

The coal swamps of the late Desmoinesian are among the most diverse of the entire Pennsylvanian, but there are some genera and many species of swamp plants with stratigraphic ranges that do not extend as high as the upper Westphalian D. A detailed list of the described taxa of permineralized plants from Euramerican coal-balls with their known stratigraphical occurrences has been compiled by Phillips (1980). The coal-ball plants of the Sahara mine (Table 7.1), with very few exceptions (*Cyathotheca, Stelastellara*), clearly belong to one of five major taxonomic groups: Lycophytina (lycopods), Filicophytina (ferns), and Sphenophytina (sphenopsids), which are lower vascular plants; the Pteridospermales and Cordaitales are gymnosperms (seed plants). The described taxa from the Herrin Coal at Sahara constitute a fairly comprehensive list of the swamp plants known from late Desmoinesian swamps. Hence, citations are given for the published descriptions. For those taxa originally described from other sites or coals an appropriate reference is prefixed by "see." The percent volume contribution of many of the taxa are given later in Table 7.5.

The floral list includes 59 genera with 68 identified species. This, of course, includes numerous organ and form genera of natural assemblages which have not yet been interconnected as conventional species. A moderate estimate of how many natural taxa are actually represented is about 29 genera and 44 species. Five new genera and 23 of the species have been described from the mine. The lycopods are probably the best established or probable natural assemblages of aerial portions at the species level with 8 genera and 10 species. This is particularly important in our vegetational analyses in the Herrin Coal since lycopods constitute two-thirds or more of the peat biomass. There are probably as many genera each of the ferns and pteridosperms with more species represented by each group. Not very many natural assemblages are fully worked out for these species, such as those of *Ankyropteris glabra* (Eggert and Taylor 1966) and *Callistophyton boyssetii* (Rothwell 1975). The relative importance of each of the major taxonomic groups in their contribution to the biomass of coal-ball peats is quite similar in VS 4 and 5, but it differs particularly among the relative importances of lycopod taxa.

Because data on the miospore flora of the Herrin Coal are so generally consistent with the peat data, plant sources of the most abundant kinds of spores (also see Courvoisier and Phillips 1975; and Millay 1979) at the

TABLE 7.1: Sahara Coal-Ball Flora

Lycophytina — *Herbaceous*
  Achlamydocarpon takhtajanii (Snigirevskaya) Schmacker-Lambry
    (see Balbach 1966; Phillips 1979)
  Polysporia mirabilis Newberry (DiMichele, Mahaffy, and Phillips 1979)
  Selaginella fraipontii (Leclercq) Schlanker and Leisman (1969)
    (Phillips and Leisman 1966)
  Spencerites cf. *majusculus* Scott (Leisman and Stidd 1967)
        Arborescent
  Lepidodendron dicentricum C. Felix (DiMichele 1979c)
  Lepidodendron hickii Watson (DiMichele 1979a)
  Lepidodendron scleroticum Pannell (DiMichele 1979a)
    Achlamydocarpon varius (Baxter) Taylor and Brack-Hanes (1977)
      (Leisman and Phillips 1979)
  Lepidophloios hallii (Evers) DiMichele (1979b)
    Lepidocarpon lomaxii Scott *sensu* Balbach (1965) (Phillips 1979)
    Lepidostrobus oldhamius Williamson *sensu* Balbach (1967)
  Paralycopodites brevifolius (Williamson)
    (Morey and Morey 1977; DiMichele 1980)
    Lepidostrobus diversus C. Felix (DiMichele and Phillips, in press)
  Sigillaria sp.
    Mazocarpon sp.
  Stigmaria ficoides (Sternberg) Brongniart
    (Frankenberg and Eggert 1969)
  Stigmaria sp. (*Lepidodendron* form)
  Stigmaria sp. (*Sigillaria* form)
Filicophytina
  Anachoropteridaceae
    Anachoropteris involuta Hoskins *sensu lato* (see Phillips 1974)
    Anachoropteris spp. (see Phillips 1974)
    Tubicaulis spp. (see Phillips 1974)
  Botryopteridaceae
    Botryopteris cratis Millay and Taylor (1980) (Phillips 1974)
    Botryopteris forensis Renault
      (see Phillips, 1974; Galtier and Phillips 1977)
    Botryopteris sp. (pseudoantiqua form, see Phillips 1974)
  Tedeleaceae
    Ankyropteris (*Tedelea*) *glabra* Baxter
      (Eggert 1963; Eggert and Taylor 1966)
    Ankyropteris sp. (see Phillips and Andrews 1965; Dennis 1975)
  Zygopteridaceae
    Zygopteris illinoiensis (Andrews) Baxter (Dennis 1974)
    Etapteris sp.
    Corynepteris sp.
  Marattiales
    Scolecopteris latifolia Graham (Millay 1979)

Scolecopteris majopsis Millay (1979)

Scolecopteris mamayi Millay (1979)

Scolecopteris minor Hoskins (Millay 1979)

Scolecopteris parvifolia (Mamay) Millay (1979)

Scolecopteris saharaensis Millay (1979)

Scolecopteris vallumii Millay (1979)

Pecopteris spp.

Psaronius melanedrus Morgan (Stidd 1971)

Psaronius cf. *chasei* Morgan (1959)

Psaronius roots (Ehret and Phillips 1977)

  Incertae Sedis

    Cyathotheca tectata Taylor (1972)

Sphenophytina

  Sphenophyllales

    Peltastrobus reedae Baxter

    Sphenostrobus iowensis (Mamay) Good (1978)

    Sphenophyllum constrictum Phillips

    Sphenophyllum multirame E. Darrah (1968) (Good 1973)

    Sphenophyllum reedae Good (1973)

  Equisetales

    Calamocarpon insignis Baxter (Good and Taylor 1974; Good 1975)

    Calamostachys inversibractis Good (1975) (Good 1977)

    Palaeostachya andrewsii Baxter (Good 1975)

    Anthropitys spp. (Good 1975)

    Calamodendron americanum Andrews (Good 1975)

    Annularia hoskinsii Good (1976)

    Asterophyllites multifolia Reed (Good 1975)

    Dicalamophyllum americanum Florin (Good 1975)

    Dicalamophyllum sp. (Good 1975)

Gymnosperms

  Pteridospermales

    Medullosaceae

      Albertlongia incostata Taylor (1967)

      Hexapterospermum delevoryii Taylor (1966)
        (Matten and Hopkins 1967)

      Pachytesta gigantea Brongniart (Taylor 1965)

      Pachytesta hoskinsii Taylor (1965)

      Pachytesta illinoensis Stewart (Taylor 1965)

      Pachytesta saharasperma Taylor (1965)

      Pachytesta stewartii Taylor and Delevoryas (1964)

      Pachytesta vera Hoskins and Cross (Taylor 1965)

      Stephanospermum elongatum Hall (Leisman and Roth 1963)

      Stephanospermum sp. (see Taylor 1962)

      Dolerotheca spp. (see Ramanujam, Rothwell, and Stewart 1974)

      Potoniea illinoiensis Stidd (1978)

      Rhetinotheca tetrasolenata Leisman and Peters (1970)

      Medullosa endocentrica Baxter (see Delevoryas 1955)

continued

TABLE 7.1:   Sahara Coal-Ball Flora (continued)

Medullosa noei Steidtmann (see Delevoryas 1955)
Medullosa sp. (see Rothwell and Whiteside 1974)
Myeloxylon
   Alethopteris cf. *lesquereuxi* Wagner (see Baxter and Willhite 1969)
   Neuropteris scheuchzeri Hoffman
   Neuropteris rarinervis Bunbury (see Oestry-Stidd 1979)
medullosan roots (see Rothwell and Whiteside 1974)
Sutcliffia insignis Scott var. *tuberculata* Phillips and Andrews
   (1963) (Stidd, Oestry, and Phillips 1975)
   Linopteris sp.
Callistophytaceae
   Callistophyton boyssetii (Renault) Rothwell (1975)
   Callospermarion undulatum (Neely) Rothwell (Neely 1951)
   Idanothekion glandulosum Millay and Eggert (1970) (Rothwell 1972)
Lyginopteridaceae
   Conostoma kestospermum Taylor and Leisman (1963)
   Conostoma platyspermum Graham (Taylor 1967; Rothwell,
     Taylor, and Clarkson 1979)
   Heterangium americanum Andrews
   Heterangium sp.
    Sphenopteris sp.
   Schopfiastrum decussatum Andrews
    (Rothwell and Taylor 1972; Stidd and Phillips 1973)
    Mariopteris sp.
Cordaitales
  Cardiocarpus oviformis Leisman (see Leisman 1961)
  Cordaianthus sp.
  Cordaites principalis (Germar) Geinitz
  Pennsylvanioxylon Vogellehner [= *Cordaites*] (Whiteside 1974)
Incertae Sedis
  Stelastellara pravula Baxter (DiMichele and Phillips 1979)

Note: Citations are given for published descriptions. For those taxa originally described from other sites or coals an appropriate reference is prefixed by "see." The percent volume contribution of many of the taxa are given in Table 7.5.
Source: Compiled by the authors.

Sahara mine are given later with a tabular summary prepared by R. A. Peppers of the Illinois State Geological Survey.

BOTANICAL CONSTITUENTS OF THE PEAT

Major Taxa

In Table 7.2, we have included the results from VS 2 reported by Phillips, Kunz, and Mickish (1977) for comparative purposes. The principal

TABLE 7.2: Percent Volume of Major Taxa in Sahara Coal-Ball Peat Profiles of Herrin (No. 6) Coal

	With Unidentified			Normalized		
	VS 2	VS 4	VS 5	VS 2	VS 4	VS 5
Unidentified	14.1	4.7	3.8			
Cordaitales	0.6	<0.1	0.1	0.7	<0.1	0.2
Ferns	13.8	14.1	16.0	16.0	14.9	16.6
Lycopods	62.6	61.8	60.9	72.9	64.9	63.4
Pteridosperms	4.7	15.4	14.9	5.5	16.1	15.4
Sphenopsids	4.2	3.9	4.2	4.9	4.1	4.4

Source: Compiled by the authors.

differences among the three coal-ball profiles is the larger component of "unidentified" material and the smaller percent volume of pteridosperm peat. With these exceptions noted, the normalized percentages are used hereafter in all comparisons, tables, and figures.

Lycopods dominate the vegetation at Sahara with 63 to 73 percent of the biomass. Ferns are usually second with 15 to 17 percent, and pteridosperms are the most variable with 6 to 16 percent. In VS 4 and 5, ferns and pteridosperms contribute almost equal amounts of the peat. The sphenopsids are consistently fourth in abundance with 4 to 5 percent and cordaites are ≤ 0.7 percent.

Organ Composition

The contributions of each of the four major taxonomic groups in the Herrin peats differ in organ and tissue composition (Table 7.3). The lycopod trees are the predominant bark (stem cortex and periderm) and root (stigmarian) peat contributors. One of the important differences between the organ composition of VS 4 and 5 is the relative amount of stem and root material. *Psaronius* tree ferns are largely represented by aerenchymatous root systems, both aerial and subterranean. Pteridosperms, mostly *Medullosa*, contribute more foliage than other groups, and the sphenopsids are largely represented by wood from stems and roots.

The ranges of percent biomass composition of organs within each of the major groups are given in Table 7.4. A few of these determinations require special explanation because they are related to quantification procedures. The consistent 15 percent fructification composition of ferns includes both the delicate *Scolecopteris* and the *Pecopteris* foliage to which it is attached; this diminishes, of course, the relative amount of leaf material for the ferns. In the medullosan pteridosperms, cortical fragments which are not clearly

TABLE 7.3: Percent Volume of Peat Contributed by Organs of Major Taxa for Vertical Series 4 and 5 in Herrin (No. 6) Coal

		Fructifications	Leaves	Stems	Roots		Totals for Taxa
Vertical Series 4	Cordaitales	0	0	<0.1	0	=	<0.1
	Ferns	2.2	1.5	0.3	10.9	=	14.9
	Lycopods	2.6	2.4	38.0	21.8	=	64.8
	Pteridosperms	0.5	13.8	1.6	0.3	=	16.2
	Sphenopsids	0.2	0.2	1.9	1.8	=	4.1
	Totals for Organs	5.5	17.9	41.8	34.8	=	100%
Vertical Series 5	Cordaitales	<0.1	0	0.2	<0.1	=	0.2
	Ferns	2.4	3.2	0.7	10.3	=	16.6
	Lycopods	5.8	2.6	21.2	33.8	=	63.4
	Pteridosperms	0.8	11.6	2.6	0.4	=	15.4
	Sphenopsids	0.3	<0.1	2.0	2.1	=	4.4
	Totals for Organs	9.3	17.4	26.7	46.6	=	100%

Source: Compiled by the authors.

TABLE 7.4: Ranges of Percent Biomass Composition of Organ Assemblages for Each of the Major Taxa in Sahara Vertical Series 4 and 5 in Herrin (No. 6) Coal

Major Taxa	Fructifications	Leaves	Stems	Roots
Cordaitales	0–4	0	83–100	0–13
Ferns	15	4–19	2–4	62–73
Lycopods	5–9	4	34–53	38–53
Pteridosperms	3–5	75–84	11–17	2–3
Sphenopsids	4–6	0.4–4	44–50	43–49

Source: Compiled by the authors.

part of a stem are included in the frond category, but the bias does not significantly inflate the foliage contribution. The root material for the pteridosperms is consistently very low and the medullosan trees are apparently the only arborescent forms without characteristic aquatic anatomical adaptations of root tissues.

Fusinized Preservation

Fusinized plant material in coal balls from the Herrin Coal has been reported as 5.0 to 7.2 percent of the total volume (Phillips, Kunz, and Mickish 1977). The fusain content of VS 4 and 5 is 6.5 to 6.9 percent and most of the identifiable portion is from aerial tissues of the lycopods. However, there is a quite variable but disproportionally higher contribution by the pteridosperms and sphenopsids in VS 4 and 5 with 10 to 14 and 7 to 17 percent of their assemblages fusinized, respectively. In VS 5, pteridosperms contributed almost one-third of the fusain. This has been observed previously by Phillips, Kunz, and Mickish (1977).

Genera and Species

The dominant kind of tree in the peat is *Lepidophloios hallii* (Fig. 7.5) with 29 to 49 percent of the peat volume (Table 7.5). It is almost twice as abundant in VS 4 as in VS 5. *Lepidophloios* also produced the most abundant seed-like units found in the swamp, *Lepidocarpon lomaxii*, and the largest microsporangiate cone, *Lepidostrobus oldhamius*. *Lepidodendron* is the second most abundant genus in biomass with 16 to 22 percent of the volume. *Lepidodendron scleroticum*, which was probably the largest tree in the swamp (DiMichele 1979a), was the most variable in biomass in VS 4 and 5 with 4 to 18 percent. *Lepidodendron dicentricum* contributed 7.3 to 8.5 percent biomass in the two profiles. *Sigillaria* and *Paralycopodites* were smaller contributors to the peat, with 1 to 2.5 and 0.5 to 5.7 percent,

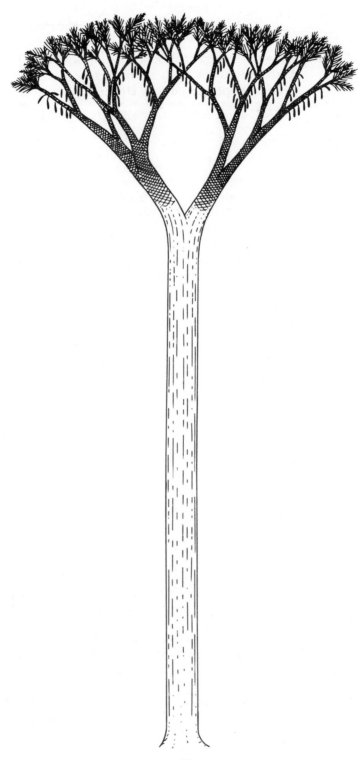

250

TABLE 7.5: **Percent Volume Contributions of Genera and Species to the Coal-Ball Peats of Sahara Vertical Series 4 and 5 in Herrin (No. 6) Coal**

	VS 4	VS 5
Lycophytina		
Lepidophloios hallii	49.2	28.6
Lepidodendron dicentricum	7.3	8.5
Lepidodendron hickii	0.8	0
Lepidodendron scleroticum	3.9	18.3
Achlamydocarpon varius	0.6	0.6
Sigillaria sp.	2.5	1.0
Paralycopodites brevifolius	0.5	5.7
Selaginella fraipontii	0.1	0.1
Filicophytina		
Psaronius spp.	14.5	15.6
Small Ferns	0.4	1.0
Sphenophytina		
Calamites	3.9	2.9
Sphenophyllum spp.	0.2	1.5
Gymnosperms		
Pteridospermales		
Medullosa spp.	13.9	12.5
Sutcliffia insignis	<0.2	<0.1
Callistophyton boyssetii	1.8	2.6
Heterangium	<0.1	<0.2
Cordaitales		
Cordaites	<0.1	<0.2

Source: Compiled by the authors.

respectively, and their abundant occurrences were largely restricted to certain zones which are discussed later.

Among the other major contributors to the peat biomass in VS 4 and VS 5 were *Psaronius* spp. with 14.5 to 15.6 percent and *Medullosa* spp. with 12.5 to 13.9 percent. This is the most consistent percent volume recorded for the medullosans from one site to another in the Herrin Coal.

On a whole seam basis *Lepidophloios* is the dominant with subdominants of *Lepidodendron, Medullosa,* and *Psaronius*; but, in the peat profile

FIGURE 7.5. Reconstruction of the aerial portion of a mature tree of *Lepidophloios hallii* (Evers) DiMichele. The crown with lateral cones is formed by infrequent isotomous branching and lacks secondary tissues in the branches. The height attained is estimated as 10 to 20 m based on the study by DiMichele (1979b). (Prepared by the authors.)

of VS 4 it is evident that *Lepidophloios* largely dominates one kind of swamp environment which alternates with more diverse assemblages. In these, the resources are shared by more highly structured communities in which *Psaronius, Medullosa*, other lycopods, and many small plants are more abundant.

Small plants, including *Selaginella, Polysporia*, the small ferns and pteridosperms, except *Callistophyton*, contribute only 0.5 to 1.0 percent of the total volume of peat. The two principal genera of small plants which are most abundant are *Callistophyton* (one species) and *Sphenophyllum*, which contribute 1.8 to 2.6 percent and 0.2 to 1.5 percent of the peat, respectively.

PEAT PROFILES OF VEGETATION

Of the three profiles of coal-ball peats analyzed thus far from the Sahara mine (VS 2, 4, 5), VS 4 (sector 1, Fig. 7.6) is the most complete and the only one in which vegetational zones could be, in part, examined for lateral continuity. Consequently, it is treated as the reference section for the vegetational sequences and their interpretations at the Sahara mine. This sequence of vegetational succession is described and then comparisons are made with VS 5 with a few references to VS 2.

The beginning and ending of the vegetational succession of the coal swamp are similar in the strong dominance of *Lepidophloios* (Fig. 7.6). In the bottommost coal-ball zone the stigmarian root systems of *Lepidophloios* constitute most of the peat. At the top of the seam profile there are fairly thick peat deposits of aerial and root material from *Lepidophloios*, beginning just above a distinctive zone of *Psaronius* root peat. These zones are also rich in fusain. The *Psaronius* zone is the maximum for root peat of the tree ferns. This distinctive pattern in the terminal phases of the swamp is the same kind as seen to a lesser degree throughout the VS 4 profile. There are repeated *Psaronius* expansions overlapping and followed by dominant development of *Lepidophloios* forests. The alternating abundances of *Psaronius* and *Lepidophloios*, in turn, relate to the other vegetational changes associated with the tree fern cycles and with the occurrences of clastic bands with which important vegetational changes occur.

Between the first and last *Lepidophloios* forests are a series of changes in vegetation in which other lycopod trees alternate in abundance with *Lepidophloios*. These include *Lepidodendron scleroticum* and *L. dicentricum*, combinations of both, and in one case each, *Sigillaria* and a mixture of *L. scleroticum* and *L. hickii*. These oscillating changes in diversity of large tree components continued up to the coal-ball zone above a pyritic shale parting where there was apparently an exceptional interruption in the swamp and a subsequent "crash" in diversity in zone 11, which is the

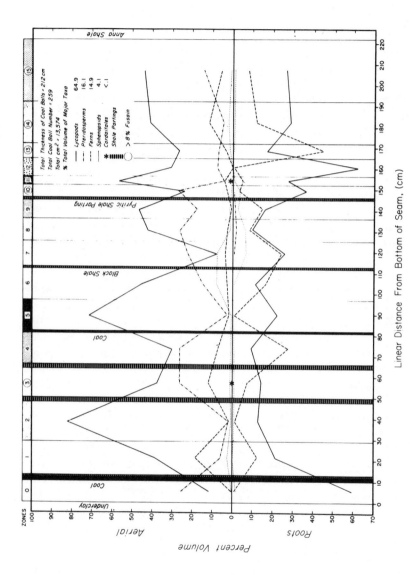

FIGURE 7.6. Sahara vertical series number 4. Percent volume of taxa in vertical section of coal balls from Herrin (No. 6) Coal, Carrier Mills, Illinois. For further explanation, see text. (Prepared by the authors.)

principal pyritic zone (62 percent) except for the bottommost (zone 0). This marks the shift toward the terminal phases of the swamp that contain the *Psaronius* root zone and it is otherwise totally dominated by *Lepidophloios* forests.

The occurrences of clastic bands or shale partings in the diverse portions of the coal-ball profiles mark important interruptions or modifications in the prevalent vegetational types and are relevant to changes in the assemblages that occur below and/or above. Above the deposition of each of the four lower shale bands there is a change in the kind of lycopod tree, a diminution in the abundance of lycopod peat, and usually expansions of tree ferns and pteridosperms. There are, however, important differences in the patterns of vegetational changes relative to the different kinds of clastic bands. The most distinctive pattern of change relating to the gray shale partings is the coal-ball zone of *Sigillaria-Paralycopodites* which occurs between a pair of shale partings. This zone also contains the maximum amount of fusain in the coal-ball profile.

While changes in the vegetation occur after deposition of each gray shale parting, there are notable changes immediately below both the black shale and pyritic shale partings in the abundance of *Lepidodendron* species (Figs. 7.6, 7.7). Pteridosperms show maintenance of maximum abundance levels or slight increases from below to above all of these clastic partings except for the basalmost one. The calamites exhibit one major interval of relative abundance immediately below and above the black shale parting. The few cordaitean fragments are restricted to coal-ball zones between the prominent pair of gray shale partings and just above the pyritic shale band.

In summary, the fluctuating conditions of the swamp result in an oscillating pattern of forests strongly dominated by *Lepidophloios* and of quite low diversity with relatively diverse forests of probably taller trees such as *Lepidodendron* or *Sigillaria* with lower stories of *Psaronius* and *Medullosa* with many small plants in the ground story. The cyclicity of the vegetational changes is determined by comparing the *Psaronius-Lepidophloios* abundances, relative abundances of the major lycopod taxa (Fig. 7.7), and, where present, the clastic bands in the coal. Medullosan peat-abundances generally overlap those of *Psaronius*, but there are significant differences in the responses to the influxes of mineral matter in the periods of clastic deposition.

The profile of VS 5 (Fig. 7.8), while composed of almost the same amounts of peat of each of the major taxonomic groups as VS 4, is quantitatively different in several important aspects. The coal-ball peat zones are thinner, the amount of root material is significantly higher, *Lepidophloios* constitutes only slightly more than one-fourth of the biomass compared to one-half in VS 4, and the profile lacks the upper clastic bands and perhaps some of the uppermost peat zones seen in VS 4. All of these

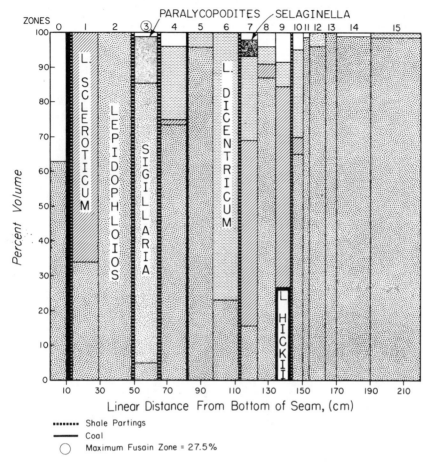

FIGURE 7.7. Relative percent of identified lycopod taxa of stems in Sahara vertical section 4, based on coal-ball peat from Herrin (No. 6) Coal. For further explanation, see text. (Prepared by the authors.)

attributes are generally consistent with just slightly higher elevation (slightly lower water table conditions on the whole) or less extreme wet conditions. Such conditions would result in greater loss of aerial portions of plants by exposure to decay and be more conducive to the development of forests less tolerant of higher water tables. If this were the case, the cyclicity of *Psaronius* and *Lepidophloios* could well be depressed quantitatively, and this appears to fit the overall pattern. In fact, there appears to be a slurring of sharp alternation of *Psaronius* with *Lepidophloios*, and in general a lack of sharp abundance peaks for either. This may be due, in part, to the loss of significant aerial portions, at least for *Lepidophloios*.

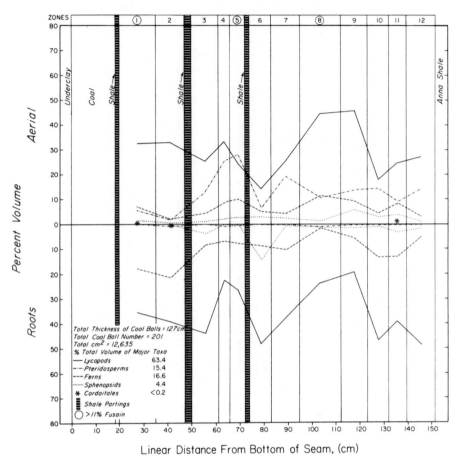

FIGURE 7.8. Sahara vertical series number 5. Percent volume of taxa in vertical section of coal balls from Herrin (No. 6) Coal, Carrier Mills, Illinois. For further explanation, see text. (Prepared by the authors.)

Where *Psaronius* peats attain maxima (total assemblages), in the lower and uppermost zones (1, 2, and 10, VS 5), the abundances of *Lepidophloios* largely overlap. In between, *Psaronius* is almost equally abundant from one zone to the next. There are still changes in the kinds of lycopods found in association with the prominent pair of gray shale partings, with marked differences in species from zone to zone (Fig. 7.9). Three zones of coal-ball peats occur between the pair of gray shale partings, compared to one in VS 4. Below the upper gray shale parting is the only occurrence of *Sigillaria*, again coinciding with the maximum fusain content as in VS 4. *Paralycopodites* occurs in the same zone but is much more abundant in the zone below,

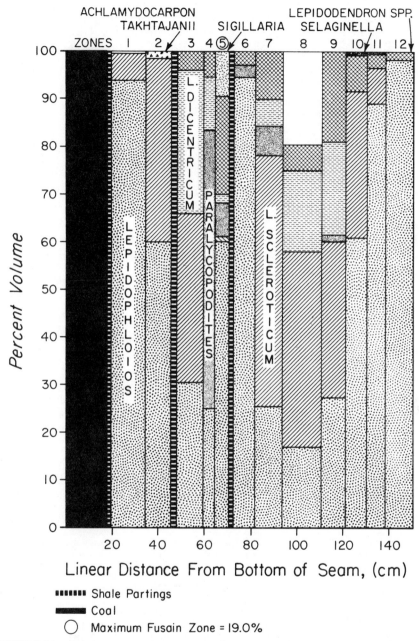

FIGURE 7.9. Relative percent of identified lycopod taxa of aerial portions in Sahara vertical section 5, based on coal-ball peats from Herrin (No. 6) Coal. For explanation, see text. (Prepared by the authors.)

and there is about an equal distribution of *Lepidodendron scleroticum, L. dicentricum,* and *Lepidophloios* in the zone below that. This suggests an ideal successively drier sequence of vegetation. Above the upper gray shale parting there is a prolonged interval of expansion of *Lepidodendron scleroticum* with abundant *L. dicentricum* which accounts for a significant amount of the total *Lepidodendron* peat in the profile, 27 percent compared to 29 percent for *Lepidophloios.*

While the peaks of abundances of the lycopods and ferns are not very sharp, compared to VS 4, there are prominent rises in the pteridosperms and sphenopsids. Medullosan peat reaches maxima in the zones of *Paralycopodites* (zone 4), *Sigillaria-Paralycopodites* (zone 5), and a *L. scleroticum* zone also with abundant *Paralycopodites* (zone 7). In between (zone 6) the sphenopsids attain their maximum. The few cordaitean fragments occur low and high in the profile (zones 1, 2, 11) in overlapping *Lepidophloios-Psaronius* rich zones. The *Psaronius* root zone in the upper part of the sequence is not as prominent as in VS 4, and it is not clear if a "crash" in swamp diversity occurred high in the sequence as in VS 4. The uppermost coal-ball zone in VS 5 does not seem markedly different from that in VS 4, but it appears that the changes in the upper zones of VS 5 are less pronounced and quantitatively exhibit more *Lepidodendron, Medullosa,* and sphenopsids with less tree fern peat prior to the final *Lepidophloios* forests.

The differences between vegetational sequences in VS 4 and VS 5 are thought to be environmentally significant in understanding variations within a small swamp area of the Herrin, as well as appreciating differences between swamps (as represented by the Springfield Coal) with similar floras but with such quantitative differences in the major taxa. This is discussed further with their beta-diversity values. One of the most striking similarities between VS 4 and 5 is the occurrence of *Sigillaria* and *Paralycopodites* below the upper gray shale. A sigillarian-rich peat zone also occurs at a comparable position in VS 2 (DiMichele 1979a; DiMichele and Phillips, in press) and the coincidences of maximum fusain level, *Sigillaria-Paralycopodites,* and the pair of gray shale partings are discussed in connection with the so-called "blue band" later.

LATERAL CONTINUITY OF VEGETATION ZONES

Lateral sampling of coal-ball zones adjacent to sector 1, VS 4 (Fig. 7.4) was carried out to check on taxonomic and quantitative continuity of the vegetation zones indicated in the reference profile (Figs. 7.6, 7.7). Five zones could be traced accurately across two or three 1-m-wide sectors with the aid of clastic bands and coal benches. The sample sizes of the additional collections are individually less in each zone of a sector than the reference section, but collectively those of a given zone approach an adequate sample size. There were 66 coal balls and 5,346 cm^2 for the five zones.

In Table 7.6, the percent volume for the major taxa in the five zones are given with data from VS 4 indicated in sector 1. Inspection of the numbers shows marked variability in all the zones per sector, but qualitatively there is continuity of abundance of the same major taxa in each, at least at the generic level. Zone 1 consistently shows an abundance of *Lepidodendron scleroticum* and *Psaronius* tree ferns. Zone 2 shows a marked difference between the *Lepidophloios* dominated peat (95 percent) from sector 1 and that of its lateral sectors. The other sectors show *Psaronius* abundant (17 to 22 percent) and pteridosperms as moderately abundant (6 to 10 percent). *Lepidophloios* still comprises two-thirds to three-fourths of the peat zone. In this particular case we understand the bias of sampling in sector 1. The massive coal balls in sector 1 consisted of a series of fallen *Lepidophloios* trunks, some of the largest (up to 24 cm in diameter) intact trunks we have encountered. This layering of logs across the meter-wide exposure has markedly excluded the other vegetation of the zone indicated by lateral sampling. Zone 7 is rich in pteridosperms, ferns, and sphenopsids, and all the samples are consistent with this, including the mixed occurrences of *Lepidodendron* species. Sector 2 contains more ferns and pteridosperms than lycopods. Zone 8 is the smallest sample size and perhaps that accounts for the great variations. It does indicate in most sectors an abundance of pteridosperms and ferns, but not consistently. Zone 10 also shows some differences in pteridosperms and sphenopsids, but is not that inconsistent with sector 1.

One of the specific reasons for examining lateral continuity of vegetation in coal-ball zones was to assess the possible patchiness of medullosan trees. Extensive sampling (>400 coal balls) at another outcrop of coal balls in the Herrin Coal has indicated that the larger the sample size per zone the lower the pteridosperm content (Phillips 1981). At VS 4 and VS 5 the abundances of medullosan pteridosperms are the most consistent at a site and between sites of any analyzed thus far. In comparisons of similar kinds of vegetation zones in both VS 4 and 5, there are reasonably good equivalents between zone 2 in both profiles, zone 3 (*Sigillaria* and *Paralycopodites*) of VS 4, and zones 4 and 5 of VS 5 and the associated gray shale partings. Immediately above that level close comparisons are not apparent, but both have abundant *Lepidodendron* zones prior to the terminal *Lepidophloios* forests. The compositional differences in patterns are referred to later in conjunction with beta-diversity values.

MIOSPORE ABUNDANCES IN THE COAL

The general consistency of miospore data from the coal and coal-ball peat information from extensive coal swamps in the Pennsylvanian (Phillips

TABLE 7.6: Percent Volume of Major Taxa in Select Coal-Ball Zones Contiguous with Those in Sahara Vertical Series 4, Sector 1, Herrin (No. 6) Coal

Sectors*	Ferns				Lycopods				Pteridosperms				Sphenopsids			
	1	2	3	4	1	2	3	4	1	2	3	4	1	2	3	4
Zones																
10	6	10	11		61	69	72		28	16	17		5	5	0.5	
8	12	0	27	13	51	89	54	49	30	11	20	37	7	0	0	0.6
7	28	39	20	18	34	20	52	49	23	34	24	17	14	8	4	16
2	3	20	17	22	95	68	74	64	2	10	6	8	0.5	2	3	5
1	31		28	22	60		65	65	6		3	8	3		4	6

*Each sector is 1 meter wide (see Fig. 7.4).

Source: Compiled by the authors.

and Peppers 1979) has prompted us to include a summary of the coal palynology prepared by R. A. Peppers (Fig. 7.10). The plant sources of most of the abundant kinds of spores are given in the tabular summary (Table 7.7). The seam was divided into four increments. *Lycospora granulata* from *Lepidophloios* dominates the spore flora of the seam with 45 to 76 percent of the spore assemblage. *Crassispora* from *Sigillaria* occurs only in the lower increment. *Cappasporites* from *Lepidodendron* is abundant above that and attains a maximum in the upper part of the seam. *Psaronius* is the subdominant of the miospore flora, particularly as represented by *Thymospora* and two species of *Laevigatosporites*. *Medullosa* is not represented because of the exclusion of such large prepollen from miospore fractions. *Florinites* from *Cordaites* occurs in two portions of the seam, in the lowest increment and in the lower part of the upper one-third. These quantitative measures and the general positions of the mentioned taxa are consistent with information from the peat profiles. In order to more precisely compare miospore and peat data from such seam profiles, it is necessary to subdivide the seam into much smaller increments. This has been done in a parallel palynological study of both the peat and the coal at Sahara (Mahaffy 1979).

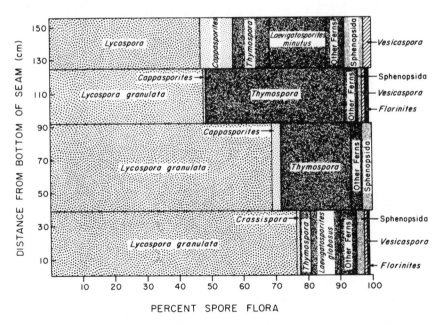

FIGURE 7.10. Relative abundance of miospore taxa in Herrin (No. 6) Coal Member at Sahara Coal Company Mine No. 6, Saline County, Illinois. The percent number of each of the major taxa in the four increments of coal is given in Table 7.7. For further explanation, see text. (Prepared by the authors from data provided by R. A. Peppers.)

TABLE 7.7: **Relative Abundance of Miospore Taxa, Herrin (No. 6) Coal Member, Sahara Mine No. 6 Sec. 30, T.9S., R.5E., Saline County, Illinois**

	A	B	C	D
	40 cm	53 cm	32 cm	32 cm
Lycopods				
Lycospora granulata	76	69	46	45
(Lepidostrobus oldhamius–				
Lepidophloios)				
Other *Lycospora*	0.5	0	2.0	2.0
Cappasporites distortus				
(Achlamydocarpon varius–				
Lepidodendron)	0	3.0	0.5	10.0
Crassispora kosankei	1.0	0	0	0
(Mazocarpon-Sigillaria)				
Pteridosperms				
Veiscaspora wilsonii	1.5	0	1.0	2.5
(Idanothekion-Callistophyton)				
Cordaites				
Florinites pellucidus	0.5	0	1.0	0
Ferns				
Marattiales-*Psaronius*				
Thymospora pseudothiesseni	5	21	44	11.5
(Scolecopteris vallumii)				
Laevigatosporites minutus	3	0.5	1.5	17.5
(Scolecopteris saharaensis)				
Laevigatosporites globosus	9	2.0	2.0	1.0
(Scolecopteris mamayi)				
Punctatisporites minutus	0	0	0	2.0
(Scolecopteris minor)				
(Scolecopteris parvifolia)				
Filicales				
Triquitrites, Raistrickia, etc.	0.5	1.5	1.0	2.0
Sphenopsids				
Calamospora breviradiata	0.5	0.5	0.5	1.5
Laevigatosporites ovalis	2.0	1.0	0.5	4.5
Others	0	1.5	0	0

Source: Quantitative data provided by R. A. Peppers with fructification sources compiled by the authors.

One of the consistent features of miospore analyses of the Herrin Coal is the relative increase in *Cappasporites* (*Lepidodendron*) in the uppermost portion of the seam. This is paralleled by increases in *Achlamydocarpon varius* in the peat profiles, but the relative amounts of *Lepidodendron dicentricum* peat is quite small in the topmost zones in VS 4 and 5 (Figs. 7.7, 7.9). In VS 2 the amount of the moderately saline tolerant nonsecretory form of *L. dicentricum* was considerably more in the top two zones. The possibility exists that *L. dicentricum* was temporarily more abundant in the very final phases of the swamp, but we have relatively little surviving peat evidence of that. The higher abundances of both *Cappasporites* and *Achlamydocarpon varius* would be consistent with that.

COAL-SWAMP COMMUNITY ANALYSES

Community Coefficients

The community coefficients for vegetation (coal-ball) zones in VS 4 (Table 7.8) and VS 5 are relatively uniform, varying mostly from 0.60 to 0.80 and averaging 0.65 in VS 5 and 0.71 in VS 4. This indicates a relatively uniform flora in the Herrin Coal, as measured by presence-absence data. As a result of such general uniformity (floristic) these values are not useful for distinguishing among the most dissimilar plant assemblages. The major discrepancy in community coefficients is in zone 12, VS 4 (Table 7.8), which is the only zone with an inadequate sample size.

Percentage Similarity and Polar Ordination

Percentage similarity (Table 7.8) is based on percent volume or biomass as the importance value and this provides quantitative means of recognizing importance similarities and vegetation types among the coal-ball zones of each peat profile. Names of the dominant or codominant taxa are given for each of the zones in VS 4 (Table 7.8). In VS 5 the principal differences were the paucity of *Medullosa* dominated or codominated communities (one compared to four) and the fewer strongly dominated *Lepidophloios* assemblages.

Initial end points for polar ordination (Fig. 7.11) of the vegetational assemblages in VS 4 were zones 2 and 3. Zone 2 is dominated by *Lepidophloios hallii* with 95 percent recorded in sector 1. Lateral sampling (Table 7.6) indicated that this figure is probably too high and *Lepidophloios* contributed two-thirds to three-fourths of the peat as the dominant. Only seven species are present, including *Achlamydocarpon takhtajanii* (putative megasporangial unit of *Lepidodendron serratum*, which has not been found in any of the profiles), which has not been previously reported from the Herrin Coal in southern Illinois. Zone 3 is dominated by *Sigillaria* and the diversity is relatively high with 14 species. The second pair of end points are zones 7 and 9. Zone 7 is a *Medullosa-Psaronius* zone. Calamites attain their

TABLE 7.8: Matrix of Percentage Similarity and Community Coefficients for Plant Assemblages in Coal-Ball Zones of Sahara Vertical Section 4, Sector 1, in the Herrin (No. 6) Coal

Percentage Similarity

Dominance	Peat Zone	0	1	2	3	4	5	6	7	8	9	10	11	12*	13	14	15
								Sahara Vertical Section 4, Sector 1									
Medullosa	0	—	24.58	26.72	34.45	61.34	29.08	34.59	47.45	57.44	29.43	72.15	34.49	48.03	32.21	33.88	46.68
Psaronius-Lepidophloios L. dicentricum	1	0.69	—	16.67	24.37	53.8	19.96	59.56	42.18	36.34	46.62	37.11	32.12	29.51	50.39	58.59	38.17
Lepidophloios	2	0.72	0.76	—	9.40	29.0	91.03	18.01	7.79	48.22	5.79	26.91	79.27	66.91	38.23	48.11	60.40
Sigillaria	3	0.73	0.65	0.78	—	34.48	11.07	33.05	34.50	30.67	31.96	38.69	19.18	18.08	19.46	23.78	31.55
Medullosa-Psaronius Lepidophloios	4	0.67	0.84	0.80	0.74	—	36.75	62.30	64.52	69.49	37.27	78.85	42.0	49.92	58.31	52.52	61.97
Lepidophloios	5	0.72	0.76	0.86	0.72	0.93	—	25.68	15.71	55.02	13.75	35.16	83.28	65.93	36.63	51.51	64.91
L. dicentricum Lepidophloios-Psaronius	6	0.67	0.77	0.80	0.74	0.94	0.93	—	47.39	40.31	33.73	59.94	31.58	34.14	55.63	52.36	47.61
Medullosa-Psaronius	7	0.62	0.79	0.75	0.65	0.82	0.81	0.94	—	51.95	40.6	60.96	18.4	24.52	39.61	27.13	37.36
Medullosa-Lepidophloios	8	0.74	0.84	0.80	0.68	0.94	0.93	0.88	0.94	—	34.05	70.79	58.31	66.20	44.53	60.73	74.50
L. scleroticum with Lepidodendron hickii	9	0.76	0.73	0.69	0.65	0.85	0.81	0.70	0.77	0.82	—	37.49	15.58	19.48	20.8	19.66	28.43
Medullosa-Lepidophloios	10	0.65	0.74	0.70	0.76	0.83	0.82	0.89	0.84	0.83	0.79	—	41.30	49.15	41.72	42.54	56.99
Lepidophloios	11	0.83	0.79	0.74	0.68	0.76	0.81	0.76	0.71	0.76	0.64	0.67	—	74.31	44.71	62.92	75.48
Lepidophloios*	12	0.53	0.42	0.44	0.31	0.40	0.44	0.40	0.36	0.40	0.36	0.33	0.47	—	45.45	61.63	81.13
Lepidophloios-Psaronius	13	0.67	0.64	0.62	0.62	0.77	0.75	0.69	0.64	0.69	0.57	0.60	0.69	0.42	—	65.35	52.11
Lepidophloios	14	0.64	0.62	0.56	0.54	0.59	0.64	0.59	0.62	0.67	0.55	0.52	0.66	0.40	0.67	—	71.48
Lepidophloios	15	0.57	0.62	0.64	0.83	0.79	0.77	0.73	0.74	0.79	0.68	0.65	0.60	0.28	0.67	0.71	—

Community Coefficient

*Inadequate sample.
Source: Compiled by the authors.

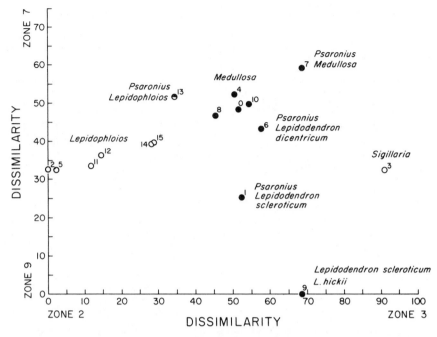

FIGURE 7.11. Polar ordination of the coal-ball zones from Sahara vertical section 4, sector 1. Each of the plant assemblages from a coal-ball zone is given taxonomic designation based on the major biomass source or sources. The dissimilarity plots are based on biomass as an importance value (negative of percentage similarity); see Table 7.8. For further explanation, see text. (Prepared by the authors.)

maximum in this zone (12 percent), the highest for any zone of both profiles. Lycopod diversity is high. Zone 9 is dominated by *Lepidodendron scleroticum* with abundant *L. hickii*, an extremely rare swamp form. There are three types of pteridosperm foliage: *Alethopteris* cf. *lesquereuxii, Neuropteris scheuchzeri,* and an undescribed form.

The composition of the initial end points of VS 5 parallels those of VS 4. A *Lepidophloios*-dominated zone (zone 2) is represented with abundant *Lepidodendron scleroticum,* and *Achlamydocarpon takhtajanii* is also present as in VS 4 at about the same zone position. Zone 4 exhibits high diversity (12 species) and is dominated by *Paralycopodites* with several other taxa in abundance. As noted later, zone 4 and zone 5, the *Sigillaria-Paralycopodites* zone just above, may be about equivalent to zone 3 of VS 5. The second set of end points are zones 6 and 8. Zone 6 is *Lepidophloios* dominated (a similarity to zone 2), but is more diverse (13 species compared to 9). Calamites reached their maximum abundance (7.3 percent) in the profile in this zone. Zone 8 is dominated by *Lepidodendron scleroticum* and parallels zone 9 of VS 4 in shared dominance with five other taxa and in the presence of *Neuropteris scheuchzeri.*

The polar ordination of assemblages from coal-ball zones of VS 4 (Fig. 7.11) and VS 5 are quite similar except the *Paralycopodites* zone represented the extreme in VS 5 compared to the *Sigillaria* zone in VS 4, and the *Medullosa* communities are well clustered in VS 4. In general the separation effected by choice of end points emphasizes *Lepidophloios* and *Sigillaria* (and/or *Paralycopodites*) zones as extremes with *Psaronius*-rich assemblages stretching from the edge of the *Lepidophloios* clusters to positions of *Medullosa* and the two common *Lepidodendron* species. This very broad amplitude for *Psaronius* is not that detectable in the polar ordination of VS 5, but *Psaronius* occurs in almost equal amounts across most of the profile. Perhaps the means of assessing its importance (aerial + 50 percent of outer root mantle) diminishes its recognition, but there were really no strong peaks for *Psaronius* (Fig. 7.9).

Dominance Diversity Curves

Dominance diversity curves for the four end points used in polar ordination of assemblages from VS 4 are shown in Figures 7.12 to 7.15. The curve for the *Lepidophloios*-dominated assemblage conforms to a steep and almost straight line indicating very strong dominance and low diversity. In contrast, that of *Sigillaria* dominance (Fig. 7.13) forms an arc indicative of weak dominance and much sharing of resources by a more diverse flora. The curve for the *Medullosa-Psaronius* codominance zone (Fig. 7.14) also indicates sharing of resources among a fairly diverse flora. The plots for the assemblage with *Lepidodendron scleroticum* dominance with *L. hickii* convey only moderate dominance (compared to *Lepidophloios* zones) and resource sharing with an understory of pteridosperms, tree ferns, and smaller plants. Three of the four end points represented previously are regarded as indicative of fairly well defined "community types" with greatest variations seen in the *Lepidodendron scleroticum* assemblages and their relationships with *Medullosa* abundances.

Beta-diversity

Data from VS 4 and 5 were analyzed to quantitatively measure the degree of change in plant assemblages (communities *sensu lato*) on a given site with time, that is, beta-diversity within a seam profile, and to compare beta-diversity patterns between sites within the geographically restricted area of the Sahara mine. This type of analysis allows assessment of swamp patchiness, provides insight into the recurring assemblages, and patterns of succession (primary or secondary), if any. It also forms the data base for

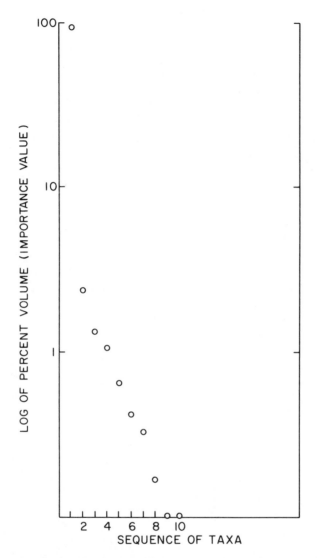

FIGURE 7.12. Dominance diversity curve for Sahara vertical section 4, sector 1, zone 2–*Lepidophloios* dominance. The curve conforms to a steep almost straight line indicating very strong dominance and low diversity. *Lepidophloios* is the dominant tree of the swamp on a whole seam basis. (Prepared by the authors.)

examining questions about widespread events and their effects on the composition of swamp vegetation.

Beta-diversity values indicate different patterns of vegetational change and levels of diversity at the sites of VS 4 and 5, within the larger vegetation type of the Herrin (No. 6) Coal. Whole profile beta-diversities of 3.1 for VS 4

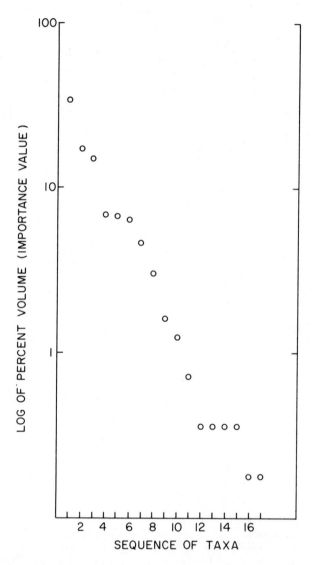

FIGURE 7.13. Dominance diversity curve for Sahara vertical section 4, sector 1, zone 3—
Sigillaria dominance. The arc of the curve indicates the lack of strong dominance and much
sharing of the resources by a diverse flora. The *Sigillaria* assemblage is consistently associated
with the maximum fusain for any peat zone and appears only once in the profile. (Prepared by
the authors.)

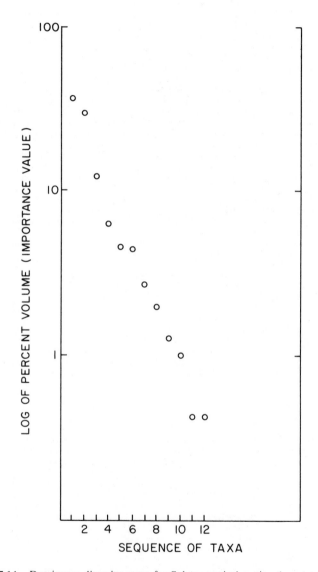

FIGURE 7.14. Dominance diversity curve for Sahara vertical section 4, sector 1, zone 7—*Medullosa-Psaronius* codominance. The curve indicates codominance with sharing of resources among a fairly diverse flora. *Medullosa* and *Psaronius* have overlapping ecological amplitudes and *Psaronius* is also linked with a variety of lycopod trees in sharing resources. (Prepared by the authors.)

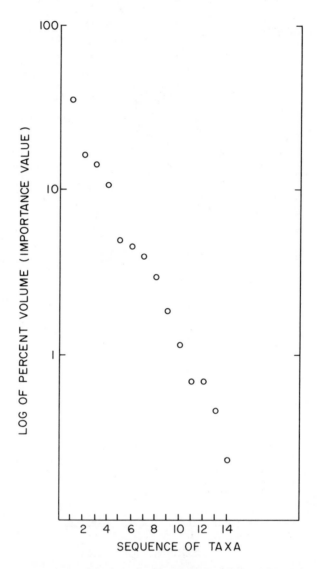

FIGURE 7.15. Dominance diversity curve for Sahara vertical section 4, sector 1, zone 9–*Lepidodendron scleroticum* dominance with *Lepidodendron hickii*. The curve indicates only moderate dominance by *L. scleroticum* (compared to *Lepidophloios*) with resource sharing by an understory of pteridosperms, tree ferns, and smaller plants. The combination of *L. scleroticum* and *L. hickii* occurs only in one coal-ball zone. (Prepared by the authors.)

and 2.4 for VS 5 indicate more homogeneity (greater floristic similarity) among the zones of VS 5 than of VS 4. Although the two sites are only 0.6 km apart, there are few compositional equivalencies at approximately corresponding seam levels between them. This indicates a conspicuous detectable level of patchiness of vegetation structure, but not in overall floristic composition. The Sahara mine area and the other sampled portions of the Herrin Coal are characterized by a relatively uniform seam flora.

There are several major quantitative differences in the types of assemblages and the patterns of variation of taxa in VS 4 and 5. Dominance of a zone by one species or by one major taxonomic group is largely lacking in VS 5, particularly the strong and recurrent dominance of *Lepidophloios* typical of VS 4. Only a single zone in VS 5 can be characterized as dominated by medullosan pteridosperms. In most of the *Medullosa*-rich zones of VS 5, resources were shared with *Psaronius* and *Lepidodendron scleroticum*. In VS 4, zones in which *Medullosa* exceeded 30 percent in volume, there were also subdominant levels of *Lepidophloios*. Zones in which *Lepidodendron scleroticum* shared dominance are much more numerous in VS 5 than in VS 4. *Psaronius* abundances, as previously mentioned, are very uniform in VS 5, averaging 19.6 percent with a range of 11.6 to 28.9 percent. *Psaronius* exceeds 20 percent abundance in seven of 12 zones. In VS 4, *Psaronius* averages 17.1 percent with a range of <1 to 44.5 percent and accounts for >20 percent of the vegetation in nine zones. The aforementioned data emphasize the greater homogeneity of the vegetational profile of VS 5, compared to VS 4, and suggest that less extreme growth conditions occurred at the site of VS 5, allowing community structure to fluctuate largely within a shared dominance and high-diversity type of vegetation.

DISCUSSION

Community Types

On the basis of data from the Sahara profiles and from analyses of other sites in the Herrin (No. 6) Coal (Phillips, Kunz, and Mickish 1977; DiMichele and Phillips, in press), several "end-point assemblages" or "community types" can be recognized. All of these have major lycopod components.

Lepidophloios Dominance with Low Diversity

After *Lepidophloios* peat exceeds 50 percent in a zone, *Psaronius* usually maintains an abundance level of 15 to 25 percent; *Medullosa* rarely persists as an important element, and the amounts of other groups and the diversity are sharply diminished. At about the 70 percent level of *Lepidoph-loios* peat, the amount of *Psaronius* drops to <10 percent and diversity is highly reduced.

Free-sporing Lycopods with High Diversity

The most important lycopods with the free-sporing (megaspore) morphology are *Sigillaria* and *Paralycopodites*. *Sigillaria* probably represented the extreme community type with *Paralycopodites* complementary under slightly more moderate environmental conditions. Most of the important kinds of swamp plants are found in the *Sigillaria-Paralycopodites* zone or zones, and the abundance of a given species rarely exceeds 20 percent of the peat. This type of assemblage is the rarest encountered at most sites in the Herrin Coal.

Lepidodendron-Medullosa Mixed Dominance

Most of the diversity in the floral composition of the Herrin Coal occurs in this general kind of assemblage. This may be because of the overlap of vegetation in dry-wet or only moderately wet sites. It is either dominated by *Lepidodendron scleroticum* or *Medullosa* (several species). *Psaronius* and *Lepidodendron* spp. vary in importance (5 to 15%). *Lepidophloios* is <10 to ≤20 percent in volume and lower with more abundant *L. scleroticum*.

Swamp Habitats

The habitats of the most important kinds of trees in the swamps are inferred from a combination of vegetative and reproductive morphology, community analyses, sequences in the peat profiles, and associated geological evidence It is essentially a deductive series of speculation about changes in vegetation along gradients of moisture, water quality, nutrients, and other parameters which ought to be internally consistent with what is known of the life cycles and the paleoecology.

Lycopods

Lepidophloios hallii is the dominant kind of tree in the swamp at Sahara and in all the Herrin peat profiles examined thus far. It is interpreted as the principal indicator of prolonged standing water and net rising water tables where salinity is not a critical factor in limiting growth or reproduction. It is likely that *Lepidophloios* is tolerant of more brackish conditions than those at Sahara, but these trees apparently could not reproductively maintain such stands in the mangrove-like environments in which cordaites were dominant. There is little evidence of saline influences in the Herrin peat profiles. The cordaitean species (*Cardiocarpus oviformis*) is rare in occurrence and not representative of the typical mangrove-like species abundant in the early Desmoinesian. Direct evidence of the terminal marine transgression in the Sahara peats is limited to the topmost coal-ball zone in VS 2 which contains marine invertebrates intermixed with the peat (Phillips, Kunz, and Mickish 1977). The saline influence on the vegetation was apparently confined to the upper two coal-ball zones which contained an ecotypic form (nonsecretory) of *Lepidodendron dicentricum* associated with such an environment (DiMichele 1978). Such zones are not evident in VS 4 or 5.

The nutrient levels probably required for *Lepidophloios* forests were minimal. Recycling from the debris in a net rising water table with such huge biomass accumulation would have been very low. In studies of the Okefenokee cypress swamp forest, Schlesinger (1978) found that major nutrient cycling was confined to the water column with peat acting as a permanent nutrient sink.

Our analyses suggest that the distribution of *Lepidophloios*-dominated assemblages was strongly controlled by abiotic factors. The inferred water depth and prolonged intervals of such conditions are consistent with the low diversity. The aquatic adaptations of the boat-like *Lepidocarpon* allowed fertilization and dissemination of the seed-like units over vast water-covered areas of the swamp (Phillips 1979). The stigmarian root system of *Lepidophloios* is, of course, very similar to that of many other lycopod trees except that the rootlets and their lacunae which provide aeration are usually much larger than in other lycopods.

Among the lycopod habitats, perhaps the opposite extreme of *Lepidophloios* is *Sigillaria*. This genus is rare in most coal swamps of the Desmoinesian, but it does occur in moderate amounts in some early Westphalian peats and is the principal lycopod-tree in the tree fern-dominated swamps of the Missourian in the Illinois Basin. Most of the fossil sigillarians are found in shale and sandstone floras and are among some of the largest lycopod trunks in cast-mold preservations. *Sigillaria* is thought to be, in general, indicative of low water tables (or alternatively wet-dry conditions with emphasis on the drier side) of predominately freshwater nature and probably moderate nutrient requirements. This may be too broad a characterization for the many species, but it serves as a general basis for relating the *Sigillaria-Paralycopodites* peat assemblages to environmental parameters. This is discussed later under the "blue band."

The *Lepidodendron* species apparently occur in habitats largely intermediate in moisture regime between *Sigillaria* and *Lepidophloios*. The two principal species have different reproductive strategies (DiMichele 1979a; DiMichele and Phillips, in press) and they are usually found in communities which are more highly structured and diverse. *Lepidodendron scleroticum* was the largest tree in the swamp and was much more abundant, 18 percent of the peat, in VS 5 (Table 7.5), which is regarded as a less extreme site on the whole. *Lepidodendron dicentricum* has an ecotypic form tolerant of moderate saline influences, but this was only encountered in the topmost zones of VS 2 (DiMichele 1978).

Tree Ferns

Some of the *Psaronius* tree ferns were probably quite complementary to the aquatic vegetative adaptations of *Lepidophloios*, being able to survive in more fluctuating water tables than most other swamp plants, up to the prohibitive level or length of time where *Lepidophloios* alone could maintain its forest stands. The adventitious and highly aerated aerenchymatous root mantles of *Psaronius* both buttressed these tree ferns as well as provided successive root systems capable of adjusting to the moisture regime. Consequently, *Psaronius* species had the capability of living over a very wide amplitude of habitats in the swamps. Until there is a good delineation of species assemblages one can not sort out specific habitat preferences. However, it should be noted that among the known species of *Psaronius*, some even have aerenchymatous stem tissue (*P. pertusus*, Morgan 1959) and a spectrum of their moisture tolerances undoubtedly extends to drier habitats of the medullosan seed ferns.

Medullosan Seed Ferns

The medullosan seed ferns are among the most abundant and diverse elements in roof shale floras of the coal swamps and their habitat requirements are thought to have been relatively high in nutrients and drier swamp conditions—ideally, exposed peat substrates (Phillips 1981). While this too may be an over generalization, it is consistent with abundances of pteridosperm peats in zones enriched by clastic sediment, higher proportional fusain content, the reproductive strategies of the medullosans and their obvious lack of aquatically adapted root systems.

Sphenopsids

The sphenopsids are generally minor elements in Desmoinesian age swamps and we do not have an adequate grasp of their habitats to suggest the likely environmental parameters. They too contribute a disproportionately high amount of fusain to the peat and their moderate abundances in swamps are in stratigraphically higher and lower parts of the Pennsylvanian, like those of *Sigillaria* (Phillips 1980). In VS 4, the greatest abundance of sphenopsid peat (mostly calamites) was immediately below and above the black shale parting. In VS 5, it is immediately above the top gray shale parting. Both partings could be regarded as indicative of a good nutrient supply—one rapid and one slow. Perhaps some of the sphenopsids had requirements somewhat similar to those of pteridosperms.

"Blue Band," Fusain, and *Sigillaria*

The sigillarian zone is noted at the same approximate position in each of the three profiles at the Sahara mine. In VS 2, the peat is mostly sigillarian with a high fusain zone just above it and there are no clastic bands. In VS 4, abundant *Sigillaria* occurs with *Paralycopodites* with maximum fusain content for the profile. This single coal-ball zone is between two gray shale partings. In VS 5, the *Sigillaria-Paralycopodites* peat is less abundant and *Polysporia* also occurs rarely. Again, it is the maximum fusain zone just below the upper gray shale parting. The maximum *Paralycopodites* coal-ball zone (the thinnest of all the zones) occurs immediately below. These two zones are sandwiched, along with a third mixed vegetative zone, between two gray shale partings.

The *Sigillaria-Paralycopodites* interval associated with maxima in fusain and gray shale partings (except in VS 2) appears to be one of the most unusual changes in the swamp sequence and might represent a key event in the swamp traceable over much greater distances. The possibility is suggested that the paired gray shale partings "sandwiching" the *Sigillaria-Paralycopodites* coal-ball zone or zones represent several events related to what is considered the "blue band" across most of the Herrin Coal. Unfortunately, there are virtually no distinctive characteristics for recognition of the "blue band" except as a single moderately thick (2.5 to 7.5 cm) gray shale somewhat below the middle of the seam. At many places there are also other persistent partings with a 1-cm thick gray band about 15 to 25 cm below the "blue band" and a thin dark shale band 46 to 61 cm below the top of the coal (Wanless 1952, p. 164). These may be referable to the bottommost gray band and the black shale parting in VS 4 (Figs. 7.6, 7.7).

The possibility exists that the "blue band" of the Herrin Coal, as interpreted from the Sahara sites (VS 4, 5), may represent a significant and diagnostic vegetational marker in the seam. The degree to which it constitutes a major interruption may vary from a complete lack of vegetation, or at least no or little peat accumulation, to only minor changes. The "blue band" and the gray shale partings in VS 4 and 5 are interpreted as evidence of rapid flooding from the Michigan River drainage system and its distributaries. The thicker pair of gray shale partings represent two successive floods intervened by a hiatus of an extreme dry period. In many areas there may have been no substantial plant growth or little peat accumulation in the interval between floodings. This "dry period" at the Sahara mine is partially represented at the three sites by *Sigillaria*, in some cases also by *Paralycopodites* and *Polysporia*, and maxima in fusain content (VS 4, 5). Comparisons of the "sandwiched" coal-ball zones between shale bands in VS 4 and 5 indicate that coal-ball zone 3, VS 4, has *Sigillaria* above *Paralycopodites* and in all probability is approximately equivalent to zones 4 and 5, VS 5 (Figs. 7.7, 7.9).

The exact relationships between the "dry period" between two major floods at the Sahara sites and the "blue band" are not entirely clear. There is a strong likelihood that the "blue band" may represent either one or both of the flood periods noted at the Sahara sites. Where both floods are represented, but with no peat accumulation between them, the "blue band" would obviously be thicker. Where only one flood is recorded by clastic deposition a prominent fusain band could occur above, below, or possibly in between; nevertheless, the peat at the Sahara sites provide some botanical evidence of the distinctive vegetation during the dry period.

One of the repeated observations concerning the "blue band" is the lack of carbonaceous plant material extruding through it. This has puzzled geologists, because there ought to be if a flood temporarily interrupted growth of swamp vegetation with a veneer of 2.5 to 7.5 cm of fine sediment among tree trunks. However, if the "dry period" preceded the first flood, there may not have been standing, living forests to interrupt. The exposed peat may have been largely oxidized. This still does not really resolve all the observations. The converse follows, if the "dry period" followed the first flood, the high fusain content would be above rather than below the "blue band." In both cases the "blue band" must have served as a thin underclay for the continuation of the swamp sequence.

Evidence generally relating to the above interpretation include observations on fusain content and reproductive biology of the pertinent lycopods. Peat zones with abundant fusain in the Herrin peat profiles from other mines have been noted above the "blue band" and both above and below the "blue band" with the maxima for fusain in the profiles usually in one or the other position (Phillips, Kunz, and Mickish 1977). The fusain content is interpreted as evidence of dryness whether the product of fire or slower oxidation (Fredriksen 1972). Fire certainly can not be ruled out in such a severe dry period and extensive loss of vegetational cover would be consistent with the depositional pattern of the "blue band" as one or two episodes.

The reproductive biology of the lycopods in the assemblage is fairly similar for *Sigillaria* (*Mazocarpon*), *Paralycopodites* (*Lepidostrobus diversus*), and *Polysporia* (Phillips 1979; DiMichele, Mahaffy, and Phillips 1979). They reproduced repeatedly under drier conditions and produced relatively small granular megaspores. Megaspores, some of which are probably referable to those of *Sigillaria*, were reported as unusually and consistently abundant in one bench of coal directly above the "blue band" by Schopf (1937, p. 28, 1941, p. 37) who stated, ". . . the greater abundance of the aphanozonate species *Triletes reinschi* and *Triletes brevispiculus* [*Tuberculatisporites mamillarius*] in the Herrin (No. 6) coal . . . in the coal bench immediately overlying the blue-band clay parting is one of the factors to be considered in explaining the origin of this type of coal. Furthermore the importance of the sigillarians as plants capable of establishing themselves on what must have been a dense clay substratum (the blue-band) must be recognized. These aphanozonate spores are by no means alone in this portion of the coal bed but, in marked contrast to some of the other species present, they are definitely more abundant there."

The interruption of the Herrin coal swamp by the "blue band" is thought to coincide with the split in the Lexington coal, into the lower Alvis and upper Lexington according to Wanless and Wright (1978, p. 21), ". . . by a clastic wedge of sediments (now a part of the Labette Shale) that moved into western Missouri, Kansas, and Oklahoma and temporarily terminated the growth of vegetation in the coal swamps." Wanless (1952, p. 166) also reported the possible extension of the "blue band" into Iowa where its northwestern expansion gradually separated the Upper and Lower Mystic Coal Members.

Origins of Coal Balls and Coal-Ball Distribution

A detailed discussion of coal-ball origins is not within the scope of this chapter, but our observations and mapping of coal balls in the Herrin Coal at sites in the Sahara mine (and elsewhere) differ from those previously published by Evans and Amos (1961) for the Sahara mine. Our observations of coal-ball distribution in the Herrin Coal are consistent with the model proposed by Phillips, Kunz, and Mickish (1977, p. 3). The topographical relationships of coal-ball zones with each other and with clastic bands, as well as the qualities of in situ preservation (fusain, compaction, collapse) and chemical data (Phillips, Kunz, and Mickish 1977) support the independent formation of successive coal-ball zones from the bottom zone upward during the temporary span of the swamp—until the terminal marine transgression. The origin of the top most coal-ball zone or zones could be related to such a transgression in places such as VS 2.

The observations of Evans and Amos (1961) were apparently made in the western portion of the Sahara Mine No. 6 (mining prior to 1966) and included the determination that beneath the underclay (one meter thick) were permeable sandstones about 13 meters thick. Their interpretations of the coal-ball distribution in the mounded areas (like VS 4) of heaviest concentration led them to believe that the centers of such areas had served as hollows for blow wells of mineralizing waters from the sandstone aquifer as a result of the hydrostatic forces of saline and estuarine waters beneath the coal-forming swamp.

One of the consistent interpretations conveyed by Evans and Amos (1961) is that in the outcrop areas of dense coal-ball occurrences, there was obvious disturbance of the underclay and seam extending into the roof shale. In some areas, the jumbled coal-ball piles had a considerable amount of silt and carbonaceous clay intercalated among the coal balls. While the possibility exists that some of these occurrences were clay dikes, seen previously in the Herrin and Springfield Coals (and at one coal-ball locality), our observations of the massive mounds of coal-ball material at the Sahara mine have not included such outcrops.

The means by which such massive amounts of calcite were precipitated in a coal-swamp environment such as that represented specifically by the Herrin Coal are uncertain. The possibilities of aquifers or ground water movement obviously seem more plausible than a terminal marine transgression, and it would be highly desirable to discover outcrops much as those diagrammatically illustrated by Evans and Amos (1961, Figs. 1–3).

Succession

There is no indication of directional succession in a predictable sequence of vegetation from the onset of peat deposition from *Lepidophloios* forests to the demise of similar ones with the marine transgression in the Herrin Coal at Sahara. Palynological studies of other coal seams in the United States, Canada, and Great Britain (Habib 1966; Habib and Groth 1967; Hacquebard and Donaldson 1969; Smith 1962, 1964) have suggested a strong directional abiotic element varying predictably from onset of peat accumulation to cessation of the swamp. Factors such as salinity changes with marine encroachment and moisture in the substrate are thought to have brought about shifts in swamp vegetation almost continuously and directionally as indicated from spore profiles.

In the coal swamp represented by the Herrin Coal, there is evidence of abiotic factors affecting the vegetational sequences; however, these oscillating abiotic influences result in repeated disruptions of plant communities and thus hardly allow secondary succession to proceed to detectable levels. One of the extremes in abiotic influences in which forests survive with continued peat accumulation is wetter and more prolonged standing-water periods of the *Lepidophloios* forests. Along a moisture gradient, the *Sigillaria* zone represents the other extreme. The remarkably uniform floristic composition of the vast Herrin Coal has not been tested in supposed transitional environments or in more western seams that are considered correlative.

Although there are strong components of abiotic control in relatively dry sites in the Herrin Coal (*Sigillaria* zone), the high diversity and often exotic taxa in assemblages (particularly small pteridosperms and ferns) indicate considerable biotic or competitive control of the floral composition and community structure at any given site. Certainly, the high diversity, compositional variability, and differences among the adaptations of plants in the *Lepidodendron-Medullosa* assemblages indicate important biotic factors. These apparently give way to abiotic control in wetter areas with prolonged periods of standing water and to a lesser extent in drier sites or prolonged dry periods.

ACKNOWLEDGMENTS

We thank R. A. Peppers, Illinois State Geological Survey, for providing the palynological data; T. D. Lee and F. A. Bazzaz, Botany Department, University of Illinois, for advice in community analyses; R. Gullic and R. Dyer, Sahara Coal Company, Harrisburg, Illinois, for their continued help and cooperation; W. J. Nelson and P. J. DeMaris, Illinois State Geological Survey for their aid in collecting; and A. Raymond, C. R. Scotese, and A. M. Ziegler, University of Chicago, for providing the paleographic map.

Computer programming assistance was provided by D. Gaines and F. Adrian, Illinois State Geological Survey. The figures were prepared by P. P. Phillips, School of Life Sciences, University of Illinois.

This research was supported in part by NSF Grant DEB 75/13695, EAR 78/12954, and an NSF Energy-Related Traineeship (1978–79).

REFERENCES

Balbach, M. K. 1965. Paleozoic lycopsid fructifications. I. *Lepidocarpon* petrifactions. *Amer. J. Bot.* 52(4):317–30.

———. 1966. Paleozoic lycopsid fructifications. II. *Lepidostrobus takhtajanii* in North America and Great Britain. *Amer. J. Bot.* 53(3):275–83.

———. 1967. Paleozoic lycopsid fructifications. III. Conspecificity of British and North American *Lepidostrobus* petrifactions. *Amer. J. Bot.* 54(7):867–75.

Baxter, R. W., and M. R. Willhite. 1969. The morphology and anatomy of *Alethopteris lesquereuxi* Wagner. *Univ. Kansas Sci. Bull.* 48(18):767–83.

Cady, G. H. 1937. The occurrence of coal balls in No. 6 Coal bed at Nashville, Illinois. *Ill. Acad. Sci. Trans.* 29(2):157–58.

Courvoisier, J. M., and T. L. Phillips. 1975. Correlation of spores from Pennsylvanian coal-ball fructifications with dispersed spores. *Micropaleontology* 21(1):45–59.

Darrah, E. L. 1968. A remarkable branching *Sphenophyllum* from the Carboniferous of Illinois. *Palaeontographica* 121B:87–101.

Delevoryas, T. 1955. The Medullosae—Structure and relationships. *Palaeontographica* 97B:114–67.

DeMaris, P. J., and R. A. Bauer. 1978. Geology of a longwall mining demonstration at Old Ben No. 24: Roof lithologies and coal balls. *Ill. Mining Inst., Proceed. (1977)*, pp. 80–91.

Dennis, R. L. 1974. Studies of Paleozoic ferns: *Zygopteris* from the middle and late Pennsylvanian of the United States. *Palaeontographica* 148B:95–136.

——. 1975. Studies of Paleozoic ferns. *Abstr. Bot. Soc. Am., Corvallis, Oregon.* Lawrence, Kansas: Allen Press, p. 19.

DiMichele, W. A. 1978. Ecotypic variation in *Lepidodendron dicentricum* Felix. *Abstr. Bot. Soc. Amer. Misc. Ser.* Pub. 156, p. 32.

——. 1979a. Arborescent lycopods of Pennsylvanian age coal swamps: morphology, evolution, and paleoecology. Ph.D. thesis, University of Illinois at Urbana-Champaign.

——. 1979b. Arborescent lycopods of Pennsylvanian age coals: *Lepidophloios. Palaeontographica* 171B:57–77.

——. 1979c. Arborescent lycopods of Pennsylvanian age coals: *Lepidodendron dicentricum* C. Felix. *Palaeontographica* 171B:122–36.

——. 1980. *Paralycopodites* Morey et Morey, from the Carboniferous of Euramerica—a reassessment of generic affinities and evolution of "*Lepidodendron brevifolium* Williamson. *Amer. J. Bot.* 67:1466–76.

——. 1981. Arborescent lycopods of Pennsylvanian age coals: *Lepidodendron*, with description of a new species. *Palaeontographica* 175B:85–125.

DiMichele, W. A., J. F. Mahaffy, and T. L. Phillips. 1979. Lycopods of Pennsylvanian age coals: *Polysporia. Can. J. Bot.* 57(16):1740–53.

DiMichele, W. A., and T. L. Phillips. 1979. *Stelastellara* Baxter, axes of questionable gymnosperm affinity with unusual habit—Middle Pennsylvanian. *Rev. Palaeobot. Palynol.* 27:103–17.

DiMichele, W. A., and T. L. Phillips. In press. Paleoecology of the Herrin (No. 6) Coal Member of the Illinois Basin: Reproductive biology and distribution of *Lepidodendron* and *Lepidophloios. C. R. Congr., 9, Strat. Geol. Carb.* (Urbana, Ill.).

Eggert, D. A. 1963. Studies of Paleozoic ferns: The frond of *Ankyropteris glabra. Amer. J. Bot.* 50(4):379–87.

——. 1972. Petrified *Stigmaria* of sigillarian origin from North America. *Rev. Palaeobot. Palynol.* 14:85–99.

Eggert, D. A., and T. N. Taylor. 1966. Studies of Paleozoic ferns: On the genus *Tedelea* gen. nov. *Palaeontographica* 118B:52–73.

Ehret, D. L., and T. L. Phillips. 1977. *Psaronius* root systems—morphology and development. *Palaeontographica* 161B:147–64.

Evans, W. D., and D. H. Amos. 1961. An example of the origin of coal-balls. *Proc. Geol. Ass.* 72(part 4):445–54.

Frankenberg, J. M., and D. A. Eggert. 1969. Petrified *Stigmaria* from North America: Part I. *Stigmaria ficoides*, the underground portions of Lepidodendraceae. *Palaeontographica* 128B:1–47.

Frederiksen, N. O. 1972. The rise of the Mesophytic Flora. *Geosci. and Man* 4:17–28.

Galtier, J., and T. L. Phillips. 1977. Morphology and evolution of *Botryopteris*, a Carboniferous age fern. Part 2. Observations on Stephanian species from Grand'Croix, France. *Palaeontographica* 164B:1–32.

Good, C. W. 1973. Studies of *Sphenophyllum* shoots: Species delimitation within the taxon *Sphenophyllum*. *Amer. J. Bot.* 60(9):929–39.

———. 1975. Pennsylvanian-age calamitean cones, elater-bearing spores, and associated vegetative organs. *Palaeontographica* 153B:28–99.

———. 1976. The anatomy and three-dimensional morphology of *Annularia hoskinsii* sp. n. *Amer. J. Bot.* 63(6):719–25.

———. 1977. Taxonomic and stratigraphic significance of the dispersed spore genus *Calamospora*. In *Geobotany (1977)* (R. C. Romans, ed.). New York: Plenum, pp. 43–64.

———. 1978. Taxonomic characteristics of sphenophyllalean cones. *Amer. J. Bot.* 65(1):86–97.

Good, C. W., and T. N. Taylor. 1974. The establishment of *Elaterites triferens* spores in *Calamocarpon insignis* microsporangia. *Trans. Amer. Micros. Soc.* 93(1): 148–56.

Habib, D. 1966. Distribution of spore and pollen assemblages in the Lower Kittanning Coal of western Pennsylvania. *Palaeontology* 9:629–66.

Habib, D., and P. K. H. Groth. 1967. Paleoecology of migrating Carboniferous peat environments. *Palaeog., Palaeoclimatol., Palaeoecol.* 3:185–95.

Hacquebard, P. A., and J. R. Donaldson. 1969. Carboniferous coal deposition associated with flood-plain and limnic environments in Nova Scotia. In *Environments of Coal Deposition*. (E. C. Dapples and M. E. Hopkins, eds.). *Geol. Soc. Amer. Spec. Pap.* 114:143–91.

Hopkins, M. E. 1975. Coal mines in Illinois. *Ill. Geol. Survey*, 1 map.

Hopkins, M. E., and J. A. Simon. 1975. Pennsylvanian System. In *Handbook of Illinois Stratigraphy* (H. B. Willman et al., eds.). Ill. *Geol. Surv. Bull.* 95:163–201.

Johnson, D. O. 1972. Stratigraphic analysis of the interval between the Herrin (No. 6) Coal and the Piasa Limestone in southwestern Illinois. Ph.D. thesis, University of Illinois at Urbana-Champaign.

Kosanke, R. M., J. A. Simon, and W. H. Smith. 1958. Compaction of plant debris-forming coal balls. *Geol. Soc. Amer. Bull.* 69:1599–1600.

Krausse, H.-F., H. H. Damberger, W. J. Nelson, S. R. Hunt, C. T. Ledvina, C. G. Treworgy, and W. A. White. 1979. Roof strata of the Herrin (No. 6) Coal Member in mines of Illinois: Their geology and stability. *Ill. Min. Note 72, Ill. Geol. Surv.*

Leisman, G. A. 1961. A new species of *Cardiocarpus* in Kansas coal balls. *Kan. Acad. Sci., Trans.* 64(2):117–122.

Leisman, G. A., and J. S. Peters. 1970. A new pteridosperm male fructification from the Middle Pennsylvanian of Illinois. *Amer. J. Bot.* 57(7):867–73.

Leisman, G. A., and T. L. Phillips. 1979. Megasporangiate and microsporangiate cones of *Achlamydocarpon varius* from the Middle Pennsylvanian. *Palaeontographica* 168B:100–28.

Leisman, G. A., and J. Roth. 1963. A reconsideration of *Stephanospermum*. *Bot. Gazette* 124(3):231–40.

Leisman, G. A., and R. L. Rivers. 1974. On the reproductive organs of *Lepidodendron serratum* Felix. *C. R. Congr., 7, Strat. Geol. Carb.* III:351–65.

Leisman, G. A., and B. M. Stidd. 1967. Further occurrences of *Spencerites* from the

Middle Pennsylvanian of Kansas and Illinois. *Amer. J. Bot.* 54(3):316–23.

Mahaffy, J. F. 1979. Profile patterns of coal and peat palynology in the Herrin (No. 6) Coal Member, Carbondale Formation, Middle Pennsylvanian of southern Illinois. *Abstr. Congr., 9, Strat. Geol. Carb.* (Urbana, Ill.), pp. 123–24.

Matten, L. C., and W. E. Hopkins. 1967. *Hexapterospermum delevoryii* from the Middle Pennsylvanian of southern Illinois. *Ill. Acad. Sci., Trans.* 60(1):98–99.

Millay, M. A. 1979. Studies of Paleozoic marattialeans: A monograph of the American species of *Scolecopteris. Palaeontographica* 169B:1–69.

Millay, M. A., and D. A. Eggert. 1970. *Idanothekion* gen. n., a synangiate pollen organ with saccate pollen from the Middle Pennsylvanian of Illinois. *Amer. J. Bot.* 57(1):50–61.

Millay, M. A., and T. N. Taylor. 1980. An unusual botryopterid sporangial aggregation from the Middle Pennsylvanian of North America. *Amer. J. Bot.* 67:758–73.

Morey, E. D., and P. R. Morey. 1977. *Paralycopodites minutissimum* gen. et. sp. n. from the Carbondale Formation of Illinois. *Palaeontographica* 162B:64–69.

Morgan, J. 1959. The morphology and anatomy of American species of the genus *Psaronius.* Illinois Biological Monographs 27. Urbana: University of Illinois Press.

Neely, F. E. 1951. Small petrified seeds from the Pennsylvanian of Illinois. *Bot. Gazette* 113(2):165–79.

Nelson, W. J. 1979. Geologic effects of the Walshville channel on coal mining conditions in southern Illinois. In *Depositional and Structural History of the Pennsylvanian System of the Illinois Basin.* Part 2, Invited Papers. (J. E. Palmer and R. R. Dutcher, eds.). Field Trip 9, *Congr., 9, Strat. Geol. Carb., Ill. Geol. Surv.* (Urbana, Ill.), pp. 151–58.

Oestry-Stidd, L. L. 1979. Anatomically preserved *Neuropteris rarinervis* from American coal balls. *J. Paleontol.* 53(1):37–43.

Phillips, T. L. 1974. Evolution of vegetative morphology in coenopterid ferns. *Ann. Miss. Bot. Gard.* 61(2):427–61.

———. 1979. Reproduction of heterosporous arborescent lycopods in the Mississippian-Pennsylvanian of Euramerica. *Rev. Palaeobot. Palynol.* 27: 239–289.

———. 1980. Stratigraphic and geographic occurrences of permineralized coal-swamp plants—Upper Carboniferous of North America and Europe. In *Biostratigraphy of Fossil Plants* (D. Dilcher, ed.). Stroudsburg, Pa.: Dowden, Hutchinson and Ross, pp. 25–92.

———. 1981. Stratigraphic occurrences and vegetational patterns of Pennsylvanian pteridosperms in Euramerican coal swamps. *Rev. Palaeobot. Palynol.* 32:5–26.

Phillips, T. L., and H. N. Andrews. 1963. An occurrence of the medullosan seed-fern *Sutcliffia* in the American Carboniferous. *Ann. Miss. Bot. Gard.* 50:29–51.

Phillips T. L., and H. N. Andrews. 1965. A fructification of *Anachoropteris* from the Middle Pennsylvanian of Illinois. *Ann. Miss. Bot. Gard.* 52:(3):251–61.

Phillips, T. L., A. B. Kunz, and D. J. Mickish. 1977. Paleobotany of permineralized peat (coal balls) from the Herrin (No. 6) Coal Member of the Illinois Basin. In *Interdisciplinary Studies of Peat and Coal Origins* (P. N. Given and A. D. Cohan, eds.). *Geol. Soc. Amer. Microform Pub. 7.*, pp. 18–49.

Phillips, T. L., and G. A. Leisman. 1966. *Paurodendron*, a rhizomorphic lycopod. *Amer. J. Bot.* 53(10):1086–1100.

Phillips, T. L., and R. A. Peppers. 1979. Pennsylvanian (Upper Carboniferous) coal-swamp communities in the Illinois Basin and relationships to vegetational patterns in Euramerica. *Abstr. Congr., 9, Strat. Geol. Carb.* (Urbana, Ill.), pp. 163–64.

Phillips, T. L., R. A. Peppers, M. J. Avcin, and P. F. Laughnan. 1974. Fossil plants and coal: patterns of change in Pennsylvanian coal swamps of the Illinois Basin. *Science* 184:1367–69.

Pryor, W. A., and E. G. Sable. 1974. Carboniferous of the Eastern Interior Basin. In *Carboniferous of the Southeastern United States* (G. Briggs, ed.). *Geol. Soc. Amer. Spec. Pap. 148.*, pp. 281–313.

Ramanujam, C. G. K., G. W. Rothwell, and W. N. Stewart. 1974. Probable attachment of the *Dolerotheca* campanulum to a *Myeloxylon-Alethopteris* type frond. *Amer. J. Bot.* 61(10):1057–66.

Rothwell, G. W. 1972. Pollen organs of the Pennsylvanian Callistophytaceae (Pteridospermopsida). *Amer. J. Bot.* 59(10):993–99.

———. 1975. The Callistophytaceae (Pteridospermopsida): I. Vegetative structures. *Palaeontographica* 151B:171–96.

Rothwell, G. W., and T. N. Taylor. 1972. Carboniferous pteridosperm studies: morphology and anatomy of *Schopfiastrum decussatum*. *Can. J. Bot.* 50(12):2649–58.

Rothwell, G. W., T. N. Taylor, and C. Clarkson. 1979. On the structural similarity of the Paleozoic ovules *Conostoma platyspermum* and *C. leptospermum*. *J. Paleontol.* 53(1):49–54.

Rothwell, G. W., and K. L. Whiteside. 1974. Rooting structures of the Carboniferous medullosan pteridosperms. *Can. J. Bot.* 52(1):97–102.

Schlanker, C. M., and G. A. Leisman. 1969. The herbaceous Carboniferous lycopod *Selaginella fraipontii* comb. nov. *Amer. J. Bot.* 130(1):35–41.

Schlesinger, W. H. 1978. Community structure, dynamics and nutrient cycling in the Okefenokee cypress swamp-forest. *Ecol. Mono.* 48:43–65.

Schopf, J. M. 1938. Spores from the Herrin (No. 6) Coal bed in Illinois. *Ill. Geol. Surv. Rep. Invest. 50.*

———. 1939. Coal balls as an index to the constitution of coal. *Ill. Acad. Sci., Trans.,* 31(2):187–89.

———. 1941. Contributions to Pennsylvanian paleobotany: *Mazocarpon oedipternum*, sp. nov. and sigillarian relationships. *Ill. Geol. Surv. Rep. Invest. 75.*

Smith, A. V. H. 1962. The palaeoecology of Carboniferous peats based on the miospores and petrography of bituminous coals. *Proc. Yorkshire Geol. Soc.* (No. 19)33:423–74.

———. 1964. Palaeoecology of Carboniferous peats. In *Problems in Palaeoclimatology* (A. E. M. Nairn, ed.). New York: Wiley, pp. 57–75.

Smith, W. H., and J. B. Stall. 1975. Coal and water resources for coal conversion in Illinois. *Ill. Water Surv., Ill. Geol. Surv. Coop. Resources Rep. 4.*

Stidd, B. M. 1971. Morphology and anatomy of the frond of *Psaronius*. *Palaeontographica* 134B:87–123.

———. 1978. An anatomically preserved *Potoniea* with *in situ* spores from the

Pennsylvanian of Illinois. *Amer. J. Bot.* 65(6):677–83.

Stidd, B. M., L. L. Oestry, and T. L. Phillips. 1975. On the frond of *Sutcliffia insignis* var. *tuberculata. Rev. Palaeobot. Palynol.* 20:55–66.

Stidd, B. M., and T. L. Phillips. 1973. The vegetative anatomy of *Schopfiastrum decussatum* from the Middle Pennsylvanian of the Illinois Basin. *Amer. J. Bot.* 60(5):463–74.

Taylor, T. N. 1962. Additional observations on *Stephanospermum ovoides. Amer. J. Bot.* 49(7):794–800.

———. 1965. Paleozoic seed studies: A monograph of the American species of *Pachytesta. Palaeontographica* 117B:1–46.

———. 1966. Paleozoic seed studies: On the genus *Hexapterospermum. Amer. J. Bot.* 53(2):185–92.

———. 1967. Paleozoic seed studies: On the structure of *Conostoma leptospermum* n. sp., and *Albertlongia incostata* n. gen. and sp. *Palaeontographica* 121B:23–29.

———. 1972. A new Carboniferous sporangial aggregation. *Rev. Palaeobot. Palynol.* 14:309–18.

Taylor, T. N., and S. D. Brack-Hanes. 1977. *Achlamydocarpon varius* comb. nov.: morphology and reproductive biology. *Amer. J. Bot.* 63:1257–65.

Taylor, T. N., and T. Delevoryas. 1964. Paleozoic seed studies: A new Pennsylvanian *Pachytesta* from southern Illinois. *Amer. J. Bot.* 51(2):189–95.

Taylor, T. N., and G. A. Leisman. 1963. *Conostoma kestospermum*, a new species of Paleozoic seed from the Middle Pennsylvanian. *Amer. J. Bot.* 50(6):574–80.

Wanless, H. R. 1952. Studies of field relations of coal beds. In Second Conference on the Origin and Constitution of Coal, Crystal Cliffs, Nova Scotia (1952), pp. 148–75.

———. 1956. Depositional basins of some widespread Pennsylvanian coal beds in the United States. In *Third Conference on the Origin and Constitution of Coal*, Crystal Cliffs, Nova Scotia (1956), pp. 94–128.

Wanless, H. R., J. R. Baroffio, and P. C. Trescott. 1969. Conditions of deposition of Pennsylvanian coal beds, In *Environments of Coal Deposition*. (E. C. Dapples and M. E. Hopkins, eds.). *Geol. Soc. Amer. Spec. Pap. 114*, pp. 105–42.

Wanless, H. R., and C. R. Wright. 1978. Paleoenvironmental maps of Pennsylvanian rocks, Illinois Basin and northern midcontinent region. *Geol. Soc. Amer. MC-23.*

Whittaker, R. H. 1975. *Communities and Ecosystems*, 2nd ed. New York: Macmillan.

Whiteside, K. L. 1974. Petrified cordaitean stems from North America. Ph.D. thesis, University of Iowa, Iowa City.

Zeigler, A. M., C. R. Scotese, W. S. McKerrow, M. E. Johnson, and R. K. Bambach. 1979. Paleozoic paleogeography. *Ann. Rev. Earth Planet. Sci.* 7:473–502.

INDEX